The heart of the wise is
But the heart of fools

UNLOCKING
WISDOM
FORMING AGENTS OF GOD
IN THE HOUSE OF MOURNING

*A canonical-linguistic exposition
of the Books of Job and Ecclesiastes*

JAMES REITMAN

21ST CENTURY
PRESS
PUBLISHING WITH PURPOSE
WWW.21STCENTURYPRESS.COM

UNLOCKING WISDOM
FORMING AGENTS OF GOD IN THE HOUSE OF MOURNING

Requests for permissions should be addressed to:
21st Century Press
2131 W. Republic Rd.
PMB 41
Springfield, MO 65807

ISBN 978-0-9779535-5-4

Key search words: 1. Job 2. Ecclesiastes 3. Wisdom 4. Hermeneutics
5. Canonical-Linguistic

Download files at: www.21stcenturypress.com/wisdom.htm

Download 1: Hermeneutical Method ("Words of Truth and Words of Purpose")

Download 2: Synthetic Chart of Job (full color)

Download 3: Synthetic Chart of Ecclesiastes (full color)

Download 4: Searchable pdf of *Unlocking Wisdom*

email author: jreitman@21stcenturypress.com
email publisher: lee@21stcenturypress.com

Cover: Lee Fredrickson
Book Design: Terry White

Visit our website at: www.21stcenturypress.com

21st Century Press
2131 W. Republic Rd., PMB 41
Springfield, MO 65807

21st CENTURY PRESS
PUBLISHING WITH PURPOSE
WWW.21STCENTURYPRESS.COM

DEDICATION

To my patient wife Peggy, who endured countless cycles of the "Hermeneutical Spiral" and set the tone for this book when I told her we were finally going to press.

She said:

"It's a good thing you're a doctor and not an author, because we would have starved by now."

ACKNOWLEDGEMENTS

I cannot overstate the contribution made by Ruben Martinez, who was my first real mentor and guided me through my early stages of foolishness after seminary. It was he who first had the courage to administer "the rebuke of the wise" (Eccl 7:5) with great compassion and love as soon as we met in 1987. I owe to him the encouragement that first motivated me to pursue my expository journey through the books of Job and Ecclesiastes. We planted a church together, but he was the one with the passion, stubbornness, and courage to shepherd Living Word EFC (Pharr, Texas) against great odds for the last 20 years.

Also of great encouragement over the years since I entered Dallas Seminary in 1981 have been Elliott Johnson and Roy Zuck. It was Elliott's *Expository Hermeneutics* that first gave me the incentive to pursue "synthetic" hermeneutics, and he invited me to join the 2006 Expository Hermeneutics study group of the Evangelical Theological Society that reignited my interest in hermeneutic methodology. Elliott and Roy have both consistently encouraged my work on this commentary since my original article on Ecclesiastes in 1997. More recently, the work of Kevin Vanhoozer and Dick Averbeck provided the main theological incentive for my paper "Words of Truth and Words of Purpose," which best articulates the hermeneutical rationale underlying the present commentary. Kevin's innovative framework for understanding the connection between textual meaning and authorial intent and his "canonical-linguistic" approach to theology have especially boosted my confidence in the soundness of the expository approach that led to the present volume.

Finally, I am indebted to the people of the Body of Christ, who for 29 years have endured my rugged individualism and loved me even when I was unlovable. I am particularly grateful for the men of "The Agency" at Fellowship Bible Church in Colorado Springs who seasoned my teaching style and tested my theological convictions in the area of "human agency." Pastor Raleigh Gresham and the "Missional Integration Boys" at FBC have been equally encouraging discussion partners. My wife Peggy has tolerated my antisocial traits for 30 years and has *really* loved me when I was unlovable. In light of the loving persistence of all these agents of the Creator, I too am now loving others a little more consistently.

TABLE OF CONTENTS

ECCLESIASTES: WISDOM IN SEARCH OF A LEGACY

ABBREVIATIONS

AB	Anchor Bible
BDB	F. Brown, S. R. Driver, and C. A. Briggs, *The New Brown-Driver-Briggs-Gesenius Hebrew-English Lexicon*
BKC	*The Bible Knowledge Commentary*
BSac	*Bibliotheca Sacra*
cf.	*confer,* compare with
cp.	compare
e.g.	*exempli gratia,* for example
esp.	especially
fn(s).	footnote(s) cited in other works
Gk	Greek
Heb.	Hebrew
HOTC	Holman Old Testament Commentary
ibid.	*ibidem,* in the same source
idem.	*idem,* same, the previously mentioned author
i.e.	*id est,* that is
ILM	*Issues in Law & Medicine*
impf.	imperfect tense
lit.	literally
LXX	Septuagint
MS(S)	manuscript(s)
MT	Massoretic Text
n(n).	footnote(s) cited in this commentary
NASB	New American Standard Bible
NCBC	New Century Bible Commentary
NET	New English Translation (The NET Bible)
NICOT	New International Commentary on the Old Testament
NIV	New International Version of the Bible
NIVAC	New International Version Application Commentary
NKJV	New King James Version of the Bible
NRSV	New Revised Standard Version of the Bible
NT	New Testament
OT	Old Testament
pf.	perfect tense
q.v.	*quod vide*, referring to the text within a work
TOTC	Tyndale Old Testament Commentary
v(v).	verse(s)
WBC	Word Biblical Commentary

Old Testament Books

Gen	Genesis	Eccl	Ecclesiastes
Exod	Exodus	Song	Song of Solomon
Lev	Leviticus	Isa	Isaiah
Num	Numbers	Jer	Jeremiah
Deut	Deuteronomy	Lam	Lamentations
Josh	Joshua	Ezek	Ezekiel
Judg	Judges	Dan	Daniel
Ruth	Ruth	Hos	Hosea
1 Sam	1 Samuel	Joel	Joel
2 Sam	2 Samuel	Amos	Amos
1 Kgs	1 Kings	Obad	Obadiah
2 Kgs	2 Kings	Jon	Jonah
1 Chr	1 Chronicles	Mic	Micah
2 Chr	2 Chronicles	Nah	Nahum
Ezra	Ezra	Hab	Habakkuk
Neh	Nehemiah	Zeph	Zephaniah
Esth	Esther	Hag	Haggai
Job	Job	Zech	Zechariah
Ps(s)	Psalm(s)	Mal	Malachi
Prov	Proverbs		

New Testament Books

Matt	Matthew	1 Tim	1 Timothy
Mark	Mark	2 Tim	2 Timothy
Luke	Luke	Titus	Titus
John	John	Philem	Philemon
Acts	Acts	Heb	Hebrews
Rom	Romans	Jas	James
1 Cor	1 Corinthians	1 Pet	1 Peter
2 Cor	2 Corinthians	2 Pet	2 Peter
Gal	Galatians	1 John	1 John
Eph	Ephesians	2 John	2 John
Phil	Philippians	3 John	3 John
Col	Colossians	Jude	Jude
1 Thess	1 Thessalonians	Rev	Revelation
2 Thess	2 Thessalonians		

FOREWORD

Through the prism of his own trials, professional disillusionment, and intense interest in medical ethics, James Reitman engages in this important exercise in biblical interpretation, mining two wisdom books for the answers to the theist's dilemma. He believes that Job and Ecclesiastes help us answer the question: why is there reason to hope, much less to live and believe in God, when life's quest for fulfillment leaves only an unshakable sense of utter futility.

For Reitman, Job turns out to be, not a shining example of faithfulness in adversity, but a believer who, like many of us, lost confidence in God's justice and care when God failed to satisfy his self-righteous expectations. Ecclesiastes is not merely a cynical tract proclaiming the futility of life without God. It points the way to an informed optimism—that those who trust in God can find a lasting legacy in his inscrutable ways.

I especially appreciate Dr. Reitman's self-conscious and meticulous hermeneutical rigor—the point at which I am most qualified to endorse his work. He explains his rationale for the format that he employs in the commentary—one that is both idiosyncratic and effective. In the commentary's organization, his careful and analytical mind excels. Each section starts with a summary statement that clearly articulates its payoff: how the author makes his case, what he intends to say, and how readers should respond. As well, readers can see for each book a Synthetic Chart that graphically depicts the Expository Outline, and for each section an Overview, Theological Correlation, and Validation. He employs a system of footnoting that traces the theological conclusions that emerge and correlates them to other sections.

Dr. Reitman is aware of the danger of leveraging the text to suit his own preferences, and he adopts the worthy goal of discovering the "author's intended meaning as expressed in the biblical text." He employs what he calls the "spiral of induction and deduction" to drill down deeper and deeper into the authors' intended overarching and composite meanings. Only then does he seek the texts' application. He tests his interpretations against the criteria of comprehensiveness, competence, coherence, and consistency. These are all laudable tactics. Would that all commentaries were so rigorous. And would that all were so satisfying in their conclusions. Beyond his attention to methodological precision, Reitman's conclusions ring true to life—always the test of a commentary's effectiveness.

William W. Klein, Ph.D.
Chair, Division of Biblical Studies
Denver Seminary

*"The heart of the wise is in the house of mourning,
But the heart of fools is in the house of mirth."*
(Ecclesiastes 7:4)

"Blessed are those who mourn..."
(Matthew 5:4)

PREFACE

Hermeneutics and the "Window" of Suffering

*Suffering is real—so real that the human psyche can only bear to con-template the depths of its reality if from the outset it is given some cause to believe that suffering is not the **ultimate** reality, not as such the last word about existence in this world. Apart from such a prospect, who would have the stamina to expose himself or herself deeply to the fact of human suffering? Without at least the hint of a promise that meaning might be found in, alongside, or beneath such suffering as human flesh is heir to, no doubt the better course would be (what in fact so many of our contemporaries do!) to avoid so far as possible any such exposure!* [1]

The Existential Crisis of Unjust Suffering

Years ago as a specialist in Internal Medicine with a background in Biblical Studies I began to feel a strange attraction to the books of Job and Ecclesiastes. To me they seemed uniquely able to "name" the kinds of dis-tress that typically surfaced among patients and their family members when they were facing overwhelming medical illness. As my interest in Medical Ethics intensified, I wondered whether these two books of Old Testament Wisdom could inform the quandaries of decision-making that frequently plague physicians confronted with end-of-life situations. Analysis of these issues in the literature of contemporary Medical Ethics struck me as particularly impoverished—ethicists seemed all too con-cerned with promoting the priorities of "autonomous" decision-making and "death with dignity," and the need to relieve or avoid suffering at all cost. When I reflected on these issues from Job's vantage point, it occurred to me that most of my contemporaries in Medical Ethics were approaching end-of-life dilemmas very much like Job's friends, and I felt that Job's rebuke directly addressed their misplaced priorities in response to suffering:

---

[1] Douglas John Hall, *God and Human Suffering* (Minneapolis: Augsburg, 1986), 94 *(author's emphasis)*.

"Did I ever say, 'Bring something to me'?
Or, 'Offer a bribe for me from your wealth'?
Or, 'Deliver me from the enemy's hand'?
Or, 'Redeem me from the hand of oppressors'?
"Teach me, and I will hold my tongue;
Cause me to understand wherein I have erred.
How forceful are right words!
But what does your arguing prove?" (Job 6:22-25)

Most chronic suffering cannot be completely eliminated without killing the patient, and chronically suffering patients at some point begin to look for some meaning in their suffering. Job's greatest need from his friends was not to relieve all suffering, or maintain autonomous decision-making, or preserve "death with dignity." But Job's friends were more concerned with appeasing his despair by giving him advice that would eliminate his suffering as quickly as possible and thereby relieve their own distress. To serve these priorities was of no benefit at all in helping Job extract some meaning out of his otherwise senseless suffering. In his rebuke Job seemed to recognize his critical need for wisdom amid the suffering that typically deprives people of their capacity to reason clearly, and Job's drama ended up portraying Elihu as the only one of Job's friends who was able to restore insight after introducing himself as Job's "advocate" or "mediator." Elihu impressed me as an ideal role model for the bedside ethicist: He engaged the sufferer in decision-making, facilitated mourning, and affirmed the redemptive potential of Job's suffering, even in the face of uncertainty and death.

Qoheleth—the voice of reflection in the book of Ecclesiastes—encountered the same existential dilemma from the viewpoint of one engaged in the earnest pursuit of lasting satisfaction in this life. Qoheleth could find no meaning at all when he witnessed unjust suffering and he expressed the overwhelming sense of futility that tends to well up inside all of us when we too witness such suffering:

And look! The tears of the oppressed,
But they have no comforter—
On the side of their oppressors there is power,
But they have no comforter.
Therefore I praised the dead who were already dead,
More than the living who are still alive.
Yet better than both is he who has never existed,
Who has not seen the evil work that is done under the sun. (Eccl 4:1b-3)

The natural inclination to recoil from such unjust suffering emerges from a deep visceral angst or dread that is so profoundly intimidating it can quickly isolate the sufferer from community—it is *contagious*. Witnesses may well consider such suffering to be worse than death itself, and when it cannot be avoided, the resulting existential crisis tends to evoke several typical responses from sufferer and bystander alike: They may seek retribution, demand restitution for their losses, or—like Qoheleth—seek to eliminate the pain at any cost. But behind all these recourses, people seek a *plausible explanation for innocent suffering that can relieve the terror of apparent meaninglessness.*

This was precisely the crisis that disrupted the lives of Job and his friends. Innocent suffering raises the most serious questions about the presence, character, and purposes of God—it seems incompatible with the existence of an all-loving and all-powerful God, especially when the suffering remains unabated or unexplained. Job's unexplained suffering shook their complacent views of God to the core—it jerked from them the cherished presumption that they were secure in their piety and led them to debate the very justice and goodness of God Himself. When Qoheleth—with his unprecedented wealth and power—tried to find a meaningful explanation for innocent suffering in the face of uncertainty and death, all he discovered was that suffering is only compounded by wealth and power. This leads to a similar starting scenario in both Job and Ecclesiastes: Human disillusionment and despair inevitably ensue amid adversity when all that is left in life's quest for fulfillment is an unshakable sense of *utter futility*.

Job and Qoheleth may thus be viewed as complementary protagonists in their disillusionment: Job reacts to the futility of unjust suffering from the perspective of *maligned victim*; Qoheleth reflects on the futility of all his achievements from the viewpoint of *ambitious oppressor*. Both dispositions are rooted in a natural human *self-sufficient* disposition toward life. The reader is thus presented with two complementary greater-to-lesser (a *fortiori*) arguments against self-sufficiency in response to disillusionment. In Job's case, if such profound suffering could befall the most "blameless and upright" of men (Job 1:1), how could any *less righteous* reader claim to be protected from suffering? Similarly, if Qoheleth had "gained more wisdom than all who were before" him (Eccl 1:16) yet found that it conferred no advantage in his self-sufficient pursuit of lasting satisfaction, how could a *less wise* reader expect to find any more? The attentive reader is thus compelled to identify with each protagonist in profound disillusionment over the futility of even the best human effort to achieve some lasting legacy or meaning in life.

The wisdom of Job and Ecclesiastes thus became for me a far prefer-able template for decision-making in end-of-life dilemmas[2] because it openly addresses the critical issue of finding meaning even when suffer-ing persists and it frames decision-making at the end of life with the right criteria to find that meaning. Yet, how could I be sure I had not "lever-aged" the text to suit my immediate purpose of arguing for a preferable alternative to the prevailing models of end-of-life decision-making? Had I read my own meanings into the texts of Job and Ecclesiastes?[3] I was compelled to test my hermeneutical integrity and I determined to com-plete a coherent exposition of both books. It has taken more than 20 years, as my task proved considerably more challenging than I anticipated, but the enterprise has taken on a life of its own.[4] It has yielded a much more valuable and enduring return than my initial aim of validating a wisdom model for decision-making: I discovered how our intended human agency in the eyes of our Creator is confounded by human self-sufficiency but secured in the fear of God (see "A Distinctive View of the Arguments of Job and Ecclesiastes," below). Moreover, significant interpretive prob-lems in the two books forced me to address critical questions of hermeneutical integrity and verify the soundness of my hermeneutical approach.

---

[2] For further analysis of wise decision-making based on the arguments of Job and Ecclesiastes in common medical settings of intractable suffering, see my arti-cles, "The Debate on Assisted Suicide," *ILM* 11:299-329 (1995); "Wise Advocacy," in Kilner et al (eds.), *Dignity and Dying: A Christian Appraisal* (Grand Rapids: Eerdmans, 1996), 208-22; "A 'Wisdom' perspective on Advocacy for the Suicidal," in Timothy Demy & Gary Stewart (eds.), *Suicide: A Christian Response* (Grand Rapids: Kregel, 1998), 369-85; "The Dilemma of Medical Futility," *ILM* 12:231-64 (1996); and "Perinatal Hospice: A Response to Early Termination for Severe Congenital Anomalies," in TJ Demy & GP Stewart (eds.), *Genetic Engineering: A Christian Response* (Grand Rapids: Kregel, 1999), 197-211.

[3] If I had not asked the question, it would ironically surface in a review of my first article on end-of-life decision-making (above, note 2) that relied heavily on the texts of Job and Ecclesiastes for ethical insight. See the review by Robert A. Pyne in *BSac* 153 (1996), 369.

[4] Annie Dillard masterfully describes how one's writing, if it is to be true and have power, will follow its own inherently determined life (*The Writing Life*, New York: HarperCollins, 1989). The inspired text of Scripture inherently governs its own interpretation and guides the expositor to the truth—one's pen follows the Spirit's inscrutable path to that truth. Yet the process of unfurling that truth cannot be isolated from all the vagaries of the expositor's own personal experience, and the enterprise cannot be constrained by editorial deadlines.

The Critical Importance of Hermeneutical Integrity

In the case of Job, the drama unfolds in the wake of a somewhat arresting wager between God and Satan over the fate of Job, a "blameless and upright man...who fears God and shuns evil" (1:8; 2:3). As Job begins to verbalize the utter meaninglessness of his unjust suffering he epitomizes our universal yearning for order, justice, and meaning in the world. The reader naturally expects the plot to resolve this dilemma by reconciling life's apparent injustice with the character of a just, loving, and sovereign God—in short, to provide a theodicy. This is the approach taken by some, including Harold Kushner in his popular treatment of innocent suffering,[5] but the argument of Job never provides this reconciliation: When God finally appears after Job has accused Him of blatant injustice in the wake of his unexplained catastrophes, not only does God fail to reconcile His justice with Job's innocent suffering, but He actually *indicts* Job for ignorance and presumption (38:1-40:2; 40:6-41:34). God's sarcastic diatribe only seems to affirm Job's failure as an exemplary servant (cf. 1:8), and Satan's original contention that God plays favorites (cf. 1:9-11) seems to be vindicated by Job's final blessing (42:10-17). Why is Job commended elsewhere for his exemplary righteousness and perseverance?[6] If God intended to communicate a distinct message and purpose in the story of Job, what meaning might we educe in view of the opening wager and Job's apparent failure?

Ecclesiastes challenges the reader with its own set of interpretive dilemmas. An anonymous editor-author (1:1-11; 7:27; 12:8-14) quotes the first person account of Qoheleth (1:12-12:7), a collector of proverbs and reflections who ostensibly matches the credentials of Solomon, the son of David and the wisest king in Israel's history (1:1, 12, 16). Yet the language of Ecclesiastes does not really match the vocabulary or expression of Solomon's known proverbs or other writings. Moreover, expositors have struggled notoriously to find some thread of logical coherence in Qoheleth's assorted reflections and aphorisms beyond the obvious resignation to life's apparent futility. Many have even abandoned all hope of tracing any coherent argument, message, or purpose in the book. Given that the author affirms that Qoheleth "pondered and sought out and set in

---

[5] Harold Kushner, *Why Bad Things Happen to Good People* (New York: Shocken Books, 1981).

[6] While Job is cited as a model of righteousness (Ezek 14:14, 20) and perseverance (Jas 5:11), these traits are best taken in the book of Job not as *object lessons* but as a *concession* that if the redemptive message applies to Job it should apply to all people, regardless of reputed righteousness or perseverance.

order many proverbs" (Eccl 12:9), how do we identify this "order" in an apparently fragmented text and piece together the textual elements in a way that accurately reflects the author's intended message and purpose? If the argument of Ecclesiastes does in fact elaborate a logical and coherent message and purpose, how do we reconcile the author's apparent misrepresentation of Qoheleth as Solomon?

Bartholomew has capably reviewed the history of interpretation of Ecclesiastes[7] and emphasizes the critical role of hermeneutical presuppositions, particularly epistemology, in approaching the book.[8] The Epilogue (Eccl 12:9-14) may very well supply the normative epistemological foundation[9] that validates the book's narrative unity.[10] Moreover, the similarity of themes and rhetorical purposes in Job and Ecclesiastes suggests that the unity of each book is mutually informed by the other.[11]

The Unity of Job and Ecclesiastes— A "Canonical Linguistic" Approach

The hermeneutical approach adopted herein affirms that the most reliable interpretation of Job and Ecclesiastes (as all the books of the Bible) comes from seeking and recognizing the "author's intended meaning as expressed in the biblical text."[12] The reliability of the method is based on the conviction that the text is inspired in its entirety and contains within itself all the clues the reader needs to recognize and validate the true meaning of the book. It might seem obvious that the most efficient way to discover this meaning would simply be to explore the text and discover these clues. However, some expositors question the authenticity or textual integrity of

---

[7] Craig Bartholomew, *Reading Ecclesiastes—Old Testament Exegesis and Hermeneutical Theory* (Rome: Pontifical Biblical Institute, 1998).

[8] Ibid., 265-270.

[9] James Reitman, "Words of Truth and Words of Purpose: Exegetical Insights into Authorial Intent from Ecclesiastes 12:9-14," presented at the 58th Annual Meeting of the Evangelical Theological Society, 2006 (www.21stcenturypress.com/wisdom.htm).

[10] Bartholomew, *Reading Ecclesiastes*, 104-107; 139-171; 265-67.

[11] This is why a "canonical linguistic" approach to interpretation (below) holds so much promise in unfolding the appropriate theology of the two books. See Kevin J. Vanhoozer, *The Drama of Doctrine—A Canonical-Linguistic Approach to Christian Theology* (Louisville: Westminster/John Knox, 2005).

[12] Elliott Johnson, *Expository Hermeneutics: An Introduction* (Grand Rapids: Zondervan, 1990), 23; see also Grant Osborne, *The Hermeneutical Spiral: A Comprehensive Introduction to Biblical Interpretation* (Downers Grove, IL: InterVarsity, 1991), 6-8; 366-7.

Job as it has been transmitted to us. Similarly, others question whether Qoheleth's collection of reflections and proverbs was ever meant to be understood as a cohesive piece of literature. But if we presuppose the inspiration, textual integrity, and cohesiveness of these books, then it makes sense to apply a consistent methodology to identify the author's *literary strategy, communicative intent,* and *strategic intent.*[13]

Our "preunderstanding" of this threefold intent is progressively adjusted in cycles as the processes of *induction* and *deduction* mutually inform each other, and the deeper nuances of intended meaning are eventually brought to light through this incremental "spiral" of recognition and exegesis.[14] Thus, the reader holds only a tentative understanding while the meaning adduced is iteratively adjusted during the interpretive process to cohere more and more precisely with the author's overarching intended meaning as it, too, gradually emerges. This incremental process continues over time until the expositor has arrived at an "accurate" interpretation; that is, a high probability (near-certainty) of having identified the intended overarching and composite meanings embedded in the text throughout the book (see Appendix). We find that even ostensibly clearer constructions can be incrementally "fine-tuned" this way; otherwise we rely too heavily on the "analogy of faith" principle—that obscure passages must be understood in light of "clearer" passages—resulting in interpretive "premature closure."

Job and Ecclesiastes can be theologically correlated with each other and the rest of Scripture only when the books are first studied as cohesive, self-contained pieces of literature. The expositions presented herein thus represent countless cycles of induction and deduction of the texts of these books, both as composite thought units and as integrated literary works. As the text incrementally yields its meanings during the interpretive process, theological correlation between the two books and with the rest of Scripture further sharpens and fills out the meanings adduced

---

[13] These are defined in the Appendix and under "Literary Composition" below. A well-argued rationale for this threefold stratification of authorial intent in the task of interpretation is offered by Kevin Vanhoozer, *Is There a Meaning in this Text? The Bible, the Reader, and the Morality of Literary Knowledge* (Grand Rapids, MI: Zondervan, 1998), 201-280, and Richard Averbeck, "God, People and the Bible: The Relationship between Illumination and Biblical Scholarship," in James Sawyer and Daniel Wallace (eds.), *Who's Afraid of the Holy Spirit?* (Dallas: Biblical Studies Press, 2005), 137-165.

[14] Osborne, *Hermeneutical Spiral,* 6; 14; 411-15; Johnson, *Expository Hermeneutics,* 75-6; 142-3; William Klein, Craig Blomberg, and Robert Hubbard, *Introduction to Biblical Interpretation* (Nashville: Thomas Nelson, 2004), 135-209.

from each book individually (see "Theological Composition" below).[15] Finally, the expositor's own "response" to the text ("application") will further inform the text on continued reflection over time.[16] When can we be confident that the understanding achieved in this mutually informing enterprise of *recognition* and *exegesis* is accurate enough to reliably represent the author's *communicative* and *strategic* intents? Before addressing this task of *validation*, let us first elaborate on the premises that support our interpretive method.

The premises that underlie the methodology are summarized below, followed by a synopsis of the distinctive interpretation that this methodology yields when applied to these two books of wisdom.[17]

Literal Composition. Consistent with the presumption of divine inspiration, our interpretive method presupposes that the book's intended meaning is embedded in the text and can be adduced by examining the text carefully. This is the literal premise, affirmed by Johnson to be the most basic to the accurate interpretation of Scripture.[18] Therefore, the true interpretation of any given section, passage, or thought unit encountered in the text must cohere under divine inspiration with the central, overarching meaning intended by the author (see Appendix). It follows that there exists an interpretive solution for each composite part of the text that harmonizes with the central, overarching meaning, so the expositor can be confident that it will be recognized in the text as it is "received" by revelation. Thus, when expositors encounter apparent inconsistencies among the various affirmations of the text, they should not conclude that the text is inauthentic, corrupt, or lacking cohesive design. Rather, they will presume that the inspired author has embedded the solution in the text and keep studying the text until they educe the intended meaning that reconciles these *prima facie* inconsistencies.

---

[15] A "canonical" reading accepts that our *present* understanding of Scripture cannot be fully consummated, since God's progressive revelation to man has not yet been completely fulfilled. For now, the best results can therefore be achieved by viewing all Scripture as derivative of a *canonical unity* and thus mutually informing. See, e.g., Vanhoozer, *Is There a Meaning?* 313-14; and idem., *Drama of Doctrine*, 239-359.

[16] The *meaning* of the text cannot be separated from its intended *purpose* (see below, "Application").

[17] *See* also Greg Parsons, "Guidelines for Understanding and Proclaiming the Book of Job," *BSac* 151 (1994), 393-413; and Craig Bartholomew, *Reading Ecclesiastes*, 226-70.

[18] Johnson, *Expository Hermeneutics*, 31-7.

The most important implication of the literal premise is that the expositor must examine the text both inductively and deductively in order to avoid *eisegesis*—the reading of one's own preconceived meanings into the text. As the reader approaches the text inductively,[19] the meanings embedded in the text are incrementally recognized. This begins with individual constructions "so central to what the author is saying that the author includes in the immediate contextual development what is needed to clarify and to specify all that he intends."[20] The reader must be attentive to the intended impact of the message on the author's audience *(communicative intent)* in the arrangement of his constructions within the literary framework of the text *(literary strategy)* in order to realize the readers' intended response to the message *(strategic intent)*.

Grammatical Composition. The next major premise affirms that in order to accurately communicate the author's intended meaning, the grammatical constructions that comprise the text are "expressed within the limits of common language usage."[21] That is, in order to address their needs as seen by God the biblical author under divine inspiration used conventions of language and grammar that were familiar to the readers at the time of writing. The expositor should thus be able to elucidate the intended meanings of the constructions in the text by appealing to grammatical conventions that prevailed at the time of writing. Can we reasonably assume that by now translators of successive versions of the Bible have thoroughly considered such grammatical conventions in order to accurately represent what the text affirms?

The problem is that even contemporary translations of Job and Ecclesiastes still vary considerably because of continuing controversy over the occasion of composition (see below) and the semantics and syntax of obscure constructions, which occur with relatively high frequency in both books. Thus, "the language of the book of Job is notable for its numerous rare words and unique examples of morphology and syntax."[22] The same can be said of Ecclesiastes, yet its own rare words and grammatical distinctives are very different from those of Job. Although Hebrew grammars, lexicons, interlinear translations, and technical commentaries can help the expositor of

---

[19] See, e.g., Hans Finzel, *Unlocking the Scriptures: Three Steps to Personal Bible Study* (Colorado Springs, CO: Victor Books, 2003); Howard and William Hendricks, *Living by the Book* (Chicago: Moody Press, 1991).

[20] Johnson, *Expository Hermeneutics*, 145.

[21] Johnson, *Expository Hermeneutics*, 38

[22] John Hartley, *The Book of Job*, NICOT (Grand Rapids, MI: Eerdmans, 1988), 5.

both books to delineate the semantic and grammatical options for obscure constructions, the primary determinant of meaning for these constructions is the context in which they are embedded, governed by an overarching literary design (see "Literary Composition"). As we evaluate these various semantic and grammatical options, they are iteratively tested for the best contextual fit with their mutually informing associated constructions, as noted above in "Literal Composition."

Historical Composition. The author's meaning is also influenced by the historical occasion for writing.[23] The historical settings of Job and Ecclesiastes are somewhat opaque and debated, yet I contend that these can also be inferred from the context. A key historical feature in both books is the unparalleled life circumstance of each protagonist. The "blameless and upright" Job is a perfect foil for his three "comforters," whose lineages can be traced to patriarchs who were originally excluded from God's promises to Abraham. By disrupting their flawed conceptions of the God of Abraham, the unexplained suffering of their "blameless and upright" friend afforded them a unique opportunity to be reconciled to God. The repeated mention of their tribes of origin during their contentious dialogue with Job should remind any reader familiar with ancient Israel of their historical alienation from God's favor and blessing.

Similarly, Qoheleth takes on the royal persona of Solomon, the wisest king in the history of Israel. Again, this singular precedent is chosen to inform the imagination of any reader familiar with Israelite history who might contemplate the inferences that Qoheleth draws as they reflect on the inevitable failure of even the greatest resources known—Solomon's unprecedented wisdom and wealth—to afford either lasting satisfaction in this life or a lasting legacy after death. The familiar historical circumstance and mindset of each protagonist in either book thus affords an ideal backdrop for dialogue and reflection designed to facilitate the reader's recognition of the author's intended meaning.

Literary Composition. If the first three premises underlying the process of interpretation are integral to a divine communication that can be understood by limited man, then it follows that the inspired author had to articulate that communication in a humanly perspicuous way. Each book of the Bible is therefore presumed to follow readily *discernible* literary conventions (genre, style) in order to express the *communicative* and *strategic* intent according to a *textual design* that would have been recognized by the

---

[23] Johnson, *Expository Hermeneutics*, 40ff.

original audience. The expositor should therefore approach each book of the Bible as literature and expect the textual design to follow a discernible *literary strategy* by which the author has embedded his intended meanings into the text.[24] The textual design thus provides a logical template for the reader to establish coherence between the various meanings embedded in the individual thought units and the overall intended meaning (see Appendix). A thorough understanding would thus dictate that the expositor meticulously examine the governing literary style(s) and composite textual design(s) into which the author embedded *both* his inspired messages *and* the kinds of responses he intended to elicit from his readers (see "Application," below).

Attention to literary strategy is particularly crucial in the book of Job. Even the average reader who accepts the book as a coherent, integrated piece of literature will over time be able to discern the main literary elements from ubiquitous clues embedded in the text. It is not difficult to identify the coordinated interplay of narrative, lament, dramatic dialogue, and legal metaphor in the argument, especially the overarching literary framework of the *lawsuit* genre. Each of these elements serves a key role in framing and elaborating the author's intended meaning. In this regard the broader mirror-image symmetry of the dramatic plot is especially important. Even short narratives in the book of Job depend heavily on these features of genre and textual design to provide the literary framework for their intended meaning, so a mere verse-by-verse approach to interpretation will fall hopelessly short of fully informing the author's message and purpose. Some of the references in the bibliography offer good insight into the plot structure and textual design of the book—the excerpts selected from Zuck's anthology[25] are especially helpful.

The literary strategy of Ecclesiastes presents somewhat more of a challenge. Although the editor-author affirms that Qoheleth selected and compiled his proverbs according to an inspired intentional textual design to yield "words of truth" and "words of purpose" (12:9-11), it is not readily apparent how these elements are woven together to produce a cohesive piece of literature. The literary premise dictates that the expositor presuppose such cohesiveness and be patient enough to eventually recognize the inspired textual design as the text is iteratively interrogated for clues to educe that design, beginning with the frame narrator's own attestation that Qoheleth "pondered, searched out and arranged many proverbs. [He]

---

[24] Ibid., 43ff.

[25] Roy Zuck, ed., *Sitting with Job: Selected Studies on the Book of Job* (Grand Rapids: Baker, 1992).

sought to find delightful words [Heb. "words of purpose"] and to write words of truth correctly" (Eccl 12:9-10).[26] A second clue is that the cumulative (pessimistic) inferences of futility ("there is no advantage") in the first half of the argument logically culminate in a crisis of disillusionment (6:1-12) that sets up the literary transition (7:1-14). The transition is set apart from the preceding and following text by its distinctive sequence of "better than" proverbs, distinguishing wise from foolish responses to disillusionment. This prepares the reader for the change in tone to *cautious optimism* of Qoheleth's object lessons in response to disillusionment in the second half of the book (7:15-12:7).

Theological Composition. The last interpretive premise hinges directly on the notion of the dual inspiration of Scripture discussed above in connection with the literal premise. If the human author's intended meaning is divinely inspired, then God's communicative acts represented in the text should reflect His character and desired relationship with the created world. Consequently, we should expect these themes to emerge progressively from the text in a way that sets forth the character of God and His purposes for man and the rest of creation.[27]

> [T]he words and actions of God in human history are related to each other as they are subsumed under one or more of the four fundamental purposes of God in history:
> - To bless man over creation,
> - To permit evil to overcome man,
> - To judge evil through the agency of man, and
> - To deliver man from the Evil One and from evil.[28]

On even a cursory reading, the prologue of the book of Job (chaps. 1-2) displays all four of these theological purposes immediately from the outset of the argument. While these same purposes are not at all transparent on a first reading of Ecclesiastes, they are ultimately surfaced in the iterative cycle of recognition and exegesis described above, becoming more evident as the direction and flow of Qoheleth's argument gradually emerge in the interpretative process. The footnotes to the present exposition follow the

---

[26] The hermeneutical implications of the author's own authentication of Qoheleth's literary *epistemology* and *teleology* in this passage are explored in detail in Reitman, "Words of Truth." Basically, the expositor cannot be content with extracting the *message* of a given text—one must also be sensitive to the author's *strategic* intent (see the first paragraph of this section and "Application" below).

[27] This is Johnson's theological premise (*Expository Hermeneutics*, 50-3).

[28] Ibid., 122.

development of these purposes in the respective arguments of both books and ultimately trace the outline for a theological anthropology that centers on man's intended role as chosen "agent" of God's redemptive work in the world.

While it is imperative that we begin our inquiry into these theological purposes by approaching the books individually as coherent literary compositions (see above), we cannot expect to adduce all that is intended from a "closed" study; the fullest possible theological understanding can come only from a "canonical" reading of the books.[29] For this reason the footnotes also provide helpful correlation of the theological purposes of Job and Ecclesiastes with other portions of Scripture, which is critical to validating a "canonical linguistic" approach to the interpretation of these books and of their appropriate application for contemporary believers (see "Theological Correlation" under "How to Use This Commentary"). Such correlation in turn informs the arguments of Job and Ecclesiastes which both initially emphasize the futility of human *self-sufficiency* and then redirect the reader's attention to the advantage of *fearing God* (see "A Distinctive View of the Arguments," below).

Validation. The notion of validation presupposes that only one interpretive solution is true for a given text, though it may be multivalent or "layered." Confidence in the validity of a given interpretation is based on probability theory[30]—the likelihood that the interpretation represents the author's intended meaning. The hermeneutical framework presented affords criteria to determine whether the interpretation of a verse, passage, or whole book of the Bible has a high probability of being embraced as the true interpretation. This process involves comparing the proposed solution with alternative interpretations of the textual data for *comprehensiveness*, *competence*, *coherence*, and *consistency* (see the definitions of these criteria in the Appendix). In the present exposition of Job and Ecclesiastes, when detailed exegetical evidence is required to validate interpretive conclusions, it is presented in the footnotes in order to facilitate the flow of the commentary proper. This step is crucial during the interpretive process, because confident and appropriate *examples* of the text depends on an accurate and decisively validated *interpretation*.

---

[29] Cf. above n. 15. For helpful history and examples, see Craig Bartholomew and Anthony Thiselton, eds, *Canon and Biblical Interpretation*, Vol. 7, Scripture and Hermeneutics Series (Grand Rapids: Zondervan, 2006).

[30] Johnson, *Expository Hermeneutics*, Part 5; see also Osborne, *Hermeneutical Spiral*, 406-8.

Application. The present approach presupposes that authorial intent can indeed be inferred from discernible, objective meaning embedded in the text.[31] That is, the author followed recognizable conventions of literary genre (i.e., he chose a *literary strategy*) to 1) compose logically coherent texts ("locutions")[32] that 2) communicate the message[s] or emotions ("illocutions") he intended the reader to identify or feel. However, if God communicated to mankind with the intent of evoking particular responses that conform to His purposes for the created world, then we should be able to adduce not only the intended *message* or *emotion* (i.e., the author's *communicative* intent) from the given text but also the intended *response* from the reader (i.e., the author's *strategic* intent);[33] he intended for his reader to respond with a particular kind of behavior ("perlocution") or *application* to the message or emotion conveyed in the text. So, the range of appropriate application for readers in any age is constrained by the author's *strategic intent*—the particular kinds of responses he intended to elicit with his text. If the author has been inspired by God to compose his text with these particular ends in mind, then it also behooves the reader/interpreter to seek out this aspect of author's intent as much as his *literary strategy* or *communicative intent.* By recognizing the strategic intents behind given texts, expositors should be able to determine what kinds of behavioral responses would fit within the range of suitable application for the individual readers within the intended audience.

Appropriate application thus involves properly identifying God's message and purpose(s) for the original audience in order to determine how those purposes apply to the contemporary reader under differing circumstances. While expositors often argue that this process—referred to as "contextualization"[34]—is a highly subjective experience, we can infer that since strategic intent is embedded in the Biblical message it affords a decidedly *objective* basis for appropriate application over time: Object lessons based on *theological* purposes (see above) should

---

[31] *See* above n. 12 and associated text.

[32] *See also* Appendix. The terms "locution," "illocution," and "perlocution" are based on Vanhoozer's use of speech-act theory to clarify this threefold stratification of authorial intent (see references in n. 13).

[33] *See* Vanhoozer, *Is There a Meaning?* 261 (cf. 228), as cited in Reitman, "Words of Truth." This is the basic premise of the field of *rhetorical criticism*, however it is my contention that discernible strategic intent is embedded in all portions of text large enough to communicate a "self-contained," logically consistent message or emotion (see Appendix).

[34] Osborne, *Hermeneutical Spiral*, chap. 15.

still be applicable to a contemporary audience and correlate with the rest of Scripture. While the *specific* applications of the biblical message may vary depending on the "context" of the contemporary reader, such applications will always be of the same *kind*.[35] The exposition in the Commentary therefore includes sufficient validation of the author's strategic intent in each passage to warrant its inclusion in the "summary statement" as a discernible component of authorial intent and thereby to help guide "suitable" application (see below, "How to Use This Commentary").

A Distinctive View of the Arguments of Job and Ecclesiastes

When this hermeneutic approach is applied, it turns out that the book of Job is less about reconciling God's character with innocent suffering than about the opportunity presented by such suffering for us to relinquish self-sufficiency and more effectively mediate God's government of Creation. Similarly, Ecclesiastes is not just a cynical tract proclaiming the futility of life without God. Rather, the author's compiled proverbs and reflections evolve from *justified cynicism* over the inevitable futility of self-sufficiency to an *informed optimism* that the one who fears God can indeed find a lasting legacy in the inscrutable work of God. In both Job and Ecclesiastes, readers are challenged to embrace the agency that their Creator has entrusted to them. This entails facing disillusionment in adversity with authentic mourning, forsaking self-sufficiency, and enlisting wisdom's advantage in the fear of God in order to accomplish God's preordained purposes and receive an inheritance in the work of God.

The experience of the protagonist in each book is explicitly depicted in order to argue from greater to lesser (or *a fortiori*) in the lives of the readers. That is, if the object lessons in these books applied perfectly to Job and Qoheleth—paragons of self-sufficient righteousness and wisdom, respectively—*much more* would the same lessons apply to the *less* righteous or wise original readers (and hearers). In each case the first half of the argument establishes the unequivocal failure of unprecedented human righteousness, wisdom, and/or wealth, and the protagonist is inexorably frustrated in his search for satisfaction until he is utterly disillusioned over the failure of self-sufficient strategies. The protagonist's disillusionment provokes a crisis: He must choose between *redoubling* his effort to make

---

[35] Vanhoozer, *Drama of Doctrine*, 126-33; 313-14, as cited in Reitman, "Words of Truth."

his life work or *relinquishing* his self-reliant strategies to fear a God who often seems absent, capricious, or even hostile. Although his choice to redouble self-effort invariably leads to entrenched bitterness and despair, the fear of God opens his heart to the benefits of true wisdom and thus equips him to fully exploit his God-given portion. In both cases authentic mourning over failed self-sufficiency prepares them to flourish as His agents in the fear of God. The overall strategic intent in both books is to *dissuade* readers with far less promising resources from clinging to self-sufficiency and instead *persuade* them to fear God in pursuit of a lasting legacy in their God-given portion.

Both arguments thus turn on man's need for a change of disposition in response to life's inevitable disillusionment. The literary transition in each book highlights the importance of this choice and provides the key to the textual arrangement of material in each book. Job had pled unsuccessfully with his three older friends to empathize with him in suffering but was then unable to find an advocate who could compel God's testimony (16:19; 19:25) to vindicate him against his friends' false charges (9:33). His bitter determination to be vindicated in the eyes of his friends prevented him from truly seeing God or prevailing as God's exemplary agent (cf. 1:8; 2:3), and the ode to Wisdom (chap. 28) sets the stage for Job's summary appeal in which he charges God with injustice (chaps. 29-31). The author then intrudes into the dialogue to formally authenticate Elihu's testimony (32:1-5). Elihu's own contention, in dramatic contrast to the other three friends, is that he is inspired (32:6-33:4)—*his* is the only truly prophetic voice. The dramatic flow of the argument thus palpably shifts as Elihu systematically reverses Satan's deception regarding God's character (33-37) and prepares Job to listen and obey when God Himself appears (38-42). By correcting theological misconceptions, Elihu's speeches thus exposed Job's need to repent of his bold presumption—his insistence that God was obligated to explain his unjust suffering, vindicate him, and restore his estate.

Job's silence in response to Elihu's correction suggests a change of heart from the progressive vituperation he displayed in response to the other three friends (chaps. 4-27). But YHWH had wagered for more than Job's *silence* in order to prevail over Satan—Job had to be vindicated as God's *exemplary servant* (1:8; 2:3). YHWH's speeches (chaps. 38-41) thus expanded on Elihu's correctives mainly to controvert Job's claim that God—by afflicting him—had subverted His own purposes in creating Job (cf. 7:17-21; 10:2-18). In reversing Job's misconceptions, Elihu convicted him of self-righteous presumption, asserting that Job had in fact already received more mercy than he deserved—he need only accept God's redemptive initiative in his life. But before Job could appropriate Elihu's wisdom and realize his role as God's chosen agent (42:7-10) he had to mourn and repent of presuming on God (42:1-6). Ironically, as soon as Job repented of his presumption and acquiesced to his Creator's prerogative of withholding blessing, he was immediately transformed into an exemplary agent of God's creative purposes and beat Satan at his own game: While still completely stripped of his estate, Job simply obeyed his commission to intercede for his friends and reconciled to God the very ones who by accusing Job had become Satan's surrogates. Thus, the drama's conclusion—Job's ultimate restoration—hinges not on his legendary perseverance through suffering (Jas 5:11) but rather on his transformed disposition in response to *hearing* Elihu and *seeing* God.

The literary transition of Ecclesiastes plays a similar structural role, dividing the argument into two stages: The first stage traces Qoheleth's account of his search for a lasting legacy to the disheartening conclusion that radical self-sufficiency can only end in disillusionment and despair (1:12-6:12), as he expresses in the concluding rhetorical question "Who knows what is good for man…?" (6:12). Qoheleth answers this question in the transitional passage by posing two radically different alternatives in response to life's disillusionment—*authentic mourning* or *false optimism*—and he describes the consequences of either choice (Eccl 7:1-14): Since the heart is edified only "in the house of mourning" (7:1-4), it is better to heed "the rebuke of the wise" than to appease despair with the "laughter of fools" (7:5-7). The choice to appease despair only "debases the heart" (7:7b) as one clings to broken dreams with entrenched bitterness (7:8-10). Those who choose to *mourn* and heed *wise rebuke* attain the benefits of wisdom and a fulfilling inheritance in the work of God (7:11-14).

The second stage of Qoheleth's argument then equips those readers with the wisdom they need to live out their intended legacy. Mankind's only hope of overcoming the inherent limitations of human depravity, uncertainty, and mortality is to relinquish self-sufficiency for the fear of God, in order to find a lasting legacy in the inscrutable work of God (7:15-12:7). The logical progression of this literary framework decisively vindicates the author's own attestation that Qoheleth arranged his selected proverbs and personal reflections according to an inspired textual design and purpose (12:9-11) and defeats the all-too-prevalent view that the book displays no apparent textual coherence.

In conclusion, the books of Job and Ecclesiastes complement one another to deliver a compelling and universally applicable message. The title of the combined exposition reflects the critical role of *mourning* in leading to the fear of God: The two arguments together challenge the pervasive mindset of self-sufficiency that characterizes mankind's natural heritage in fallen Adam. The *a fortiori* object lessons exemplified by both protagonists are perfectly designed to dissuade the reader from pursuing the same self-sufficient strategies to find meaning in life. Once each protagonist is profoundly disillusioned by adversity, his natural penchant for self-sufficiency is displaced by mourning in order to attain the crucial disposition of brokenness and dependency before God. Once the readers—like Job or Qoheleth—are disillusioned enough in adversity to mourn the utter failure of their own self-sufficiency, they are similarly equipped in the fear of God to overcome their inherent human limitations and realize their own preordained purposes as agents of the Creator. Those who choose to avoid such mourning will only fall short of their calling and their God-given legacy as His chosen agents.

How to Use this Commentary

The following material provides the rationale for the format used in the Commentary. Stylistically, we have chosen boldface type to indicate **emphasis** and italics to indicate *themes* and *direct quotes* from Scripture.

Expository Outline. This outline provides the basic thematic template for the Overview and the Synthetic Chart and displays the vertical organization of the Commentary proper, subdivided by the level of expository detail: The higher-order section titles (Roman numerals) best represent the overall flow of the argument in the Commentary proper, while the lowest-order titles are matched by the greatest expository detail in the Commentary proper (including the lexical and syntactical analysis in the footnotes). The reader can thus explore the exposition at whatever level of detail desired, comparing the exposition in the Commentary at parallel subsections of the Expository Outline. These subsections must cohere thematically with the larger sections to which they belong. The intermediate section titles in the outline (designated by Arabic caps or numerals) are reproduced in the diagonal portion of the "Synthetic Chart."

Synthetic Chart. Preceding the Overview and exposition of both Job and Ecclesiastes is a Jensen-style "synthetic" chart[36] that frames the

[36] *See* Irving Jensen, *Independent Bible Study* (Chicago: Moody Press, 1963). Other helpful resources on the use of synthetic charts to visually sharpen the interpretive process include a web-based supplement to Finzel's *Unlocking the Scriptures*; and Hendricks and Hendricks, *Living by the Book*, chaps. 24, 37.

exposition by graphically representing the book's literary structure and coherence. Each chart is a visual representation of the synthesis of the overall textual design and flow of the argument of each book as the Commentary took its final form and is meant to help expositor and reader alike visually integrate the expository details with the author's overall message and purpose. The upper section of the chart represents the central themes and major stages of the argument. The diagonal portion of the chart is drawn from the intermediate tier of section titles from the Expository Outline to horizontally display the logical flow of the argument as it contributes to the overarching intended meaning (see diagram in the Appendix). The lower section of the chart draws from the expository discussion and the footnotes to distill the major theological themes and horizontally trace their sequential development in the argument.

Overview. A literary and thematic overview of the argument of each book is offered in advance of the exposition in order to orient the reader to the author's overarching literary strategy, communicative intent, and strategic intent. These broad conclusions are presented first, because the expository process is itself informed by the overall direction and flow of the argument, thus protecting both reader and expositor from getting lost in the exegetical "weeds." While the reader and expositor alike are "gambling" that the conclusions reached in the Overview are refined enough by this cyclical interpretive process to accurately reflect the author's intended meaning, the process is naturally self-correcting: From the standpoint of *synthesis*, the Overview, Expository Outline, and Synthetic Chart have all been repeatedly adjusted and refined over the years to incorporate the results of progressively detailed exegesis of the composite portions of the text, thereby forestalling the natural tendency toward interpretive "premature closure." From the standpoint of *exegesis*, by representing the distilled product of countless cycles of recognition and exegesis, the Overview serves as a test of *coherence* of the tentative results of the detailed exegesis of the composite passages (see Validation) and forces the expositor to return to the text when these results do not adequately cohere.

Summary Statements. All but the lowest-tier subsections of the exposition are headed by summary statements. These statements give the reader a quick synopsis of the argument of each section with respect to 1) the aspects of literary genre and textual design that distinguish it from other sections *(literary strategy)*; 2) what the author intended to say in that section *(communicative intent)*; and 3) the author's intended purpose for the audience in that section *(strategic intent)*. Each statement illustrates the *competence* and *comprehensiveness* of the interpretation (see

Validation) to account for the textual data in that section and summarizes how it contributes to the overall argument of the book. The summary statements at parallel levels of the Expository Outline can be compared to document their coherence within the overall argument.

The first clause of each summary statement describes the author's *literary strategy*—the *genre* and *textual design* the author employed in that section of the argument to express the message summarized in the second clause (below). To indicate the instrumental role of this textual design, the first clause is introduced with the preposition "by" (or when preferable, "in" or "with"). Like interlocking puzzle pieces, the textual designs of all the smaller sections should fit together to comprise the literary structure of larger sections and in turn the argument as a whole. The first clause of each summary statement can thus be compared at corresponding levels of the Expository Outline to show how each section contributes to the overall literary structure.

The second clause of each summary statement (**bold type**) presents the author's *communicative intent* and begins with the subject "Qoheleth..." or "the author..." to express the core *message* the author intended to convey to his target audience in that section. This clause would match the statement found at the corresponding level in a standard exegetical outline and can be compared with the corresponding clauses of the other summary statements at the same level of detail in the Expository Outline. The message should *cohere* with the book's overarching message and the developing argument and be *consistent* with theological truth adduced from the rest of Scripture (see Theological Composition and Validation). It should also provide the logical incentive at each level of the argument to elicit the appropriate reader response, as summarized in the third clause.

The third clause of the summary statement describes the author's *strategic intent* or "final" purpose[37] in that given section. It relates the truth of his message to the needs of his target audience and expresses the desired response that the inspired author intended to elicit from his readers with his message. The clause is introduced by the purpose marker "in order that..." or "so that..." to indicate the suitable "kinds" of response author hoped to elicit from his readers (see Application, above). By establishing how the author's object lessons were intended to influence the historical audience, this clause helps to contextualize the message for the contemporary reader. Again, this "final purpose" in each section should also cohere with the overarching purpose of the book.

---

[37] Vanhoozer, *Is There a Meaning?* 218 (cf. 228), as cited in Reitman, "Words of Truth."

Expository Discussion. The expository discussion cites the key evidence gathered from the expositor's study of the text in the iterative cycle of recognition and exegesis to justify the interpretive conclusions represented by the summary statement. Sufficient exposition is included to explain and validate each component of the summary statement and warrant reader confidence in the interpretive synopsis. By highlighting the textual constructions that link the passage to its near and remote context, the discussion clarifies how the passage fits into the argument as a whole: It establishes the literary, historical/relational, and logical coherence of the composite thought units of the given section of text and explains how the embedded meanings and purposes contribute to the overarching meaning and theological purpose(s). The meaning educed from more opaque constructions in the text is supported by more detailed exegetical and theological validation in the footnotes.

Footnotes. The analytical detail in the footnotes is largely meant to complement the synthetic emphasis in the main exposition; the footnotes should thus be viewed as facilitating rather than fragmenting the flow of the argument, clarifying how initially confusing textual data most likely contributes to the author's logic. However, these footnotes serve a broader range of purposes than those of more technically oriented commentaries: Besides validating the interpretive solutions for more controversial or opaque constructions, the footnotes help develop a theology—especially theological anthropology—that is internally consistent and correlates with other portions of Scripture. Footnotes addressing similar theological content are therefore extensively cross-referenced to facilitate the reader's incremental grasp of this theology. Some of the footnotes also cite relevant excerpts from popular authors to help the contemporary reader apply the Biblical author's message. The footnotes are thus an integral part of the commentary—they help to elucidate and validate the less obvious interpretive conclusions; enhance the contemporary reader's understanding of the books' theology; and bring into focus the fitting response of God's agents to His message in these two books.

Theological Correlation. The Postscript ("The Significance of Ecclesiastes") that concludes the commentary continues the theological development begun in the footnotes. It is theological reflection from a "canonical" perspective, summarizing the relevance of Ecclesiastes as illuminated by the rest of Scripture, especially the book of Job. To this end an extensive subject index has been provided to facilitate correlation of similar theological topics throughout the exposition of both books of

Wisdom (esp. in the footnotes), as well as the discussions in the Preface, Introduction, and Postscript. Two "Personal Notes" are also offered, one in the Introduction to the exposition of Job and the other in the afterword to the exposition of Ecclesiastes, as a kind of "inclusio of application." By thus demonstrating how the book's theology correlates with the rest of Scripture and is also "true to life," the Postscript and Personal Notes demonstrate the *consistency* of the interpretation (see Validation).

Bibliography. The references selected in the three bibliographies help validate the hermeneutical foundation (see above) and the interpretive conclusions reached in the two commentaries. The references are generally accessible to the reader interested in more in-depth study. Especially valuable are the two anthologies compiled by Roy Zuck on the lexical, grammatical, historical, literary-structural, and theological issues entailed in the composition of Job and Ecclesiastes. Several popular treatments are also included in the bibliography and excerpted in the footnotes where appropriate for their clear insight into the topics of self-sufficiency, mourning, and disillusionment in adversity. While these do not typically cite either Job or Ecclesiastes *per se*, they well express the key theological purposes woven into these two closely related, inspired books of Wisdom.

Appendix

Adapted from "Words of Truth," www.21stcenturypress.com/wisdom.htm

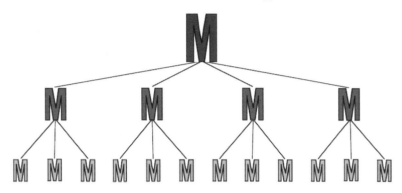

- It is presupposed that the inspired author wrote a literal message with a specific purpose in mind ("authorial intent"), that the meaning is embedded in the text itself, and that the text is woven together with literary integrity—each part of the text coheres with the overarching message and purpose of the book:
- The largest "M" represents the author's overarching meaning (message and purpose) to his readers and governs the intended message(s) and purpose(s) of all the composite texts within the book
- The book's major sections are represented by intermediate "M's" and govern the meaning of the smaller portions of text subordinated under them but all cohere with the overarching "M." There may be several intermediate tiers, but all the "M's" in the same tier should flow logically from one to the next as the author develops his argument in the book
- The most basic unit of meaning, represented by the small "M" in the lowest tier of the diagram, is the "thought unit"—this is often represented in the biblical text as a paragraph

"Synthesis" with a Synthetic Chart, Expository Outline,
and Summary Statements
- A Jensen-style "synthetic chart" serves as a graphic aid to help put the whole book together
- Each of the units of "meaning" can be epitomized in an expository outline consisting of pithy "section titles" to help the expositor quickly recognize how the related sections cohere thematically
- The logic of the argument in any given section of the expository outline can then be expressed in a three-part "summary statement" that represents the author's:

- **literary strategy** within the first clause, starting with the preposition "by," "with," or "in" to reflect the *literary genre/textual design* used in that section to communicate the intended message and purpose
- **communicative intent** within the second clause, beginning with the phrase "the author with affirms [illustrates, warns, urges, exposes, reveals]…" to reflect the *intended impact of the message* in that section on the reader
- **strategic intent** within the last clause, starting with the phrase "so that the readers/we might…" to describe the *intended response to the author's message* in that section—*the readers' appropriate "performance" before God*

The Hermeneutical Process: How Do We Get There?

This involves *initial recognition* of the more obvious features of textual design and the related communicative acts in the text, followed by *iterative testing* of the more obscure texts for conformity to the emerging intended design and meaning, as it is incrementally refined over time. Thus, "I am…spiralling nearer and nearer to the text's intended meaning as I refine my hypotheses and allow the text to continue to challenge and correct…alternative interpretations….The preliminary understanding derived from the inductive study and the in-depth understanding unlocked through research interact and correct one another…the inductive and deductive…together to understand the 'meaning' of the text" (Osborne, *Hermeneutical Spiral*, 6, 14). This cyclical inductive-deductive interchange applies to elements of both textual *design* and *meaning:* Our progressive recognition of each of these mutually informs the other to clarify textual constructions that are initially opaque, thus incrementally sharpening our (pre)understanding of the intended meaning (Klein et al, *Biblical Interpretation*, 166). Finally, the reader's understanding of this meaning is further refined throughout life, as *correlation* and *application* of the message continue to inform his/her understanding.

Validation: How Do We *Know* We Are There?

By comparing section titles and summary statements with each other and with each of the textual elements in their respective sections, the proposed interpretation is tested for:

- *Comprehensiveness*—are *all* the textual elements addressed by the interpretation?
- *Competence*—does the solution for each element *adequately* explain the textual data?
- *Coherence*—do all the elements in context contribute to a *unified* meaning and purpose?
- *Consistency*—is the proposed meaning *true to life* and does it *correlate* with the rest of Scripture?

Selected Bibliography

Averbeck, Richard. "God, People and the Bible: The Relationship between Illumination and Biblical Scholarship." In *Who's Afraid of the Holy Spirit?* ed. James Sawyer and Daniel Wallace, 137-165. Dallas, TX: Biblical Studies Press, 2005.

Bartholomew, Craig. *Reading Ecclesiastes—Old Testament Exegesis and Hermeneutical Theory.* Analecta Biblica. Rome: Pontifico Istituto Biblico, 1998.

Bartholomew, Craig, Scott Hahn, Robin Parry, Christopher Seitz, and Al Wolters, eds. *Canon and Biblical Interpretation.* Scripture and Hermeneutics Series, ed. Craig Bartholomew and Anthony Thiselton, vol. 7. Grand Rapids: Zondervan, 2006.

Finzel, Hans. *Unlocking the Scriptures: Three Steps to Personal Bible Study.* Colorado Springs: Victor Books, 2003.

Hendricks, Howard, and William Hendricks. *Living by the Book.* Chicago: Moody Press, 1991.

Jensen, Irving. *Independent Bible Study.* Chicago: Moody Press, 1963.

Johnson, Elliott E. *Expository Hermeneutics: An Introduction.* Grand Rapids: Zondervan, 1990.

Klein, William, Craig Blomberg, and Robert Hubbard. *Introduction to Biblical Interpretation.* Nashville: Thomas Nelson, 2004.

Osborne, Grant. *The Hermeneutical Spiral: A Comprehensive Introduction to Biblical Interpretation.* Downers Grove, IL: InterVarsity, 1991.

Parsons, Greg W. "Guidelines for Understanding and Proclaiming the Book of Job." *Bibliotheca Sacra* 151 (1994): 393-413.

Reitman, James. "The Debate on Assisted Suicide—Redefining Morally Appropriate Care for People with Intractable Suffering." *Issues in Law & Med.* 11 (1995): 299-329.

_____. "Wise Advocacy." In *Dignity and Dying: A Christian Appraisal,* ed. John F. Kilner, Arlene B. Miller, and Edmund D. Pellegrino, 208-22. Grand Rapids: Eerdmans, 1996.

_____. "The Dilemma of 'Medical Futility'—A 'Wisdom Model' for Decisionmaking." *Issues in Law & Med.* 12 (1996): 231-64.

_____. "A 'Wisdom' Perspective on Advocacy for the Suicidal." In *Suicide: A Christian Response,* ed. Timothy J. Demy & Gary P. Stewart, 369-85. Grand Rapids: Kregel, 1998.

_____. "Words of Truth and Words of Purpose—Exegetical Insights into Authorial Intent from Ecclesiastes 12:9-14." Paper presented at the 58th Annual Meeting of the Evangelical Theological Society, November, 2006. Available at www.21stcenturypress.com/wisdom.htm.

Reitman, James S., Byron C. Calhoun, and Nathan J. Hoeldtke. "Perinatal Hospice: A Response to Early Termination for Severe Congenital Anomalies." In *Genetic Engineering: A Christian Response,* ed. Timothy J. Demy & Gary P. Stewart, 197-211. Grand Rapids: Kregel, 1999.

Vanhoozer, Kevin J. *Is There a Meaning in this Text? The Bible, the Reader, and the Morality of Literary Knowledge.* Grand Rapids, MI: Zondervan, 1998.

_____. *First Theology: God, Scripture & Hermeneutics.* Downers Grove, IL: InterVarsity Press, 2002.

_____. *The Drama of Doctrine—A Canonical-Linguistic Approach to Christian Theology.* Louisville: Westminster/John Knox, 2005.

Zuck, Roy B., ed. *Sitting with Job: Selected Studies on the Book of Job.* Grand Rapids: Baker, 1992.

_____, ed. *Reflecting with Solomon: Selected Studies on the Book of Ecclesiastes.* Grand Rapids: Baker, 1994.

JOB:
SUFFERING AGENT
OF THE CREATOR

Seeing the God of Redemptive Purposes

INTRODUCTION

What Do You Mean, "Agent"?

A Personal Note

It is especially difficult to be humbled by adversity in front of people whose approval and respect we seek. When circumstances keep us from realizing our expectations, we naturally want to be proven right in spite of appearances to the contrary; the last thing we want to hear is "I told you so." Job, a man who was deemed "blameless and upright, who feared God and shunned evil" (1:1), had earned the approval and respect of others as "the greatest of all the people of the East" (1:3). So, when Job is unfairly devastated by adversity, we want to see "right" prevail. It seems entirely warranted and appropriate that Job sought so passionately to be vindicated in the eyes of his friends and to regain their approval and respect. It seems unfair, even cruel, of God not to vindicate him after such undeserved devastation; in short, we can sympathize with Job.

During my exposition of the book of Job I had to endure a lengthy ordeal of my own, and the resulting disillusionment gave me deeper insight into the mind of the author. Although I had done very well as a military physician I became increasingly disenchanted with the incursions of managed care into military medicine. It seemed that my colleagues were capitulating without a fight and that I was the only one who would stand up for the way things ought to be. As I continued to resist the inexorable erosion of my professional "world" I was determined that I would vindicate my views against this insidious philosophy of healthcare. I argued for several years to convince my superiors that I was right, but my efforts were repeatedly thwarted. Ironically, as my disillusionment grew to the point of despair, I was in the midst of a major revision of this commentary on the book of Job.

An unhealthy contrariness began to dominate my style of relating to others which seemed reminiscent of Job's attitude towards his three friends, and I was reported to my superiors several times over the last few years of my career. My wife Peggy was deeply concerned that I might throw away everything I had worked for and tried desperately several times to convince me that I was depressed and needed help, but I was not about to give in to my adverse circumstances. The crisis came to a head one day after several co-workers complained to my supervisor, and my oppositional attitude again came to the attention of the chain of command.

I was called in, reprimanded, and strongly "encouraged" to change my behavior, even as I earnestly tried to "defend my ways"[1]—I was **right** and the system was **wrong**. Although I backed away from frank insubordination I was deeply disillusioned—I could not change the system alone and didn't know how I would be able to endure this last tour of duty. I was broken and ready to mourn.[2]

The next morning a civilian co-worker who was a believer knocked on my door—I had confided my situation to her the day before. When she told me she had prayed for me and asked how it went, I dissolved into tears; I was overwhelmed that she cared at all. In my medical clinic that same afternoon I saw a new patient, a retired senior military officer. As we discussed his health history, this gentleman seemed to take an interest in me and asked about my interests. Still stinging from my reprimand the day before, I was not in a mood to chat but I did mention that I was writing a commentary on the book of Job. With a look of surprise, he related the story of his son's brutal murder 14 years before; he described the prominent role that the book of Job had played in mourning over his son's death and he wanted to talk with me more.

A week later he gave me a copy of the book his wife had written, recounting their experience of mourning.[3] As I read the book that evening I was deeply moved and again shed tears. The next morning my own depressed mother committed suicide. Thus began my own extended journey of mourning, triggered by the convergence of this event and my crisis of disillusionment over the developments in my career.

I reflected on the difficult circumstances that preceded my mother's death and pondered our broken relationship. I was soon convicted of how poorly and selfishly we both related to others in general. I saw in retrospect how seldom others were ever led by me to see God more clearly. As it dawned on me what God was doing in my own struggle I developed a deeper appreciation of God's redemptive purposes, as exemplified in Job's life. Had God been preparing me all along for this redemptive intrusion into my life? Had He permitted all my frustration so I could learn to

---

[1] Cf. Job 13:15b.

[2] For a similar account by a former military psychiatrist who was also deeply disillusioned by the "system" of military medicine and ultimately broken in his attempt to change it, see M. Scott Peck, *The Different Drum* (New York: Simon & Schuster, 1987), 48-50. This sequence of disillusionment leading to despair and ultimately to brokenness is the main thrust of Ecclesiastes 1-6.

[3] Mary A. White, *Harsh Grief, Gentle Hope* (Colorado Springs: NavPress, 1995).

mourn? I began to identify with Job as one whom God had called **through** suffering to bless others as an agent of His grace, and the truth is, I have never "recovered."

Nearly daily I am touched by what I see and hear. I mourn my own inadequacy in this fallen world as I am learning to identify more with the fallen-ness of others. I rejoice more in God's merciful intent, His redemptive purposes toward those He created to be a blessing…those He loves enough to transform from powerless victims of adversity into vitalized agents of His redemptive grace. While I still mourn my own inadequacy in this calling to bless others, the experience has breathed new life into my relationships with other believers—"children of Abraham"—but also with those who remain "alienated from His promises" (like Job's three friends).

Not only did this "journey of mourning" open my eyes to God's purposes in the book of Job, it also clarified for me how Job and Qoheleth are related in the outworking of these purposes. I decided to combine both expositions into a single comparative "theological" exposition, while remaining true to the integrity of both books as individual, coherent literary entities of their own. While the Postscript is primarily concerned with evaluating the canonical significance of Ecclesiastes—which remains a subject of significant controversy—the theology of Ecclesiastes is in my view more deeply and mutually informed by the theology of the book of Job than any other in the canon.

Job and Qoheleth

From the time I set out to develop a wisdom model for decision-making in Medical Ethics I was motivated to look for theological parallels between Job and Ecclesiastes.[4] Why were both of these books considered "wisdom literature"? One facet of the literary structure of the book of Job that has befuddled some expositors is the question of why chapter 28, the so-called "ode to wisdom," is situated between Job's dialogue with his three friends (4-27) and his summary defense before God (29-31). Only when I began to unpack Qoheleth's own struggle with the inscrutability of the work of God (Eccl 3; 8:16-9:10; 11:1-6) did it dawn on me that there is a key connection between true *wisdom* and the *fear of God* in the arguments of both books.[5]

---

[4] *See* "The Existential Crisis of Unjust Suffering" in the PREFACE to the commentary.

[5] *See* Job 28:28; Eccl 7:16-18, as also in the other books of Wisdom (Ps 111:10; Prov 1:7, 29; 2:5-6; 9:10; 15:33).

Job knew he was right in his seemingly endless dispute with his three friends but he had no clue what God was doing or why—he was torn between his demand for vindication and his desire to see what God was doing and why. He sensed intuitively that true wisdom was missing in his debate with the three friends and he acknowledged the inherent connection between wisdom and the fear of God (Job 28:28). Yet Job's thirst for justice prevailed over his yearning for wisdom. He pined over his past when he gloried in his influence over younger men who sought out his life-giving counsel (Job 29). When Job's estate was obliterated by one calamity after another, he intuitively sensed that his God was responsible but he could not fathom why God refused to reach down, pick him up, and restore him (Job 30). So he succumbed to his demand for vindication and sued his Creator for restitution (Job 31).

Job thereby forfeited the opportunity to gain any true wisdom until Elihu reaffirmed God's redemptive purposes amid adversity and invited Job to accept God's gracious offer to restore him (Job 33:14-30; 36:1-16). Although Job's obsession with vindication in the eyes of his friends prevented him from interceding on their behalf before God and thus serving as their redemptive bridge to God, there was still something deeply **right** about his longing to return to his previous position of influence and glory (Job 29); that yearning was **not** the reason why he was chastised by God (Job 38-41). Indeed, when Job finally repented, retracted his lawsuit against God (42:1-6), and then obeyed God's directive to intercede on behalf of his three friends (42:7-9), God responded by restoring his influence and glory two-fold as a witness to the intended influence and glory of his role as an agent of the Creator.[6]

When I began to see the God of Job as a Creator intent upon transforming fallen man into an effective agent of His redemptive purposes, I also began to scour the text of Ecclesiastes—which clearly shares with Job the themes of *self-sufficiency*, *adversity*, *suffering*, and *mourning*—for evidence that man might also be portrayed as an "agent of the Creator" in that book of OT Wisdom. While doing my research in Medical Ethics, I had sensed intuitively that both books seemed to speak with one voice to the critical role of mourning in man's pursuit of meaning during his limited life on earth. However, in the face of Qoheleth's thoroughgoing skepticism and disillusionment it took some time of studying both books independently before I recognized the complementary roles exemplified by Job and Qoheleth as agents of the Creator.

---

[6] Job 42:10-17. See nn. 119 and 226; cf. Ps 8; Heb 2:5-8.

The two protagonists are quintessential models of human self-sufficiency that argue forcefully for seeing the critical role of adversity in dislodging this entrenched disposition from fallen mankind: Even Job's unprecedented righteousness could not provide the wisdom he needed to see what God was doing in his life until he repented (Job 42:1-6), and not even Qoheleth's unprecedented wisdom could enable him to realize the work of God until he *feared before Him* (Eccl 7:16-18; 8:12-13). Neither Job nor Qoheleth could accept his "portion" in the work of God until he endured the crucial transition of mourning his self-sufficient inability and entrusted himself to God's wisdom by fearing before Him. The only difference, then, between Job and Qoheleth in their mutual aspiration for a legacy in the inscrutable work of God was whether their presumption issued from the mindset of a self-sufficient **victim** or **oppressor**.

Job devoted himself to serving God but could not see God's greater redemptive purposes; his presumption stemmed from a victim's complex that drove him to demand vindication. Job's adversity finally drew his attention to the redemptive legacy that God had reserved for him—one he would never gain through self-sufficiency. Qoheleth contended against the "portion" God had ordained for him and set out to discover (or forge) his own legacy with the resources at his disposal, even at the cost of oppressing others with his selfish ambition. The suffering caused by selfish ambition draws the reader's attention to the overwhelming futility of self-sufficient effort and Qoheleth's conclusion that it is far more restful and life-giving to simply accept and enjoy one's portion from God.

I eventually realized that Qoheleth's skepticism and disillusionment were resolved by the end of Ecclesiastes only in recognizing the supremely high value of man's agency in the eyes of God: Qoheleth's compiled reflections end with a series of hope-filled imperatives to the "young man" (11:9-12:7). He is above all to "remember his Creator" as soon as possible in life (12:1a), before he has "no further purpose" as a valued agent of that same Creator (12:1b-7). This climactic exhortation is just as central to Qoheleth's argument as Job's redemptive intercession (42:7-9) is to the argument of Job. What remains in the forefront by the conclusion of both books is *the crucial role mankind was created to serve in the outworking of God's purposes.* In both books adversity leads to mourning, and mourning to the *fear of God*, the primary requisite of fruitful human stewardship ("agency") and inheritance in the work of God.

The portraits of Job and Qoheleth are thus "mirror images" in that both protagonists contend with God for a self-determined legacy. Job speaks to suffering readers who feel deprived of a legacy with no clue that their Creator has greater purposes in store for them as agents of the

Creator. Ecclesiastes should capture the attention of those who try to compensate for the inscrutability of God's purposes by exploiting God-given resources in pursuit of their own dreams yet who disregard the oppressive consequences of their selfish ambition, both to themselves and to others. The argument of Job sets the stage for Ecclesiastes by expanding the reader's perspective beyond preconceived notions of meaning in life to a larger view of mankind's intended role and legacy in the work of God. Qoheleth then goes on to explore wisdom's role in equipping man to maximize his God-given portion in view of the continuing inscrutability of the work of God.

Job lamented the inscrutability of God's whereabouts when he tried to pin God down about why He had afflicted Job (cf. 9:10-11; 23:3-9). However, Elihu's defense of God's justice—specifically, the arguments of 34:29-37 and 37:13—indicts Job for his arrogance and lack of wisdom when he presumes in his affliction to be able to deduce the target and scope of God's judgment and activity. The distressing implications of the inscrutability of God's activity that were surfaced by Job's dilemma in turn establish the backdrop for Qoheleth's further exploration of man's uncertainty in the book of Ecclesiastes. In light of man's penchant for self-sufficiency Qoheleth goes on to explain how wisdom rooted in the fear of God can better position the reader for maximum success and fulfillment as an agent of God, notwithstanding the unsettling inscrutability of God's work in the world.

EXPOSITORY OUTLINE OF JOB

LITERARY STRUCTURE OF JOB

	PROLOGUE (PROSE)	DIALOGUE: GOD'S CHARACTER ON TRIAL (POETRY)		GOD'S SOVEREIGNTY CONFIRMED		EPILOGUE (PROSE)	STRUCTURE
	EVIL PERMITTED	GOD'S PURPOSES CHALLENGED				SATAN DEFEATED	
		"Friendly" Debate		Elihu's Rebuttal	Yahweh's Challenge		
Verse references	1:1 – 2:13 · 3:1	Round One (4–14) · Round Two (15–21) · Round Three (22–27) · Wisdom Found in the Fear of God (28) · Job Sues for Full Restitution (29–31)	31:40	32:1 · God's Spirit-Filled Mediator (32:1–33:7) · God's Redemptive purposes (33:8–33) · Job's Rule Determines His Justice (34) · Job's Self-Righteous Presumption (35) · God's Sovereign Instruction (36–37) · 37:24	38:1 · God's Absolute Knowledge of Creation (38:1–40:5) · God's Absolute Power over Evil (40:6–42:6) · 42:6	42:7 – 17	
Content boxes	God's Exemplary Agent (1:1-5) · Satan Attacks Job's Loyalty (1:6-2:10) · Job Comforted in His Grief (2:11-13) · Job's Grief Expressed as Death Wish (3)	Appeal for Compassion · Confidence of Vindication · Obsession with Revenge				Reconciled to God, Job Mediates Redemption for His Enemies (42:7-9) · God Blesses Job with Health and Double Wealth (42:10-17)	
THE PLOT AS COURTROOM METAPHOR	"...Job did not sin nor charge God with wrong"	JOB FACES UNJUST CHARGES, CALLS GOD AS *WITNESS*, AND SUES FOR RESTITUTION BEFORE GOD AS *JUDGE*		JOB FACES THE EVIDENCE OF GOD AS *CREATOR*, PROVING JOB IS UNQUALIFIED TO TRY HIS CASE BEFORE GOD AS *JUDGE*		THE LAWSUIT RETRACTED, THE JUDGE REDEEMS	
SATAN'S REBELLION AGAINST GOD	SATAN CHALLENGES JOB'S AGENCY	SATAN USES SUFFERING TO CONFOUND GOD'S CHOSEN AGENTS, ENLISTS THEM TO *SUBVERT GOD'S SOVEREIGN RULE*		GOD SENDS HIS SPIRIT TO REVERSE THE DECEPTION, CONFIRM HIS SOVEREIGNTY, AND *REIGN IN HIS AGENTS' HEARTS*		JOB OBEYS, HIS AGENCY RESTORED	
GOD'S REDEMPTIVE PURPOSES SUSTAINED	JOB FEARS GOD AND PERSEVERES IN SUFFERING	JOB DOUBTS GOD'S JUSTICE, TRUSTS IN HIS OWN RIGHTEOUSNESS, SUCCUMBS TO THE FALSE HOPE OF RETRIBUTION		ELIHU INTERCEDES FOR JOB, AFFIRMS GOD'S PURPOSES ARE REDEMPTIVE	GOD EXPOSES SELF-RIGHTEOUS PRESUMPTION; JOB REPENTS	IN FEARING GOD, JOB MEDIATES REDEMPTION	
A MEDIATOR	1:5	5:4; 9:33; 10:7; 16:21; 19:25; 23:7; 29:12		33:6, 23-28; 34:23, 28; 36:15		42:8-10	

OVERVIEW OF JOB

By dramatizing Job's adversity and God's answer to Satan-inspired mis-conceptions of God's purposes, **the author affirms that even when God's purposes remain inscrutable, He rules over all creation with perfect wisdom and power and seeks through suffering to redeem mankind's intended agency**, *so that readers in adversity might replace self-sufficient presumption with calm confidence in God's redemptive character and thus be restored and blessed as chosen mediators of His redemptive purposes to others.*

It is not surprising that Job's profound devastation provoked heated debate with his closest friends over whether he was guilty or God was unfair in the wake of Job's unexplained calamities. Mankind has an inherent yearning to find order and justice in the universe. Random tragedy and unexplained human suffering make us very uncomfortable and believers struggle to reconcile such events with God's justice and care. Yet the book of Job was never intended to be a theodicy:[7] God never tells Job why he had to suffer or why a God who is absolutely sovereign in power and knowledge would ever knowingly permit evil. This exposition proposes that the author of Job expounded on the disturbing unfairness of Job's innocent suffering in order to dislodge complacent, self-serving notions of God and replace them with new confidence in a God who desires to be seen and known as sovereign but extravagantly redemptive in the very midst of suffering, even when His purposes remain completely unfathomable.[8]

---

[7] "It is a mistake to characterize the book of Job as 'grappling with the problem of God and human suffering.' To make the book of Job, and especially God's answer to Job out of the whirlwind, an answer to the problem of evil is to try to make the book answer a question it was not asking" (Stanley Hauerwas, *Naming the Silences: God, Medicine, and the Problem of Suffering* [Grand Rapids: Eerdmans, 1990], 45). Hauerwas goes on to explain how the work of theodicy reflects man's need to maintain confidence in God when faced with inexplicable loss. The way suffering and evil is reconciled with God's character depends on how it has impacted the person who feels the need to explain it; however, this is not the purpose of Job (ibid., 39-58).

[8] Philip Yancey (*Disappointment with God: Three Questions No One Asks Aloud* [Grand Rapids: Zondervan, 1988]) reflects on his own initial misconception of the purpose of Job and how he eventually grasped the principal issue at stake in the dramatic development:

> I once regarded Job as a profound expression of human disappointment... with direct biblical sanction...however, I discovered that it does not really

The interpretation of the book depends critically on how we view the dramatic roles played by Job and his somewhat mysterious younger friend, Elihu.[9] God's scathing reply to Job (38:1-3) should lead us to question whether Job should be viewed more as a paragon of faithful endurance through suffering (a popular perspective[10]) or rather as a believer who like many of us loses confidence in God's justice and care when God fails to satisfy our self-determined expectations.[11] For those who adopt the former view, Elihu comes off as an angry, self-inflated gadfly who only intensifies Job's unjust suffering. In the latter view, however, Elihu becomes God's

---

represent the human viewpoint...[ibid., 186]

When people experience pain, questions spill out—the very questions that tormented Job. Why me? What's going on? Does God care? Is there a God? This one time...we the onlookers—not Job—are granted a view behind the curtain....As nowhere else in the Bible, the book of Job shows us God's point of view, including the supernatural activity normally hidden from us.

Job has put God on trial, accusing him of unfair acts against an innocent party. Angry, satirical, betrayed, Job wanders as close to blasphemy as he can get....His words have a startlingly familiar ring because they are so modern. He gives voice to our most deeply felt complaints against God. But chapters 1 and 2 prove that, regardless of what Job thinks, God is not on trial..., Job is on trial. The point of the book is not suffering: Where is God when it hurts? The prologue dealt with that....The point is faith: Where is Job when it hurts? How is he responding? [ibid., 188-9]

[9] One's views of Job and Elihu are necessarily related: If Job is seen as essentially justified in his demand for vindication, then Elihu's argument is basically unfair, like the other "comforters." However, if Job's misconceptions of God have led to a growing presumption and arrogance on his part, then Elihu's role should be seen as both *prophetic* and *priestly*, revealing the truth of God's redemptive purposes and mediating Job's reconciliation to God.

[10] *See*, e.g., Mike Mason, *The Gospel According to Job* (Wheaton, IL: Crossway Books, 1994). Job **is** cited in the NT for his legendary endurance (Jas 5:11). James' purpose for citing Job's example was to foster hope in "the end intended by the Lord," which refers in context to eschatological blessing at "the *parousia*" (5:7-11). This in turn raises the question of what analogous "end" was "intended by the Lord" in Job's endurance through suffering (Job 42). This issue will be explored at length in the Commentary.

[11] Views that portray Job primarily as an exemplar of perseverance through suffering do not sufficiently account for YHWH's opening sarcastic confrontation (Job 38:3) *Who is this who darkens counsel with words without knowledge?* or Job's final response: "He does not say, 'Ah, at last I understand!' but rather, 'I repent.' He does not repent of sins that allegedly brought on the suffering; he repents of his arrogance in impugning God's justice, he repents of the attitude whereby he simply demands an answer, as if such were owed him. He repents of not having known God better" (Donald Carson, *How Long, O Lord? Reflections on Suffering and Evil* [Grand Rapids: Baker, 1990], 174).

inspired spokesman and Job's longed-for mediator (cf. 9:33; 16:19; 19:25). Yet he does not vindicate Job, as Job had demanded; rather, he affirms God's sovereign but persistently redemptive character and he exposes Job's foolish presumption that God owed him anything. Elihu offers Job hope of restoration not to his former estate, but to a **transformed** righteous agency for God (33:23-28).

The text supplies the evidence to conclude that though Job was without precedent, *blameless and upright* and a model of perseverance in suffering, he allowed his plea for vindication in the eyes of his friends to distract him from knowing God more intimately. Similarly, while Elihu may at first appear to some as pretentious and bombastic he must in the end be seen as the ardent advocate of God's perspective on Job's problem—his teaching prepared Job for his encounter with God.[12] The acrimonious debate (chaps. 4-27) serves to elicit the reader's sympathy for Job. If the gambit succeeds, then both Job **and** the reader are "nailed" in the crucible of suffering: Elihu's speeches expose our own self-sufficiency before God and challenge us to fear God.

LITERARY STRUCTURE AND LEGAL METAPHOR IN THE ARGUMENT[13]

The symmetrical design of the argument helps define the dramatic roles of Job and Elihu. Comprised of Hebrew poetry framed by a prose prologue (chaps. 1-2) and epilogue (42:7-17), the plot takes the form of a dramatized lawsuit that provides the literary template for the book's argument. In the

---

[12] "Elihu's role [is] different from that of the comforters....[His] name, which means 'he is my God,' intimates that he functions as Yahweh's forerunner....he prepares Job to hear what Yahweh will say and to surrender his case against God" (John E. Hartley, *The Book of Job* NICOT, [Grand Rapids: Eerdmans, 1988], 28-29). "Elihu...[advances] the discussion by suggesting that Job's greatest sin may not be something he said or did **before** the suffering started, but the rebellion he is displaying **in** the suffering" (Carson, *How Long, O Lord?* 170, emphasis his). Cf. Greg Parsons, "The Structure and Purpose of The Book of Job" (reprinted in Zuck [ed.], *Sitting with Job: Selected Studies on the Book of Job*, Grand Rapids: Baker, 1992), 20-1.

[13] See the chart, "The Literary Structure of Job." The symmetry of the argument helps to define the issues in tension (Hartley, *The Book of Job*, 35-37) and sharpens the intended contrasts between and within subsections (ibid., 43-47). See also Norman Habel's treatment of Job's form and structure ("Literary Features and the Message of The Book of Job," reprinted in Zuck [ed.], *Sitting with Job*, 97-104) and the legal metaphor (ibid., 108-11), as well as helpful general discussions of the book's dramatic and verbal irony by both Habel (ibid., 104-7) and Parsons ("Literary Features of The Book of Job," reprinted in Zuck [ed.], ibid., 38-42).

first half, the reader is immediately confronted with God's disturbing permission of unjust suffering and evil in the life of a faithful servant (chaps. 1-2). Job's friends are so distraught by his nihilistic soliloquy (chap. 3) they are compelled to explain his suffering and falsely charge him with sin, thus igniting an acrimonious debate over their presumption of Job's guilt and his countercharge of God's injustice (chaps. 4-27). The resulting legal stalemate triggers an appeal for wisdom (chap. 28), and Job pleads before God as both **defendant**—for summary judgment and vindication—and **plaintiff**—for restitution of his former estate (chaps. 29-31).

A prose editorial (32:1-5) serves as the literary hinge between the two acts, validating Elihu's speeches as the prophetic reply to Job's claim of divine injustice. Elihu plays the dual courtroom role of advocate for Job and attorney for God's defense[14]—he gives Job hope of restoration but also refutes Job's complaint (chaps. 32-37). God then intervenes as Judge, citing incontrovertible evidence from Creation to revoke Job's standing to sue (chaps. 38-41). Job finally "sees" God, retracts his lawsuit, submits to God, and in restored fellowship mediates his Creator's redemptive purposes (chap. 42). The lawsuit thus serves as a literary template to frame Job's changing disposition before God.

JOB'S EVOLVING DISPOSITION AND NEED OF A MEDIATOR

The reader's attention throughout the drama is thus riveted on Job's evolving disposition. His attitude is repeatedly highlighted in the prologue (1:22, 2:10c); his soliloquy (chap. 3); the hostile debate with his friends (chaps. 4-27); his summary appeal (chaps. 29-31); Elihu's rebuttal (cf. 33:12; 34:5-9, 36-37; 35:2-3, 16; 36:16-21); and God's final climactic confrontation (cf. 38:2; 40:1-5, 8; 42:1-6) and commission (42:10).

Following Job's agonizing initial "death wish," Job expresses growing exasperation with his friends and ambivalence toward God in a series of highly emotional exchanges. Job complains that God remains hidden yet continues to persecute him; he pleads with God to warrant the affliction, abate it, or just show up to hear his case. Unable to secure testimony that can vindicate him in the eyes of his friends, Job pleads for a *mediator* to

---

[14] Elihu in his self-introduction takes great pains to **affirm** that he is Job's advocate, lit. his "mouth before God" (33:6) and also inspired by the very Spirit of God (32:17-33:4) to **refute** Job's complaint (33:5).

bridge the gaping distance between him and his elusive God,[15] Job's vexation escalates with each round of the debate, finally erupting in open acrimony toward his friends: Having pled in vain for God's vindication, Job harshly dismisses them (chap. 27). Following a poetic interlude that betrays the desperate need for *wisdom* in the *fear of God* (chap. 28), Job laments his lost estate and status in the community, charges God with injustice, and issues a brazen subpoena for God to appear in court (chaps. 29-31).

At this point the author introduces Elihu as the mediator Job truly needed.[16] He affirms that Elihu's rebuttal is warranted by both Job's self-justification at God's expense and his friends' unsubstantiated condemnation (32:1-5). By confidently affirming God's redemptive intent towards the oppressed, Elihu refutes both Job and his friends, mollifies Job's obsession with vindication, and prepares him for a direct confrontation by God (chaps. 32-37).[17] God responds to his subpoena but never explains the reason for Job's suffering, bluntly exposing Job's pathetic ignorance and impotence in light of His own all-wise, all-powerful rule (chaps. 38-41). In response to God's scathing irony and sarcasm Job repents of his presumptuous disposition, is reconciled to God, and he himself mediates[18] his friends' redemption (42:1-9). As a direct result of his submissive intercession, Job is rewarded with the two-fold restitution of his former estate (42:10-17).

The striking reversal in Job's attitude is underscored by the mirror-image symmetry of the drama. Whereas Job's debate with his three friends featured blistering invective in retaliation for their unjust charges, culminating in blatant self-righteous presumption before God Himself (chaps. 4-31), his response to Elihu's compassionate rebuttal and God's blistering confrontation is characterized by silent, self-effacing humility (chaps. 32-41, cf. 40:1-5). Job's initial self-focused nihilism amid suffering (chap. 3) is completely replaced by God-focused repentance, even while still suffering (42:1-6). Finally, Job's fear of God on first being stripped of his estate (chaps. 1-2) is mirrored by faithful obedience to God's redemptive commission, and his

---

[15] Job initially has no hope of *any mediator between us* (9:33a) to secure his vindication (9:2-35, cf. esp. 9:2b, 28b). He then continues to lament the absence of someone to plead his case (16:21) but begins to express confidence of his vindication, *Even now...my witness is in heaven, And my advocate is on high* (16:19, NASB). Though Job despairs of living to see his vindication (chap. 17), his confidence of deliverance (n. 23) ironically escalates to the settled conviction that he will not only be vindicated (19:23-27) but will also avenge his aggravated suffering at the hands of his friends (19:28-29, cf. 19:2-22).

[16] Parsons, "Structure and Purpose," 20-21 (cf. fn. 15); 30-32 (cf. fn. 76).

[17] Ibid., 20-21.

[18] Ibid., 32 (cf. fn. 77).

submissive agency for God is rewarded by the restoration of full fellowship with his Creator and with others (42:7-17).

THEOLOGICAL RESOLUTION BY AN UNEXPECTED MEDIATOR—THE GOSPEL ACCORDING TO ELIHU

Embedded in the debate over Job's guilt and God's justice are the deeper theological issues at stake for the reader. These issues emerge in a shadow plot featuring Satan's continued attack on God's sovereign rule through the unwitting complicity of fallen mankind.[19] While Satan is no longer mentioned after the prologue he continues to wage a subtle campaign against God's rule by cultivating distorted perceptions of God's character. His strategy is to exploit the adversity of unjust suffering in order to confuse God's servants regarding the revealed truth about God: If Satan could undermine mankind's confidence in God's redemptive character, it would subvert mankind's intended role as God's agent in the outworking of His redemptive purposes.[20] God's purposes would remain inscrutable, and God would appear unable or unwilling to protect His servants, who would then stop trusting Him for life and blessing.

Having been covertly influenced by the Accuser's insinuation that Job's guilt was the proximate reason for his unremitting suffering, Job's three friends naively depict YHWH throughout the debate as a God of

---

[19] This has always been Satan's *modus operandi*. Satan's original ambition is accurately represented in Ezekiel 28:12-16 and Isa 14:12-15 as incarnated in human kings who clamor for position on God's "holy mountain," the image of God's sovereign rule (cf. Isa 14:13-14; Ezek 28:14-16). Once Satan is banished from this dominion (Ezek 28:16; Isa 14:15), his strategy for attacking God's sovereignty is to undermine man's capacity to serve Him in fear (see below). The quintessential example of this subversion by Satan is the narrative of the Tower of Babel (Gen 11:1-9), which accurately depicts Satan's determination to exploit mankind in order to fulfill his vow to "ascend above the heights of the clouds" in order to "be like the most High" (Isa 14:14).

[20] God's plan from the beginning (Gen 1-2) has been for mankind to assume responsibility as co-regent of His dominion over the world—a human agency epitomized by Christ Himself (Heb 2:5-9; cf. Ps 2, 8, 110). Herein lies Satan's opportunity: If God has made His rule contingent on human agency (how absurd! cf. Ps 8:3-6), Satan can exploit unjust suffering and twist the truth about God enough to convince a righteous man like Job that God is holding out on him (cf. Gen 3:1-6). Satan will then seem to have successfully subverted God's plan to redeem the world through the agency of men *who fear God and shun evil* (cf. Job 1:1, 8; 2:3). But God in His redemptive love has fully anticipated human failure, so the only issue that ultimately hangs in the balance is whether Job (or the reader) will choose to fulfill his appointed role in God's plan.

one-for-one retribution and blessing. Job succumbs as well by inferring from his unrelenting adversity that God had unjustly abandoned him to unwarranted persecution (chaps. 3-31). Elihu decisively refutes these misconceptions in five unanswered speeches that reveal God's true character (chaps. 32-37). Through this "court-appointed" mediator the Spirit of God reverses Satan's deception,[21] affirming God's righteous, albeit unfathomable, rule and His persistently redemptive love.

This shadow plot pitting Satan's rebellion against God's sovereignty develops within the argument's legal metaphor. The devil initially presents before God's throne among the other angels (1:6) as Satan—"the Adversary"—in a transparent ploy to accuse God's chosen servants of being rebellious at heart (1:8-11). After enlisting Job's wife to plant the seed of rebellion in the fertile soil of Job's adversity (2:9), Satan exploits Job's affliction to co-opt Job and his friends into colluding with him as unwitting co-conspirators: In a tortured debate laced with dramatic and verbal irony, they **each** argue their respective cases to conclusions that twist the truth about God (chaps. 4-27).

The key question of the debate is "Can a man be righteous before God?"[22] While Job's suffering suffices as de facto evidence in the eyes of his friends to convict Job of sin, Job is equally convinced of his innocence but unsuccessful in his attempts to coerce God into vindicating him in their eyes. This **legal** deadlock reflects the underlying **theological** deadlock: Since Job's friends can neither refute Job nor compel him to confess, and Job cannot get God to testify and exonerate him, both sides keep misconstruing God's power to *deliver*.[23] Job insists that a "redeemer" will

---

[21] While Parsons ("Structure and Purpose," 25) contends that Elihu "fail[ed] to divorce himself from the dogma of divine retribution (see 34:11, 25-27; cf. 34:33; 36:17; 37:13)," the Commentary will establish that these same verses actually **correct** the dogma to vindicate God's justice.

[22] The question is stated rhetorically three times during the debate (4:17; 9:2b; 25:4a). In the mouths of Job's friends (4:17; 25:4a) the implication is that any man under the cloud of sin (as logically inferred from Job's suffering) cannot be **considered** righteous before God and must therefore be judged guilty. However, the same question in the mouth of Job (9:2b) implies that he can't be **declared** righteous in the absence of the only testimony capable of vindicating him, given the "indictment" of his suffering.

[23] Eliphaz infers that Job is guilty, a fool with *no deliverer* (*nāṣal* [Hifil], 5:3-4), but that God would yet *deliver* him (*nāṣal*, 5:19) if he would repent (5:8-27). In a subsequent lament when Job asserts *there is no one who can deliver* [*nāṣal*] *from Your hand* (10:7b), he means "deliver" from the *unjust* punishment God levies on the *innocent* (10:7a). The same sense is connoted later by the term *pālaṭ* (23:7). A third term (*mālaṭ*) ironically portends the kind of deliverance that God

deliver him not only by vindication but also by avenging him against his "comforters" (19:21-29; 27:7-23).

In answering Job's need for a deliverer, God solves the problem of man's unrighteousness in His eyes by revealing His redemptive character, even **before** Job's suffering is abated. Elihu ends up serving as Job's mediator but not at all as Job had expected.[24] Rather than vindicating Job, Elihu exposes his true need to submit to God as His chosen agent. Satan had used unjust suffering to convince Job that his own righteousness exceeded God's, so Job was arguing that God "owed" him the restitution of his estate and vindication before his friends. Elihu refocused Job's perspective by placing his suffering in the context of God's sovereign, inscrutable yet redemptive purposes: Since God had chosen mankind to fulfill His creative purposes He would not shrink from using suffering to "deliver"[25] mankind from self-destruction. Indeed, God would even send a *ransom* to redeem them to serve those purposes by restoring to them *His righteousness*,[26] thereby quashing Satan's rebellion (cf. 1:8; 2:3).

God finally appears in court to give irrefutable testimony from Creation and renders Job's complaint moot by divesting him of any legal standing in the case: Job had ignored the ubiquitous evidence of God's

---

did intend, both in Job's self-portrayal as a *deliverer* (29:12) and in Eliphaz's unwitting prediction of his own vicarious *deliverance* (22:30) through Job's intercession (cf. 42:7-9; n. 20). See also Elihu's use of the term *ḥālaṣ* and YHWH's use of the term *yāša'* (n. 25, below).

24 Job had sought an *adjudicator* (9:33a) who could exonerate him of false charges, and a *redeemer* who would raise him from death to see his vindication (19:25). But in his self-righteous pursuit of vindication Job lost sight of his calling as God's chosen agent. In perhaps the pivotal irony of the entire drama Elihu served as God's exemplary agent, not to adjudicate Job's legal dispute with God and his friends but to expose Job's failure as God's agent by revealing God's redemptive purposes in suffering (33:14-30). Job would indeed see his Redeemer (33:23-28), but One who would restore Job's agency for God, so that Job might in turn mediate God's redemptive purposes in the lives of others (42:8-9, cp. 1:5).

25 Elihu contributed the key theological corrective to the concept of *deliverance* (n. 23) by promising that God would *deliver* (*ḥālaṣ* [Piel], 36:15) the afflicted only if they listen to Him, repent, and obey (36:8-21). YHWH Himself echoes this same sense when he dares Job to *deliver* himself (40:14, *yāša'* [Hifil]). This implied that Job was in fact guilty, but not for some imagined heinous offenses committed prior to his affliction, as his other friends had asserted (n. 23); it was for his failure as God's agent to listen to instruction **while** he was suffering.

26 In probably the most fascinating pericope of the entire book Elihu lays the foundation for the propitiation of God's wrath by substitutionary atonement. Elihu explained that God uses suffering to get self-sufficient servants to listen to Him (33:14-22) and realize that they are delivered from death and reconciled to God by virtue of His imputed righteousness (33:23-30) through the provision of a ransom (*kōpher*, 33:24).

sovereign, creative activity (chaps. 38-41) and had limited God to blessing him on **his** terms, not allowing that a sovereign God could in fact bless
through suffering. By apprising Job of God's intimate *knowledge* of
Creation, His persistent *desire* to deliver man from the Pit, and His sovereign *power* to deliver (chaps. 32-37), Elihu prepared Job to truly "see"
God (chaps. 38-41), repent of his self-righteous presumption (42:1-6), and
be transformed in suffering into a righteous intercessor (42:7-9). By submissively mediating God's deliverance of his friends,[27] Job himself
served God's redemptive purposes **through** his suffering, and God in turn
delivered him and rewarded him with full fellowship and a double inheritance (42:10-17)—the picture of abundant Kingdom blessing in return for
faithful human agency.

GOD'S INTENT FOR THE READER:
RIGHTEOUS CO-REGENCY

Job's ordeal exemplifies God's creative intent for all mankind as His chosen agents: to serve as mediators of His redemptive purposes. But as
things stand, we do not know our Creator well enough to serve Him as
intended. By revealing how Job's agency was preempted in adversity by
his self-righteous presumption—undermining his fear of God and thereby
subverting God's wisdom[28]—the author invites his readers to a greater

---

[27] The notion of *deliverance* (nn. 23, 25) thus comes full circle: Eliphaz had
promised in his first speech that Job would be delivered from punishment if he
repented (5:19) yet he ironically predicted **his own** deliverance by proposing in
his last speech that God would *even deliver one who is not innocent...by the purity of your hands* (22:30). The verb *deliver* (*mālaṭ* [Piel]) is not the same word used
to promise Job's deliverance; it bears the sense of *letting one escape.* That is,
Eliphaz predicted that Job's repentance would be so valuable to God, his restored
righteousness would even cover the sin of those who are guilty and let them "off
the hook," which is exactly what happened when Job interceded for his "comforters" (42:7-9, cf. Jon 2-3): God fulfilled Eliphaz' prediction by ironically allowing Eliphaz—himself the guilty one—to escape punishment on the basis of Job's
imputed righteousness (n. 26) and intercession (n. 23).

[28] Larry Crabb studies Job's disposition in response to adversity and describes
what he calls "demandingness" when suffering is prolonged without any answer
from God (*Inside Out* [Colorado Springs: Navpress, 1988], 131-151). Such an attitude emerges in Job's demand for the relief or justification of his suffering. Crabb
underscores how presumptuous this attitude really is, thus explaining why the
demanding sufferer needs to repent, as Elihu implicated (34:36-37). Such presumption is exposed in Ecclesiastes 5:1-7, in which Qoheleth advises *Do not be
rash with your mouth, And let not your heart utter anything hastily before God.
For God is in heaven, and you on earth; Therefore let your words be few* (5:2).

confidence in God and to seek to know Him better, even under the most oppressive circumstances. As long as we contend for self-sufficient control in this life we will capitulate to Satan's strategy of exploiting adversity to co-opt God's agents into complicity with his own subversive purposes. But God uses suffering to get our attention, so that we may know our Creator as fully redemptive, reigning wisely over His Creation. Those who respond in suffering by seeking God are "perfected" as His chosen agents[29]—"regents made righteous" who can thus carry out His rule over Creation.[30]

Readers who experience innocent suffering but resent God in light of that suffering emulate Job: While we may be genuinely approved of God we risk becoming mired in self-pity, self-righteous, and vindictive when adversity destroys our dreams for no discernible reason. Like Job we demand an explanation of suffering and seek vindication and relief at any cost. Yet, only by seeking God out of brokenness will self-pity and self-righteous presumption yield to the calm confidence that God is fully sovereign and can deliver us. Despite Satan's continued testing we can then see God as fully redemptive and, like Elihu and (ultimately) Job himself, serve as mediators of His redemptive grace to others in need of deliverance with the hope of a Kingdom inheritance.

Similarly, when we, like Job's three friends, are spared such adversity we can easily succumb to the false notion that God in this life invariably

---

The context of this exhortation concerns man's natural, self-sufficient response to suffering, especially when it is inflicted by others (4:1-3ff; 5:8-9). Particularly relevant is Qoheleth's advice to *draw near to hear rather than to give the sacrifice of fools, for they do not know that they do evil* (5:1). The *sacrifice of fools* and their *dreams and many words* (5:3, 7) refer to a self-sufficient person's attempts to cajole God into blessing selfish ambitions. Such presumption only "does evil" (Eccl 5:1c) by accommodating Satan's strategy of deception (n. 20). It is wiser to listen in silence for God to reveal himself (Eccl 5:1a; cf. Job 40:1-5, Heb 12:25).

[29] In this respect the NT teaching on the role of suffering in the life of Christ is extremely illuminating: That a sinless Christ should undergo temptation by Satan (Matt 4, Luke 4) and then suffer makes sense only when we realize that *He learned obedience by the things which He suffered* (Heb 5:8) and was thereby *perfected* (Heb 5:9) as God's chosen High Priestly intercessor on behalf of sinful man (Heb 5:1-7). Christ in suffering exemplified God's plan for fallen mankind to be perfected as His chosen mediator of redemption by relying completely on the Father. Job exemplifies in turn how this "perfection" is meant to develop in the as yet "un-perfected" reader who was created to be a reliable servant or "agent" of God on earth.

[30] The repeated question *"Can a man be righteous before God?"* in the mouths of Job and his friends (n. 22) thus takes on crucial significance from God's perspective when we finally appreciate this overarching strategic intent in suffering.

blesses those who obey and punishes the wicked—we see affliction only as retribution for personal sin and try to ignore the disturbing reality of innocent suffering. Falsely assured by the delusion of self-righteousness, we see unexplained suffering and cannot bear to consider that we too could be similarly afflicted. The reality of Job's innocent suffering disrupts myopic, preconceived notions of God's justice, exposes our lack of compassion for others who suffer, and reminds us of our own need of deliverance from self-righteous pride to the true righteousness of God as His representatives to this world.

Prologue

SATAN'S DARE

Mankind's Agency Subverted

Job's Integrity Challenged (Job 1-2)

By describing how God permitted Satan to test the allegiance of an upright servant without ever explaining the cause of his affliction, **the author shatters the myth that our own righteousness can protect us from unjust suffering,** *in order to challenge our self-serving strategies to earn God's favor and disrupt our complacency over the supernatural battle for our allegiance as human agents of our Creator.*

The structure of the prologue[31] helps frame the author's meaning and purpose. The introduction establishes Job's initial state of blessing, faithfulness, and lack of culpability (1:1-5). His initial wealth (1:2-3) serves as a stark contrast to his condition after devastating affliction: utterly destitute and bereft of blessing (2:11-13). Sandwiched between these two extremes is Satan's challenge, detailed in parallel narratives that demonstrate his characteristic opposition to God's kingdom (1:6-22; 2:1-10). Each narrative emphasizes the supernatural origin of Job's testing: 1) God allows testing but places limits on its extent; 2) the details of Job's catastrophes testify to divine design and end up affirming Job's steadfast innocence—*In all this Job did not sin* (1:22; 2:10c).

The prologue clearly establishes the theme of unjust suffering and sets the stage for the ensuing arduous debate over Job's guilt and God's justice (chaps. 4-27). The author repeatedly affirms Job's lack of culpability for the calamities that befall him (1:1, 8, 22; 2:3, 10), so that the reader remains under no illusion: The actual issue is not deserved retribution, but innocent suffering. Since Job and his three friends are never made aware of the celestial wager between Satan and the Lord they must grapple with the questions about God's justice and Job's righteousness that his suffering raises, but without recourse to the reader's inside knowledge of the wager.[32]

The reality of Job's innocent suffering compels the reader to ask, What can we assume about the righteousness of those who suffer? Anyone who has

---

[31] Chapters 1-2 are arranged in chiastic parallel (x:y / y':x'), where x = 1:1-5; y = 1:6-22; y' = 2:1-10; and x' = 2:11-13. Sections x and x' are meant to be compared with one another, and y with y'. By contrast, sections 1:6-22 and 2:1-10 are each internally arranged in alternate parallel (a:b / a':b'), where a = 1:6-12; b = 1:12-22; a' = 2:1-7a; and b' = 2:7b-10. Such parallelism is critical to the understanding of other key passages in Job as well (cf. Robert Gordis, "The Language and Style of Job," reprinted in Zuck [ed.], *Sitting with Job*, 89-90).

[32] *See* Yancey's comments above (n. 8) regarding the reader's privileged insight in chaps. 1-2.

suffered unjustly and like Job cannot explain their suffering or assumes that it must be deserved punishment can now be consoled that suffering may have little or nothing to do with personal guilt. On the other hand, the complacent and self-righteous reader who has convinced himself that God will always bless the righteous and punish the wicked and has rested in the false notion that he merits God's favor must now face the unsettling reality that not even the righteous are immune to suffering. We should all therefore pause before resorting to complacent, simplistic solutions to the dilemma of innocent suffering[33] and reflect on how we judge the victims of that suffering when we, too, remain unaware of how supernatural prerogatives may be exercised in specific situations.

The truth is that we are usually unaware of the causes of suffering we encounter in life. The audience is left with no recourse but to empathize with Job as innocent victim and face with him the deeper questions surfaced by the dilemma of unjust suffering: If those who are blameless are not invariably blessed, then what should motivate us to serve God? How can those who experience unrelenting adversity like that of Job serve God faithfully? Should adversity change one's perspective toward God or others? If so, how? These questions should be kept in mind as the reader continues to identify with Job, bearing silent witness to his evolving attitude toward both God and his companions during the ensuing debate (chaps. 43-27).

A. Job's Initial Right-Standing with God (1:1–5)

*By attesting to Job's initial state of bountiful blessing in right-standing with God, **the author establishes Job's lack of culpability beyond any doubt**, so that readers cannot attribute Job's calamities to any sin on his part and are therefore compelled to identify with him in his innocent suffering.*

---

[33] Hauerwas addresses our natural compulsion to fix the problem of suffering and recasts suffering as a question to be asked in light of God's redemptive purposes (*Naming the Silences*, 78-79):

> The problem of evil is not about rectifying our suffering with some general notion of God's nature as all-powerful and good; rather, it is about what we mean by God's goodness itself, which...must be construed in terms of God as the Creator who has called into existence a people...so that the world might know that God has not abandoned us. There is no problem of suffering in general; rather, the question of suffering can be raised only in the context of a God who creates to redeem.

Empathy in the one who observes suffering should thus stem from this redemptive aspect of the character of God for whom suffering is not a "problem"—precisely the perspective that Elihu will supply in Job 33.

Job's opening characterization as *blameless and upright, and one who feared God and shunned evil* (1:1) precludes any later presumption by the reader that Job bore any hidden guilt that could possibly have justified his affliction. The long list of large numbers quantifying the various possessions in Job's estate (1:2-3) exemplifies his great blessing and poses a stark contrast to his impending state of utter destitution (2:11-13). Job's right-standing with God is depicted in his regular faithful worship as priest over his family (1:4-5).[34] Job's daily concern over whether his sons *may have cursed God* (1:5c) conspicuously portends the substance of Satan's wager (cf. 1:11; 2:5), the brazen dare of Job's wife (cf. 2:9), and the eventual speculation of his friends (cf. esp. 8:4).

The author curiously omits Job's lineage at the outset, in contrast to his comforters whose ancestries are clearly identified as soon as they are introduced (2:11). This may well be to facilitate the reader's identification with Job in his innocent suffering, since he is tied to no specified heritage that might evoke feelings of partiality on the part of the reader.[35] He seems to be "everyman" (as far as patriarchs are concerned). The gratuitously lavish description of Job's estate leaves the average reader—who could hardly match Job's wealth—unlikely to have suffered greater loss than Job, so the object lessons from Job's experience would apply *a fortiori* to any readers facing innocent suffering.

B. Job's Allegiance Tested by Confiscated Blessing (1:6–22)

*By dramatizing the total devastation of Job's earthly estate, **the author depicts Satan's attempted subversion of the sovereign rule of God, who allows His chosen servant to afflicted by unjust suffering**, so that readers might begin to question the true basis for God's blessing in life and reflect on how they would respond in Job's place.*

---

[34] The adjectives *blameless* (*tām*) and *upright* (*yāšār*) (1:1) set Job apart as unparalleled in his moral behavior or culpability for sin in the eyes of men. The question of *righteousness* (*ṣedāqâ*) before *God* is not raised (cf. n. 22) or resolved (33:23-26) until later. But Job's right standing relates to his ongoing state of confession: The regularity of his sacrifices attests to his awareness of his fallenness as a man (and that of his children) and of sin's potential to disrupt fellowship before God, as Job himself admits (1:5c).

[35] The story of Job was known to at least pre-exilic Israel (cf. Ezek 14:14, 20), notwithstanding uncertainty over the date of the text (cf. Hartley, *The Book of Job*, 17-20). The Jewish reader would find the ancestry of Job's comforters excluded from the promise to Abraham (1:11, n. 45), so the natural bias would be to identify with Job against the "comforters" and to be wary of their arguments during the ensuing debate.

As this scene unfolds among *the sons of God*,[36] Satan—"the Adversary"[37]—is portrayed responding evasively to God's question regarding his whereabouts.[38] The author clearly intends to depict Satan's rebellious agenda and deceitful character as he deals with God and man. However, it should be noted that it is *the Lord* who first seems to bait Satan by presenting a man—*Have you considered Job?* (1:8)—who by all appearances has been completely loyal to God. Only then does Satan propose his wager, a challenge based on the premise that Job's worship is contingent on God's blessing (1:9-12). Even so, it is God who clearly dictates the terms of the wager.

Four catastrophic events are then seen to destroy all of Job's possessions, including his children, in such rapid succession and with such utter finality, that Job could not reasonably attribute the convergence of these events to chance. This desired effect is emphasized with each calamity: Three times the author introduces the calamity with the phrase *While he was still speaking;* four times he concludes with the phrase *I alone have escaped to tell you!* This unmistakable mark of supernatural design is not lost on Job, who even amid his grief (1:20) continues to worship God and acknowledges His sovereign prerogative to allow such overwhelming devastation (1:21). Rather than succumb to Satan's temptation and ascribe evil motives to God in permitting this affliction (cf. 1:11), *Job did not sin nor charge God with wrong* (1:22). Satan has clearly lost the first round of the wager.

This dramatic sequence of events assaults the reader with unstated but obvious questions: What kind of God would barter away His blessing of a righteous man in an ostensibly capricious wager with a subversive enemy? What was God trying to prove? This unequivocal evidence that the "righteous" can suffer unjustly is a sobering challenge to the reader's conception of God's goodness. At this point the honest reader should be

---

[36] This title for God's angels underscores their identity as beings created to serve His purposes.

[37] This translates Heb. "the Satan," the Accuser of the servants of God (Hartley, *The Book of Job*, 71-72, cf. Zech 3; Rev 12:10). By impugning Job's motivation, Satan assumes the role of subversive insurrectionist against God's sovereign rule, intending to achieve his own purposes by duping mankind into complicity (cf. nn. 19 and 20).

[38] The parallels between Job 1:6-2:10 and Gen 3:1-12 are striking. Satan's answer to the Lord's question (Job 1:7, 2:2) belies his shifting, evasive strategy (cf. Gen 3:1; 1 Pet 5:8). When the Lord asks Adam of **his** whereabouts to expose his co-optation by Satan's offer to be like God (cf. Gen 3:5), Adam adopts a similarly evasive blame-shifting tactic (Gen 3:9-12)—he indicts the woman. For the reader who recognizes these parallels the obvious question is, Will Job also succumb to Satan's time-tested strategy (cf. n. 8)?

filled with ambivalence, wondering whether God can be "trusted" and how we might respond should we also be faced with such overwhelming adversity. This crisis of confidence in God's benevolence and justice sets the stage for Job's debate with his three friends (chaps. 4-27) and the looming prospect of Job's defection as God's touted faithful servant (1:8; 2:3).

C. Job's Allegiance Tested by Subversive Suggestion (2:1–10)

By dramatizing Job's intensified suffering and his wife's cynical response, **the author exposes Satan's strategy of "subversive suggestion" in undermining God's sovereign rule**, *so that readers might recognize Satan's strategy amid suffering and realize the high stakes of serving God faithfully as agents of his sovereign rule.*

This scene completes a sequence of events insinuating that Job has been completely abandoned by God. The additional challenge is occasioned by Satan's failure to dislodge Job's allegiance to God after the first affliction. Satan presents himself exactly the same way as before (2:1-3) and demonstrates that his agenda of subverting God's rule has not changed. The *Lord* responds to Satan's claim—that man will continue to worship God only as long as his health remains—by permitting Satan to attack Job's health (2:4-6): He is allowed to afflict virtually every square inch of Job's skin,[39] and Job assumes a posture of total personal collapse *in the midst of the ashes* (2:7-8), which in turn provides the backdrop for the final scene (2:11-13).

Job's wife intervenes at this point and inadvertently accommodates Satan's strategy of inciting Job to turn away from God.[40] Aware of Job's blamelessness and unable to discern any basis for his suffering, she impugns God's justice by ridiculing Job's steadfast devotion as he refrains from "charging God with wrong" (2:9, cf. 1:22). By suggesting that he *curse God and die*, she succumbs to Satan's temptation and seems perfectly willing to accept the consequence of certain death as God's expected retribution for

---

[39] Readers familiar with the Law of Moses would assume that this disease marked the sufferer as cursed by God. Hartley (*The Book of Job*, 82-83 [fn. 4]) points out that one of the deuteronomic curses for disobedience (cf. Deut 28:35) involved being smitten with the same kind of skin condition that afflicted Job.

[40] Satan preserved Job's wife in both catastrophes even though he was apparently free to kill her (cf. 1:12). Apparently, Satan reserved the woman's persuasiveness—just as in the case of Adam (Gen 3:1-6, cf. n. 38)—as an "ace up his sleeve": Since Job failed to buckle under the first catastrophe, Satan would "outflank" Job's steadfast devotion through the influence of Job's wife in order to incite Job to rebel against God.

such a curse.[41] Her suggestion only incites Job's righteous indignation: Rather than accede to her proposal he accuses her of foolishness (2:10a, cf. 1:21), and the author concludes with the ominous statement, *in all this Job did not sin with his lips* (2:10b).[42]

To the reader this second sequence of events may only seem to add insult to the injury of losing his whole estate but it exposes Satan's strategy of using the power of suggestion amid adversity to pervert mankind's conception of God's justice and goodness: It undercuts his confidence as God's chosen agent, and thereby subverts God's rule. For the time being Job's steadfastness seems to seal Satan's defeat, but how long will Job refuse to *sin with his lips*? Will Job ultimately take his wife's advice and impugn God's righteousness (cf. 1:22) in the face of protracted suffering?

Although Satan is not explicitly mentioned again in the entire book, Job's potential to capitulate to Satan's suggestion amid adversity sets up the ensuing dialogue with his friends as the pretext for Elihu's redemptive correction of his misconceptions about God's character. By now the reader should recognize the subtlety of Satan's strategy: Since God Himself had affirmed that Job suffered *without cause* (2:3), no reader can justifiably hold Job accountable for what has happened to him. So, when his three friends do exactly that they only capitulate to Satan's strategy and underscore the high stakes of preserving God's reputation as His chosen agents in the face of adversity.

---

[41] Job's wife is not suggesting that he take his own life by cursing God, only that he resign himself to what she sees as a logical conclusion of her understanding of retribution. That is, she knew Job was innocent and believed he was therefore entitled to blessing. By urging Job to curse God, she implied that Job's own righteousness was greater than God's. And if God was going to be that unfair, Job might as well curse God and die rather than give Him the perverse satisfaction of continuing to persecute Job. (Logically, if God had perpetrated such horrendous calamities when Job was **innocent**, what retribution would be left to punish Job for **cursing** Him other than certain death?) Behind the suggestion of Job's wife is the ancient counterfeit appeal of self-righteousness so well depicted in Gen 3:5 that readily accommodates Satan's subversive agenda, as illustrated in the ensuing narratives of Genesis (cf. Gen 4:12, 16-26; 6:1-7; 11:1-9).

[42] If indeed "the fear of the Lord is wisdom" (Job 28:28, cf. Prov 1:7, 9:10; Ps 111:10), then surely cursing God is the epitome of foolishness, as Job affirms. But this passage is as significant in what it portends as it is in testifying of Job's faithfulness (for the time being): Job will soon show his own lack of wisdom and attendant verbal foolishness, as Elihu, God, and eventually Job himself with all attest (cf. 34:34-37; 38:2; 42:3).

D. Job Consoled in his Separation from God (2:11–13)

By portraying Job's consolation in the death-like devastation of his unjust suffering and perceived separation from God, **the author depicts the crucial importance of fellowship with God amid suffering,** *so that readers might fully acknowledge Job's apparent abandonment by God and identify with Job's ensuing despair and yearning for a mediator who can bridge the gap back to his Creator.*

Job's collapse and isolation represent the complete reversal of his initial state of blessing and fellowship (1:1-5). The news of Job's affliction draws his three friends to visit him (2:11), thus initiating a new line of dramatic tension that will be resolved only in the final scene. Their natural assumption would be that God has abandoned Job and no longer desires to bless him, so they mourn with him in silence for seven days.[43] Their reaction— *each one tore his robe and sprinkled dust on his head toward heaven* (2:12)—depicts profound vicarious agony over Job's suffering and apparent abandonment by God. Silent consolation is all they can offer for now, because words cannot capture the magnitude of his suffering, and they are undoubtedly confused about how something like that could have happened to one whom they know so well (2:13).

By similarly identifying with Job in his suffering, the audience is also forced to grapple with the unsettling questions raised about God's character by Job's unjust suffering. Since God seems to have abandoned Job to suffering, how much more must Job endure before God abates his suffering and is reconciled to him? Is God really just? Does He really care about man, or is man simply a pawn He uses to accomplish His sovereign objectives (chaps. 3-31)?[44] But the scene also raises questions

---

[43] This may be symbolic of Job's own death. Zuck (*Job*, 20, fn. 12) points out that the usual time of mourning for the dead was seven days for the patriarchs (cf. Gen 50:10), the monarchy (cf. 1 Sam 31:13), and the exilic period (cf. Ezek 3:15). Since Job was now mourning with his friends on another "day" some time after the death of his children (cf. 2:1), the period of mourning for his children should have long since passed, and the present seven day period may signify his own figurative death from the standpoint of the reader.

[44] This is the very question that concerns Ps 8 and Heb 2, texts that place man at the center of God's creative purposes as His intended agent, as exemplified by Abraham and Christ his seed (cf. nn. 20, 29). The present exposition contends that this question is central to the author's strategic purpose for the readers (see "Application" in the PREFACE to the Commentary), who share Job's intended human agency and are therefore just as valued and essential to the fulfillment of God's creative purposes.

about Job's relationship with his three gentile friends,[45] whose own understanding of God is now challenged to the core—how will they explain his suffering?[46] How will they define their relationship with him, now that he is a mere shell of a man? We the readers must wonder how we, too, might respond under similar circumstances.

---

[45] It is somewhat surprising that expositors of Job have not generally explored the significance of lineages in the drama (cf. n. 35). It is of interest that while the author leaves Job in relative anonymity (cf. 1:1-5) he does identify the lineages of his friends (2:11; cf. Zuck, *Job*, 20; Hartley, *The Book of Job*, 85-86). Any reader who is familiar with Israel's history would recognize Job's friends as descended from famous ancestors who were closely related to but estranged from God's promised seed. Eliphaz is the very namesake of Esau's firstborn son and also of the line of Teman, the principal chief of Edom—both were the progeny of *daughters of Canaan* (Gen 36:2, 15). Bildad may well be the descendant of Shua, the Canaanite father of Judah's wife (Gen 38:2), who bore the promised seed to Judah. Zophar is tagged with the name of Naamah, the one daughter singled out in the genealogy of Cain (Gen 4:22), possibly the prototype of the estranged *daughters of men* (Gen 6:4). While Zophar could not be a direct descendant of Naamah because of the Flood, it might well strike the reader as his "spiritual lineage," like that of the Nephilim who reappeared through the line of Canaan after the Flood (Num 13:33, cf. Gen 6:4). If this analysis is accurate, then we are incessantly reminded of these lineages during the ensuing debate with each repeated introduction of Job's friends (chaps. 4-25). By the end of the book it should shock the reader who is familiar with these lineages that God intended from the beginning to reconcile to Himself Job's friends (42:7-9)—the very ones so obviously estranged from His promises to Abraham.

[46] For the time being, Job's friends can only *sympathize with him and comfort him* (2:11, NASB) and do not ascribe (at least overtly) his suffering to sin, as they do later in the drama. But once they are verbally engaged by his grief (chap. 3), so great is their vicarious discomfort that they will soon seek relief by trying to explain his suffering, as Job astutely observes (6:14-21). Only then does their lack of understanding of God's justice surface, along with their own need for redemption (cf. n. 27 and related text).

Act I

CREATOR IN COURT

"Can a man be righteous before God?"

God's Creative Purposes Challenged
(Job 3-31)

By framing the debate over Job's guilt and God's justice with "lament" and by culminating the debate with a plea for wisdom, **the author illustrates how self-righteous presumption to know God's purposes in suffering only serves Satan's objective of subverting mankind's intended agency by distorting the truth about God***, so that readers facing adversity might resist the temptation to ascribe all suffering to personal sin or indiscriminate punishment from God and instead seek wisdom in the fear of God.*

Structurally, this major section consists of a long, acrimonious debate (chaps. 4-27) culminating in an ode to wisdom (chap. 28) and framed by extended lament (chaps. 3 and 29-31).[47] The enclosed debate features three sequential rounds of indictment by each of Job's friends, except for the third round in which Zophar demurs.[48] Each indictment is followed by an immediate rebuttal, the last of which merges into the ode to wisdom with no literary marker (chaps. 26-28). The speeches in 27:13-23 and chap. 28 are stylistically quite distinct from the surrounding text, but we may reasonably deduce that they belong to Job and are integral to the

---

[47] This view of the structure is well argued by Claus Westermann ("The Literary Genre of The Book of Job," reprinted in Zuck [ed.], *Sitting with Job*, 51-63, cf. 54-57). It is notable that this largest portion of the book begins and ends with Job's invocation of curses upon himself (3:1-10; 31:5-40), thus forming an inclusion for the entire section.

[48] Although Hartley (*The Book of Job*, 322-3) contends that this anomaly makes it "quite obvious that this cycle has suffered severely early in its transmission," Greg Parsons ("Structure and Purpose," 19) provides a cogent explanation for the disruption of the third cycle of debate:

> One should recognize that this alteration of structure contributes to the development of the argument of the book. There are two basic lines of interaction which run through Job—Job's crying out to God and Job's disputations with his three friends. The absence of the third speech of Zophar is consistent with the fact that each of the speeches of the three friends is progressively shorter in each cycle and that Job's responses to each of the friends (which also are progressively shorter) are longer than the corresponding speech of the friends. This seems to signify Job's verbal victory over Zophar and the other two friends. It is also indicative of the bankruptcy and futility of dialogue when both Job and the three friends assume the retribution dogma (which for the friends implies Job's guilt and for Job implies God's injustice). Consequently, this structural design marks a very gradual swing toward a focus on Job's relationship and interaction with God in contrast to the earlier primary interaction between Job and his friends.

author's meaning and purpose.[49] Thus, 27:13-23 is best viewed as a frustrated concluding tirade in which Job dramatically dismisses his three friends then pleads for wisdom (chap. 28). Following this plea, Job appeals directly to God for summary judgment (chaps. 29-31).

This structure governs the flow of the argument, which develops as a legal metaphor. Job's initial soliloquy is an eloquent three-part lament that regrets his very creation by God (chap. 3). His friends are so deeply disturbed by his existential despair that they try to appease his suffering by soliciting his repentance for imagined sins; but this only antagonizes him and fuels a progressively vitriolic dispute over the evidence for God's justice and Job's guilt (chaps. 4-27). The dispute surfaces their desperate need for wisdom in the fear of God (chap. 28), and Job abandons the debate to sue God for restitution: He laments his lost honor as an agent of blessing (chap. 29), cites evidence that he was wrongfully dispossessed of his estate (chap. 30), and calls for God as Judge to unseal His indictments, daring God to convict him if He can (chap. 31).

The escalating invective exchanged by Job and his friends reflects faulty notions of God's justice and redemptive grace. As Job's disposition evolves, it becomes clear that he mistakenly shares his friends' presumption that God is bound by a simplistic notion of one-to-one retribution and blessing; he can only infer from his innocent suffering that God must be unjust.[50] Job's initial

---

[49] To those who see 27:13-23 (in view of its retribution theology) and chap. 28 (because of its sudden change in tone and theme) as necessarily voiced by Bildad or Zophar, Zuck responds that

> seeing the section as Job's is to be preferred for these reasons: (1) the section is consistent with Job's imprecatory desire that his enemy (the three friends considered collectively) become "as the wicked" (27:7-10). (2) Job had never denied that the wicked will eventually be punished; he only questioned why they continue to prosper. This idea is similar to Job's previous words (24:18-25). The *ultimate* judgment of the wicked contrasts with the *immediate* and sudden destruction of the wicked, which Zophar had expounded (chap. 20). (3) The fact that several statements in 27:13-23 are similar to Zophar's words in chapter 20 could just as easily argue for their being Job's words. Frequently, Job threw the friends' arguments back on them by using their own words. What more effective way to accuse them of being wicked than to employ against them their own words about the fate of the wicked? (4) The absence of a speech by Zophar is consistent with the fact that the speeches of the three friends become progressively shorter, and it suggests Job's verbal victory over Zophar. (5) Chapter 28 appears to be a continuation of 27:13-23, thus suggesting the same speaker. But chapter 28 is inappropriate for Zophar. [*Job*, 121, emphasis original]

[50] Carson clarifies this aspect of Job's faulty reasoning as his attitude evolves:

> Job may be innocent..., but that does not give him the right to charge God with injustice. There is a sense in which Job himself has been snookered by a simplistic doctrine of mathematically precise retribution. The major difference

poignant lament over his catastrophic loss (chap. 3) evolves into impatient disillusionment over his friends' lack of compassion (chaps. 4-27) and culminates in a petulant, self-righteous lawsuit to compel his vindication (chaps. 29-31). While Satan can clearly exult in the auspicious degeneration of Job's attitude as God's exemplary agent, the ode to wisdom (chap. 28) portends God's ultimate victory.

The point of the drama is therefore not to present Job as a paragon of faith amid adversity. By nature we seek to feel more secure in an uncertain world and attempt to explain unjust suffering by ascribing purposes to God that make sense in our own eyes: Like Job, we may color God capricious and unfair or, like Job's three friends, we may glibly absolve God of any purposes that would ever allow unjust suffering.[51] The futile debate tests

---

between Job and his three friends is not their underlying views of retribution, but their views of Job's guilt or innocence. [*How Long, O Lord?* 169]

[51] Harold Kushner epitomizes the danger of falling prey to either fallacy in his now famous book *Why Bad Things Happen to Good People* (New York: Shocken Books, 1981). Kushner (ibid., 43-45) goes to amazing lengths to twist the obvious logic of YHWH's speeches to Job in order to arrive at the conclusion that God does not in fact have the power he claims in His speech. Carson provides keen insight regarding Kushner's failure here:

> Many have sought to "solve" the problem of evil by denying that God is omnipotent...If evil and suffering take place, it is because someone or something else did it. God not only did not do it, he could not stop it; for if he could have stopped it, and did not, then he is still party to it....The most famous expression of this viewpoint in recent years is the widely circulated book by Harold Kushner, *When Bad Things Happen to Good People*. Kushner lost his son, and his grief drove him to question his traditional Jewish faith. Though a rabbi, Kushner came to believe that God could not have prevented his son's death. He is frank: "I can worship a God who hates suffering but cannot eliminate it, more easily than I can worship a God who chooses to make children suffer and die."...[T]he paperback edition soon topped one million. Clearly, Kushner had hit a nerve: people in pain were looking for answers, and many of them thought Kushner had provided one. [*How Long, O Lord?* 29]

By embracing this less-than-omnipotent God, Kushner must then contrive a monstrous explanation for how a "good" God can minister to those who die as innocent sufferers—he claims that all God can do is to work through living survivors: "The dead depend on us for their redemption and their immortality" (*When Bad Things Happen*, 138). Kushner views the role of religion as "help[ing] us feel good about ourselves when we have made honest and reasonable...choices about our lives" (ibid., 97). Kushner's theodicy is no more than a disingenuous, thinly veiled humanism that adopts the disposition of Job's wife (cf. n. 41) without being as honest. See the excellent analysis of Kushner's thesis by Peter Kreeft (*Making Sense Out of Suffering* (Ann Arbor, MI: Servant, 1986, 37, 47-49); Philip Yancey (*Disappointment with God*, 207-9); Douglas Hall (*God and Human Suffering*, 150-8); and Stanley Hauerwas (*Naming the Silences*, 44-59 [esp. fn. 25]).

our preconceived notions of God's character, fostering ambivalence as we yearn for dramatic resolution but are offered instead the *fear of God* (28:28).

The honest reader will allow Job's plight to challenge stereotyped views of God's justice and to expose our ignorance regarding God's sovereign purposes in suffering. Only by admitting our own inadequacy amid suffering will we forsake self-righteous presumption or the demand for quick relief or reassuring explanations and instead seek to know God better as His chosen agents. Even when we remain deeply ambivalent over unexplained suffering we can still accept His redemptive grace. Just how God reveals Himself amid suffering to evince this response will be addressed in Elihu's rebuttal (chaps. 32-37), YHWH's challenges (chaps. 38-41), and Job's eventual repentance and restoration as chosen mediator of God's redemptive purposes (chap. 42).

A. Job Laments His Creation (Job 3)

By articulating Job's grief with a disturbing nihilistic lament, **the author poignantly depicts how acutely Job's created purpose as God's servant is jeopardized by suffering,** *in order to disrupt reader complacency over mankind's crucial role in God's purposes and draw us to identify with Job in the ensuing battle over his continued allegiance to God.*

This chapter supplies the literary bridge to the lengthy debate between Job and his three friends. It is distinguished from the prologue by a shift from prose to poetry, which characterizes the bulk of the book. Job's soliloquy should therefore be considered the opening passage of the section that follows. The three-part structure of Job's lament[52] gives voice to the perceived meaninglessness of his entire existence by now—his very created purpose is at stake.[53] This elicits such profound discomfort in his friends that it triggers the entire ensuing "courtroom controversy" (chaps. 4-31).

Having spent seven days of silent grief in a state of utter collapse (2:13), Job can no longer contain himself. His despair is so crushing that he would prefer extinction: He curses the day of his birth—even God's creation "decree"—for allowing the light of that day to dawn (3:1-10). He then laments his birth because it has robbed him of comfort and rest (3:11-19)

---

[52] Job's lament violently disrupts the preceding silence (2:11-13) and quiet resignation to God's will (1:20-22; 2:10-11). It begins with an extended imprecation—a series of curses that couldn't seem more at odds with his prior disposition—calling for the annihilation of the day of his conception/birth (3:1-10). This leads to a formal lament composed of two rhetorical questions that express Job's preference for extinction (3:11-12; 21-23), in the light of the *rest* attained by those who are already dead (3:13-19) and the intolerable suffering and existential dread of continued living (3:24-26).

[53] Hartley cites M. Fishbane's work relating Job 3:3-13 to Jer 4:23-26 and hypothesizing that the "curse" here is a "counter-cosmic incantation" that in effect "negates each stage" in the order of creation (*The Book of Job*, 88-89; 101-102). He also points out that Jer 20:14-18 is nearly identical to Job 3:3, 7-8, 10-11 and suggests that the curse genre was borrowed from a common source as a literary means of investing grief with greater substance (ibid.). No doubt the perceived irreverence of this curse provoked Job's friends to respond after seven days of silence (David Clines, "A Brief Explanation of Job 1-3," reprinted in Zuck [ed.], *Sitting with Job*, 251-2). Cf. also n. 46. Job may well have hoped that his curse would move his friends to compassion (cf. 6:14) and he later used a curse to try to force God to respond to his complaint (see exposition, chap. 31).

and exposed him to the dreaded suffering he is still experiencing (3:20-26). While Job's initial worshipful response (1:21) had attested to his confidence that God was in full control of his destiny, the reader must now admit that Job's resolve to accept the bad along with the good (2:10) seems to be crumbling; Satan's chances of prevailing in his wager with God seem improved.

Did Job *sin with his lips* (2:10c), as his friends presumed when they were scandalized by his bold death wish (chap. 3, cf. 6:14b)? Does he show a lack of faith in his desire to "subtract" himself from God's creative plan (cf. 6:11)? Why then his impassioned plea to God for apparently trashing a creation as valuable and carefully fashioned as he had been (10:3, 8-12)? It seems best, rather, to view Job's lament here as "rhetoric of outrage"[54] designed to give full voice to the unmitigated suffering of his meaningless devastation and to direct such expression to the God who unmistakably permitted it to occur. The lack of explanation for Job's suffering eventually leads to a legitimate plea for wisdom (cf. chap. 28) but it also leads Job to *charge God with wrong* (chaps. 30-31, cf. 1:22) and thereby appears to facilitate Satan's agenda.

By so poetically expressing the unrelenting misery of Job's grief, the author intends to dislodge any residual complacency in the reader's

---

[54] Carson discusses the role of the disturbing nihilistic and imprecatory rhetoric in Job 3:1-13 and compares this with similar rhetoric in the Psalms:

> Not every expression of moral outrage is to be taken as concrete description, or even as considered desire....[T]he vividness of the outrage would be diluted were it replaced by a bland abstraction....It follows that we must ask whether some of the malediction language in the psalms is in the same way not the language of considered address but the *rhetoric of outrage*. Its purpose is not to inform but to ignite.... [*How Long, O Lord?* 97-98, emphasis added]

Hauerwas underscores the legitimacy and importance of such rhetoric:

> The psalms of lament do not simply reflect our experience; they are meant to form our experience of despair. They are meant to name the silences that our suffering has created. They bring us into communion with God and one another, communion that makes it possible to acknowledge our pain and suffering, to rage that we see no point to it, and yet our very acknowledgment of that fact makes us a people capable of living life faithfully...
>
> We are encouraged to express our pain and suffering not simply because that provides a "healthy release".... [O]ur willingness to expose our pain is the means God gives us to help us identify and respond to evil and injustice. For creation is not as it ought to be. The lament is the cry of protest schooled by our faith in a God who would have us serve the world by exposing its false comforts and deceptions. [*Naming the Silences*, 82-83]

Cf. Dan Allender and Tremper Longman (*The Cry of the Soul* [Colorado Springs: NavPress, 1994], 29-39).

imagination. We know what led to Job's affliction and cannot help but be drawn into Job's grief with a strong sense of injustice, realizing that Job seems initially to be little more than a pawn in a supernatural wager. This forces us either to try, like Job's friends, to justify God's obvious permission of evil[55] or to silently empathize with Job, recognizing the unequivocal reality of unjust suffering.[56] Either response should provoke us to question God's purposes in allowing a human to suffer this level of despair.[57]

[55] Hauerwas explains how the author confronts the natural tendency of the reader to want to placate Job's anguished cry with theodicy (*Naming the Silences*, 45-46 [fn. 10], quoting Terry Tilley, "God and the Silencing of Job," *Modern Theology* 5 [Apr. 1989], 267-68):

> Serious readers...can either read Job as silencing the voice of suffering or allow Job to silence claims about how God and suffering are related. The book...displays the cost of providing the "systematic totalization" a theodicy requires: silencing the voice of the sufferer, even if she/he curses the day she/he was born and accuses God of causing human suffering....The comforters are "academics" in the worst sense of that term, ineffective observers of the terrors of human suffering, or tormentors who intensify that suffering by the ways they respond to suffering. Job reveals the worth of such academic responses to real evil. Perhaps the better alternative is for the reader to remain silent.

Christ Himself implied the uselessness of theodicy for the observer of suffering (cf. n. 7) when he summarily dismissed attempted attribution by witnesses of tragedies (John 9:1-3; Luke 13:1-5). Just as Christ treated these occasions as opportunities for silent self-examination leading to redemptive change (cf. Luke 13:3, 5), so does Job's apparently meaningless suffering provide similar opportunities for the reader.

[56] The observer of suffering and evil can develop his own "rhetoric of outrage" (n. 54), which may result in cynicism and existential despair. This is well portrayed by Qoheleth, who in his quest for true meaning reflects on the apparent futility of life as we see it. He expresses profound dejection as he witnesses the boundless suffering of those unjustly oppressed by others with greater power (Eccl 4:1-3; cf. 3:16, 5:8). He reacts—like Job—by asserting that non-existence seems eminently preferable to the utter futility of innocent suffering (Eccl 4:2-3). Although it expresses legitimate outrage and grief, such existential despair may evolve into bitterness and cynicism (Eccl 7:8-10) rather than the fear of God that brings true hope (cf. Eccl 7:18; 8:12-13). In the so-called "enjoyment passages" (Eccl 5:18-20; 9:7-10; 11:9-12:1) Qoheleth, like Elihu, expresses God's true heart for those who suffer.

[57] A simple explanation of the meaning of his suffering might have satisfied Job (cf. 7:20; 13:20-24), but this would not meet his need to know and experience God more intimately. Job's lament supplies the point of departure for the ensuing discourses involving his friends (chaps. 4-27), Elihu (chaps. 32-37), and God Himself (chaps. 38-42) in his quest to "figure God out."

> A person who laments may sound like a grumbler—both vocalize anguish, anger, and confusion. But a lament involves even deeper emotion because [it]

Behind Job's anguish and restless despair is the nagging question: Will Satan's strategy succeed in subverting Job's created purpose as God's agent in order to win the wager?

For the moment it seems impossible to assuage the existential anguish of Job's unabated torment—*the thing I greatly feared has come upon me* (3:25).[58] We expect God to provide the ultimate explanation for his affliction and for Job to be vindicated. However, with no obvious justification for Job's suffering forthcoming, Job's friends can no longer silently endure his torment and they feel intense pressure to provide some explanation for his suffering and some hope for his eventual relief that can placate their own deep unease. The intensity of Job's anguish should heighten our curiosity about God's purposes in permitting such suffering and vilification by others (chaps. 4-27).

---

is truly asking, seeking, and knocking to comprehend the heart of God. A lament involves the energy to search, not to shut down the quest for truth. It is passion to ask, rather than to rant and rave with already reached conclusions. A lament uses the language of pain, anger, and confusion and moves toward God. [Dan Allender, "The Hidden Hope in Lament," *Mars Hill Review/Premier Issue* (Littleton, CO: Saint Domaine Group, 1994), 27]
See also Allender and Longman, *Cry of the Soul*, 245-8.

[58] Job concludes *I have no rest, for trouble comes* (3:26b). His greatest fear was that he would die in eternal restlessness (cf. Eccl 6:3-6)—this supplies the critical subtext behind the debate (Job 4-27) and Job's final appeal (cf. 29:18-20).

— 2 —

B. Debate over Job's Guilt and God's Justice (Job 4–27)

By staging an increasingly vitriolic debate between Job and his friends over the question of his guilt and God's justice in adversity, **the author reveals mankind's need to know God better in view of the inscrutability of God's purposes in unjust suffering,** *so that his readers might better tolerate ambiguity and uncertainty in adversity, recognize their need to know God better, and learn God's patience with those who are suffering.*

This section consists of three rounds of challenge and response between Job and his friends. The controversy revolves around the allegation by Job's friends that he is culpable for his own suffering and grief. But the deeper and more unsettling issue concerns the question of God's justice and care, which Job repeatedly thrusts back into the dispute because of God's transparent permission of unjust suffering. Job is therefore embroiled in two simultaneous struggles: to vindicate himself of the false charges of his friends and to plead with an ostensibly absent and unconcerned God to abate his unjust suffering. As Job fails in both missions he repeatedly appeals for an unknown arbiter or mediator to plead his case before God and solicit God's judgment against his friends.

Although in every round of the debate Job seems to express unequivocal confidence in God (13:15-16; 19:25-27; 23:10-12), his statements are made in the context of growing ambivalence: Job is torn between God and his friends as to who is more likely to be moved by his appeal. Each round of the debate displays progressive disillusionment over his three friends' obstinacy—they seem totally incapable of showing comfort or compassion or of even hearing him in his inconsolable distress. Their failed advocacy finally forces him to turn exclusively to God, although not out of a disposition of humble submission; he assumes the posture of a litigant as both defendant and plaintiff before God, demanding the vindication of his honor and the restitution of his losses.

The first round of the debate (chaps. 4-14) lays the foundation for retribution theology. Job's friends assert a one-to-one correspondence between man's sins and God's present retribution; to their credit, they do seem to appreciate the depravity of man. With even greater presumption they assert that God will fully restore Job in exchange for his repentance. Job responds in turn by trying to convince his friends of his innocence and pleading for their compassion. With each response Job also pleads with

God either to explain or abate his suffering in hopes of vindicating him in the eyes of his friends. But he finds neither compassion nor relief: He winds up disgusted by his friends' intransigent refusal to genuinely consider his argument or comfort him in his pain and he despairs of ever being restored or of even surviving to see his vindication.

Job's growing frustration explains the increasingly rancorous tone of the second round of the debate (chaps. 15-21). Job's friends are astonished at what they view as his defiance in the face of God's justice and mercy while they continue to hammer home their retribution dogma but now conspicuously omit the promise of restoration by God in exchange for his repentance. When Job realizes they will never take his claim of innocence seriously or show the slightest hint of pity or compassion he all but gives up trying to convince them. Instead he adopts an attitude of growing bravado and cynicism and warns them of their own liability to judgment: Although he has lost all hope of ever being restored before he dies he gains confidence that *in the end* an avenger will arise to vindicate him *in his flesh* before God and punish his friends (19:25-29, NIV).

The third round (chaps. 22-27) finds Eliphaz condescending to extend one final invitation for Job to repent (chap. 22). Bildad is reduced to inferring Job's guilt (indirectly) by restating his conviction about man's depravity in the face of God's sovereignty (chap. 25), but Zophar offers no retort at all, Job having refuted Zophar's prior argument point-by-point.[59] By contrast Job grows even bolder, his argument further fueled by intensifying vengeance and self-pity. With self-righteous confidence he asserts that if God would only appear to hear his arguments He would weigh Job's righteousness and promptly exonerate him (chap. 23). At the conclusion of the debate Job expands his prior claim (19:29) that his friends were liable for judgment; with mocking sarcasm he indicts them for their persistent abuse and invokes God's retribution (chap. 27).

The author's message now begins to crystallize. Job's friends have clearly failed to show any compassion or truly consider Job's complaint before judging him. Their opinions are repeated almost *ad nauseum* to underscore how difficult it can be to dislodge such attitudes, even when the sufferer has been a close friend. The cheap suggestion that God will restore Job in return for his repentance is rooted in their fear of suffering. They are completely closed to the possibility that they might be wrong about Job's guilt and forced by his innocent suffering to rethink

---

[59] Zuck (*Job*, 98) has nicely demonstrated the one-to-one correspondence between Zophar's assertions in chap. 20 and Job's rebuttals in chap. 21. This may help explain why Zophar has no response by the third round (cf. n. 48).

their misconceptions about God's justice. They are unmasked as Pharisaic moralists who cannot empathize with Job because of their entrenched belief in performance-based acceptance by God—they essentially deny any role for true compassion or grace.

On the other hand, Job's own growing obsession with vindication has inflamed his vengeful spirit toward his friends and his increasingly demanding and presumptuous disposition toward God. As a result he has "sinned with his lips" (cf. 1:22, 2:10c), disrupted his fellowship with God (cf. 1:5, 20-21; 2:10), and all but abandoned his commitment to worship, thereby promoting Satan's agenda. The author portrays this evolving disposition in prolonged discourses saturated with lament and invective, so that the reader will fully absorb Job's emotional distress yet grow increasingly uncomfortable with his escalating self-pity, cynicism, and presumption, culminating in a formal lawsuit demanding vindication from God Himself (chaps. 29-31).

Since so much of the dispute consists of statement and restatement of the faulty doctrine of retribution, one may legitimately ask why the author devotes such a large portion of his argument to this debate. From the outset the audience is fully aware that any attribution of Job's suffering to retribution from God is ill founded, and therefore—at the very least—it is erroneous to apply the doctrine without qualification. Thus for the reader, as far as the contentions of Job's friends are concerned, the debate is over before it starts. What then does the author intend to teach the reader as the debate proceeds? How does he expect us to respond to Job's dilemma?

Ironically, the manifest futility of Job's sheer determination to solve his unjust suffering by vindicating himself in the eyes of his friends drove him to seek God's wisdom—even as he prepares for his bold confrontation with God Himself (chaps 29-31), Job seems to concede that this wisdom comes only by forsaking self-sufficient strategies to secure relief and by submitting in the fear of God (chap. 28). Hopefully, our increasing uneasiness over the attitudes displayed by Job and his friends will promote an awareness of our own disposition in suffering and of the inescapable fact that in this life we can demand neither genuine compassion from others nor immediate relief of suffering from God. The only alternative is to fear God and seek His wisdom.

— 3 —

1. Round One: Pleading for Compassion (Job 4–14)

*In describing Job's futile appeal to his friends for compassion and his plea to God to relieve his suffering, **the author shows that neither compassion from others nor relief from God are guaranteed in this life**, so that his readers might look to God in the face of unexplained suffering with greater tolerance for ambiguity and uncertainty and greater compassion for others.*

The first round of dialogue features the literary device of "interchange," alternating between Job's debate with his non-empathic friends and dramatic "asides" in which he openly laments his miserable estate before a silent and unresponsive God. The debate stems from Job's poignant death wish (chap. 3), which profoundly disturbed his friends. To this point they had been grieving together with him in silence but now felt compelled by his distressing verbal nihilism to correct his distorted view of God. They try to counter his grief-deranged thinking by offering a more rational explanation for his suffering: He must have done something terribly wrong to warrant such "punishment" (4:1-21; 8:1-4; 11:1-12). Their own anxiety and intimidation by the sheer magnitude of his suffering too quickly leads them to falsely reassure him of full restoration to health and wealth if he will only repent (5:1-27; 8:5-22; 11:13-20); this is the only answer they can see that will ever mitigate his suffering.

In his laments Job squarely affixes the blame on God for willful— even capricious—persecution (6:4; 7:17-21; 9:21-31; 13:26-27) even though he remains uncertain of the real reason behind his suffering. Why does God refuse to intervene and set the record straight? He pleads with God to either relieve (7:11-16; 10:13-22; 13:28-14:6) or justify (7:17-21; 10:1-12; 13:20-25) his unremitting affliction and expresses growing fear that he will die and never be restored to see that his life had any meaning (14:7-22). Job displays obvious ambivalence as he vacillates between his comforters and God, seeking sympathetic advocacy; thus far all he has received is repeated attempts to console him with the false promise of restoration in exchange for repentance.

Confident that he has done nothing to warrant such suffering, Job sees through the hypocrisy of their misguided efforts to console him; his friends are seeking only to appease their own fear and anxiety over his suffering (6:14-23; 12:1-6; 13:1-12). Job is astonished that they continue to insist that he must in some way be responsible for his own suffering so he repeatedly tries to clear up the false indictment in hopes of motivating them to show some compassion (6:24-30; 9:1-3, 14-16; 12:7-12). He finally loses patience with his friends (13:1-12) and threatens to enlist God as a witness against their accusations (13:13-19). However, he does not become truly embittered until the next round of debate, when it becomes clear that his main objective has escalated from the simple relief or explanation of his suffering to decisive vindication by God and retribution against his unfeeling friends (chaps. 15-21).

The reader cannot help but identify with Job during this first round of the debate. The fact that we are fully aware of the circumstances leading to Job's affliction in chaps. 1-2 precludes the option of accepting his friends' presumption of Job's guilt, so we are left to identify with Job's ambivalence. Is it possible for the just to suffer unjustly? Why would God allow an innocent man to continue suffering just to prove a point to Satan? What would that imply about the character of God? It seems especially unfair that God would maintain steadfast silence when Job's friends' repeatedly ascribe his affliction to justified retribution from God, so Job's disappointment over their lack of compassion is clearly legitimate. On the other hand, the debate surfaces Job's nagging awareness that God had created him with particular care to represent Him as His agent on earth. This underscores the high stakes of faithful stewardship and should also lead us to reflect on how we might respond in adversity and whether we would remain true as agents of God when faced with comparable adversity.

a. Eliphaz: *"Only sinners warrant such destruction. Admit your sin, repent, and surely God will restore you." (Job 4–5)*

Presumably the oldest and wisest of Job's friends (cf. 32:4, 7), Eliphaz is the first to respond to Job's lament (chap. 3). After briefly crediting Job's prior reputation for good works (4:2-6) he immediately insinuates that Job must be guilty, for only sinners would reap such destruction at the hand of God (4:7-11). Eliphaz then proceeds to quote a spirit that "spooked" him in a night vision (4:12-16)[60] and asked him a rhetorical question, *Can mortals be*

---

[60] Eliphaz's reaction to this "spirit" suggests visceral fear of a supernatural being that Eliphaz misconstrued as a messenger from God, so that he falsely attributed the spirit's assertions (4:18-21) to God. It may well have been a demon commissioned by Satan to recruit Eliphaz with the false theology implied by the spirit's rhetorical question (4:17) and further elaboration in 4:18-21. See n. 19.

righteous before God? (4:17).[61] This spirit then explained that a man's punishment reflects his lack of righteousness before God (4:18-21). By ascribing this theology to a supernatural being, Eliphaz feels entitled to vilify Job and provide an easy solution (paraphrasing): "You have *no deliverer* [5:1-5][62] since you did something wrong to bring on such grave afflictions [5:6-7].[63] If I were you I would confess my sin in the hope that God would restore me [5:8-16]—God will surely *deliver* those who accept His chastening [5:17-27]."

b. Job: "You're so intimidated by my pain, you can't see me— look at me; hear my case, then teach!" (Job 6)

Job responds to Eliphaz as the representative of all three of his friends. He initially expands his lament to further underscore the great pain of his suffering (6:1-13), which his friends seem to have missed completely (6:14-23). Their false insinuation of guilt is initially of less concern to Job than his desperate need for true compassion ("kindness," 6:14a). But Job promptly senses their reticence to truly minister to this need:[64]

---

[61] So NRSV. Whereas NKJV, NIV render Heb. *min* as comparative—*"Can a mortal be **more** righteous than God? Can a man be **more** pure than his Maker?"*—this sense does not fit the context, since the spirit immediately goes on to compare men with *angels* in their common liability to judgment *before* God (4:18-19; cp. Ps 8:4-5). The sense is that Eliphaz is acknowledging mankind's natural propensity to sin, so that when one sins (as Job must have) he cannot justify himself *before* (= *min*) God. This issue becomes the main point of contention in the debate, and the rhetorical question is later repeated by both Job and his friends without this same ambiguity of *min* (9:2b; 25:4a, cf. n. 22).

[62] Eliphaz is responding to Job's quest for one who can deliver him by vindicating him in light of all the evidence for his guilt. He justifies Job's lack of an advocate in court (5:1) by alluding to the liability of his children *in the gate* (5:4). In Job's day legal matters would typically be judged at the city gate by a respected elder (cf. 29:7, where Job himself had served this role), so the hidden presumption is that Job's children must have died as judgment for Job's guilt (Job had consistently offered sacrifices to atone for his children's guilt, cf. 1:5). The word *deliverer* (*nāṣal* [Hifil participle], 5:4, cf. n. 23) anticipates Job's more explicit quest for an advocate or vindicator who can get him acquitted before God and avenge him against his friends who have charged him (cf. 9:28-33, 10:7, 16:19-21, 19:25-28).

[63] While the oft-quoted *For man is born to trouble, as the sparks fly upward* (5:7, NASB) affirms the universal depravity of mankind it serves in context to substantiate the preceding assertion, *For affliction does not come from the dust, Nor does trouble spring from the ground.* Eliphaz thus means to justify the meting out of punishment by God as predictable retribution warranted by man ("born to trouble") for evil deeds done before God ("as the sparks fly upward").

They are so squeamish when confronted with his "irreverent" death wish (*he forsakes the fear of the Almighty*, 6:14b) that they lavish him with false optimism that is only swallowed up by his boundless grief (6:15-20). Job then exposes the selfish motivation that drives their attempted reassurance: They are so terrified by Job's suffering (6:21) they seek to appease it with unsolicited simplistic solutions intended merely to assuage their own terror (6:22-23),[65] yet they completely dismiss the true cause of Job's anguish—his unjust suffering. Job begs his friends first to give him an honest hearing and only then to provide the wise counsel he needs in his state of despair and confusion (6:24-30).[66]

(To God) "Why do you pester me to the point of death? What have I done to You to deserve this?" (Job 7)

Understandably frustrated over his friends' inability to respond effectively to his need, Job uses images of rapidly fleeting time to lament his

---

[64] The failure of Job's friends to address his true need leaves Job even worse off than before in his time of trouble (cf. Prov 25:19), which explains his growing bitterness in response to their arguments.

[65] Witnessing the apparent meaninglessness of unjust suffering provokes such existential dread, that the observer may desire to circumvent the suffering at all cost, proffering some rationalization or quick solution (cf. *bribe*, 6:22). This provides Satan with an ideal opportunity to subvert God's purposes in Job's suffering (cf. nn. 19-20). Edith Schaeffer elucidates Satan's agenda behind the "bribe" (*Affliction: A Compassionate Look at the Reality of Pain and Suffering* [Grand Rapids: Baker, 1978], 62-3):

> As part of the battle, [Satan] chooses the affliction he attacks us with and then he himself whispers the temptation to us to get out from under it...and we will then be relieved immediately....We are tempted to get rid of afflictions through shortcuts....The "wiles of the devil" were pitted against Job in his afflictions....The devil "dishes up on the same plate" both the affliction and a false way of getting rid of it, so that we face a double temptation: cursing God and complaining against Him, and then turning away from Him toward something or someone else.

[66] Job's rejoinder accurately reflects the truth of Eccl 7:5, 7: *It is better to hear the rebuke of the wise than for a man to hear the song of fools...Surely oppression destroys a wise man's reason, and a bribe* [Heb. *mattānâ*] *debases the heart*. His friends' desperate attempt to appease his suffering was only a *bribe* (6:22b, Heb. *šāḥad*) that preempted the true compassion (6:14a) and wise counsel (6:24) he needed in his despairing condition (6:26). Rather than patiently witnessing the profound devastation of Job's suffering, they tried to extinguish his despair with cheap theology (*the song of fools*; cf. also Prov 25:20). Job will soon sense the growing contempt of his friends (cf. 12:5) and expose them as *worthless physicians* (13:4) and *miserable comforters* (16:2), unable to show any compassion (19:21-22) or mitigate his grief at all (16:4-5). See further my more extended analysis, "A 'Wisdom' Perspective on Advocacy for the Suicidal," in Timothy Demy & Gary Stewart [eds.], Suicide: A Christian Response (Grand Rapids: Kregel, 1998), 369-85.

unremitting suffering (7:1-6) and "eye" images to remind God of His limited opportunity to "see" him before he dies (7:7-10).[67] Since his days are numbered, he pleads with God to at least relieve his intolerable affliction on the way to death (7:11-16) then punctuates his plea with logical questions: If there is no basis for punishment in Job's past behavior, why is he singled out for persecution (7:17-18)?[68] Even if he **had** sinned, why not explain it so he can be restored[69] as God's valued agent rather than perish in futility (7:19-21)?

c. Bildad: "Your suffering only proves God is just; if you would only repent, surely He would bless you again" (Job 8)

Bildad loses patience with Job's *blustering* (8:2, NIV) and replies with a rhetorical question to justify Job's affliction, *Does God pervert justice?* (8:3, NIV): Job's children must have sinned to warrant their deaths (8:4). Bildad virtually echoes Eliphaz, inviting Job to repent so that at least he can be restored to his former state of blessing (8:5-7). He smugly challenges Job to learn the age-old axiom (8:8-10) of proportional retribution for *all who forget God* (8:11-13), since Job has trusted in a "house of cards" (8:14-18).[70] Bildad considers his explanation very generous and

---

[67] The imperative singular (*remember*, 7:7) shows that Job is now addressing God, and the chiastic link between *eye* and *see* (7:7-8) depicts God's former individualized attention. Job is aware that God had created him with particular purpose and care and he will challenge God in the next aside (10:1-13) with the apparent contradiction posed by his unjust suffering. As the debate intensifies, however, Job's awareness will ironically cut both ways: He himself is still accountable to serve as God's exemplary agent, even in adversity.

[68] Job's catastrophes bore the clear mark of divine purpose (see exposition of 1:6-22), so in 7:17 Job "echoes" Ps 8:4 with unmistakable sarcasm to challenge God's purposes in Job's suffering (n. 44). With a likely *double entendre* (Heb. *pāqad* can mean both "appoint" and "examine, scrutinize") Job insinuates that in **his** case God has inexplicably reneged on His original *creative* intent to "appoint" man over the world (Ps 8:4) and now aims to "scrutinize" Job with *destructive* purposes in mind (Job 7:18a, cf. 10:8-13). The parallel verb in 7:18b (*bāḥan*) also means "scrutinize."

[69] Job's unfailing practice of offering sacrifices bore witness to his sensitivity to sin (cf. 1:5, n. 34), so that if God would only inform him of the sin, Job could abate his suffering by making the proper atonement (7:20-21a).

[70] The imagery of flimsy dwellings that collapse or vanish with the slightest opposition depicts Job's former prosperity as only a charade that covers his sin but will inevitably collapse to expose his hypocrisy (cf. 8:13b). Bildad went a step further than Eliphaz by insinuating that Job was **intentionally** deceitful, thus inciting Job to react by exposing Bildad's own hypocrisy (9:27-31).

exudes the same sanctimonious confidence as Eliphaz that God would surely restore Job (8:19-22, cf. 5:8-27).

d. Job: "On the contrary, though I am innocent, God's punishment in effect condemns me, so why even try?" (Job 9)

Job's response this time is less sanguine than his first, but he still attempts to help his friends see his predicament: Job heartily agrees (9:1-2a) that *God will not cast away the blameless* (cf. 8:20a) but contends that in fact he is *righteous before God;* he just can't persuade God to declare it publicly (9:2b-3).[71] With biting sarcasm he speculates that God must be too busy exercising his creative wisdom and powerful justice on a grand cosmic scale to answer Job's trivial complaint (9:4-12).[72] Yet, even if Job could successfully subpoena God as a witness he still could not successfully argue his case before God as Judge (9:14-16), *for He crushes* and suffocates Job, making him look guilty even though he is innocent[73] (9:17-20). So the fact that Job is *blameless* leaves him with no alternative but to attribute his affliction

---

[71] Following Habel, Hartley (*The Book of Job*, 166) explains how Job's repetition of the rhetorical question *How can a man be righteous before God?* (9:2b) has **forensic** significance in contrast to the **moral** connotation intended by Eliphaz (4:17, n. 61). The infinitive construct *lārîb* (9:3a) means "to dispute in a court of law, or to enter into litigation" (ibid.). "The interrogative indicates that Job does not think there is any likelihood of winning a case against God. Yet his conviction that God does not pervert justice prods him to contemplate the impossible, i.e. of pursuing litigation against God" (ibid.). Job thus answers his friends by implying that he is already **morally** righteous but can't compel God's **forensic** testimony to exonerate him and abate his punishment.

[72] In these verses Job ironically anticipates the later speeches of Elihu and YHWH (chaps. 36-41), who make the same points about God's cosmic wisdom and omnipotence (cf. e.g., 37:18, 38:31) in order to justify the opposite conclusion: In His omniscience God in fact cares very much about Job's welfare and actually goes to great lengths in his efforts to get Job to know Him better through affliction (cf. esp. 36:5-21).

[73] Job's logic is impeccable. Job needs God as a witness in court to testify to his innocence in order for him to successfully prove that his punishment is unjust. Yet, God is also the Judge who sits in judgment. If they were to face each other in court, God has already deflated his case (cf. 9:18a), because *though* Job is *righteous*, his ongoing affliction would force him to *beg mercy of my Judge* (9:15). Job is therefore caught on the horns of a dilemma: On the one hand, Job can't appeal to God's power to spare him, for that is the very power that *crushes* him; on the other hand, if he tried to subpoena God's testimony to seek *justice* (i.e., vindication), *who* would *summon Him* (9:19, NASB [after LXX])? A defendant begging mercy of his judge amounts to admitting guilt; hence, *my own mouth would condemn me* (9:20a). Thus, Job cannot logically plead for both justice and mercy at the same time.

to the capricious and unjust judgment of God—who else could it be (9:21-24, cf. 9:24)?

Job is convinced he will soon die (9:25-26) so he can only conclude that Bildad's optimism (cf. 8:20-22) is completely unwarranted—it is ludicrous to "put on a happy face" (9:27): Since Job's suffering continues in effect to corroborate the indictment of his friends, they would never acquit him; they would only continue to condemn him (9:28-31).[74] Job's only recourse is therefore to appeal to God to abate his suffering, but given Job's lack of legal standing before God (9:32),[75] he can only lament the lack of *any mediator* to arbitrate his dispute with the God who terrifies him (9:33-35).

(To God) "Why did you create me with such care only to crush me? If you don't back off, I will surely die!" (Job 10)

Job's exasperation with Bildad leads him to appeal to God for some explanation of his suffering (10:1-2). He appropriately invokes God's creative purpose for him, *the work of Your hands* (10:3), by asking why He would have *fashioned* him *into an intricate unity* (10:8) with such loving care only to crush him on false charges before he could ever realize that purpose (10:3-13).[76] Job presumes that God must be actively scrutinizing his every action—trumping up allegations of sin with no chance for acquittal—in order to justify His continuing persecution (10:14-17). This leads Job again to lament the fact that he was ever born (10:18-19, cf. chap. 3) and

---

[74] Job shifts to the second person in 9:28b-31, raising the question of whom he is addressing. Most translations assume it is God who will *not acquit* him (9:28b, NASB). However, Job's primary agenda here is to convince his **friends** of his innocence; thus, 9:27-31 is best viewed as unmasking Bildad's hypocrisy: Job asks sarcastically why Bildad should even try to cheer him up (9:27, cf. 8:5-7) and answers him in alternate parallel (9:28-29): Since his ongoing afflictions (9:28a) still *condemned* him (9:29a, cf. n. 73), Bildad would still refuse to *acquit* him (9:28b, cf. NASB), and Job's best efforts to establish his innocence in their eyes would be futile (9:29b)—*If I washed myself...and my hands..., you would plunge me into a slime pit* (9:30-31a, NIV).

[75] *See* nn. 15, 24. Since Job's affliction subverted his standing as defendant to appeal to God's power or justice to secure his acquittal (cf. 9:14-20, n. 73), it is obvious he needed an advocate to plead his case.

[76] The drama hinges on Job's appeal to God's creative purpose (cf. n. 20)—a powerful argument to abate his affliction, **if** his premise is valid, that God has forgotten him. The strategy behind Job's assertion here is thus to draw the Creator's attention to his own creative design (cf. n. 68) and force Him (if He is even listening) to either **reaffirm** His original intent or **concede** the nihilistic premise of Job's initial soliloquy (chap.3, cf. 10:18-22).

plead for some relief before his created life is lost in meaningless darkness forever (10:20-22).

e. Zophar: *"God can see through your empty claims of innocence—if you would only repent!" (Job 11)*

Zophar is the least diplomatic of all three of Job's friends, even implying that Job has been positively deceitful by trying to mask his guilt with his *multitude of words* (11:1-3). He answers Job's claim of innocence by asserting that God's wisdom—should He testify, as Job was demanding—would only trump Job's words[77] by exposing even more sin and thus warrant more punishment than God had already imposed (11:4-6). He boasts that God's unfathomable wisdom easily roots out deceitful motives and that His justice will not allow the hidden sin to go unpunished (11:7-11). Zophar therefore infers that Job is *empty-headed*[78] (11:12) and—like Eliphaz and Bildad—also urges Job to repent, so that God can restore him to a secure existence (11:13-20, cf. 5:8-27; 8:5-7, 20-22).

f. Job: *"God alone is behind this, you worthless doctors—He will explain, and I'll be vindicated!" (12:1–13:19)*

Provoked by Zophar's attempt to match wits with him by impugning his wisdom and motives, Job loses all patience and sarcastically accuses his friends of hypocrisy in restating the obvious about God's wisdom (12:1-3): They can easily mock the *just and blameless* from their own comfort and security, which shields their smug perspective on guilt and justice from genuine challenge (12:4-6).[79] Job retaliates by unmasking the

---

[77] NKJV distorts the meaning of 11:6a. The Heb. reads "and disclose to you the secrets of wisdom, for sound wisdom is *double*..." The sense here is that if God were to testify He would "call" Job's bluff by unmasking even more sin ("double") than was apparent from Job's punishment. A modern analogy would be the game of bridge, in which a bid can be unmasked as foolish by "doubling" the bid, such that the penalty for failing to make the bid is double.

[78] Or *witless* (NIV). Zophar's true motivation—to "match wits" with Job—is ironically unmasked, so that his ensuing offer of restoration in exchange for Job's repentance is really only condescension. When trying to reason with one who is suffering (cf. 6:24-27), it is all too tempting to justify their continued punishment as due to their stubborn refusal to confess purported sin; thus Zophar's analogy of a donkey giving birth to a man (11:12b) is only a "cheap shot" meant to further denigrate Job as stubborn.

hypocrisy of having insinuated that Job lacks wisdom because he presumes God cannot detect his hidden guilt (cf. 11:7-12): He advises Zophar instead to examine the obvious evidence[80] that *the Lord has done this*[81] (12:7-10)—it is Zophar who lacks the *wisdom* of *aged men* (12:11-12) to recognize that God's *wisdom and strength* can make prisoners and fools of even the wisest and most powerful men (12:13-25).[82]

Job concludes that he knows as much as them all[83] (13:1-2) and must therefore appeal directly to God (13:3)—they are lost in untruth (*forgers of lies,* 13:4a) and *worthless physicians* (13:4b, cf. also 16:2-4), bereft of any capacity to provide real insight or compassion. In a burst of sarcasm he tells them that their best wisdom is to keep their mouths shut (13:5); with serial rhetorical questions he insinuates that their deceitful attempt to defend God will only incur His judgment (13:6-12). Job demands that they be silent and listen as he threatens to sue for certain vindication, even if God slays him (13:13-18).[84] And Job feels entirely justified for he believes that his only other alternative is to die in silence (13:19, NASB).

---

[79] NKJV translates MT *lappîd* (12:5) as "lamp," implying that Job's friends had disparaged his insight, but *lappîd* is elsewhere used to denote the fire of judgment (BDB, 542a, b), not the fire of "illumination." While the passage mainly responds to Zophar's sniping at Job's wisdom (12:2-3), the immediate context (12:4-6) shifts back to Job's perceived failure of justice. Thus, "it seems best to divide this word into the preposition *lᵉ-* plus the definite noun *pîd*, 'ruin, disaster'" (Hartley, *The Book of Job*, 206 [fn. 3, on 12:5], so NASB, NIV). The sense of 12:4-6 is therefore to lament an ironic paradox of injustice: "I have become a joke to my friend—I, the one who used to call on God, and He answered him; I, the righteous and blameless, a joke. He who is at ease can dismiss disaster as reserved for those who stumble, [yet] the tents of destroyers are at ease—those who provoke God are secure, he whom God holds in His hand." Job is insinuating that while he is the righteous one who is being punished, the bands of Sabean and Chaldean "destroyers...who provoke God" by destroying Job's estate (1:13-17) are ironically being **protected** by God.

[80] In a burst of sarcasm Job suggests that if Zophar ("you" is singular) would only inquire, even the simplest of creatures could inform him (12:7-8).

[81] Job infers in 12:9 that God, not Job, is the "guilty" party behind his affliction. The astute reader will perceive that this comes close to "charging God with wrong" (cf. 1:22, n. 50).

[82] Job's point is that it is blatantly presumptuous of Zophar to claim enough understanding of God's inscrutable judgments that he can so smugly ascribe Job's affliction to preexisting guilt. Ironically, when Elihu later defends God's justice he throws this very argument back at Job (chap. 34).

[83] Job reverts to the plural "you" as he now addresses how poorly all three have responded to his initial plea that they *Teach me....Cause me to understand wherein I have erred* (6:24, cf. n. 66).

(To God) "You're terrifying me—please tell me what I did wrong! Can I hope to ever live again?" (13:20–14:22)

Even after boldly rejecting the "counsel" of his friends, Job remains ambivalent. Although still terrified of further persecution by God, he nonetheless pursues his vow to argue his case before God (13:20-22, cf. 13:3). Job ascribes all his suffering to a vendetta from God (cf. 13:24, *Why do You...regard me as Your enemy?*), citing retribution that seems utterly out of proportion to his trivial sins (13:23-25)[85] given that he continues to be hemmed in and consumed, to the point of impending extinction (13:26-28).[86]

As he loses all hope of surviving Job resigns himself to the imminent termination of the short, preordained life to which he is heir (14:1-5). Pleading with God to at least leave him in peace for the few days he has left (14:6), Job laments that even a felled tree has more hope of being restored than a man so doomed (14:7-11) with no prospect of resurrection

---

[84] As Hartley explains (*The Book of Job*, 221 [fn. 2]), the apodosis of v. 13:15a has two textual traditions: "...I would not [*lō'*] have hope" (Ketib) or "...yet will I trust in Him [*lô*]" (Qere). But the Piel of the verb *yāḥal* in the Ketib most naturally reads "wait," as in 14:14 (BDB, 404a[1]); this would yield "Though He slay me, *I surely will not wait*" as the logical introduction to Job's avowed intent to sue before God in 13:15b-19 (cf. 13:3, 6, 13). In light of Job's dogged determination to be vindicated in the eyes of his friends we should revisit his long-revered "statement of faith" (Qere); as Crabb aptly notes (*Inside Out*, 141):

> Job had become convinced he had a case. No longer did he pray for relief, he was ready to demand it. The intensity of his conviction is reflected in his well-known statement, "Though he slay me, yet will I hope in him." This verse is often held up as an example of fervent faith, but notice the second half of the verse: "I will surely defend my ways to his face"....He goes on to say, "Now that I have prepared my case, I know I will be vindicated. Can anyone bring charges against me? If so I will be silent and die" (Job 13:18-19)....Far from humbly yielding to the decisions of a sovereign God, Job strongly asserts that he deserves better treatment than he's received. If God takes his life, Job pledges to go to his grave convinced that if the facts were known, it would be clear to everyone that he's been mistreated.

[85] Job instinctively recognizes the injustice of disproportional retribution. Job's allegation is all the more ironic to the Jewish reader, in that the uncontrolled excesses of disproportional retribution are the very basis for God's repeated affirmation of *lex talionis* in the Law of Moses (cf. Exod 21:24; Lev 24:20; Deut 19:21).

[86] NKJV poorly reflects the logic of 13:26-28, which consists of an explanatory *kî* ("for"), followed by four clauses joined by simple conjunctive *waw*, the last of which bears consequential force: "*For* You sentence me to bitterness *and* make me inherit the sins of my youth *and* put my feet in the stocks *and* scrutinize all my paths to restrict my movement, *so* I decay like something rotten, like a moth-eaten garment" (cf. NIV).

(14:12, *So man lies down and does not rise....They will not awake*). Job hopes to live again (14:13-17)[87] but nevertheless[88] warns God that He is inexorably destroying a man's hope (14:18-19), overpowering him with unremitting pain and grief (14:20-22, cf. NIV).

---

[87] Cf. 14:14, *If a man dies, shall he live again?* Job displays a remarkable grasp of the conditional role of propitiation (14:13, 16-17, cf. NRSV) in redeeming his preordained agency through the hypothetical future restoration of his created purpose (14:15b, *you would long for the work of your hands* [NRSV], cf. n. 76). Job's hope is that God would finally respond to the many sacrifices that he had offered to atone for his sins and those of his children (cf. n. 34).

[88] The strongly adversative compound conjunction *we'ûlām* (14:18a) emphasizes the striking dichotomy between Job's present condition (14:18-22) and the restoration that would accompany propitiation (n. 87); Job is lamenting the rapid erosion of any hope of seeing this restoration.

— 4 —

2. Round Two: Confident of Vindication (Job 15–21)

*By displaying Job's increasing contempt for others in his obsessive quest for vindication, **the author illustrates how an unrelenting disposition of victimization and self-righteousness only resists the Creator's purpose of vindicating human agency**, so that readers might realize how easily we can subvert mankind's crucial role as God's chosen agent by pursuing our own vindication rather than seeking God's mercy in the face of suffering.*

In this round of the debate Job's ambivalence toward God continues to grow, and his responses to his friends and to God are less clearly distinguished. Also conspicuously absent are his friends' prior assurances of restoration in exchange for his repentance, indicating that whatever meager sympathy they had has now yielded to a mutual obsession with winning the debate. Job's deep disappointment over God's continuing failure to relieve his suffering (16:7-17) leads him to despair of any possible restoration (17:6-16). Yet the failure of his friends as advocates (16:1-6; 19:1-6, 21-22) ironically fuels his conviction that this same God will indeed vindicate him of their false charges (16:18-17:5; 19:23-29). Deeply wounded by their relentless insistence that he is guilty, Job replies with escalating vindictiveness and closes with a decisive rebuttal of their theory of retribution, counter-indicting them for their own intransigent ill will toward him (chap. 21).

The trouble is that Job's real needs will not be met by seeking vindication against his friends. This agenda drives him to approach God no longer out of a desire to know Him better or rely on His grace for restoration but out of the presumption that he merits vindication. Ironically, Job's previous despair of any possible restoration is completely displaced by a growing vengeance, which culminates in his obsessive confidence that a redeemer will even raise him from death to witness his ultimate vindication and avenge the persecution he suffered from his friends (19:25-29). While the author continues to emphasize the crucial importance of extending comfort and sympathy to the sufferer he also exposes the self-righteousness and foolish presumption of demanding that justice be served in order to bring any meaning to suffering.

Job's increasing obsession with vindication should strike a sympathetic cord in the reader, since it is obvious that Job is in no way responsible for his suffering. However, once the reader is hooked into "rooting" for Job to prevail in this courtroom controversy, it becomes increasingly clear that none of the verbal strife helps reveal God's purposes in permitting Job's suffering. The reader is aware of God's initial wager with Satan but still can't see how Job's quest for a courtroom mediator (16:19-21) would serve God's purpose in the wager—to present Job as *a blameless and upright man, one who fears God and shuns evil* (1:1, 8; 2:3). Even if a redeemer were to raise Job from the dead, it would only satisfy his thirst for revenge (19:25-28). Ironically, Elihu ultimately serves as Job's ideal mediator, not by vindicating him but by revealing to him God's redemptive purposes in adversity (chaps. 32-37).

a. Eliphaz: "By defying God, you deserve a wicked man's judgment!" (Job 15)

Eliphaz is annoyed that Job keeps arguing so earnestly in the face of his obvious judgment and uses ironic wording to imply that Job's impious words betray signs of Satan's deceit[89] (15:1-6). He is offended by what he sees as Job's arrogant rejection of his friends' efforts to comfort him on God's behalf (15:7-13, cf. 15:11, *Are the consolations of God too small for you, and the word spoken gently with you?*) and he asks Job why God should pay any attention to him—a mere mortal who is *detestable and corrupt* in the eyes of God—when He doesn't even trust His own angels[90] (15:14-16, NASB). Consequently, Eliphaz cites presumably unbroken traditional wisdom (15:17-19) to warrant Job's suffering as the judgment one should expect (15:20-35) for so boldly defying God (cf. 15:25-26) and he withholds his previous offer of God's restoration in exchange for Job's repentance (cf. 5:8-27).

---

[89] Eliphaz's insinuation *you choose the tongue of the crafty* (15:5b) is a transparent allusion to Gen 3:1, in which exactly the same word (*'ārûm*) is used to characterize the serpent's deceitfulness.

[90] This third echo of Ps 8 (cf. 4:18-19; 7:17; and nn. 44, 61, 68) again compares man (15:16) with angels (15:15, *His holy ones*, NASB). By translating *holy ones* as "saints" (15:15a) the NKJV misses the *a fortiori* comparison with angels: While Eliphaz intends to denigrate Job as an archetypal representative of sinful man by asserting that Job is far less righteous than the angels in the eyes of **God** (15:16), the outcome of the opening wager hinges on whether Job will be deemed righteous in the eyes of the archetypal angel, **Satan** (15:15, cf. 1:6; 2:1; n. 38). This profound irony in Eliphaz's rejoinder casts him as Satan's complicit though unwitting "accuser" (cf. n. 37), a testimony to the author's literary skill in continuing to portray Job's controversy with his friends in light of the original wager even though Satan remains unseen and unmentioned.

b. Job: *"Miserable comforters! Even though I am near death, surely God will vindicate me!" (Job 16–17)*

Job responds by taking further umbrage at the verbal attacks of his *miserable comforters,* who only manage to continue haranguing him in the face of his unmitigated pain (16:1-3). He suggests that they should instead be extending *words* of sympathy to *comfort* him in his downtrodden, grief-stricken state (16:4-5).[91] Job concludes that it makes no difference whether he complains or remains silent—he still has no relief (16:6). God has surely and specifically marked him out for persecution, which brands him a pariah among his friends and robs him of companionship, since all they do now is scorn him (16:7-14).[92] This keeps him in a state of continuous grieving with no prospect of relief, even though he remains innocent

---

[91] Man's natural yearning for *comfort* amid suffering (cf. 16:2) plays a central role in Job's debate with his friends. The alternate parallelism in 16:4-5 describes how they could have comforted him in his distress (cf. 6:24-30, n. 66): Job affirms the importance of edifying speech (16:4a,b, cf. Prov 10:19-21; 12:18, 25; 15:1-2, 4, 28; 25:11-13) by comparing the derogation he has received from his friends (*heap up words against you,* 16:4c) with the edification his words would have provided if their roles were reversed (*strengthen you with my mouth,* 16:5a). Job then employs facial imagery to underscore the importance of *sympathy* or *compassion* (16:4d/5b): With a Heb. play on words Job compares the effect of "shaking" (*nûaʿ*) the head (16:4d)—an expression of mockery—with *the comfort* [*nîd,* lit. "quivering"] *of my lips* (16:5:b)—a clear gesture of sympathy, as if one were about to cry. In both 2:11 and 42:11 the Heb. *nûd* ("nodding," as of the head in sympathy)—from which *nîd* is derived—is rendered *mourn* or *console* and also linked with *comfort* (*naḥam,* same as *comforters* in 16:2). The same connection of *sympathy* with *comfort* is seen in Ps 69:20: *I looked for someone to take pity* [*nûd*]*, but there was none;/ And for comforters* [*naḥam*]*, but I found none.* A contemporary illustration is found in Paul Brand and Philip Yancey, *Pain: The Gift Nobody Wants* (New York: Harper Collins, 1993), 277-9. See also the present author's "Wise Advocacy," in Kilner et al (eds.), *Dignity and Dying: A Christian Appraisal* (Grand Rapids: Eerdmans, 1996), 218-19, and Mark R. Littleton, "Where Job's 'Comforters' Went Wrong," reprinted in Zuck (ed.), *Sitting with Job,* 254.

[92] Job's ambivalence emerges again as he now describes his persecution at the hand of God. Whereas in 16:1-6 Job had addressed his friends collectively in the second person plural he now refers to God as his adversary in both the second and third person singular in the hearing of his friends. He also cites former acquaintances in the third person plural in 16:10-11, but it is not clear whether those whom he labels *ungodly* and *wicked* (16:11) are the comforters or other men who once respected him (cf. chap. 29). If they are the former, then Job's claim that *They have slapped me on the cheek with contempt* (NASB) is figurative for their verbal contempt (16:10) to which he alluded in 16:1-4.

and his *prayer is pure* (16:15-17).

This again leaves Job pleading for a *witness in heaven* who can exonerate him—an *advocate* (NASB) who can intercede on his behalf before God, his courtroom adversary (16:18-21),[93] in view of his impending death (16:22-17:1). Out of desperation Job dares to ask God for a pledge that He will vindicate him against his friends, who mock him out of ignorance and thus deserve their own retribution[94] (17:2-5). He vows that in spite of the guilt falsely conveyed by his inexorable demise (17:6-8), his unwavering righteousness will ultimately prevail (17:9). He sarcastically dares them to nonetheless[95] *try again* to defend their vacuous optimism (17:10, NIV) that he can be restored in the face of his impending hopeless fate, death (17:11-16).[96]

---

[93] Job now builds on his plea in 9:33 for a mediator between God and himself (cf. n. 15) and uses three different words in these verses to characterize this *arbiter.* The Heb. *'ēdî* (16:19a, *my witness*) is paralleled in 16:19b by the Aramaic *śāhᵃdî,* "my defender, witness" (Hartley, *The Book of Job,* 262 [fn. 3], cp. NIV, NASB), which is preferable to NKJV's *evidence.* The Heb. *lîs* in 16:20a is best translated *intercessor* (NIV) or *mediator*—just as in 33:23—to parallel Job's yearning in 16:21 for a man to plead his case; "scoffers" (NASB) or "scorn" (NKJV) seems misplaced in context (16:19-21). Cf. Parsons, "Structure and Purpose," 30. Elihu's use of the same term in 33:23 only heightens the irony of Job's plea, in that he exposes Job's need for an entirely different kind of *mediator,* one who reveals God's redemptive purposes in Job's suffering (cf. nn. 24-26).

[94] The NKJV rendering of 17:5 is misleading. It is likely a proverb that Job cites as a veiled threat of retribution, *If a man denounces his friends for reward, the eyes of his children will fail* (NIV). The implication is that his friends are mercenaries who would falsely accuse Job for the "reward" of placating their own unease over his unexplained suffering (17:5a, cf. nn. 65, 66).

[95] Job again uses the adversative compound conjunction *wᵉ'ûlām* (cf. n. 88) to introduce his concluding remarks. The sense is that of sarcastic provocation: Even though Job is certain to prevail in his pursuit of vindication against their false indictments (17:9), they are welcome to *try again* and marshal all the lame arguments they can to continue opposing him but they will *not* be found *wise* (17:10, NIV).

[96] The sense of foolish optimism is transparently projected in Job's accusation that his friends *turn night into day* (17:12, NIV), alluding not to their accusations of his guilt (which they inferred from his suffering) but to their repeated promises of God's restoration in return for his repentance (5:8-27; 8:19-22; 11:13-20). In a closing swipe at his friends, Job asks sarcastically how this purported restoration could confer any hope when the only "family" he can see now inhabits his impending grave (17:13-15). Do they have the courage of conviction to accompany him to this promising future of *dust* (17:16b)?

c. Bildad: "Why do you scorn us so? It should be obvious that your own wickedness justifies your punishment." (Job 18)

Stung by Job's bitter sarcasm, Bildad replies by berating him for his long-winded defense and suggests sarcastically that Job himself *gain under-standing* before he speaks and excoriates them as *stupid* (18:1-3, cf. 17:10b). Feeling Job's growing contempt, Bildad (like Eliphaz) withholds any further promise of restoration (cf. 8:19-22) and accuses Job of stubbornly resisting the obvious (18:4) before offering his own gratuitously detailed rebuttal: Citing a litany of self-indicting afflictions of the *wicked* (18:5-19),[97] he argues that anyone would deduce[98] from Job's afflictions that he is *wicked* and *does not know God* (18:20-21). This proves to be a flashpoint for Job's smoldering obsession.

d. Job: "By persecuting me like this, you yourselves merit God's punishment—I know God will vindicate me!" (Job 19)

Job answers their incessant slander[99] and the inference that he has *erred* (19:1-5) by countering *that God has wronged me* (19:6).[100] He substantiates his claim by citing his unanswered cries *concerning wrong* (19:7) and God's relentless attack that has stripped him of any vestige of dignity and hope (19:8-12), leaving him completely alienated from friends and family (19:13-20). Job thus redoubles his appeal for them to *have pity* and not *persecute me as God does* (19:21-22) and he vows again to sue for his ultimate vindication (19:23-29, cf. 13:15-19; 16:19).

Job pleads that his testimony might be preserved forever (19:23-24), indicating that although he has resigned himself to the probability of dying soon (cf. 16:22-17:16) he is so determined to vindicate himself in the eyes of his friends, that nothing else is more important. He is so certain of his

---

[97] Culminating Bildad's list of afflictions is his recognition of man's overriding hope for a legacy and "remembrance" (*zeker*) that will last beyond the grave (18:17-20). This same concern for lasting remembrance culminates Qoheleth's initial reflection over meaning in life in the face of his ultimate demise (Eccl 2:16, NASB). The hope of retaining some legacy or remembrance plays a key role in the dramatic/rhetorical resolution of both Job (42:7-17) and Ecclesiastes (9:4-10; 11:9-12:14).

[98] Bildad uses merism in 18:20 (*west...east*) to rhetorically claim universal agreement that Job must be guilty (18:21).

[99] With obvious hyperbole Job cites *ten times you have reproached me* (19:3), twice the actual number recorded in the dialogue so far.

[100] Note the dramatic contrast of this claim with Job's initial refusal to *charge God with wrong* (1:22b, cf. n. 42).

eventual vindication that he brazenly presumes that after he dies he will ultimately see his testimony prevail—restored by a *redeemer*[101] who *shall stand* on the day of judgment,[102] so *that in my flesh I shall see God*[103]

---

[101] Expositors have long debated the identity of Job's *Redeemer* (19:25a) and what Job really understood about him. The Heb. (*gō'el*) is the same as for *kinsman redeemer* (cf. Zuck, *Job*, 89; Hartley, *The Book of Job*, 292-294) and typically refers elsewhere in the OT to the God of Israel or to the relative who redeems the heritage of a dead or wronged brother. Albert Barnes effectively rules out any conscious expectation of Messiah on Job's part, as the context shows Job is seeking an *avenger* or *vindicator* ("Job 19:25-29," reprinted in Zuck [ed.], *Sitting with Job*, 285-6, 294-5). Job thus sees this *redeemer* as the *arbiter* (9:33), *witness* (16:19) or *intercessor* (16:20-21, NIV) he had sought earlier to plead his case before God (cf. Parsons, "Structure and Purpose," 30-32; Elmer B. Smick "Mythology and The Book of Job," reprinted in Zuck [ed.], *Sitting with Job*, 228, 235). With dramatic irony this expectation foreshadows Elihu's inspired promise of a deliverer (cf. n. 62) who would instead restore Job's intended agency for God (33:23-30, cf. nn. 20, 24) in the face of his own self-sufficient pride.

[102] The term *at last* or "in the end" (19:25b) may well denote judgment at the end of the age (Hartley, *The Book of Job*, 294). The Heb. for "'rise, stand up' is here a technical legal term meaning 'to stand up' as a witness in court [cf. Deut. 19:15-16; Ps. 27:12; 35:11]. Job is thus saying that his kinsman will fulfill his responsibility as redeemer by giving the decisive testimony in Job's defense" (ibid.). Such a vindication of OT saints at the end of the age is foreseen in Dan 12:1, where the testimony of a witness (Michael) is needed in connection with the resurrection of *every one...written in the book* (cp. Job 19:23). If this is the testimony Job was anticipating "in the end," then against whom does he hope to see judgment declared? The notion that "Job is beseeching the God in whom he has faith to help him against the God who is punishing him" (Hartley, *The Book of Job*, 295) requires an "abrupt break" at 19:25 (ibid., 292) and wrenches 19:25-27 out of the context of Job's case against his friends (19:21-29). It makes more sense and preserves the palistrophic structure of 19:21-29 (cf. Habel, "Literary Features," reprinted in Zuck [ed.], *Sitting with Job*, 101) to see Job as so bent on avenging his persecution by his friends that he can imagine nothing sweeter than God's judgment against them (19:28-29). This tarnishes Job's oft-cited confidence in a future resurrection, for his hope that *in my flesh I shall see God* only reflects an obsession with vengeance. Even if the correct reading is *apart from my flesh* (see below), the author clearly intends to illustrate the continued deterioration of Job's attitude as a negative example for his readers—notwithstanding his legendary patience (cf. Jas 5:11).

[103] Barnes ("Job 19:25-29," 293-6), Zuck (*Job*, 91-92), and Hartley (*The Book of Job*, 295-6) argue here that the notion of bodily resurrection is at odds with (1) ancient beliefs, (2) the preferred rendering "[apart] from my flesh" (19:26b), and (3) the grave doubts Job had already expressed about his future restoration after death (cf. 7:9, 21; 10:21-2; 14:7-22; 16:22; 17:16). However, such a resurrection was anticipated by at least some patriarchs (cf. Heb 11:17-19, 35), and Job's previously expressed doubts about future restoration now only heighten the dramatic irony of his declaration in 19:25-27: After having lost all hope of survival, he is now so convinced

(19:25-27). Job has clearly given up pleading for compassion from his friends (cf. 19:21-22) and concludes instead by warning them of God's retribution (19:28-29).[104]

e. Zophar: *"Your rebuke that reproaches me will not save you from God's just and discerning judgment." (Job 20)*

While Zophar was undoubtedly stung by Job's previous response (12:1-13:19), it is the immediately preceding threat of judgment (19:21-29) that especially provokes his *anxious thoughts* and forces him—somewhat petulantly—to justify his stance on behalf of all three friends (20:1-3).[105] He resorts to the most insulting word pictures yet to convey Job's reputed wickedness.[106] Like Eliphaz, he leans on tradition (20:4, cf. 15:17-19) to attribute the swift and complete reversal of Job's fortune to natural retribution for a wicked man's arrogance[107] (20:5-11, cf.

---

of God's justice prevailing that he presumes God would ultimately be obligated to resurrect him in order to vindicate him (cf. R. Laird Harris, "The Doctrine of God in The Book of Job," reprinted in Zuck [ed.], *Sitting with Job*, 176-7).

[104] Job imagines what his friends must have been thinking in order to treat him the way they do, *'How shall we persecute him?'* (19:28a). In view of their stubborn insistence that Job must be guilty (*Since the root of the matter is found in me*, 19:28b), he threatens his recalcitrant friends with the very judgment from God they claimed Job had warranted (19:29, cf. 13:7-12).

[105] Zophar is the least original of Job's three friends: He mimics Job's preceding complaint by whining that Job's *rebuke...reproaches me* (20:3a, cf. 19:3a). He plagiarizes Eliphaz's *anxious thoughts* (*śe'ippîm*, 20:2, cf. 4:13) and *spirit of...understanding* that *causes me to answer* Job (20:3b, cf. 4:15-16, n. 60) and he gratuitously embellishes Eliphaz's prior allusion to the serpent (20:12-16, cf. 15:5b, n. 89).

[106] Zophar accuses Job of more than just ordinary wickedness—he aligns Job with the most notorious of rebels against God. He borrows primordial figures from Genesis (*since man was placed on earth*, 20:4) to impugn Job's character, including the arrogance exemplified at the Tower of Babel (20:6, cf. Gen 11:4) and the cunning deceitfulness of the serpent (20:12-13, cf. nn. 89, 105). Zophar also stoops to the crudest imagery yet by inferring that Job will *perish forever like his own* excrement (20:7a); it is small wonder that Job is even more sarcastic and vengeful by the next round of the debate.

[107] The main point of the pericope (20:4-11) is to link the wicked man's sudden and permanent destruction to his own rebellious pride (vv. 5-6), so the mention of the wicked man's *children* in 20:10 seems awkward (cf. NKJV, NASB). NIV clarifies that his loss is so complete, the next generation will have to pay back the poor who were exploited to accumulate his wealth. Zophar's position that such exploitation requires complete restitution is further developed in the following pericope (20:12-22).

18:5-21). This is because a wicked man's deceit[108] invariably backfires as the predictable outcome[109] of exploiting the poor (20:12-22) and God inevitably exposes[110] such wickedness to justify His judgment (20:23-29).

f. Job: "Why then do the wicked prosper? God's judgment is not at all apparent from their earthly fate" (Job 21).

Job counters Zophar's inference of deceit (cf. 20:12-13) by exposing his friends' own profound hypocrisy:[111] If they were genuinely interested in *consolation*[112] as they had claimed they would *listen carefully* (21:2) and take his argument seriously and only then, if they must, *keep mocking* (21:3). He humors their hostility by insisting that his *complaint* is not with them but with God and that his *impatience* is justified (21:4, cf. 4:2, 5). Rather than mock him they should *look at* him *and be astonished;* they should observe his terror in silence[113] as he *remembers* his affliction (21:5-6). Job then proceeds to systematically refute Zophar's claim that we invariably see God's retribution against the wicked:

---

[108] The key figure of Zophar's rebuttal—a man who spews deceit like a serpent but is poisoned by his own venom (20:12, 14, 16)—ironically illustrates the fact that he himself had become Satan's dupe (cf. 1:9ff, n. 20).

[109] This "lesson" of reciprocal retribution is driven home with revolting gastronomic imagery: A wicked man tries to *swallow* (20:15, 18) but *vomits* (20:15) whatever fills his *belly* (20:14, 15, 23).

[110] The image of God's arrow piercing the wicked man's body to reveal the *gall* inside (20:24-25) graphically depicts Zophar's contention that God will reveal the *venom* of his hidden *evil* (20:12-14).

[111] With the exception of 21:3b, Job addresses all three of his friends in the second person plural (21:2-3a, 5, 27-29, 34). He pricks them with their own hypocrisy by the skillful use of rhetorical questions imbued with heavy sarcasm; the chapter is loaded with them.

[112] *See* 15:11, where Eliphaz had used the same word (*tanhumoth*) to characterize their "good-faith" attempts to console him.

[113] The facial imagery here is similar to that used by Job in 16:2-5 (n. 91). The imperative *put your hand over your mouth* (21:5b) is intended as a graphic contrast to the sarcastic *keep mocking* (21:2b). All along Job's friends have been claiming to comfort him by promising God's restoration in exchange for his repentance, but this has been more to palliate their own anxiety and fear when tragedy strikes so close to home. Job had long since pled for them to *please look at me, And see if I lie to your face* (6:28), but they refused to acknowledge how terrifying his suffering really was, even after he had surfaced their profound existential dread (cf. 6:14-23 and nn. 65-66).

In fact, *the wicked* flourish (21:7-13) as they defy God (21:14-16),[114] who only *distributes* calamity at random (21:17-18). Why claim that *God lays up a man's iniquity for his children*—shouldn't he himself be punished before he dies (21:19-21)?[115] The truth be told, death is utterly impartial (21:22-26). Job can only surmise that his friends had cited his calamities to intentionally malign him (21:27-28). If they would just ask, even the "man on the street" would inform them (21:29)[116] that *the wicked* are often spared despite their evil deeds (21:30-31);[117] in fact, a wicked man commonly dies an honorable death (21:32-33).[118] Such common sense reasoning only confirms Job's contention that his friends' efforts to *console* him are futile; *nothing is left of* their *answers* to his suffering *but falsehood* (21:34, NIV; cf. 16:2; 21:2).

---

[114] Given the rebellion of the wicked (21:14-15), their prosperity must come from God (21:16a); yet even so, Job refuses to align himself with such a disposition (21:16b), as his friends had insinuated (cf. 20:12ff).

[115] Job argues that Zophar's claim that a man's children will pay for his sin (20:19, cf. 20:10, n. 107) makes no sense, *for what pleasure would he have in his descendants after he is dead?* (21:21, my translation). Job's point is that once such a man is dead he could no longer be punished by suffering the vicarious punishment of his children. (cf. 5:4) makes no sense at all—it certainly says nothing about his own guilt (cp. Eccl 3:18-21).

[116] Job's sarcasm is expressed by two rhetorical questions, the second of which is awkward in NKJV. The NRSV best captures the intended sense, *Have you not asked those who travel the roads, and do you not accept their testimony...?* (cf. also NIV, NASB).

[117] The logic of 21:30 is misconstrued by the NKJV, NASB, and marginal NIV readings, which would better support Zophar's argument. NRSV best conveys Job's intended sense, *that the wicked are spared in the day of calamity, and are rescued in the day of wrath* (cf. also NIV). This sense is in turn supported by the self-evident reflections conveyed in the rhetorical questions of 21:31.

[118] Job's logic in 21:30-33 substantiates his point in 21:13 that the wicked prosper and then die before they can be held accountable for their deeds, which is echoed by the argument of Eccl 8:10-11.

3. Round Three: Obsessed with Revenge (Job 22–27)

In the unwittingly ironic responses of Job's opponents to his escalating obsession with vindication and revenge, **the author affirms both the depravity of all mankind and the universal scope of God's redemptive purposes amid adversity,** *so that readers might recognize in Job's disposition their own natural inclination toward self-righteousness and the attendant risk of falling short of their own role as agents of God's redemptive purposes.*

Although the arguments of Job's opponents in this final exchange are shorter, the level of dramatic irony is further heightened. Eliphaz prophetically anticipates Job's restoration as an agent of God who will mediate God's propitiation of the guilt of others (chap. 22), and Bildad identifies this need for propitiation among all mankind (chap. 25); thus, they unwittingly affirm the universal scope of God's redemptive activity. In effect, as Eliphaz urges Job to be reconciled with God he predicts his own deliverance (22:21-30); and as Bildad asserts that no one can justify himself before God (25:4-6), the "blameless" Job himself proves the point in his own driven quest to vindicate himself (23:1-12; 27:1-6), refute his opponents' theology (chap. 24), and even invoke God's revenge upon them (27:7-23).

In his self-absorbed obsession Job has lost sight of his calling as an agent of the Creator, and this has subverted his worship and his commitment to intercede for others (cf. 1:4-5). If God's permission of suffering could neutralize **Job**—*a blameless and upright man...the greatest of all the people* (1:1, 3b, 8; 2:3)—what hope in adversity would a reader of **lesser** stature have? In the ironic assertions of Job's opponents alert readers will recognize the real problem that they and Job alike share, as well as God's redemptive solution: No one on their own can be *righteous before God*, but God will use suffering to get their attention and restore to them His righteousness, transforming them—like Job—into effective agents of His blessing to others (chaps. 32-37).[119]

---

[119] As dramatic irony develops in the debate, it becomes increasingly evident that God intends to bless mankind by commissioning human mediators of His redemptive grace. This is the great commission of the Abrahamic covenant (Gen 12:1-3) and the cornerstone of Elihu's entire argument (Job 32-37, nn. 24-25), which thus parallels the argument of Genesis 12-50, exemplifying God's providential transformation of his chosen covenant mediators.

a. Eliphaz: *"Your case will never prevail before God; be reconciled to Him, and He will bless others through you."* (Job 22)

In his final speech Eliphaz marshals his best arguments to persuade Job.[120] He aptly cites Job's obsession with justifying himself (22:1-4) yet continues to insist that Job's suffering must be the consequence of *great wickedness* (22:5) and he justifies Job's punishment by citing his presumed oppression of others (22:6-11).[121] Eliphaz contends that God can see it all (22:12) then quotes Job's claim in order to refute him:[122] Job had argued that God does not *judge* fairly in that *He cannot see* (22:13-14)[123] and thus lets *the wicked* prosper (22:17-18a); moreover, Job had claimed to have avoided their evil counsel (22:18b). Eliphaz counters Job's argument by insisting, however, that *you keep to the...way* of *wicked men...who* are *cut down before their time* (22:15-16); *the righteous* rejoice as the wicked are *cut down* (22:19-20).[124] Once more Eliphaz urges Job to *submit to God and...accept instruction* (22:21-22, NIV); if he

---

[120] Eliphaz offers Job a three-part rebuttal with both positive and negative incentives to repent: He (1) reasserts the logic of retribution in view of Job's obsession with vindication (22:1-11); (2) tries to refute Job's argument that man's iniquity is not reflected by his judgment (22:12-20, cf. 21:7-34); and (3) again invites Job to be reconciled, promising even more advantages to repentance than before (22:21-30, cf. 5:17-27).

[121] In the midst of addressing Job in the second person, Eliphaz alludes to another man in the third person. NIV construes this as a sarcastic allusion to Job himself, a man who became *powerful* and *honored* in the land by dispossessing those less fortunate (22:6-9); NKJV/NASB imply that the *mighty* and *honorable* the one Job allowed to dwell comfortably in the land (22:8) at the expense of the defenseless (22:6-7, 9). Either sense satisfies Eliphaz's intent to justify Job's punishment.

[122] The ensuing pericope 22:13-20 makes the best contextual sense when read as Eliphaz's rebuttal in a two-step alternate parallel response (22:15-16, 19-20) to his quotation of Job's own claims (22:13-14, 17-18). See the argument in NET (fns. on 22:13-18).

[123] The initial particle in 22:13 is adversative: The gist of Eliphaz's opening assertion in 22:12 is contradicted (*"But you have said..."*, NET) by the opposite claim ascribed to Job in 22:13-14—that God is so far removed *He cannot see* the works of *the wicked* (as claimed by *the wicked* in Ps 73:11, cf. NET fn. on Job 22:13). Thus, Eliphaz is answering Job's purported claims in order to unmask the duplicity he alleges is behind Job's claims: He counters that Job was **presuming** he could hide from God the evil deeds that his friends alleged he had done (22:13-14, cf. 22:5-9) while at the same time **claiming** that God is unfair to refrain from judging the wicked yet **denying** his own evil which warrants exactly the same judgment (22:17-18).

[124] Eliphaz refutes Job's prior claim that *the wicked* profitably defy God (22:17-18a [NIV], cf. 21:14-16) by describing how *the righteous* celebrate their sure and decisive destruction (22:19-20).

renounces all iniquity and lust for gold he will be so lavishly restored (22:23-25),[125] that his intercession will be able to bless others vicariously (22:26-30).[126]

> **b. Job:** "*I would make my case if I could get His attention, but He terrorizes me, while the wicked get away with murder! Though justice is delayed it will prevail!*" *(Job 23–24)*

Job again laments the fact that he can't bring his petition directly to God (23:1-7, cf. 16:18-21) because he is stymied by God's apparent inaccessibility (23:8-9, cf. chap. 9). If he could only gain a hearing he is certain that his integrity and obedience to God would prevail in his favor (23:10-12).[127] Yet he doubts he can change God's mind and is resigned to his *appointed* fate of terror (23:13-16), though it will not stop him from pressing his case for vindication (23:17).[128] So he laments God's tardiness in judging evil (24:1),[129] citing the overwhelming evidence that wickedness

---

[125] The conditional logic "If..., then...; if... [23], and..., and... [24]; then... [25]" is better expressed in NASB than NKJV. The sense is that if Job repents of sin and gives up rights to his own wealth, ironically anticipating the final scene, he will have **God's** wealth (42:7-17).

[126] Eliphaz's promise that the *purity of your hands* would save even the guilty (22:29-30; contrast 9:30-31) is ironically fulfilled when his own sin is eventually remitted by Job's righteous intercession (42:7-9, n. 27). Elihu will later expand on Eliphaz's prediction of Job's reconciliation (33:25-28; n. 26).

[127] Job's third renowned "statement of faith" must again be questioned (cf. nn. 84, 102) in light of the context. Job felt that God was obliged to hear his testimony and exonerate him for his proven integrity and obedience (23:4-12). While his claim *When he has tested me, I shall come forth as gold* (23:10b) ironically portends Job's ultimate restoration in 42:10-17, Job prevails not by forcing God to vindicate him but by repenting and becoming a blessing (42:1-9). Job's present disposition shows no trace of repentance; it is instead imbued with the arrogant presumption that God should be held accountable for His judgments. Larry Crabb observes that "when all happy passions were smothered by grief, something came alive within Job as he courted the idea of challenging God. Nothing more closely masquerades as true vitality than arrogance" (*Finding God* [Grand Rapids: Zondervan, 1993], 88).

[128] The verse is difficult, but if as in NIV the logic begins in 23:15 with a context of justified resignation (*That is why I am terrified...*), then the opening *kî* in 23:17 has concessive force, "*though* I have not been silent because of the darkness" (cf. NET; NIV; NASB). That is, Job still refuses to give up his claim.

[129] This verse serves as a literary hinge, its parallel rhetorical questions best conveyed by NIV: *Why does the Almighty not set times for judgment? Why must those who know him look in vain for such days?*

still flourishes (24:2-17).[130] Job then abruptly shifts his focus to the future and takes comfort in the consolatory conviction that God will ultimately settle all accounts: The present thriving of the wicked by God's sovereign permission will eventually dry up and yield the barren legacy that has been warranted all along by their *wickedness* (24:18-25).[131]

Job's argument in this response may at first seem inconsistent, since his point in 24:18-24 seems diametrically opposed to what he claims in 24:2-17; in fact, it appears to confirm his opponents' case that the wicked are punished for their evil deeds.[132] Yet, if Job is to argue his case successfully (23:1-7) he must show that God's justice **will** ultimately prevail and prove him innocent, while the wicked are judged guilty and suitably punished. Therefore, Job's main contention is that God allows the wicked to prosper by delaying His justice, while Job's opponents have stubbornly contended that his affliction proves that God's justice is invariably swift and decisive. With this understanding, Job's argument logically falls into place,[133] and he concludes with a veiled threat of retribution upon his opponents (24:25, cf. 27:7-13).[134]

---

[130] This passage consists of three lists of unpunished civil injustices (24:2-8; 9-12; 13-17) that Job cites to refute his opponents by illustrating God's open permission of evil. The first two lists answer the allegations Eliphaz had trumped up to indict Job as an **oppressor** (22:6-11, 15-20) by comparing Job's unrelieved distress with that of the **victims** of such crimes (cf. 24:4b-8; 11-12b). The last list contradicts Bildad's contention (chap. 18) that Job is suffering predictable retribution: Job borrows Bildad's light/dark imagery (cf. 18:5-6, 18) to illustrate how the wicked actually do get away with their evil (24:13-17) when *God does not charge them with wrong* (24:12c).

[131] NKJV takes the impf. verbs in 24:18-25 as jussive or modal, but Job is **affirming** (not just **hoping**) that the wicked will be judged with a barren legacy (24:20, cp. Ps 58); thus, every "should" or "would" (NKJV) should read "will."

[132] For this reason "many commentators…identify this unit as a misplaced part of the speech of Zophar" (NET, cf. n. 49). However, to construe the pericope as Job's quotation of his opponents' ideas (so NET) would produce a *non sequitur* for Job's conclusion (24:25).

[133] If Job's basic premise is that God is just but delays the execution of His justice, then the argument becomes transparent: Job cannot gain a hearing before God to prove his innocence (23:1-12) and must therefore continue to suffer in terror (23:13-17), because God has *not set times for judgment* (24:1, NIV). Thus, the wicked do indeed get away with murder (24:2-17) until God finally decides to cut them down (24:18-24; cf. the analogous reasoning in Eccl 8:9-15).

[134] Job concludes for now by daring his opponents to prove him wrong (24:25), the veiled implication being that his opponents will also eventually "get theirs" (cf. 19:29). This threat becomes explicit in 27:7-23.

c. Bildad: "Your righteousness is nothing to God— man is but a maggot in His sight." (Job 25)

Bildad is in a bind. He realizes that Job is still trying to justify himself (cf. 23:1-12), but Job has "stolen his thunder" by now conceding that God does indeed mete out retribution to the wicked (24:18-25). Bildad therefore addresses Job's demand for an audience with God (cf. 23:3-9)[135] and explains why Job cannot find God *and be at peace with Him* (as Eliphaz had so "charitably" offered in 22:21, NIV): Job should ascribe *Dominion and fear to Him* who only *makes peace in...high places* (25:2). However, since God's righteousness is even greater than all the host of heaven (25:3, 5),[136] man in his depravity (*maggot...worm,* 25:6)[137] must therefore span a huge gap in order to be reconciled to God. Bildad implies that since Job's goal is rather to justify himself, he can therefore never *be righteous before God* (25:4).[138]

d. Job: "You hypocrite! You are all my enemies now and will surely be punished, just as the wicked!" (Job 26–27)

Job replies with a flurry of sarcastic rhetorical questions implying that Bildad's advice on human depravity had restated the obvious and was therefore worthless to those who need true comfort (26:1-4, cf. 13:4; 16:5). His preaching had skirted the real issue—whether Job's punishment

---

[135] The passage responds to 23:3-9 and has a chiastic structure: "Verse 4, standing at the center of the chiasm, bears the emphasis. Verses 3 and 5 focus on the heavenly host; the stars and the moon (v. 5) are numbered among God's troops (v. 3). Verses 2 and 6 are antithetically parallel: the greatness of God (v. 2) stands in contrast to the insignificance of mankind (v. 6)" (Hartley, *The Book of Job*, 355).

[136] Bildad's final rebuttal is imbued with dramatic irony as he unwittingly affirms the true basis for God's ultimate victory over Satan, the very issue in question since the opening wager: God's righteousness prevails over the *moon* and *stars*, which are figurative for Satan and the angels (cf. also 15:14-16, n. 90).

[137] Eliphaz had previously affirmed man's universal depravity (5:7; 15:14). The recurring irony is that none of Job's opponents seems to have any awareness of how their own depravity has been exposed by their tenacious insistence on punishing Job and their reticence to show true compassion.

[138] With this third appearance of the rhetorical question *"How can a man be righteous before God?"* (25:4a, cf. 4:17; 9:2) Bildad combines the moral and forensic senses of the word *righteous* (cf. n. 71) to refute Job's claim to merit a hearing from God and thereby be reconciled to Him ("make peace," cf. 25:2): Bildad quite accurately affirms Job's inadequate righteousness, as Elihu will confirm (chap. 35), yet he still fails to acknowledge the inscrutability of God's judgment in the present world and Job's real need for compassion, as Job will remind him (chap. 26). Although Bildad blessedly refrains from echoing yet again the dogma of simplistic retribution, this does not deter Job from launching his final contemptuous tirade (chap. 27).

could legitimately be attributed to his own sin. Job thus exposes Bildad's hypocrisy by trapping him with his own argument: Yes, God's dominion is so high it commands the fear of even the greatest forces in all creation (26:5-13, cf. 25:2), but *these are the fringes of His ways, and how faint a word we hear of Him, so*[139] *who can understand His mighty thunder?* (26:14, NASB).[140] In other words, how incredibly presumptuous of Bildad to infer Job's guilt from his circumstances alone—God's *ways* are too inscrutable to assign indiscriminate one-for-one blame simply on the basis of Job's calamities.

Fed up with his friends' hypocrisy, Job then proceeds to excoriate them all[141] with openly contemptuous invective. He refuses to admit that they are right and vows that he will maintain his integrity and righteousness to his death (27:1-6, cf. 13:13-15). He now considers them his *enemy* and invokes upon them retribution suited to the *wicked* and *unrighteous* (27:7), asking rhetorically whether they think they can escape God's judgment (27:8-10, cf. 19:29). He spitefully threatens to *teach* them *about the hand of God* (27:11)—a liability that they don't seem to understand, considering their willful and persistent persecution of him (27:12).[142] Consequently, Job's attitude toward his friends descends even further into frank bitterness: He adopts their own tactic[143] of enumerating the terrible

---

[139] The opening *waw* in the final clause of 26:14 is inferential (cf. NIV) rather than adversative (as NKJV).

[140] Job argues from Bildad's own tidy assertion that God's righteousness is infinitely *high* (25:4-6) that God's judgment is therefore equally inscrutable from the far removed realm of man's existence *below*, thus contradicting Bildad's prior claim to have inferred from Job's affliction precisely how God's judgment was operating in his life. Ironically, Elihu will later remind Job of this exact point in order to convince him that God's judgment is still just when He allows Job's affliction within the broader scope of His transcendent rule (37:23-24, cf. 34:29; 37:13).

[141] Zuck observes that "you" in 27:5 is plural (contrast 26:2-4, addressed to Bildad alone), so that chap. 27 constitutes part of "grand finale to all three contestants" (*Job*, 115). While Zuck takes this "grand finale" to end with chap. 31, the sudden change in tone of chap. 28 suggests instead that Job is "done" with them after his climactic counter-threat of revenge in 27:13-23.

[142] Job's vow regarding *the hand of God* implies that their antagonism warrants the retribution of God, and he is surprised that they do not recognize their liability: *Look, you have all seen it* [the hand of God] *so why do you vainly persist in this futility?* (27:12, my translation). It is irrational for them to keep on pressing their futile case that Job is guilty in view of God's impending judgment on **them** (27:13-23).

[143] Some commentators do not assign 27:13-23 to Job (n. 49) because it echoes the retribution theology of his friends (cf. 18:5-21; 20:4-29; 22:6-11). Yet, this is fully consistent with his escalating vindictiveness (cf. 19:28-29, n. 104) and confidence in the final judgment of the wicked (cf. 24:18-25, 26:5-14, nn. 133, 134), with whom he now aligns these same friends ("you" in 27:11 is still plural, cf. n. 141).

judgments that God reserves for *wicked oppressors* (27:13-23),[144] insinuating that his former friends are just as wicked and liable to judgment.

Such a disposition should strike the reader "in the know" as remarkably disparate for a *blameless and upright* servant of God (cf. 1:8; 2:3),
and Satan must certainly be "licking his chops" as he observes the down-
ward spiral in Job's attitude. If the reader also understands the high stakes
of God's opening wager, it should not come as a surprise that the following text is an ode to Wisdom which ends up magnifying the importance of
the *fear of God* (28:28) at this critical juncture in the drama.

---

[144] Job introduces these judgments as the *portion* (*ḥēleq*) and *heritage* (*naḥălâ*)
of *the wicked* (27:13). The sense is that while the wicked seem to be getting away
with their oppression now, they will be judged with an empty legacy when they
are dead (cf. 24:18-25 [n. 134] and Eccl 3:16-17; 8:13-14).

6

C. Plea for Wisdom—Does Job Fear God? (Job 28)

By comparing the pursuit of wisdom to the difficult excavation of useful metals and precious jewels, **the author affirms that the hidden wisdom of God is precious and can only be found in the fear of God,** *so that readers might not presume to discern God's purposes but instead seek His wisdom in submission to His sovereign prerogatives.*

There is an obvious shift in literary style and tone—Job's bitter vow of revenge (chap. 27) now runs headlong into this lofty ode to Wisdom. The poem is divided into three parts by a repeated question (28:12, 20) that clearly establishes the importance of pursuing wisdom but implies that it is hidden from plain view. The first pericope (28:1-12) implies that since it is reasonable for mankind to mine and purify valuable metals from the earth, it is just as reasonable for him to mine Wisdom. The next pericope (28:13-20) esteems the value of Wisdom above that of gold and precious stones, again implying that it is not easily found. The final pericope (28:21-28) explains that God has hidden Wisdom within His creative design and implies that God did this so that mankind would find Wisdom only by forsaking evil to fear God.

The poem transparently compares Wisdom with naturally occurring precious metals and jewels: (28:1-11), but[145] it is even harder to find Wisdom (28:12), for it is rarer, more intangible, and deeper (28:13-14). Even precious jewels can't compare with it (28:15-19), so where can Wisdom be found (28:20-21)? God has hidden it in His original design for all creation (28:22-26),[146] so man's only hope of finding it is in *the fear of the Lord, that is wisdom* (28:27-28). Since there is no opening marker at 28:1, this indicates that Job the protagonist of the drama (cf. 27:1) is still speaking in the presence of his three friends, insinuating that their foolish opposition[147] is rooted in a failure to fear God and *depart from evil* (28:28).

---

[145] The opening *waw* in 28:12 is mildly adversative: It introduces a rhetorical question that is then logically substantiated by the contrast in 28:13-14.

[146] If placed in the mouth of Job (n. 49), these verses ironically prefigure both Elihu's teaching (36:27-37:24) and God's own testimony (38:4-38) of His full command over all Creation.

[147] Job's last direct address was a rhetorical question *Why then do you act foolishly?* (27:12b [NASB], cf. n. 142); the verb *act foolishly* (derived from *hebel*, "futility") thus supplies the pretext for Job's plea for wisdom in 28:28.

Ironically, however, Job has identified his **own** need: When he dared to *charge God with wrong* (1:22), his fear of God gave way to self-righteous presumption. In context the poem thus warns prospective servants of God that we will only forfeit God's wisdom when we presume to understand God's inscrutable purposes and try to mitigate unjust suffering on our own (chaps. 4-27). By fearing God instead, we will encounter His hidden wisdom, a precious resource for maintaining our faithfulness and integrity in adversity (cf. 1:8; 2:3). Job's self-righteous presumption is thus all the more apparent in his summary appeal to God (chaps. 29-31). His foolish disposition will only change when he freely accepts God's redemptive overture in the face of death, as God's spokesman, Elihu, will teach him (chaps. 32-37).

7

D. Job Sues for Full Restitution (Job 29–31)

In Job's summary appeal before God, in which he sues God for vindication and demands restitution for his lost estate, **the author shows how self-righteous presumption serves Satan's agenda of subverting godly agency,** *so that readers in adversity might realize how seriously the nurturing of a disposition of victimization and self-righteous pride will jeopardize their capacity to bless others and worship God.*

The opening marker *Job again took up his discourse...* (NASB) signifies the beginning of a new section that returns to the genre of extended lament and completes the major section that began with chap. 3.[148] While Job no longer addresses his opponents directly, they are still present during this final lament to witness what amounts to a legal showdown with God in court.[149] The first of the three subsections features a lament over **past** blessing lost (chap. 29). The second subsection shifts the focus to **present** misery with the opening marker *and now...* (chap. 30). The final subsection looks to a **future** judicial solution with a series of conditional curses, each introduced by the phrase *If I have...*, in effect demanding that God execute justice (chap. 31). The distinctive closing marker *The words of Job are ended* (31:5-40) sets the stage for the author's reappearance in his own words to mark the major turning point in the drama (32:1-5).

The argument takes the form of a pleading in civil court. Job's opening statement *Oh, that I were as in months past...when God watched over me* (29:2) intimates that he is suing for restitution of his former estate. In order to substantiate his claim Job first recalls how he was previously

---

[148] *See* n. 47 and related text regarding the literary design of Job 3-27.

[149] Michael Dick ("The Legal Metaphor in Job 31," reprinted in Zuck [ed.], *Sitting with Job*, 330) observes that

> chapters 29-31 signal a new strategy....Job recapitulates the internal dialectic of his earlier speeches by completely turning away from his friends to face his real..."opponent," God. C. Westermann assigns these...chapters...to the genre of lamentation. Chapter 29 describes Job's former fortune—a feature most common in the "lament of the people"; chapter 30 is a more standard lamentation pattern. However, instead of completing this lamentation with the customary plea for help, the author of Job has altered the pattern so that it culminates in the trial request before a judge.

That Job's friends are still present, however, is subsequently attested by the author (32:1). Job intends to compel their presence as witnesses when he is vindicated in their eyes by God.

blessed by God and had in turn blessed others (chap. 29). He then cites the necessary evidence to indict God Himself for wrongful confiscation of his estate (chap. 30, cf. 30:19-26). Job's final challenge (chap. 31) is cleverly designed to force God to declare Himself openly: Like his opening statement, the closing statement is expressed as a wish, thus forming an inclusion to serve God a formal subpoena: *Oh, that I had someone to hear me! I sign now my defense—let the Almighty answer me; let my accuser put his indictment in writing* (31:35, NIV). Job aims thereby to compel the adjudication of any sealed indictment that God might be holding against him **and** to counter-sue for the full restitution of his lost estate.

Job's gambit is brilliant from a human perspective: Since he knew that God was responsible for his suffering he felt justified in calling God to appear as Judge and then either convict Job as defendant or exonerate him and restore his losses as plaintiff. By challenging God's justice he hoped to precipitate a final resolution of his restless dread (cf. 3:25-26). However, the drama must ultimately be seen in the context of God's original wager with Satan (1:6-2:10): In demanding justice on his own terms, Job yielded to Satan's strategy of co-opting God's agents to subvert God's kingdom authority.[150] While God yielded none of His authority by refusing to answer Job on his own terms, the outcome of the wager and fulfillment of God's creative purposes still hinged on whether Job would choose to drop his lawsuit and be restored as God's faithful agent—*a blameless and upright man...who fears God and shuns evil* (1:8; 2:3).

Job's lawsuit masked a proud self-sufficiency that in light of Job's preceding plea for wisdom (chap. 28) only preempted the fear of God, thus forfeiting God's wisdom (cf. 28:28).[151] So, even if Job's clever ploy were to prevail and he was exonerated, he would still fail to serve God's purposes wisely as God's chosen agent. Ironically, God responds to Job's ploy by enlisting another agent (Elihu), not to reconcile God's justice with Job's unjust suffering but to disclose how God in His providence uses suffering to redeem his agents (chaps. 32-37). The author's purpose is served as

---

[150] Cf. nn. 19, 20.

[151] This logical link between Job 28 and 29-31 is further elucidated by Eccl 7:7-14: To live skillfully amid adversity and uncertainty requires humble dependence on God's wisdom (Job 28, cf. Eccl 7:11-14). Yet, the already negative influence of adversity on Job's wisdom (Job 6:22-30, cf. Eccl 7:7; n. 66) was only intensified when his initial humble resignation (1:20-21; 2:10) yielded to the false hope of stubborn self-sufficiency—his foolish obsession with his former prosperity (Job 29, cf. Eccl 7:10), his entrenched bitterness (Job 30, cf. Eccl 7:9), and his impatient demand for full restitution (Job 31, cf. Eccl 7:8).

soon as the reader realizes that he too is God's chosen agent, intended for blessing and to be a blessing. Observing in Job's example the high stakes of nurturing an attitude of victimization and proud self-sufficiency, self-sufficient readers will recognize that they also need to be rescued from the ravages of such a disposition and restored to productive agency.[152]

1. Job Dwells in the Past, Deprived of Former Blessing (Job 29)
The key construction governing the sense of this section is *the days when* (29:2). This phrase is followed by a series of clauses each introduced by *when* to denote Job's reminiscence over times past (29:3-7). Job recounts how abundantly God had blessed him (29:2-11) and then ascribes[153] his blessing to his exemplary behavior as a deliverer of the oppressed (29:12-17). The reason why Job described his former state of blessing in such detail becomes clear in the final pericope,[154] where he touts his stellar reputation as God's favored servant (cf. 1:8; 2:3): Job fully expected to *multiply* his *days* in favor with God and to die at rest—full of *glory* (29:18-20)[155]—as an exceptional mediator of blessing to the oppressed (29:21-25).[156]

Job's wistful reminiscence ironically illustrates God's continuing purpose for Job to serve as His agent on earth—a prototype of man representing the image of God. Job's former days of blessing depicted not only how God intends to bless man but also how He intends for man to be

---

[152] The outcome of the drama centers on whether Job will be restored to his intended agency (cf. n. 44). Larry Crabb superbly expresses the profoundly adverse effects of a self-sufficient mindset that demands freedom from suffering (*Inside Out*, chaps. 4-7): Those who consider themselves entitled to relief are more readily seduced by Satan's counterfeit promises to satisfy their legitimate needs for security and influence in the world, rather than relying on God to supply and superintend these functions of vital agency for God.

[153] The second pericope is introduced by the conjunction *kî* (29:12), which in context retains its standard causal force ("because") to indicate that Job believed his former state of blessing was God's reward for his good deeds.

[154] The final pericope is introduced by a *waw* with a clearly inferential thrust "*so* I said" (29:18a) to denote the inference that Job drew from his former state of blessing.

[155] In 29:18-20 Job cited the dashed hope of his expectation of a well-earned legacy (cf. 3:13-15) as grounds to sue God for robbing him unfairly (Job 31).

[156] The imagery in 29:21-25 depicts men desperate for the benevolent counsel that Job unexpectedly provided: *I smiled at them; they couldn't believe it* (29:24, my translation). Their surprise implies that they were outcasts of society—the same men who now turned on him to mock his cruel fate (30:1-15). In his former life Job had freely bestowed what he himself now sought in vain—freely given *comfort to mourners* (29:25, cf. 13:2; 16:2-4; 19:21-22). Job now felt entitled to the same comfort as a *mourner* himself—one whom even God refused to comfort (30:20-31, cf. v. 31).

a blessing to others.[157] However, Job's determination to dwell in the past and sue for full restitution of his former estate only deferred the necessary mourning (30:31)[158] that would enable his full restoration as God's chosen mediator.[159] The message for the reader as God's prospective agent is that it is foolish presumption to dwell on past glory and expect it to be restored.[160]

2. Job Displays His Evidence, Charges God with Injustice (Job 30)

This section is distinguished by a shift from the past to the present tense, as denoted by the repeated marker *and now...* (30:1, 9, 16) which governs the textual design of his argument that God has unfairly robbed him of blessing. Job contrasts his former days of blessing with his present circumstances to establish why the confiscation of his estate was unwarranted: *Now* he is mocked by the same young men he had previously blessed, the very dregs of society (30:1-8, cf. 29:7-17, 21-25);[161] *now* he is totally disgraced by *their* relentless *taunting* (30:9-15, cf. v. 13b, *No one restrains them,* NASB); *now* God Himself ignores Job as his very *life ebbs away* in relentless *suffering* (30:16-17). Not only does God fail to *answer* Job's *cry* for help (30:20) but He even *turns* to *attack* Job and *bring* him *down to death* (30:18-19, 21-23).[162]

---

[157] In this respect Job's reminiscence in chap. 29 perfectly depicts the key tenets of the Abrahamic covenant, wherein God promised to *bless* His chosen agent and his seed (Gen 12:2b; 22:17, cf. Job 29:1-11) yet He expected them in turn to *be a blessing* (Gen 12c-3; 22:18, cf. Job 29:12-25) and thereby to exemplify His character. The Abrahamic covenant thus encompasses God's redemptive design for his agents after the fall of mankind (nn. 20, 119). Seen in this light the entire plot of the controversy in Job revolves around the implicit question of whether and how Job can again become a blessing to others, even in his adversity.

[158] Job's heart would have to be softened considerably through mourning (cf. n. 156) before he would be fully receptive to the wisdom that both Elihu and YHWH would offer to rescue him from his dogged self-sufficiency, so that he might fear God and serve Him wisely (cf. Job 28:28) as His chosen agent. The word *mourning* (*'ēbel*) in 30:31 is the same as in Eccl 7:4 and promises the same benefits of wisdom (cf. Eccl 7:4-5).

[159] Whereas Job characterized himself as one who had *delivered* [*mālaṭ*] *the poor* (29:12), his insistence on full restitution of his former estate ironically only forestalled his mediation of God's purposes in his present suffering: to deliver his own friends (cf. n. 23).

[160] This is exactly the point of Eccl 7:10; cf. n. 151.

[161] Job points out the irony of their present mocking in light of their own ignoble past when he had blessed them (cf. n. 156); thus the entire pericope (30:1b-8) should be voiced in the past tense, as in NIV.

[162] The sense of the entire pericope 30:16-23 is best rendered by NIV, here indicated in italics.

Job's closes by appealing to the obvious,[163] *Surely no one lays a hand on a broken man when he cries for help in his distress* (30:24, NIV)—which is how Job views his treatment from God: being "kicked while he is down." Despite the fact that Job consistently had shown mercy on the downtrodden (30:25, cf. 29:12-17), now that he himself was desperate and *looked for good* (30:26a, c), all God gave him was *evil* and *darkness* (30:26b, d). Job's concluding imagery depicts the physical and emotional harm he suffers in his present affliction (30:27-30), so[164] his only music is *mourning* (30:31). Yet his closing lament betrays a presumptuous sense of entitlement:[165] Job pleads for mercy on the basis of his own righteousness in showing mercy to others (cf. 30:25-26).

3. Job Demands His Day in Court, Serves God a Subpoena (Job 31)
Verses 1 and 38-40 at first seem misplaced but likely denote inclusion:[166] These affirmations typify Job throughout as a man of unimpeachable moral integrity. The enclosed text is comprised of interwoven rhetorical questions, vows, and curses that call down punishments matched to a variety of hypothetical transgressions by moral category.[167] Job renews his fundamental confidence in proportional retribution (31:2-4) to justify his repeated plea for an open trial to exonerate him of all charges before God (31:6, cf. 23:3-12). However, Job betrays his own hypocrisy when he indirectly indicts God for injustice (31:23).[168] In so doing he escalates his complaint to the level of

---

[163] Cp. Job's logical appeal to common sense in 21:29, cf. n. 116.

[164] The opening *waw* in the final verse has consequential force ("therefore" or "so," cf. NASB).

[165] Ironically, Job's *mourning* would benefit him (n. 158) only when he acknowledged his arrogant presumption.

[166] Citing Habel, Good observes, "From the cultic covenant of verse 1 to the covenant with his agricultural land in verse 38-40, he ranges over the sins he has not committed and the attitudes he has had" ("Job 31," reprinted in Zuck, ed., *Sitting with Job*, 339, citation omitted). Each of these "covenants" topically matches the cluster of hypothetical sins in which it is grouped (n. 167).

[167] Verses 1-12 deal with sins of sexual enticement and their consequences, quite reminiscent of Prov 5; verses 13-23 address sins of discriminatory or inhumane treatment of the disenfranchised (cf. Jas 1:27-2:17); and verses 24-40 deal with the root causes of greed, idolatrous pride and prejudice (cf. Eccl 5:8-17; Jas 4:1-5:6).

[168] Job contrasts his fair regard for the needy and afflicted with what he sees as God's unjust and capricious treatment (31:23, cf. 30:24-25). Ironically, while he touts his exemplary past behavior toward those who hated him (31:29-30) he remains oblivious to the vengeance he has displayed toward his erstwhile friends (27:7-23) and devotees (30:1-15). Job's hypocrisy reaches a climax when he dares to contrast his own candor before God with Adam's deception after the fall (31:33-34, cf. Gen 3:8-10).

overt challenge, culminating in a brash and presumptuous subpoena (31:35-37).

If in fact God is bound by proportional retribution as an invariable requirement of His justice, Job's strategy is designed to "call God's bluff": By invoking curses on himself for any of a variety of imagined sins, Job dares God to reveal the evidence for his guilt—which does not exist—and execute judgment.[169] Job again touts his exemplary behavior toward widows, orphans, and the poor (31:13-22, cf. 29:12-17) and is so confident of his vindication that he even includes failures of altruism and hidden sins of the heart in his catalog of hypothetical sins.[170] By daring God to judge such mere lapses of piety, Job acquits himself as the archetypal "religious man."[171]

Job formalizes his demand for justice by convening a hearing (31:35a). He dares to serve God a subpoena[172] bearing his own seal (31:35b), enjoining God to reveal His hidden indictment (31:35c), so that

---

[169] If God is bound by the doctrine of simplistic retribution, Job has the leverage to force summary judgment and has little to lose by doing so, since all he has left is his wife and the bare vestiges of life: If he is innocent, none of the curses will strike him, and he must be exonerated; if guilty, he would incur judgment but, ironically, by losing his life he would end his suffering—a "win-win" situation (cf. 6:8-10; 30:23; and n. 41).

[170] *See* n. 167. By virtue of his exemplary background as a righteous judge in municipal court (29:7-17), Job deemed himself eminently qualified to determine the appropriate list of hypothetical sins that needed to be covered in order to fully vindicate him in the eyes of his friends (cf. 31:36-37). If Job itemized only flagrant, externally visible sins, they could still have accused him of sins of the heart or sins of omission that only God could see (cf. e.g., 31:1, 7, 9, 26-28, 33-34).

[171] Job epitomized in his behavior the practitioner of "pure and undefiled religion" (cf. Jas 1:27). Ironically, even the best of man's religion is only religion: Job is still estranged from God by his continuing misperception of God's righteousness as fundamentally *retributive* and not *redemptive*.

[172] Job's pivotal demand for litigation is laden with dramatic irony: Originally, Job had all but given up hope of being vindicated before God (9:2-3, cf. n. 71), admitting the utter presumption of opposing God (9:4) and lamenting the fact that no one could arbitrate the differences between mortal man and a terrifying God (9:32-35). By his next rejoinder, however, Job was willing to die, just to defend his righteousness to God's face (13:14-15). He trusted a "witness on high" to vindicate him (16:19, cf. 19:25-27, n. 101) but continued to lament his inability to contend with God in open court (16:21; 19:7). By 23:3-7 he broached the possibility that God might actually hear his case and reason with him, still terrified of God's presence yet with unequivocal confidence that his righteousness would prevail (23:10-17). Now he throws caution to the winds and doesn't even ask for a trial; he **demands** it to God's face! It may seem even more ludicrous that God actually responds to such audacity (38:3; 40:7; cf. Sylvia Scholnick, "The Meaning of *Mišpāṭ (Justice)* in The Book of Job," reprinted in Zuck [ed.], *Sitting with Job*, 349-58).

Job might gain his all-but-assured acquittal and display it for all to see (31:36-37)! The inherent presumption of Job's brazen ultimatum[173] is magnified by the repeated inference that his own righteousness surpassed God's (cf. 30:24-26; 35:2) and thus compels fair judgment from a God who **should** show justice. This amounts to *charging God with evil* (1:22), so that Job has traversed the full gamut from self-effacing worship (1:5, 20) to self-glorifying pride (chap. 31). The reader can only wait with baited breath to see how God answers this outlandish demand, the suspense only intensified by Elihu's interposed speeches (chaps. 32-37).[174]

---

[173] The imagery in 31:36-37 recalls Job's prior desire to inscribe his testimony in stone for all to see (19:23-24). What has become obvious by this point is that Job is no longer willing to accept the lot God has chosen for him and is openly "contending" with God for a different lot (cf. Eccl 6:10-11).

[174] Elihu's speeches clearly expose Job's self-righteous presumption and inadequate appreciation of God's redemptive character. These speeches will be seen in retrospect by the reader as God's gracious provision that laid the groundwork for Job to see God as fully redemptive and repent of his presumption (42:5-6, cf. n. 12). The reader who at this point still identifies with Job's demands is thus also targeted for the gracious rebuke Job receives.

Act II

PLAINTIFF & MEDIATOR

*"He delivers the afflicted
and opens their ear"*

God's Spokesman Expands Job's Perspective
(Job 32-37)

In Elihu's inspired rebuttal of Job's charges, **the author corrects Job's presumptuous misconceptions of God by revealing His redemptive nature and just rule over Creation**, *so that readers might depend on God's sovereignty and redemptive grace to serve Him effectively as chosen agents of His redemptive purposes.*

Our understanding of the author's role for Elihu in the drama is critical for a cohesive grasp of the message and purpose of the book.[175] The text supports the view that Elihu's speeches avoid the errors of the comforters' rebuttals and that they are more substantial. The introductory editorial (32:1-5) seems designed to warrant Elihu's arguments, and there is enough internal evidence to confirm that they are indeed inspired and authoritative:[176] Elihu repeatedly claims that his words are inspired (32:8, 18; 33:3-4; 36:2-4), which protects them from human bias (32:9-12, 21-22); the reasons for Elihu's wrath—Job's self-justification and his friends' faulty presumption (32:1-3)—are the same ones that arouse God's wrath (40:8; 42:7); God validates Elihu's key assertions;[177] his speeches are not contested by Job or the other friends,[178] nor are his words rejected by God like those of the others (cf. 42:7); and finally, the account of God's irruption into the drama *out of the whirlwind* mirrors Elihu's own imagery (38:1, cf. 37:2-6, 9).

In four uninterrupted speeches Elihu's teaching is primarily directed at Job.[179] He aims first to cultivate a receptive frame of mind, so that Job

---

[175] This point is developed at length in the OVERVIEW OF JOB. Some expositors are disturbingly ambiguous about Elihu's role (cf., e.g., Parsons, "Structure and Purpose," 25; Mason, *Gospel According to Job*, 333ff).

[176] For a historical development of the controversy over the validity of Elihu's speeches and a cogent argument supporting this conclusion, see Waters, "The Authenticity of the Elihu Speeches in Job 32-37."

[177] Cp. 38:2 with 35:16; 40:2a with 33:13; 40:2b with 34:37b; and 40:8 with 35:2.

[178] Of 106 imperatives in the book of Job, only 7 are in the "long" form, taken by some expositors as a polite form (personal communication, Hélène Dallaire) and six of these are spoken by Elihu (32:10; 33:1, 5 [x2]; 34:16; 37:14). While Arnold and Choi dismiss this nuance (*A Guide to Hebrew Syntax* [New York: Cambridge University Press, 2003], 64-65), Elihu's use of the form is virtually exclusive in the book, which seems significant and may imbue his rebuttal with a more "humanizing" tone than the arguments of the other three friends.

[179] In 34:1-15 Elihu addresses the older friends but then shifts his focus back to Job (Zuck, *Job*, 149). Similarly, 37:2-13 begins by addressing "you" plural (ibid., 156), but Job himself is the main object.

can truly *listen* to the truth about himself and God (cf. 33:10-11; 34:5-6; 35:2-3; 36:23), rather than continuing to justify himself out of self-righteous presumption. Elihu accomplishes this objective by connecting with Job as none of his other friends could: He maintains credibility as his inspired and empathic spokesman for God (32:6-33:7, cf. 36:1-4).[180] Thus engaged—and without attributing Job's suffering to any prior sin, as the other friends had done—Elihu presents an accurate view of God as intent on redeeming man from destruction (33:14-33). With this foundation of hope for Job's restoration, Elihu can credibly answer Job's claim that God has deprived him of justice (cf. 33:8-13).[181]

Elihu refutes this claim in his next two closely linked speeches: By explaining that God's justice is necessarily dictated by his vast inscrutable rule (chap. 34), Elihu justifies God's silence in response to man's self-righteous presumption (chap. 35). He concludes by affirming that all Creation is subordinate to God's sovereign rule (chaps. 36-37). By exposing Job's presumptuousness and disclosing the redemptive basis for man's relationship with God, Elihu reverses Satan's deception regarding God's character, defeats Satan's subversive purposes in Job's suffering,[182] and offers Job the incentive to repent of his contempt for his friends and alienation from God (cf. 34:36-37; 36:16-17).

The author has clearly invested Elihu with the main role of teaching the audience about the character of God and His relationship with mankind.[183] Given that Job remains silent (cf. 33:5, 32-33) in the face of Elihu's repeated invitation to *listen* and *hear*,[184] the reader who identifies with Job is vicariously invited to also receive Elihu's teaching. The author intends through Elihu to expose misconceptions about the nature of God's righteousness (33:8-12; chap. 35) and recast suffering as the perfecting instrument of God's consistently redemptive purposes (33:14-30; 36:15-16), fully congruent with the execution of His perfect justice, even when

---

180 *See* Stephen J. Lawson, *Job*, HOTC (Nashville: Holman, 2004), 271-2, 279-80, cf. n. 12.

181 The order of Elihu's speeches is critical: For Job to confidently accept Elihu's correction regarding how his own righteousness relates to God's absolute sovereignty and justice (chaps. 34-35, cf. 33:8-13) he must first be convinced that God is fully redemptive. Elihu gains credibility as God's empathic spokesman only because he is entirely faithful to this priority (33:14-33; cf. n. 33).

182 In order to prevail in his wager with God, Satan has successfully "worked" Job and his friends throughout the preceding drama (chaps. 3-31, cf. nn. 19, 20, 60, 65, 150 and related text).

183 *See* Larry Waters, "Elihu's Theology and His View of Suffering," *BSac* 156 (1999), 143-59.

184 Cf. 32:10; 33:1, 31, 33; 34:2, 10, 16, 34; 36:2, 10; 37:14.

we cannot see it (chap. 34). The concluding elegant exposition of God's infinite knowledge of, and absolute rule over, Creation (36:24-37:24) prepares Job for his direct confrontation by God (38:1-42:6).

— 8 —

A. God's Spirit-Filled Mediator (32:1–33:7)

*By authenticating Elihu as an inspired and empathic spokesman in response to the futile debate over Job's guilt and God's justice, **the author validates Elihu's teaching as authoritative**, so that the reader might seriously reflect on the truth that Elihu spoke and take note of Job's subsequent response to God.*

The author emerges in a brief dramatic interlude to introduce Elihu and validate his rebuttal of the arguments of both Job and his friends by summarizing their errant dispositions and misconceptions: 1) Job was righteous in his own eyes (32:1) and *justified himself* at the expense of God's justice (32:2), and 2) Job's friends *found no answer* to warrant Job's suffering yet condemned him nevertheless (32:3).[185] Although Elihu had shown proper deference to the age and experience of Job's older friends (32:4) he was angry that they could not *answer* Job's faulty reasoning (32:5). But in order for Elihu to discredit their arguments and for his own correctives to be taken seriously he first had to establish the authority of his words in contrast to theirs.

Elihu starts by affirming that inspired insight is always more authoritative than age or experience (32:6-9). His forbearance to this point had afforded him the opportunity to test the validity of their arguments, which he found ineffective (32:10-14).[186] Since the older friends were silenced by Job's rebuttals, Elihu will finally answer Job—he can no longer refrain from telling what he knows[187] (32:15-20), which he affirms is impartial,

---

[185] Hartley (*The Book of Job*, 428 [fn. 6]) prefers a variant text of 32:3 which asserts that Job's comforters made God out to be guilty rather than Job. That is, if their retribution dogma is in fact valid it logically portrays God as *unjust* in the face of Job's innocent suffering. Hartley argues that this more difficult reading was subsequently altered in the MT. Either reading is plausible and consistent with God's later judgment (42:7).

[186] The sense of 32:13 is best expressed as in NIV but only if Elihu's quotation of the other friends ends with the first line, as in NKJV, thus: "Do not say, 'We have found wisdom'; let God refute him, not man." Cp. Acts 5:38-39.

[187] Many translations read "opinion" or "what I think" in 32:17 yet read "knowledge" for the same word in 36:3 and 37:16. Heb. *dēa'* (derived from *yada'*, "to know") is used only by Elihu and should also read "knowledge" in 32:17. Thus, Elihu was bursting to impart his pure *knowledge* of God (cp. 36:4) and not just opinion (cf. 32:6, 10). Habel therefore unfairly construes Elihu's confidence as the "arrogance" of a "bloated fool" ("Wisdom in The Book of Job," reprinted in Zuck [ed.], *Sitting with Job*, 311). Cf. n. 190.

as opposed to the appeasing logic offered by Job's other friends (32:21-22).[188] Directly addressing Job, Elihu claims in fact that the Spirit of God has guaranteed the sincerity and truth of his words (33:1-4, cf. 32:8) so he even invites Job to challenge them (33:5). Job need not fear him, for he is Job's spokesman,[189] the compassionate advocate Job was seeking, one who could share his experience of human frailty before God (33:6-7).[190]

By devoting so much text to validating Elihu's rationale and authority (32:1-33:7), the author authenticates his speeches for the reader. Since the reader is already aware that Job's other friends were in error, it is necessary to distinguish Elihu's mediatory role from the other comforters; he is God's chosen agent to reach Job and correct his misconceptions about God—particularly those the reader may share. While Elihu may seem at first to follow the other three friends in criticizing Job, his teaching radically subverts their arguments and reveals God's redemptive purposes—even when suffering appears to have no present redeeming value in the life of God's chosen servant.

---

[188] Job's friends were so consumed by placating his despair that they were unable to show true compassion (cf. 6:14-23; 12:5). Therefore, Job had no confidence that anything they had to say was in his best interests (cf. 6:24-28; 16:2-6; 19:2-6, 21-22; and n. 66). Their attempts at reassurance ("flattery," cf. 32:21-22) were rooted in a desire to avoid disillusionment or confusion, rather than speaking truth in love. Since Elihu is keenly aware of Job's justified skepticism he takes great pains to assure Job that his (Elihu's) words are not similarly biased and self-serving (32:21-33:5).

[189] The dramatic effect of Elihu's speeches turns on the irony of the fact that Elihu finally answers Job's quest for a mediator (cf. 9:32-35; 16:19-21; 19:25; 23:3-4; 30:20; 33:6), but it is not to vindicate Job as he had hoped (cf. nn. 74, 93, 101): Elihu literally states he is "like your mouth before God" (33:6a, cf. NKJV; Hartley, *The Book of Job*, 437 [fn. 3]), which is unclear in NIV, NASB. That is, Elihu claims he is Job's attorney or mediator before God but also serves as Job's Spirit-inspired teacher (32:17-33:4).

[190] Although often mischaracterized (cf. n. 187), Elihu stands with Job as an empathic advocate before God, unlike his other friends; he is the "comforter" Job sought (Job 16:2, translated "paraclete" in the LXX; cf. n. 91) and thus exemplifies the Holy Spirit, the abiding agent of mankind's ultimate Advocate, Christ (cf. John 14:16; 16:8-11; 1 John 2:1; Heb 2:14-18; 4:14-16).

B. God's Redemptive Purposes (33:8–33)

With Elihu's "good news" of a loving God who uses suffering to persist-ently reach down and redeem mankind from destructive self-sufficiency, **the author refutes the misconception that God is unresponsive or capri-cious and reveals Him instead as fundamentally redemptive,** *so that suf-fering readers might be more receptive to God's efforts to rescue them from self-sufficiency and restore them as His chosen agents.*

Though incensed by Job's compulsion to justify himself (32:2), Elihu wisely sought first to restore Job's hope by repairing His flawed percep-tions of God's character and His purposes in suffering. Although Elihu began to address Job in 33:1-7, his formal rebuttal begins in 33:8 with a simple two-step argument, first citing Job's misunderstanding of God's motives in suffering, then correcting it with the truth about God's funda-mentally redemptive character: Job's attack on God's justice and his dogged pursuit of vindication is based on the erroneous assumption that God is unresponsive to his needs and bent on destroying him (33:8-13); on the contrary, God uses affliction to get man's attention and redeem him from his destructive self-sufficiency (33:14-30).

Job had convinced himself that because of God's opposition, his only interest in staying alive was to be fully vindicated in the eyes of his friends.[191] Thus, Elihu begins by first citing Job's claims (33:8) to be *pure, without transgression...innocent...no guilt in me* (33:9, NASB), yet God *invents pretexts against me; He counts me as His enemy*[192] (33:10-11, NASB). Elihu counters that Job's claims are not justified (33:12a), for *God is greater than man* (33:12b); it is presumptuous to complain to God that He does not explain everything He does (33:13).[193]

---

[191] This is the pervasive thrust of 9:1-35, 13:15-19; 16:18-17:5; 19:23-29; 23:1-12; 27:1-6; and chap. 31; cf. nn. 71, 74, 84, 102, 127, 149, 171, 172.

[192] Cf. 7:11-21; 9:15, 21-24; 10:7, 13-17; 13:24-27; 16:7-17; 23:11, 13-17; 30:16-31.

[193] The clause in 33:13b is not explanatory (so NKJV) but rather declarative ("that"); thus, Elihu's rhetorical question (33:13) rebukes Job for complaining (*rîb*) against God, *that He does not give an account of all His doings [dābār]* (NASB). At issue is Job's contentiousness (cf. 40:2; cp. Eccl 6:10b): Job had accused God of ignoring him (9:11, 16; 13:24; 23:1-9; 30:20) and insisted that He justify His treatment of Job (7:20-21; 10:2; 13:3, 13-23; 17:3-5; 23:2-12; 31:35-37). Elihu will further explore and defend God's apparent silence in Job 34-35 (esp. 34:29-33a; 35:9-16).

Indeed,[194] Elihu contends, God repeatedly[195] tries to communicate with man (33:14a), but man ignores it (33:14b), which in turn explains why God may permit suffering: He is so thoroughly committed to man's restoration that He may well resort to adversity in order to gain man's attention and rescue him from his inherent proclivity to self-destruction (33:15-30).

Elihu's reasoning sharply contradicts the logic of Job's "comforters," who insisted that suffering could only be seen as retributive punishment for preexisting sin. Rather, he declares, God proactively seeks to guide men according to His word: He *may speak...in a dream* or *a vision to seal their instruction*[196] (33:14-16) *in order to turn man from his deed, and keep him from pride* (NIV) and thus avert the destructive consequences of his self-determined deeds (33:17-18). To this end, man may even be *chastened with pain* and come close to perishing as he wastes away (33:19-22).[197] If God can thereby gain man's attention He can finally redeem him from destruction through a process that Elihu now meticulously describes (33:23-30).

Elihu first confirms for Job that there is indeed a *mediator*,[198] a unique *messenger*[199] who would come not to vindicate Job but rather to

---

[194] The opening *kî* is clearly asseverative ("indeed," so NASB), emphasizing Elihu's rebuttal to Job's claim.

[195] The Heb. reads "once...and twice" (cf. NASB), which may be rendered "over and over" or "repeatedly."

[196] Hartley (*The Book of Job*, 441 [fn. 5]) discusses alternate textual readings for 33:16b. NKJV and NASB (*seals their instruction*) is echoed in 36:10, while NIV (*terrify him with warnings*) reflects LXX and may be viewed as Elihu's answer to Job's complaint in 7:14. The former best fits the intent of 33:14, but both translations are consistent with the aim of turning man from his pride and self-destructive works (33:17-18) and with Eccl 3:11-15, affirming that God's communication is mediated through man's conscience or cosmic awareness in order to keep him accountable before God.

[197] Man's search for meaning does not make much progress until he comes to grips with his own mortality (cf. Ps 90, Eccl 7:1-14; 11:7-12:8). God's communication through "chastening" is always for our profit, to mold redeemed man in righteousness (Heb 12:4-11, cf. Job 33:23, 26). Without such opposition to frustrate his own pride, man typically fails to seek God (cf. Crabb, *Finding God*, chap. 15; Peter Kreeft, "Job: Life as Suffering," in *Three Philosophies of Life* [San Francisco: Ignatius, 1989], 59-95).

[198] The Heb. for *mediator* (33:23) is *lîs*, the same word used by Job in 16:20a, "My *intercessor* is my friend" (NIV, cf. n. 93). Elihu's revelation of God's redemptive initiative conclusively answers Job's lament over the absence of a mediator between him and God. Ironically, Elihu himself exemplifies the very *mediator* or *intercessor* of which he is now informing Job (cf. nn. 190, 199).

[199] The Heb. *mal'ak* is translated "angel" or "messenger." "The phrase *one among a thousand*...from the way [it] is used in 9:3...is better understood as having very restrictive force....He may be identified with 'the angel of Yahweh' " (Hartley, *The Book of Job*, 447). In his self-representation as Job's "spokesman" before God (33:6, cf. n. 189) Elihu prefigured this unique *messenger* or *angel* (33:23a).

declare to him the true nature of *uprightness*[200] in God's eyes (33:23). This messenger is then instructed to mediate God's grace by providing a *ransom* that can redeem a man from destruction and restore his *youthful vigor* (33:24-25, NASB). When he prays (33:26a), God *will delight in him* (33:26b), which leads to joyful reconciliation (33:26c), since by virtue of the ransom (cf. 33:24b) God can now justly *restore to* him *His righteousness* (33:26d).[201] As a result of this gracious restoration, man will "sing"

---

[200] The word *yāšār* lit. means "uprightness," from the same stem as "upright," used to describe Job in 1:1. The *messenger* is declaring either the true standard for "what is right" (cf. NASB, NIV, matching its use in 33:27) or displaying the very righteousness of God Himself (cf. NKJV). Either sense fits the context: If the former, the point would be that the messenger is mediating God's perfect Law to bring man to faith (cf. Gal 3:19-24). If the latter, it reflects the sense of John 1:18—he models God's perfect righteousness. In either case the "uprightness" declared by the messenger is meant to expose the inadequacy of mankind's own righteousness—including Job's—and establishes his need for vicarious atonement and justification before God (33:24-26).

[201] The contribution of 33:26 to the passage is best viewed as explaining how man appropriates the benefits of atonement just described in 33:23-25: God's messenger first shows man the perfect standard of *uprightness* (33:23) then mediates the gracious provision of a *ransom* to *deliver* him from deserved death (33:24) and redeem him to vitality (33:25). The ransom is appropriated by prayer (33:26a), which initiates the logical (not temporal, as NASB) sequence of the benefits of propitiation (33:26b-d): Man *prays to God* (33:26a, i.e., to confess his sin, 33:27), and God restores to him *His righteousness* (33:26d). The logical connection between praying and restoration of righteousness to man is explained in the middle two lines: God *will delight in him* (33:26b), implying that the ransom (cf. 33:24) suffices to pay the penalty for sin, so that *he shall see His face with joy* (33:26c), denoting the reconciliation accomplished by this propitiatory payment.

The pronominal suffix of the noun *ṣidqāthô* (his righteousness) is ambiguous— *God's* or *man's* righteousness?—and conveys nuances of both justification and transformation (cf. n. 204). Elihu is responding directly to Job's hope of being *declared righteous before God* (justification), but his emphasis is on the restoration of mankind's *righteous agency for God* (transformation), precisely what was at stake for Job (1:1-11, cf. n. 87) and still is for us (cf. 1 John 2:29-3:2). The logic of Job 33:23-26 is so evocative of Christ's agency in revealing and mediating God's righteousness (cf. John 1:14-18; Rom 1:17; 5:19-21; Col 1:15, 19; Heb 1:1-3) by atoning for man's sin (cf. Mark 10:45; 2 Cor 5:21; 1 Tim 2:3-6; Heb 2:9-10; and n. 29), that it seems misplaced in Elihu's speech. Yet the notion of revelatory agency was implicit in the giving of the Law (cf. John 1:17; Heb 2:2) and that of mediatory agency inheres in the Law (cf. Gal 3:19ff), the Prophets (cf. Isa 52-53) and the Psalms (cf. Ps 34:6-7). Virtually the same language of atonement (Job 33:24) is found in Ps 49:7-9 (Hartley, ibid., 445 [fn. 1]; NET); moreover, mankind's need of a ransom for sin is implicit in Job's own sacrifices (1:5; 3:25; nn. 34, 69) and in the sacrifice of Isaac (Gen 22).

to his fellow men the testimony of his restoration from sin to abundant life (33:27-28).[202]

If Elihu can thus convince Job that God desires to restore him as a representative of God's righteous character to others and redeem him to abundant life, then Job can no longer claim that God has made him an enemy. But Elihu's characterization of man in God's eyes also presupposes an inherent propensity to pride and self-sufficiency that naturally resists God's redemptive efforts (cf. 33:14-18). Elihu thus hastens to reaffirm that in order to keep man from perishing, God tries **repeatedly** to reach man and restore him to life (33:29-30).[203] If Elihu's argument succeeds, then Job will gain a sufficiently renewed hope in his restoration to acknowledge his need for God's righteousness, accept God's grace, and be vindicated in His eyes (33:31-33).[204]

Elihu's opening message of God's redemptive grace in response to man's innate propensity to self-destruction should thoroughly abolish any hope that the reader could ever vindicate himself as a self-sufficient or self-righteous agent of God. The suffering reader should reflect on whether he—like Job—is so focused on his own victimization that he too has become deaf to the message of grace conveyed by the "megaphone"

---

[202] By rendering all of 33:27-28 as a quote from the redeemed man, NASB is preferable to NKJV (see Hartley, *The Book of Job*, 445 [fn. 7] and 447). We may thus modify the NASB to read "He will sing to men and say, 'I have sinned and perverted what was right, but it did not profit me. He has redeemed my soul from going to the Pit, and my life shall see the light.'" Such a "song" or "testimony" is later exemplified by Job's own confession (42:1-6) and his redemptive mediation on behalf of his three friends (42:7-9). Cf. Ps 51:12-19. The imagery of *light* (33:28, cf. 33:30) projects more than a mere understanding of truth about God; it denotes a truly animating principle, the promise of "meaningful life" or "vitality" that directly answers Job's fears of a meaningless death (cf. 7:7-10; 17:11-16) and is ultimately fulfilled in his two-fold restoration (42:10-17). Cp. the analogous imagery of *light* in Eccl 6:3-5.

[203] God's "perseverance" in this regard is well illustrated in 2 Pet 3:8-9 and in the parables of Matt 20:1-16 and Luke 15. See Hall, *God and Human Suffering*, chap. 4, for further exposition of this redemptive goal of suffering (cf. n. 181).

[204] The benefits of propitiation (n. 201) should be seen as ongoing. By saying *Speak, for I desire to justify you* (33:32), Elihu affirms Job's need to be vindicated (cf. 9:2, 33:26; n. 71), i.e., proved righteous. He assures Job that he intends to serve as his advocate (cf. 33:6-7; n. 188) and again invites Job to refute him if he can (cf. 33:5). Job needs to *listen* to *wisdom* (33:33) concerning *righteousness* (cf. 33:23b, n. 200): If Job would accept Elihu's teaching on God's just rule (chap. 34) and his own inadequate righteousness (chap. 35) he might then confess and repent of his presumption (cf. 33:26-27) and thus allow God to *restore to* Job *His righteousness*; i.e., reconstitute him as His righteous agent (33:26d, cf. 1 John 1:9; 2:1-2; 2:29-3:3).

of suffering.[205] Such a reader is now disposed to receive God's correctives through Elihu, intended to expand his perspective regarding God's justice and righteousness (cf. 33:8-13) and elicit the responses God seeks amid the affliction He has permitted. The logic prepares us to resign ourselves to the appearance of injustice in this life in light of our own inadequate righteousness (chaps. 34-35) and submit to God's instruction in light of His creative wisdom and power (chaps. 36-37), so that we may serve God effectively as righteous agents of His redemptive purposes.

---

[205] Cf. 33:14b, 16, 19-22. C. S. Lewis' renowned quote goes as follows: "God whispers in our pleasures…but shouts in our pains. Pain is His megaphone to rouse a dulled world."

— 10 —

C. God's Sovereign Rule is Just (Job 34)

With Elihu's explanation that God's justice is grounded in the contingencies of His Sovereign Rule, **the author affirms that even when His reasons for specific judgments remain inscrutable, God's sovereign rule over all creation is inherently responsive and just,** *so that the reader might learn to trust God's just rule, even when His purposes in judgment remain inscrutable.*

The arguments of Elihu's second (chap. 34) and third (chap. 35) speeches are integrally related. Having grounded Job's hope in God's redemptive character (33:14-33), Elihu now recapitulates his opening challenge to Job's complaint against God (34:5-6, cf. 33:8-13), then systematically refutes Job's claim that he was innocent and that God had deprived him of justice: Elihu first illuminates Job's myopic perspective on God's justice by taking into consideration the vast domain of God's sovereign, inscrutable rule (34:7-37) then exposes Job's self-defeating self-righteous presumption (chap. 35), thus preparing Job to submit to God's all-wise and powerful rule (chaps. 36-37).

Elihu prefaces his rebuttal of Job's charge that God was unjust by turning to Job's friends[206] and inviting them to weigh the merits of Job's case more carefully (34:1-4).[207] They should do so, he argues, because Job's claim that God has made him look guilty by wounding him and has denied him justice by refusing to hear his case (34:5-6)[208] invites severe criticism (34:7). Indeed, Elihu adds, Job aligns himself

---

[206] *You* is plural (34:2, cf. n. 179).

[207] Job had used the figure *palate* (6:30, NASB) to invite his friends to test the merits of his case—a challenge they had not accepted (cf. 6:28-30; 13:17-18). By using the same figure Elihu now accepts Job's challenge and invites them to join him (32:3-4) in evaluating Job's prior claims (34:5-6, cf. 16:17; 27:3; see Scholnick, "The Meaning of *Mišpāṭ*," 354). Elihu's use of *mišpāṭ* here rather than *yāšār* (33:23, n. 200) indicates he is inviting them to test Job's case against God (34:4a, *let us* "discern" *justice*, cf. NIV) to see what holds up under scrutiny (34:4b, *let us know...what is good*) (Scholnick, ibid., 353-4). Ironically, this also prepares the "comforters" for their own confrontation by God (42:7-9).

[208] The text and sense of 34:6a is debated (Scholnick, ibid., 354 [fn. 8]) but only confused by most English translations. This is clarified by the chiastic structure of 34:5-6 with its pivotal wordplay on *mišpāṭ* in 34:5b, 6a (cf. n. 207): "For Job claims 'I am righteous, yet God has denied me *justice;* the *judgment* against me is false—my wound fatal—[yet] I am guiltless'."

with overt evildoers by further insinuating that man wastes his time to *delight in God* (34:8-9).[209]

Elihu then begins his rebuttal by pointing out where he differs from Job's other friends (34:10a)—Elihu agrees with them that God would never do wrong and He does reward *man according to his work* (34:10b-11), acknowledging His perfect justice (34:12, cp. 8:3). Yet His justice is not based on present retribution—as Sovereign Ruler over all the earth, He answers to no one above Him (34:13). He would still be perfectly just even if He were to allow *all* life to expire (34:14-15)![210]

Elihu now addresses Job directly[211] and expands on his thesis that God's sovereign rule must also be just (34:16-20, cf. 34:12-13). How absurd for the ultimate Ruler of all the earth to disdain justice, as Job had claimed (34:17):[212] God demonstrates His justice when He judges earthly rulers as *worthless* and *wicked* (34:18, NASB); he remains completely impartial to those whom He has ordained to wield His authority on earth (34:19). This is manifested by their equal vulnerability to death, which

---

[209] Although Job had not stated this explicitly, it can be inferred from his complaint (cf. 34:5-6): Why serve God when He's framed you? Elihu is pointing out Satan's insidious influence on Job's ideation (cf. nn. 19, 20).

[210] Elihu's logic here is that God's judgments on earth are dictated by the parameters of His sovereign rule and by no other standard of justice (34:12-13), including the deeds-based system of retribution theology so tenaciously touted by Job's comforters. All such theology is gutted when one realizes that God in His sovereign rule could justly extinguish all life (34:14-15); the fact that man survives at all implies that his continued existence must serve the inscrutable purposes of God's sovereign rule and is therefore inherently just. Job's claim of injustice (34:5-6) therefore fails out of ignorance of God's sovereign purposes and not because his other friends were right that Job sinned to warrant his punishment. Elihu's argument later develops the implications of this divine inscrutability for mankind (34:29, 32).

[211] "You" shifts to singular in 34:16-20, indicating that Elihu is now focused on Job (cf. n. 179). This next step is the "linchpin" in Elihu's argument that God's justice is determined by His absolute rule.

[212] The logic of 34:17 is reflected in Christ's reasoning with the "rich young ruler." Just as Christ questioned the standard by which the young man judged "goodness" (Matt 19:16-17), so Elihu questioned the standard by which Job could judge God's justice and his own righteousness: If Job could legitimately impugn God's justice (*condemn Him who is most just*), it would nullify the absolute standard of justice by which all others are governed (34:17). This point is then substantiated by the logic of 34:18-20 (NASB): God demonstrates his absolute standard of justice by judging some rulers as *worthless* or *wicked* (34:18), and death is His instrument to hold even the greatest of these rulers fully accountable, so that their exercise of power remains completely subject to His perfect rule (34:19-20). With this point Elihu ironically reminds Job of his own argument in 12:13-25.

God employs to subject their authority to His own rule and restrain their abuse of power *without* any help from man[213] (34:20). *For* He is fully aware of *the ways of man*—no evil deed escapes His view (34:21-22)—and[214] *He need not* respond to a man's lawsuit, as Job had demanded,[215] in order to judge evil fairly (34:23).

God demonstrates such awareness of evil when *without inquiry* He smites wicked, arrogant rulers who in their rebellion (34:24-27) have caused the poor to cry out, so that He might hear and then restrain their oppressors (34:28, 30).[216] Parenthetically, Elihu accounts for such cases as Job's—when God seems not to attend to evil—and justifies God's silence (34:29):[217] That is, even when a gross injustice like Job's suffering cries out for explanation, finite man can't condemn God's silence as unfair—he simply cannot comprehend the vast array of concomitant concerns that God needs to balance in order to harmonize His judgments fairly in all spheres of His sovereign domain.[218]

---

[213] A play on words depicts the perfect harmony between God's rule *through* His chosen agents (*the work of His hands*, 34:19c) and His justice *apart from* human agency (*without a hand*, 34:20c) to limit abuse by these same human agents of the power God has conferred on them. This point is then substantiated in 34:21-30.

[214] The *kî* that initiates 34:23 parallels the opening *kî* ("for") in 34:21 and is thus distributive in force ("and").

[215] The phrase *go before God in judgment* (34:23b) should be translated "sue for *justice* before God" (cf. nn. 207-208), which was exactly what Job did to ensure that God would judge fairly (9:1-20; 23:1-9; 30:20; 31:35; 33:13; 35:12, cf. nn. 149, 169 and related text). Elihu is insinuating that Job's demand for a hearing before God reflects unwarranted skepticism over whether God fully appreciates the evil of his suffering; this skepticism supplies the continuing pretext for Elihu's observations in 34:24-30.

[216] Verses 34:24-30 should be seen as the logical substantiation of Elihu's point in 34:19-20 (cf. n. 213): God overthrows the wicked who oppress the poor and rebel against him (34:24-28), so that the wicked are prevented from overruling His purposes (34:30).

[217] The text is difficult (cf. Hartley, *The Book of Job*, 456 [fns.], 459) but it is clearly parenthetical to 34:28 and 30. It shows an a:b/a':b'/c parallelism that should be construed as justifying God's silence when it seems to those who are suffering like Job that God is not judging evil: "But if He remains silent [i.e., we cannot "hear" His verdict over evil in any given case], who can condemn Him?/ If He hides His face, who can see Him [i.e., who can discern the scope of His judgment], whether [it is] against man or nation alike?" (cf. NIV).

[218] One cannot assume that a given affliction is direct punishment from God, since individual suffering may be woven into a much broader tapestry of related events that are within God's purview but beyond human understanding, so the reasons behind that affliction remain inscrutable (cf. 33:12b-13; 34:13; n.193). This logic expands the point made in 34:23 (n. 215; cf. also 37:13), as Crabb clarifies:

In light of Elihu's compelling argument linking God's justice to His sovereign rule, the impropriety of Job's attitude now emerges: How absurd for someone to tell God that he has been punished in spite of being innocent and then insist that God explain to him how he has transgressed so that he might be restored (34:31-32)![219] Should Job be allowed to dictate the *terms* of his restoration just because he disavows guilt for sinning in ignorance (34:33a, cf. 34:5-6)?[220] Following this rhetorical question Elihu admonishes Job to reassess the validity of his demands (*"you must choose,"* 34:33b) and rather than speculate over God's inscrutable purposes in his affliction (cf. 34:32a) *speak* only *what* he *knows* is true (34:33c).

Elihu concludes that any wise person who has followed Job's argument would agree that Job's claims have been foolish (34:34-35, cf. 34:7) and that he should thus be held accountable for rationalizing like wicked men (34:36, cf. 34:8). Elihu justifies this harsh judgment by explaining that Job's persistent charge of injustice amounts to rebellion against God's

------

Sometimes it's hard to know what God is doing. He informs us that he withholds nothing good from his children. I take that to mean that *there is nothing that perfect goodness coupled with absolute power should be doing that isn't being done—right now.*...We all rage at God, demanding he do more than he is doing. He remains quietly unthreatened, saddened beyond words that we think him cruel or indifferent, but unswervingly committed to the course he has set. He refuses to redesign the plot of the book, having already written the last chapter and knowing that the ending is very, very good, and that every thread in our story is necessary to that conclusion. [*Finding God*, 187, emphasis his]

[219] The text of 34:31-32 is also difficult. Zuck suggests that the phrase *I will offend no more* (34:31c) is more accurately translated "I did not act corruptly" (*Job*, 151 [fn. 32]). Since the verb is imperfect rather than perfect, the amended text should thus read "For has anyone said to God, 'I have borne chastening yet *I do not act corruptly;* Teach me what I do not see; If I have done iniquity, I will do no more'?" Elihu's rhetorical question exposes Job's presumption as bold but ludicrous: While insisting he is innocent he also demands that God explain to him why he is guilty so he can repent. Job had in fact made several such comments during the debate (Zuck, ibid. [fn. 33], cf. Job 7:20; 10:2; 13:23).

[220] The logic of 34:33a is directly related to that of 34:31-32. On the surface it appears that Elihu is arguing the same point that Job's other friends had argued: that Job was protesting too much about his unfair treatment in order to cover up some secret sin that had brought on legitimate retribution from God. However, Elihu's rhetorical question does not contradict Job's disavowal of guilt for some pre-existing sin. It is rather to point out the presumption of placing himself at the center of God's concerns and demanding restitution on the basis of pure speculation as to the cause of his suffering; so he says *Therefore speak* [only] *what you know* (34:33c). This sense accords well with the prologue of the book and the rest of Elihu's argument here, including his harsh conclusion (34:34-37, see below).

sovereignty and only compounds his sinful vindictiveness over the ill-treatment he has suffered at the hands of his friends (34:37).[221]

Elihu's indictment should challenge the readers' continued loyalty to Job. They must either impugn Elihu's motives or hear him as God's inspired messenger and realize the glaring disparity between Job's disposition in adversity and his intended role as God's servant. The reader must remain focused on the key concern at stake in the drama—Satan's attempt to subvert God's kingdom rule by co-opting God's chosen agents to serve his own ends.[222] The fact that Job's godly agency is jeopardized by his arrogant insistence on full disclosure reflects the reader's own need to trust in God's perfect rule amid suffering, even when His purposes remain inscrutable. Elihu thus proceeds to defend God's continued silence in the face of Job's self-righteous ultimatum (chap. 35).

---

[221] Although this verse is singled out by some to prove that Elihu also deemed Job "guilty of sin before his suffering" (Parsons, "Structure and Purpose," 25; cf. above n. 21), closer inspection reveals that Elihu was indicting Job for present sin in his attitude toward both God and man: With chiastic parallelism (a:b / b':a') this verse explains why Job's *answers are like those of wicked men* (34:36b): Not only does Job manifest *sin* in his disposition toward his friends, in that he *claps his hands among us* (i.e., he ridicules them, cf. esp. 27:7-12 and 30:1-8), but he also *adds rebellion* in that he *multiplies his words against God* (i.e., he presumptuously charges God with injustice). Elihu's judgment may seem harsh but it is a critical turning point in the argument, underscoring what is truly at stake in the remainder of the drama: Job's poisonous contempt for his gentile friends (n. 45) must yield to God's redemptive design for them before Job can fulfill his role as the chosen agent of their redemption (42:7-9, cf. nn. 24, 29, 157, 159). With this connection in 34:37 it now emerges that Job's *sin*, like Jonah's disdain for the Ninevites (Jon 4), was rooted in his *rebellion* against God's redemptive purposes. The rest of the drama focuses in turn on Job learning and bowing to God's sovereign wisdom and power.

[222] *See* nn. 14, 20.

— 11 —

D. Job's Self-Righteous Presumption (Job 35)

By exposing the presumption behind Job's self-righteous demand that God either warrant or relieve his suffering, **the author emphasizes the self-destructive effect of self-righteous presumption,** *so that suffering readers in adversity might forsake self-righteous presumption and instead wait patiently and humbly for God's life-giving wisdom and compassion.*

The author himself had already introduced Elihu as being angry with Job *because he justified himself rather than God* (32:2), and Elihu now vindicates the author's assessment.[223] Elihu began his entire rebuttal by citing Job's contention that he was innocent and that God had therefore treated him unjustly (33:8-11). Elihu again cited Job's claim as the pretext for his defense of God's justice (34:5-6) and he now alludes to it for the third time (35:2) to continue the case he had begun to build in chap. 34. After harmonizing God's justice with the sovereign, inscrutable orchestration of His redemptive purposes (chap. 34), Elihu now exposes the self-righteous presumption behind Job's charges against God and his dogged resistance to God's attempts to restore him (cf. 33:14-30) to his intended role as God's mediator of those same purposes.

Elihu again argues logically and directly. Job's complaint that he was innocent and that God had therefore robbed him of justice (cf. 33:8-11; 34:5-6) is tantamount to asserting that he was more righteous than God and had therefore wasted his diligence in avoiding sin (35:1-3, cf. 34:9).[224] Elihu again counters Job's contention by broadening his perspective to account for the vast domain of God's rule (35:4-5, cf. 34:13-30). Elihu's bold assertion could not be more contradictory to the claims of either Job or his friends: Whether Job is righteous or wicked

---

[223] That Elihu's anger is warranted is attested not only by the author but also by YHWH Himself (n. 177).

[224] If the first line of 35:3 is a direct quote, Job is claiming that neither God ("You") nor Job ("I") is benefiting from Job's righteousness (cp. 10:3); however, "you" more likely refers to Job in indirect discourse, *"For you ask what it will profit you,"* which is then rephrased as a direct quote in the parallel second line, *"'What more do I gain than if I had sinned?'"* This reading fits the context of Elihu's two-stage argument better in that it restates then expands his opening charge (34:9). Elihu is addressing Job's inference that there is no advantage in continuing to serve God with righteous behavior when it is left unrewarded.

is inconsequential to the outcome of God's preordained will[225] and only affects men like Job (35:6-8).[226] Since God is unmoved, Elihu shows how Job's disposition has instead moved him from God by emulating the arrogant presumption of people[227] who do not truly fear God (35:9-16).

Although people naturally (cf. 35:8) cry out to God for relief from their oppression (35:9) they refuse to listen patiently for God's nurturing consolation and wisdom, provided in His way and His time (35:10-11).[228] God does not respond to such vain cries for relief, because they stem from evil pride, demanding that God respond according to mankind's own terms (35:12-13, cf. 34:33).[229] Much less, therefore, will God respond

---

[225] Yancey misinterprets Elihu to be saying in 35:6-8 that it is "absurd to believe that one human being...can make a difference in the history of the universe" (*Disappointment with God*, 196). He asserts that "Elihu... was flat wrong. The opening and closing chapters of Job prove that God was greatly affected by the response of one man and that cosmic issues were at stake" (ibid.). However, the point of the narrative in those chapters is that it was Job's faith or *fear of God* that would move God and make a difference in history, not Job's *righteousness*, which was worthless to God. Parsons ("Structure and Purpose," 25) correctly affirms that "Elihu was right in pointing out the fallacious nature of Job's position, which implied that God owed a man something for his righteousness (35:3-8)." In so arguing, Elihu flatly but properly contradicts the positions of both Job ("I am righteous, and God should admit it") and his friends ("By repenting of prior sins, Job can move God to bless him"), just as the author had signaled in the text (cf. 32:2-3; 34:4). The inability of mankind's righteousness to elicit God's favor is further developed in Eccl 7:15-29.

[226] Ironically, Job's vitriolic response to his friends had made him an oppressor (see nn. 141-144 and related text, cf. also Eccl 4:1-3). Elihu's rebuttal is meant to provoke Job to reflect on whether he has in fact been righteous or wicked toward them and should remind him how his disposition as God's agent is intended to bless other people not victimize them (cf. n. 119).

[227] A study of Eccl 5:1-7 further clarifies the nature of Job's presumption by exposing the natural tendency of people to manipulate God without taking His transcendent purposes into account.

[228] Elihu's reasoning is paralleled in Isa 64. Man is presumptuous to think that he can possibly fathom the vastness of God's preordained will (Isa 64:4 [I Cor 2:7-9]; cf. Job 35:5). While God desires a righteous response to the revelation of "His ways" (Isa 64:5a, cf. Job 35:10-11), mankind's ways are sinful and completely inadequate to save him (Isa 64:5b, cf. Job 35:2-3). Mankind's righteousness has no impact on God at all (Isa 64:6, cf. Job 35:6-8). Job's demand that God relieve his suffering on his terms amounts to nothing more than a sinful failure to listen to God or trust His righteousness (Isa 64:7; cf. Job 35:9-11).

[229] The argument of 35:9-13 is echoed by Jas 4:1-3: When God fails to respond to man's agonized cries for relief (4:3), it is not based on a failure of His redemptive character but on man's own selfish lusts and desire for revenge (4:1-2). While this characterization may seem nothing like the *righteous* Job of Ezek 14:14, 20 it attests the miserable state to which his attitude had degenerated (cf. nn. 84, 127, 142, 151,

when Job cries out that he cannot see Him and must wait interminably for God to adjudicate his case (35:14, cf. NIV);[230] nor will He answer when Job charges that He ignores evil and allows wickedness to run rampant (35:15, cf. NIV).[231] Elihu therefore concludes that Job's complaining is futile, in that *He multiplies words without knowledge*[232] (35:16).

In coupling Elihu's defense of God's justice (chap. 34) with his indictment of Job for self-righteous presumption (chap. 35), the author hopes to challenge readers who sympathize with Job to be more concerned about Job's presumptuous demands and his self-righteous pride than his

---

152). Crabb argues that Christians may display such self-righteous defiance and he ascribes God's inaccessibility in just these situations to "our fallen structure. *When we approach God with this structure still in place he will not listen to us*" (*Finding God*, 91; emphasis his). This clearly reflects Elihu's assessment of Job's disposition: God is not obligated to account for His purposes (cf. 33:13) nor will He respond at all whenever a man's cries arise out of stubborn pride (35:9-13).

[230] NKJV is misleading as it seems to suggest that Elihu is encouraging Job to wait patiently on God's justice (35:14b, cf. chap. 31); however, that is exactly what Job had already vowed to do (n. 172). Elihu is more likely paraphrasing Job with indirect discourse from 35:14b through 35:15 (so NIV), citing his demand for God's summary judgment (now that Job's *case* was laid out *before him*, cf. nn. 207, 215), in order to further justify God's disregard for his *empty cry* (35:13, NIV; cf. nn. 84, 127, 171, 229).

[231] The NKJV and NASB renditions of 35:15 convey the sense that Elihu is telling Job he has been spared deserved punishment, just as Zophar had claimed *Know therefore that God exacts from you less than your iniquity deserves* (11:6b). However, v. 35:15 is best rendered as continued indirect discourse (so NIV, n. 230), in which Elihu paraphrases the charges Job had previously made, i.e., that God fails to judge evil in a timely fashion (cf. 24:1-17). Elihu clearly differs from Job's other friends in that he views Job's survival thus far not as retribution withheld but rather as grace extended by a long-suffering and loving God (cf. 33:29-30; 36:15-16) who endures Job's present defiance (cf. 35:14a) in order to ultimately be seen. Crabb again describes God's character here in a way that helps shed light on Elihu's intended sense (*Finding God*, 107):

> God wants to be found. He delights to be known. He rejoices when we are close to him. But our search for him must be on his terms. And those terms involve a radical shift away from our natural inclination to evaluate his goodness. He will not tolerate anyone sitting in judgment of him. We are not the judges. We are rather the judged, the forgiven, and the invited...

[232] The figure *multiply words without knowledge* alludes back to 34:35, 37c, where Elihu pointed out that Job was arguing out of ignorance (cf. n. 221). Here Elihu expands the sense to include willful defiance and anticipates the point of departure for YHWH's first speech (38:2), which uses the same phrase. The construction *many words* plays a similar role in Ecclesiastes (cf. n. 28; Eccl 5:3, 7; 6:11 [NASB]), where it signifies human self-sufficient presumption in attempting to fulfill selfish ambitions without considering God's inscrutable ways (cf. Reitman, "Structure and Unity of Ecclesiastes," 304, 310 [fns. 35, 58]).

victimization by unjust suffering (cf. 34:37). Elihu's admonition should prompt similarly suffering readers to replace their own demands—rooted in a victim's mindset—with an attitude of humility and receptivity to God's redemptive intent to restore them. This sets the stage for Elihu to further explain God's "instruction" to the afflicted (cf. 33:16, 24-28) which—when they hear it—He uses to avert their destruction and restore them to vitality (chaps. 36-37).

— 12 —

E. God's Sovereign Instruction (Job 36–37)

In Elihu's admonition that Job 1) learn from his suffering in view of God's sovereign control; and 2) hear God's voice, by which He rules His created order, **the author reaffirms that God's instruction informs people of their sin and that God has the desire and power to restore them,** *so that readers might listen for God's instruction as accountable agents and trust in His redemptive power to restore them to fruitful agency.*

Elihu's final speech expands on and concludes his initial exposition (33:14-33) of God's redemptive intervention when mankind is on the path to self-destruction. Following a brief reminder of Elihu's qualification to speak as God's inspired spokesman (36:1-4, cf. 32:6-33:7), the speech comsists of 1) an exposition of God's use of suffering to gain mankind's attention to his need for restoration (36:5-33); and 2) a plea for Job to listen for God's instruction in order to obediently serve his Creator (37:1-24). The text of these two sections is distinguished by repeated imperatives to *"behold"* (cf. 36:5, 22, 26, 30) and then *"listen"* (cf. 37:2, 14), in effect preparing Job for his impending rebuke and instruction by God Himself (38:1-42:6).

Job cannot stubbornly maintain his self-sufficient disposition and also assume his intended role as faithful agent of God's dominion. After frankly labeling Job's demands as *rebellion* against God (34:37) and presumptuous *words without knowledge* (35:16), Elihu now invites Job to respond to God's redemptive overture (36:1-4): The confidence that God is fully aware of the affliction of the oppressed yet also sees their sin is intended to **convince** Job of his need for restoration as God's servant and **motivate** him to acknowledge his transgression, repent of his rebellion, and properly exalt God (36:5-33). Elihu's depiction of God's commands as the *thunder of His voice*[233] is meant to **silence** Job to listen for His instructions, so that he may serve his created purpose within God's sovereign decree (37:1-24). Elihu's imperatives thus set the stage for Job's restoration as a clear example for the reader's own agency.

---

[233] The word *voice* (*qôl*) occurs four times in 37:2, 4 alone, along with repeated allusions to the *rumble, thunder, sound,* or *command* of God's voice (36:29, 33; 37:2 [twice], 4 [twice], 5, 6, 12); or to His *mouth* or *breath* (37:2, 10).

1. God Teaches in Affliction; *Behold* His Sovereign Rule (36:1–33)

Elihu invites Job to *bear with* his rebuttal a little longer (36:1-2, cf. 33:6-7); he intends to confirm God's *righteousness*, reminding Job that he draws this truth from God's *perfect knowledge* (36:3-4, cf. 32:8; 33:3-4). His formal argument then begins in 36:5 (*"Behold..."*) with an exposition of the role of human suffering in orienting God's servants to His righteous activity. He will not tolerate *iniquity* among his servants and may even *bind* them with *cords of affliction* to alert them to *their transgressions*, so that they might *obey* and prosper rather than *perish* in disobedience (36:7-14). A conspicuous shift to the second person in 36:16 then alerts the reader that Elihu is now applying his teaching on suffering (36:15) to Job's particular case.

If indeed God is righteous (cf. 36:3) He *does not despise* those who suffer but is "mighty of heart" (35:5): He does not preserve *the wicked* and ignore *the righteous* but rather *gives justice* to the *afflicted* and seats *the righteous* among *kings forever, exalted* (36:6-7).[234] Yet when the righteous **are** afflicted, God may use that affliction to expose their sinful deeds, rooted in defiant self-sufficiency (36:8-9):[235] *He opens their ears to instruction* (36:10a) and *commands them to repent* (36:10b, NRSV)[236] in hopes of eliciting their obedient service, so they may be restored to full health and vitality (36:11).[237] *But if they* ignore His overture they *die without*

---

[234] Verses 6-7 have an alternate parallel structure (a:b/a':b') which I have rendered here as a:a'/b:b' to illustrate the intended link between *affliction* and *the righteous*—exactly Job's situation. Elihu understands this, and it is this that most distinguishes his perception of Job from the other three friends. See OVERVIEW OF JOB.

[235] Cf. 36:9b, *they have magnified themselves* (NASB). Elihu has been referring to *the righteous* who are suffering (cf. 36:7) yet now speaks of turning them from *their transgressions* and *iniquity* (36:8-9); this is transparently aimed at Job's self-righteous presumption (cf. 34:35-37; 35:14-16). When *the righteous* revert to self-sufficiency, God will use suffering to show them their willful resistance to God.

[236] Elihu's teaching here recalls his initial lecture on suffering as God's instrument to gain mankind's attention to the imminent danger of self-destruction (33:14-22); He must first use suffering to *open the ears of men and seal their instruction* (33:16; n. 196, 205) before He can *restore* to them *His righteousness* (33:23-30, cf. nn. 197, 201, 204). This function of suffering is so important that Elihu explicitly repeats it when he turns to Job (36:15ff) with a view to securing Job's obedient response to the *voice of God* as an agent of His redemptive purposes (chap. 37; n. 233).

[237] Elihu thus anticipates Job's ultimate restoration for his obedient intercession (42:7-17). While the three friends rightly recognized God's desire to restore the repentant sinner (cf. 5:17-27; 8:5-7; 11:13-20; 22:21-30), only Elihu identifies the value of obedience **learned** through suffering (36:11-12, 22; cf. Heb 5:8-9, nn. 29, 57). See Carson (*How Long O Lord?* chap. 5), Kreeft, (*Making Sense,* 95-101, 111-14),

knowledge—in fact, *the godless* at *heart lay up anger; they do not cry for help when He binds them* and *they die* completely estranged from God (36:12-14, NASB).[238] Elihu then warns Job explicitly that he himself is at a crossroads, faced with this same choice (36:15-21).

God *delivers the afflicted by their affliction,* using *adversity* to *open their ears* (36:15, NRSV). And *indeed,*[239] He has *enticed* Job *from* his *distress*[240] to a *broad place, full of fatness* (36:16, NASB); but[241] Job is accruing *the judgment due the wicked* (36:17, cf. 36:6)[242] for he is letting his anger *entice* him to self-sufficiency[243]—to turn down the *great ransom* that God has

---

Crabb (*Finding God*, chap. 15), and Francis I. Andersen ("The Problems of Suffering in The Book of Job," reprinted in Zuck [ed.], *Sitting with Job*, 185-8).

[238] Elihu is comparing the fate of *the afflicted* who stubbornly persist in self-sufficiency (cf. n. 235) in response to their affliction (vv. 12-13, *they do not cry for help*, cf. 35:9) with the fate of *the godless* (v. 14): Taken to the extreme, defiant self-sufficiency among God's intended agents robs them of the wisdom they need (*they die without knowledge*) and they die as estranged from God as idolatrous temple prostitutes (cf. NRSV marginal reading).

[239] The Heb. conjunction w^{e}'*aph* clearly associates the emphatic affirmation of 36:16 with the truism restated by Elihu in 36:15 (cf. n. 236) in an *a fortiori* sense (BDB, 65a[2]): "*Even more* is this [36:15] true for *you*, Job."

[240] Note that the author will conspicuously use the same words *entice* (*sûth* [Hifil]) and *distress* (*şar* [substantive, lit. "narrow" or "constricted"]) to compare the "allure" of God's **might** (36:15-16, cf. 36:5) and Job's anger-provoked **self-sufficiency** (36:18-19) in competing to *deliver* Job (36:15a) *from distress* (36:16, 19). Regarding the critical notion of *deliverance* in the dramatic flow of Job, see nn. 23 and 25; regarding the translation "self-sufficiency," see n. 243

[241] The text of 36:17-21 is difficult. Most translations of 36:17 correctly identify the adversative sense of the opening *waw* as Elihu now applies the immediately preceding warnings to Job as one of *the righteous* who are *afflicted* (36:6-9) but also at grave risk of suffering the consequences of ignoring God's *instruction* (36:10-14). In fact, his logic in 36:17 is directly linked to his opening redemptive initiative (36:15-16), entreating Job to listen to God's offer of restoration before his *present* attitude in suffering destroys him. The translations miss this connection and make Elihu sound like the other three friends (but see nn. 9, 12, 21, 25, 221, 231, and below).

[242] Elihu may **seem** to be warning Job that he risks eternal condemnation, but Job is clearly one of *the righteous* (36:6-7, cf. n. 234) who is out of fellowship with God, and repentance in response to God's voice would *deliver* him (36:15, n. 25) from dying prematurely—a key theme of Ps 95. This speaks to the issue of how God deals with the disobedient believer and echoes warnings in Heb 2:1-4; 3:7-19; 5:11-6:8; 10:26-31; 12:25-29; Jas 1:13-15; and 1 John 5:16. Job's bitterness and vindictive spirit had seriously compromised his devotion and fellowship (cf. Heb 12:14-17). Thus, Elihu is promising full restoration to both vitality (36:11, cf. 33:25-30) and fellowship (cf. 33:23-28; 35:16; 36:15-16; and nn. 46, 231) if Job will repent of his all-consuming vindictive disposition. See further Zane Hodges, *Harmony with God—a Fresh Look at Repentance* (Dallas, TX: Redención Viva, 2001).

paid to restore him (36:18).[244] For even if Job on his own could restore his *wealth* and *all* his strength, it *would not* keep him from *distress* (36:19, cf. NIV). Elihu therefore warns him not to pursue *the night, when people are cut off in their place* (36:20)—an allusion to the grim fate of *hypocrites* who refuse to seek God's *help* (cf. 36:13-14). Job should *take heed* and *not turn to iniquity,* for *this* is what he has *chosen* by clutching self-sufficiency in his pride *rather than* humbly hearing from God in his *affliction* (36:21).[245]

Elihu thus concludes by exhorting Job again to consider God's great *power* (36:22a), learn from His unparalled *teaching* (36:22b), and acknowledge the futility of trying to second-guess His inscrutable *ways* (36:23).[246] Elihu reminds Job instead to *magnify*

---

[243] Heb. *sepheq* is a *hapax* of dubious origin (BDB, 706d), variously translated as *riches*, *scoffing* (or *mockery*), *blow* (or *stroke*), or *chastisement*. However, if the word is actually the textual variant *śepheq* (BDB, 974a) as in 20:22, where Zophar argues that Job's *plenty* or *self-sufficiency* (NKJV) would not protect him from *distress*, then it should be rendered the same in 36:18. Elihu may well have plagiarized Zophar's last speech (20:22; cf. n. 105), using the same words *self-sufficiency* (36:18) and *distress* (36:16, 19) to expose Job's self-sufficient disposition in response to adversity. The context suggests that this indeed is Elihu's emphasis (36:19, cf. 36:9b, n. 235). The sense is that Job had let his self-righteous anger get the best of him to this point, insisting on vindicating himself before God rather than swallowing his pride to accept God's life-giving ransom.

[244] The word ransom (*kōpher*) occurs in Job only here and in 33:24, again suggesting a direct connection (n. 236). The difficult Heb. of 36:18 reads lit. "For wrath—lest it entice you to self-sufficiency [n. 243] and do not let greatness of ransom turn you aside." The sense is that Job's pride is keeping him from accepting God's redemptive offer (cf. 33:23-30); Elihu is now appealing for Job to accept the *great ransom* (cf. 33:24).

[245] The figure "choosing affliction" alludes to the initial affirmation of this pericope that *affliction* is meant to *open their ears* (36:15, NRSV; n. 236). The injunction to *not turn to iniquity* ironically recalls the conclusion to Job's prior reflection on the value of wisdom—to *fear the Lord* and *depart from evil* (28:28). Job's self-sufficiency is hardly consistent with the *fear of God*, which is the real issue at stake in Job's angry demands (chaps. 29-31): His full restoration to righteous agency (cf. 33:26, n. 201) depends on whether he **persists** in his proud self-sufficiency (36:21a, cf. n. 243) or humbly **listens** for God's wisdom in his *affliction* (36:21b, cf. 36:15). The same choice is posed in Eccl 7:8-14, which contrasts the devastating consequences of nursing one's anger in response to oppression with the rich wisdom that attends humble submission to God's sovereign purposes (cf. nn. 151, 160 and related text). For the remainder of Elihu's speech (36:22-37:24) the obvious hope is that Job will choose the latter alternative.

[246] Ironically, Job's logic regarding the futility of second-guessing God's judgments is now thrown back at him. Elihu's rhetorical question *Who has assigned Him His way, Or...said, 'You have done wrong'?* (36:23) echoes Job's own response to Bildad, *who can hinder Him? Who can say to Him, 'What are You doing?'* (9:12). Cf. also 34:29, 37; 35:16.

His work, which *men* like him have readily observed and celebrated (36:24-25). To substantiate his exhortation Elihu draws Job's attention to God's inscrutable command over the elements (36:26-30), by which He executes His sovereign judgment, depicted by lightning (36:31-32). Elihu closes with a touch of sarcasm: *God's thunder announces* His impending judgment; *even the cattle* take note (36:33, NIV).[247] The allusion to *thunder* serves as a literary transition by introducing the theme of *God's voice* (chap. 37), which in turn anticipates His impending appearance out of the thunderstorm to confront Job verbally (chap. 38).

2. God Rules through His Instruction; *Listen to* His Voice (37:1-24)
Given that God's main purpose in Job's suffering was to focus Job's attention on His sovereign rule (cf. 36:1-33), Elihu now clarifies what God intends to teach Job. The order of the "storm" imagery is now reversed: God's presence displays *lightning* first—signifying His judgments—to create an expectation of *thunder* to follow (37:3-4), so that God's creatures will listen attentively to what He speaks (37:2, 5-8). This order governs the textual design: Once God gets man's attention with His judgments He speaks in the elements, *that all men may know His work* and be prepared to heed His instruction (37:1-8). Job is to be so confident of God's sovereign yet inscrutable rule over all creation (37:9-13) that he will stop presumptuously second-guessing the purposes of God (37:14-20) and instead fear God in appreciation of His powerful but excellent judgment (37:21-24).

Elihu is excited to heart-skipping awe in anticipation of God's thunder following the execution of His sovereign judgments (37:1, cf. 36:33) and invites Job also to *listen closely to the thunder of His voice* (37:2, NASB). God *sends...His lightning to the ends of the earth* in advance of the *thunder* of His *majestic voice*—He holds nothing back, so that[248] *His voice* may be *heard* (37:3-4). *God thunders with His voice* and accomplishes His inscrutable purposes

---

[247] The contextual sense of the difficult Heb. is best reflected in NIV: The implication is that if *even the cattle* are unsettled by the impending judgment announced by thunder, surely Job should also take note of the obvious warning, repent of his obstinate self-sufficiency, learn from his affliction, and accept God's provision to avert the impending threat of premature death (cf. 36:17-21 and related notes). Virtually the same object lesson is repeated in 37:8.

[248] The opening *kî* in the last clause of 37:4 is rendered with temporal force ("after") in NKJV, NASB, NIV, NRSV. However, the context suggests a preferable *modal* sense for the verb and *telic* sense for *kî* to explain the purpose for lightning's wide distribution (37:3), "*so that* his voice *may be* heard."

when[249] He commands the elements (37:5-6) to direct the acts of men, *that* they *may know His work* (37:7)[250] and obey as instinctively as *the beasts* (37:8).[251] He orchestrates the elements (37:9-12a) to *do whatever He commands them* to carry out His worldwide, mutually contingent purposes (37:12b-13).[252]

Elihu therefore invites Job to *stand still and consider the wondrous works of God* (37:14, cf. 36:24) and sarcastically exposes Job's ignorance of the complexity of God's creative rule (37:15-18).[253] How absurd to suggest that a man who is in *darkness* should argue his case before God who is *perfect in knowledge* (cf. 34:23; 36:4; 37:16b) and thereby risk being *swallowed up* (37:19-20)! Accordingly,[254] just as *no one can look at the sun, bright in the* sky

---

[249] In this context, the opening *kî* in 37:6 is occasional ("when") and not causal (as in NKJV, NASB, RSV).

[250] The NKJV or NASB *He seals the hand of every man, that all men may know His work* accurately reflects the sense of the Heb. This is the central concept of the chapter: God intends to carry out His inscrutable purposes through the obedience of mankind, and His control over nature directs men in order to realize these purposes.

[251] Elihu displays sarcasm here, using dumb beasts as an object lesson (cf. 36:33, n. 247) to teach God's intelligent but stiff-necked human agents the obvious logic of also submitting to God's voice.

[252] Elihu asserts (37:13) that *He causes it to come* [or *makes it happen*], *Whether for correction, Or for his land, Or for mercy*, implying that God's control over the elements serves inscrutable overarching purposes that contribute to the coherent out-working of His sovereign plan. Such purposes could include *correction* (as was Job's current need), or *for His land* (as in the many prophetic judgments on Israel and her neighbors throughout history), or *for mercy* (as when God delivers man from the consequences of his sin, cf. 33:18, 25, 28-30). Although man often cannot fathom the purposes that God serves with His specific judgments in nature (cf. 34:29 [n. 218]; 36:26, 29; 37:5b; and Eccl 11:1-6), they nevertheless point man to the transcendent design in God's absolute rule (cf. 36:24-25; 37:7b; 37:14; Eccl 3:11, 14-15; n. 196; and Isa 55:8-11). In contrast to Job's other friends, Elihu viewed Job's suffering not as punishment but as part of a much broader sovereign plan (cf. 34:29; 36:26). Ironically, Job himself had previously refuted Bildad by citing the same truth about God's inscrutable rule (26:14, n. 140).

[253] Elihu's rhetorical questions in 37:15-20—like those of God Himself in 38:4-38—are laced with sarcasm to underscore the presumption of demanding that God listen to Job's advice on how to improve His justice. Such sarcasm regarding Job's intrusion into the inscrutable may strike the reader as crass and unfeeling; in fact, it was the most gracious way of drawing Job's attention to his need to repent (cf. 36:9-11; n. 236). Similarly, when Christ was told about the deaths that occurred in two recent calamities (cf. Luke 13:1-5, n. 55), he left them unexplained yet bluntly warned them of their own liability to judgment and consequent need for repentance. (See also the excellent discussions of this point by Carson, *How Long, O Lord?* 66-8, and Paul Tournier, *A Listening Ear* [Minneapolis: Augsburg, 1987], 85-6.)

[254] The phrase *wᵉ 'attâ* ("and now") completes the logic begun in 37:14 and is therefore to be read inferentially ("now, therefore," BDB 774b[2b]), rendered here as "accordingly" to introduce the understood analogy, "[just as]…, [so]…."

after the wind has swept it *clean,* so *God comes in awesome majesty* (37:21-22, NIV), *the Almighty—we cannot* figure *Him* out;[255] *He is exalted in power* and does not violate *justice* or *abundant righteousness* (37:23, NASB). *Therefore, men* should *fear Him*; He pays no attention to those who are wise in their own eyes (37:24; cf. 28:28).[256]

By challenging Job's understanding of God's sovereign control over the elements, Elihu aimed to further unmask Job's presumption. Elihu understood what was truly at stake in light of Job's self-sufficient disposition—how critical it was for him to submit to God's power and learn from God's instruction as His accountable servant (cf. 1:6-2:10). In the same way the author aims to convince readers who might also presume to challenge God's justice in suffering that they also should repent of their self-sufficiency and instead fear God. As the inspired mediator between Job and God (cf. 32:18-33:6) Elihu has thus completed his instruction on mankind's appropriate response to God amid suffering. His admonition—especially the sarcastic and humiliating tirade in 37:14-20—is ideally suited to prepare Job and the self-sufficient reader to face God's own impending challenge in chaps. 38-41.[257]

---

[255] The analogy is between man's inability to gaze directly at the unobscured sun and his equal incapacity to discern God directly from His acts in the world. Elihu is therefore justified in exhorting Job to appreciate His *wondrous works* (37:14) without trying to "figure Him out" (*māṣā'*, "find out"), i.e., figure out what He is "up to" (37:23a)—the inscrutability of His work does not mitigate His righteousness or justice (cf. 34:29)

[256] MT reads "he does not see all the wise of heart." The context would imply that "wise of heart" is clearly pejorative (cf. "overly wise," Eccl 7:16), at apparent odds with the favorable connotation of similar constructions elsewhere in the OT, such as Prov 11:29 (Hartley, *The Book of Job*, 483-4 [fn. 3]). However, such favorable instances are likely distinct (cf. *heart of the wise*, Eccl 7:4; 8:5) from what Elihu intends here. Elihu is insinuating that Job's fear of God had given way to self-sufficient wisdom (cf. Job 28:28, n. 151), so that the label *wise of heart* was likely Elihu's ironic allusion to Job's own prior warning: God who is *wise in heart* will not be successfully *defied* (9:4, NASB)—not even by the likes of Job who is *wise of heart* (37:24b).

[257] Elihu's irony and sarcasm anticipate the tone of the ensuing Yahweh speeches (chaps. 38-41) in promoting humble repentance (cf. n. 253). Tournier thus echoes Elihu's thrust in appealing for
> an attitude of humility. The humility to recognize that there are no answers to the problems in our minds....[T]he leader of a Muslim sect...once said to a journalist who asked him if suffering came from God, "I do not permit myself to ask that question." That is a lesson for us, and entirely within the biblical perspective. God has mysteries. God has secrets which we cannot penetrate. In fact I ought to be silent....I speak in order to point out that there is no answer, that the...line is not to penetrate the mysteries of God, but to bow before them. (*A Listening Ear*, 88). See also Charles Swindoll, *The Mystery of God's Will* (Nashville: Word Books, 1999).

Act III

CREATOR IN CONTROL

*"Would you condemn Me that
you may be justified?"*

Job Confronted by a Sovereign God
(Job 38:1-42:6)

*In dramatizing YHWH's challenge to Job's legal standing to take God to court and in Job's repentant response to this challenge, **the author affirms that God's perfect justice is guaranteed by His all-wise and all-powerful rule over all creation and the forces of evil**, so that readers might repent of self-sufficient strategies to mitigate suffering and injustice, and instead trust in God's sovereign control and submit to His sovereign prerogatives.*

This section consists of two parallel speeches by YHWH that affirm His sovereign control over all creation (38:1-40:5) and the powers of evil (40:6-42:6). The speeches each consist of 1) a formal reply and legal challenge to Job's charges (38:1-3; 40:1-2, 6-14); 2) transparent examples of God's total awareness and control that magnify Job's total inadequacy (38:4-39:30; 40:15-41:34); and 3) Job's brief response (40:3-5; 42:1-6). The text comprises a straightforward legal argument: For Job to convict God of injustice he must be able to cite the evidence and then enforce the verdict himself; i.e., govern all Creation and overrule the powers of evil. Job can't even begin to claim such capability, so his lawsuit is rendered moot and withdrawn for lack of standing.

Even though Elihu had cogently addressed all the salient theological points to be made in the YHWH speeches, God still appears and speaks.[258] Elihu had effectively disarmed Job's claim of injustice by expanding his perspective on the vast scope of God's inscrutable yet just rule over evil oppressors (34:1-33); he incisively challenged Job's self-righteous pride (33:8-13; 35:1-15) and bold presumption to ascribe motives to inscrutable events (34:34-37; 35:16); and he brilliantly revealed God's redemptive plan and righteous power to execute it (33:14-30; 36:1-37:22). Since the text strongly insinuates that Job could not refute Elihu's contentions, one may well ask, What further purpose is served by YHWH's direct intrusion into the theological exchange?

Elihu had clearly argued that his own speeches were inspired (cf. 32:17-33:4) and that God's character was self-evident from His work of Creation (cf. 36:24ff), so it is not at all clear that God's speeches were

---

[258] Habel ("The Design of Yahweh's Speeches," reprinted in Zuck [ed.], *Sitting with Job*, 413) observes that "God's earlier silence, the wager of the prologue which has never been disclosed to Job, and the traditional theology of Elihu, which provides a legitimate answer for Job, prepares the audience for the appropriate silence of God. To our surprise God does appear and does speak."

needed to corroborate Elihu's teaching *per se*. In fact these speeches don't even recapitulate the central focus of Elihu's teaching; that is, God's persistent desire to instruct Job through affliction, thereby redeeming him from self-sufficiency and restoring him to fruitful service.[259] Some readers are understandably frustrated that God did not reveal to Job what led to his suffering.[260] However, this would have nullified Elihu's key point about the inscrutability of God's rule (chap. 34) and subverted Elihu's goals for Job and the author's purposes for the reader:[261] to elicit the fear of God and invite repentance in response to God's inscrutable—yet completely just and redemptive—design for all creation (cf. 37:13-24).

Rather, Job's silence in response to Elihu's rebuttal implies that Elihu had in fact argued effectively (cf. 33:5, 32-33) but was still unable to elicit Job's confession and repentance. This suggests that YHWH's entry into the controversy was occasioned by the continued resilience of Job's pride. The most conspicuous clue that this is the case can be found in the tone of the YHWH speeches—they are laden with irony and deep sarcasm.[262] While Elihu approached Job cautiously as he logically exposed Job's presumption and self-righteous pride, YHWH very bluntly skewers Job with the utter absurdity of consigning the Creator of the universe to the narrowly focused mission of vindicating Job and relieving his suffering. Thus, God's vicious sarcasm completely withers Job's angry attitude of victimization and entitlement and deflates the impact of his lawsuit that was rooted in self-sufficient resolve.

By removing these barriers to authentic mourning, God's intrusion can be viewed as opening the door to Job's repentance and restoration

---

[259] *See* 33:14-33; 36:6-23; and nn. 234, 243, 245.

[260] Carson (*How Long, O Lord?* 173) suggests that the disappointment of intellectuals like George Bernard Shaw and Elie Wiesel with God's failure to justify Job's suffering stems from their assumption

> that everything that takes place in God's universe ought to be explained to us…, that there cannot possibly be any good reason for God not to tell us everything we want to know immediately. They assume that God Almighty should be more interested in giving us explanations than in being worshipped and trusted.

Such responses to the plain implication of God's speeches are rooted in a thoroughly humanistic response to suffering (n. 51). See also Yancey, *Disappointment with God*, 291-3, and Tournier, *A Listening Ear*, 92.

[261] Dwelling on the cause of Job's suffering would not "silence the reader" with the impact of Job's direct experience of God (n. 55) or challenge the self-righteous, "victimized" sufferer to repentance (cf. n. 240).

[262] The subtle irony and sarcasm woven into Elihu's speeches (cf. nn. 199, 212, 226, 241, 246, 251-253, 256-257) pales in comparison with that of YHWH's blunt and overpowering rejoinder to Job's charges.

(36:17-21). However, if God's speeches in effect force a recalcitrant Job into submission, it would hardly seem a "fair" way to win the wager with Satan; how could such blatant coercion meet the prescribed contingency of Job's **voluntary** loyalty (cf. 1:8-11; 2:3-5)? And how would the scathing and punitive tone of God's speeches possibly promote faithful stewardship? In the final analysis, although such methods seem unreasonably harsh they are perfectly designed to meet Job at his point of deepest need.

The problem is resolved when we recognize God's appearance as a **forensic** response to Job's litigious presumption.[263] In order to secure Job's complicity in his rebellion, Satan had exploited Job's misconception of God's justice and man's righteousness. But when Job demanded a hearing before God in court—challenging God's justice—he also committed to know God more intimately. By acceding to his demand, God condescends to battle Job in the arena of litigation yet still reveals Himself as completely sovereign over Creation while also honoring Job as His intended steward.[264] When God cites irrefutable evidence and prevails as Defendant (chaps. 38-41), Job truly "sees" God and mourns (42:1-6), so that God defeats Satan's rebellion by completely reversing his deception. Now freed from bitterness, Job can rest in God's sovereign control to serve confidently as His chosen agent (42:7-9) and inherit the abundant blessing reserved for his obedience (42:10-17).

---

[263] "Matching [Job's] request in 13:22, Yahweh in 38:3 and again in 40:7 challenges Job to participate in a lawsuit....The author of Job draws on the forensic usage of the request to 'gird the loins' [to show] that Job is challenged to oppose God" (Scholnick, "The Meaning of *Mišpāṭ*," 355-6). See also nn. 172, 215.

[264] Scholnick ("Poetry in the Courtroom: Job 38-41," reprinted in Zuck, ed., *Sitting with Job*, 423) pinpoints the ironic power of YHWH's condescension to appear in court:

> Paradoxically, by entering the court of law, God has the opportunity to lead Job beyond the narrow confines of this legal order to...the divine perspective. By accepting accountability in man's forensic forum for what Job charges is injustice in his role as Judge of mankind, God enlightens the hero about his design for the cosmos where human juridical categories cease to be central and where man must assume accountability for his proper role in the Lord's kingdom.

YHWH's condescension reflects the redemptive self-effacement of Christ (cf. Phil 2:5-11), and Job's change in disposition after the legal confrontation reflects Jacob's transformation after wrestling with God (Gen 32).

— 13 —

A. God's All-Wise Rule over Creation (38:1–40:5)

*With YHWH's deeply sarcastic reaffirmation of His all-inclusive aware-
ness and control over both inanimate and animate creation,* **the author
discredits any attempt to indict God for ignoring unjust suffering**, *so that
readers might confide in God's infinitely wise government and His care
and concern for them and then reflect on their own role in God's creative
purposes.*

The textual design follows a three step pattern that continues the legal
metaphor of the argument: challenge (38:1-3; 40:1-2), substantiation (38:4-
39:30), and response (40:3-5). God challenges Job's charge that God is
unjust or unaware with the countercharge that Job himself is ignorant (38:1-
3). God substantiates His countercharge in a withering deposition that
reveals Job's complete lack of evidence to substantiate his charges and vindicate himself (38:4-40:2). When Job concedes that he has no legal standing to sue God (40:3-5), God as the prevailing Defendant is then "free" as
Judge to teach Job about His sovereign chain of command (40:6-41:34).
When Job repents and retracts all charges (42:1-6), God the Judge then
delivers His judgment (42:7-9).

Job had previously impugned God's wisdom by implying that God was
unaware of Job's innocent suffering and would surely respond if He would
only pay attention and take note of Job's resilient righteousness amid suffering.[265] Now God finally appears and immediately surfaces what should
have been obvious—that it is **Job** who was not paying attention—by challenging his ignorant presumption that he could possibly teach God anything
(38:1-3). God cites example after example of Job's dwarfed understanding
of what should be plainly evident in all Creation: God's intelligent design
and sustaining care (38:4-39:30). Overwhelmed by the irrefutable evidence
that God is completely aware and involved, Job can marshal no evidence to
answer God's repeated challenge (40:1-5).

God's appearance and direct confrontation accomplish two purposes
for Job that have direct relevance to the reader. First, even with no explanation for Job's suffering, the very **fact** of God's appearance should convince Job that He cares enough about him as Creator to respond to his
attempt to find Him—it is the ultimate confirmation of his value as God's

---

[265] Cf. 13:15-19, 22; 23:3-12; 31:35-37.

agent and should gain his attention to God's redemptive goals, of which Elihu had duly apprised him (33:14-33; 36:5-16). Then, the **content** of God's speech is designed to assure Job of the universal scope of his awareness and control over the created order, so that Job need no longer be concerned about the ultimate solution to what so far appears totally **out** of control—his unmitigated suffering. To thus assure Job is to give him enough security in God to relinquish his demand for vindication and the relief of his suffering. Job's reply to the incontrovertible evidence against him is the only logical "legal" response: "no contest" (40:3-5).

1. God Confronts Job's Ignorant Presumption (38:1–3)

The immediately preceding imagery *"Out of the north he comes in golden splendor; God comes in awesome majesty"* (37:22, NASB) serves to introduce God who now appears to *answer Job out of the whirlwind* [266] (38:1). Elihu had criticized Job's ignorant speculation concerning the basis for God's judgments (cf. 34:37; 36:21; 37:19-20); Job had claimed knowledge he did not possess (cf. 34:35; 35:16), and God now confirms it: *"Who is this who darkens counsel by words without knowledge?"* (38:2). YHWH takes on the role of Attorney for the Defense and challenges Job to *brace* himself *like a man* (38:3, NIV) for a tough deposition designed to expose the foolish presumption of his final appeal[267]—the absurdity of charging God with unlawful seizure.[268]

Elihu had laid the foundation for God's challenge when he made it clear that God does not need to hear man's testimony in order to judge fairly (cf. 34:21-30; 37:19-20). Thus, Elihu had already exposed the foolish presumption of Job's claim that God had ignored his cries for justice, arguing that Job's insistence on taking the case to trial is thoroughly misguided (cf. 34:34-37; 35:12-16); this will be duly corroborated in God's withering deposition (38:4-39:30). More importantly, however, by deigning to appear at all and formally responding to Job's charges, God ironically shows Job the respect

---

[266] God's sovereign appearance *out of the whirlwind* ($s^{e'}\bar{a}r\hat{a}$, so also in Ezek 1:4) accords with Elihu's prior depiction of God's presence as a *storm* or *whirlwind* ($s\hat{u}ph\hat{a}$, 37:9).

[267] *See* the exposition of chaps. 29-31 and related notes, esp. 149; 155; 172.

[268] Scholnick (ibid., 426-29) argues effectively that this is the thrust of God's interrogation:

> God dismisses through a series of cross-examining interrogatories any possible prior claim to title that Job might make....The creator has original title. If Job cannot establish his participation in the work of creation, he would have no grounds for any claim to the property he has charged was unlawfully seized [ibid., 427].

due a valued servant: He honors the integrity Job displayed in doggedly pursuing a deeper understanding of the God he has misperceived.[269]

2. God Challenges Job's Knowledge about Creation (38:4–39:30)

YHWH's deposition is designed to preempt Job's lawsuit by proving that he lacks the evidence needed to bring his case to trial. The text consists of a series of rhetorical questions that repeatedly challenge Job to disclose how the created order is sustained in its two principal spheres: the inanimate cosmos (38:4-38) and all animate Creation (38:39-39:30). God's repeated invitation to *Tell Me, if you have understanding* (38:4b, 18b) echoes Elihu's previous invitation (33:5, 32) and evokes the same conspicuous silence,[270] thus stripping Job of any legal standing to sue God. But in this process YHWH also cites enough evidence of His creating and sustaining activity to affirm that He can indeed complete His creative purposes for Job (cf. 10:3-18). The evidence is sufficient to instill in Job the obedient fear of God; the question is, Will Job respond appropriately?

God first confirms His comprehensive awareness and rule over **inanimate** Creation by echoing Elihu's rhetorical questions (37:14-18) affirming God's absolute control of the elements to execute His purposes.[271] The activities God cites in displaying His absolute rule bear witness to His orderly Creation and government over the inanimate cosmos, yet with no clue as to how He "pulls it off." Job is interrogated with scathing sarcasm:[272] *Who laid the foundations of the earth* and contained *the sea* (38:4-11); can *you* manage *the wicked* (12-15) by gaining access to the *gates of death* or the *dwelling of light* and *darkness* or the *expanse of earth* or the *storehouses* of elements *reserved for the time of trouble* (16-23, NRSV)? *Who* marshals the resources that bring forth life (24-30); can *you* govern *the constellations* or dictate *the laws of the heavens* in order to exercise *dominion over the earth* (31-38, NIV)?

God then expands on Elihu's earlier affirmation of the exemplary

---

[269] This was the transparent motivation of Job's questioning in 7:11-21; 10; 13:20-14:22; 16:18-17:16.

[270] Cf. n. 184 and related exposition.

[271] Job had previously questioned this truth (cf. n. 269). YHWH's description of His command over the elements closely follows Elihu's own exposition (cf. 34:13-30; 36:27-37:24).

[272] Four groups of rhetorical questions are distinguished by predominating pronoun and arranged in alternate parallel (*Who; you/Who; you*), beginning with the particle *Where…?* (38:4, 24). The four groups portray: a) God's original **design** of Creation (38:4-11); b) His orchestration of cosmic resources to **manage** an unruly Creation (12-23) and c) bring forth new life to **sustain** Creation (24-30); and d) His *wisdom* to **govern** the *heavens* (31-38).

obedience of *animals* to the voice of God[273] in order to challenge Job's grasp of the design of **animate** Creation (38:39-39:30): The examples chosen naturally reflect God's unfailing sustenance of all His creatures as they accomplish their appointed purpose: Job is again interrogated (but less severely) regarding *who provides food for* wild animals and *when...they deliver their offspring* (38:39-39:4); how *wild* beasts *serve* as God intends (39:5-12), even the stupid *ostrich,* whose *labor is in vain* (13-18); how the noble warhorse *mocks at fear* (19-25); and how the bird of prey *spies out* its *prey* (26-30).

God's heavy use of irony and sarcasm to expose Job's total inability to govern or even fathom Creation implies that his main problem in God's eyes was not as much the misattribution of his suffering as his proud self-sufficiency. God's questions concerning inanimate Creation prove Job's charge of injustice to be unfounded in light of God's total awareness and absolute rule.[274] Yet God also intends to rescue man and restore to him vitality, as Elihu had affirmed (33:14-30; 36:1-21), and this in turn clarifies why God also questioned Job regarding animate creation: If God so intentionally accomplishes His preordained purposes for far **lesser** creatures,[275] much more will He endeavor to realize Job's own appointed purpose,[276] so why not give up contending against

---

[273] *See* 36:33 and 37:8; cf. nn. 247, 251.

[274] God's speech was intended to replace Job's obsession to see justice done with full confidence in God's perfect control over Creation. As Scholnick explains ("Poetry in the Courtroom," 430):

> He does this first by describing his primary role in the universe as that of King rather than Judge, so that the hero can realize that the treatment he is receiving from God is not the result of a juridical decision but an administrative one. And second, God answers the complaint that he acted unjustly by defining for Job the true nature of divine justice as sovereignty. The redefinition frees the hero to see the divine action as the prerogative of the Ruler.

[275] Even God's heavy sarcasm and irony cannot mask the message of His tender care in this portion of His speech; indeed, it seems to echo the reassuring truth of Matt 6:26-30 and 10:29-31.

[276] God's intentionality with respect to the animals in Job 38:39-39:30 reflects His original design to entrust the dominion of his Creation to man (cf. Gen 1-2; Ps 8; Heb 2:5-9; and n. 20). The activities God prescribes bear witness to the kinds of activity He originally intended for man as His agent—to *be fruitful and multiply* and then *subdue* and *have dominion* (Gen 1:28-30). Carnivores *hunt prey for* their *young* (38:39-41); herbivores *bear young* (39:1-4); *wild* beasts of burden wait to be domesticated (39:5-12); even the ostrich's *eggs* survive and bear *her young* (39:14, 16). *The horse and rider* (39:18b) depict the harnessed *strength* of the warhorse, exemplifying God's *majesty* and *power* (39:19-25, cf. 37:22-23) as He exercises His dominion through man. The *eyes* that *spy out prey* from *on high* (39:27-29) symbolize His sovereign vigilance to see that it is done (cf. Ezek 1:4 [q.v. *whirlwind*, n. 266] and 18 [q.v. *eyes*]).

God's preordained calling like the contrary ostrich?[277]

3. Job Claims "I am Insignificant" and Keeps Silent (40:1–5)

God again dares Job, *who contends*[278] *with the Almighty,* to *answer* His questions (40:1-2, cf. 38:3)—just **try** and negate the overwhelming evidence that refutes Job's charge of unlawful seizure. Job merely replies that he is *insignificant*[279] (40:3-4a): His knowledge is dwarfed by God's creative wisdom; his claim is buried in the vast array of God's sovereign concerns. He capitulates by vowing that he will no longer *answer* God or even speak at all (40:4b-5, cf. 31:37), not because he has given up his defiance (cf. 34:37) but because he has no hope of contending with God, just as he feared (cf. 9:14-15). The sense at this point is thus that Job is sulking rather than repenting.

Job's self-denigration as *insignificant* is completely at odds with the thrust of God's first speech—His highly intentional care for all creatures and the key role He designed for man to superintend His Creation.[280] Job is thus more important than he is willing to acknowledge but still reluctant to accept his role as God's chosen mediator of blessing.[281] The reader is to recognize the sulking obstinacy of Job's self-denigration: Job concedes God's total awareness of his circumstances but still does not confess his self-righteous pride, which thus provokes YHWH's second speech. If the

---

[277] Flapping its wings *wildly, though its pinions lack* [the stork's] *plumage* (cf. NRSV), the ostrich reflects the noisy futility of Job's presumptuous charges (39:13). The neglect of her offspring stems from her innate lack of wisdom (39:14-17), thus portraying Job's foolish preoccupation with vindication which only distracts him from God's commission that he be a steward over created life (notes 24, 25). *When she lifts herself* and *scorns the horse and rider* (39:18) she defies God's power and majesty (39:19-25, n. 276), an ironic caricature of Job's futile contention in rejecting his own preordained calling (cp. 40:2 and Eccl 6:10-11, cf. n. 173) to be God's agent of redemption.

[278] The verb *rîb* ("dispute in court") again invites an *answer* (cf. 38:3; n. 263) and thus serves to delineate this section from the preceding one as Job's formal legal response to God's deposition; see Scholnick (*Poetry in the Courtroom*, 424) on this use of *rîb* in 40:2, as also in 10:2; 13:6; 19; 23:6; 31:35; 33:13.

[279] Job is not admitting sin here. NKJV reads *I am vile*, but a more appropriate rendering is *I am insignificant* [Heb. *qālal*] (NASB, cf. Zuck, *Job*, 175 [fn. 27]).

[280] Job is claiming that he can play no significant role in light of God's admittedly all-inclusive administration of the entire universe. But this is tantamount to negating mankind's creation commission (cf. n. 276); it is no wonder that YHWH proceeds to escalate His sarcasm in His ensuing speech.

[281] Cf. chap. 29 and n. 157. Note again the parallel with Jonah's notorious reluctance as God's chosen agent (cf. n. 221).

readers were to accept Job's silence as a sign of appropriate humility and fear in response to YHWH's first speech, then it makes no sense for God to intensify Job's humiliation in the following speech.[282]

---

[282] "Because Job did not admit to…sin, God found it necessary to continue with a second speech, to speak not only once, but twice" in response to Job's claim (Zuck, ibid., 175, cf. 40:5b). This is a testimony to the resilience of Job's pride but should hearten the reader, for if by this point God did not give up on Job—with all his arrogant presumption—He will not give up His efforts to restore any ordinary person (cf. 33:14-30).

— 14 —

B. God's All-Powerful Rule over Evil (40:6–42:6)

*In God's display of absolute control over humanly invincible creatures, **the author affirms the negligible impact of human self-righteousness on evil in the world but depicts God's sovereignty as secure against Satan's rebellion**, so that readers might—like Job—repent, forsake self-righteous pride and presumption, and rely on God alone to instruct them in adversity.*

God's first speech had shifted Job's focus to God's absolute rule, subordinating the apparent injustice of his confiscated estate to God's greater dominion over all Creation. The imagery was designed to underscore Job's role as God's chosen agent of dominion, and God expected more than a plea of "no contest" in response to His implicit invitation for Job to accept that role. The second speech thus repeats the three step design of challenge (40:6-14), substantiation (40:15-41:34), and response (42:1-6) but is imbued with more intense sarcasm to expose the arrogant presumption[283] of Job's claim that his own righteousness exceeded God's (40:8).[284]

God now affirms what Elihu had suggested more diplomatically,[285] that it is absurd for Job to think he could ever justify himself at God's expense (40:6-14; cf. 32:2). This is substantiated with *a fortiori* reasoning that unmasks Job's presumption: In order to justifiably discredit God's justice yet still deliver himself from affliction (cf. 40:14), Job must himself be able to subdue and control all the evil forces sustaining his affliction. However, Job's power is in fact totally eclipsed by the forces of evil, signified by the most indomitable of God's creatures; yet these same forces are completely subordinate and submissive to God's sovereign rule (40:15-41:34). Thus confronted with his hopelessly inadequate wisdom

---

[283] Of all the themes mentioned in the second YHWH speech, the *subjugation of pride* is conspicuous at the beginning (40:11-12) and end (41:34, cf. 41:15) and is probably the predominant theme by inclusion. It is therefore not surprising that YHWH resorts to such a conspicuous "rhetoric of humiliation" to address Job's problem (cf. nn. 257, 262).

[284] Cf. 13:13-19; 19:21-29; 21:7-21; 23:10-12; 30:1-15; 31:35-37; 33:8-13; 34:5-9; 35:2-13; 36:17-21.

[285] After patiently reassuring Job of God's care and justice (chaps. 32-34) in the face of human pride (33:17), Elihu explicitly confronted Job with his own pride (35:2-8, 12; n. 262). Thus, Job's silence could not be blamed on lack of knowledge; it was his undiminished self-righteous pride that prompted God to speak.

and righteousness in light of God's absolute command of all Creation (38:1-40:5) and control over all evil (40:6-41:34), Job finally retracts his charges and repents (42:1-6).

The bluntly preemptive sarcasm of YHWH's speech is transparently aimed at disillusioned but stubbornly self-righteous readers who are blind to their own hypocrisy and rebellion[286] against God's purposes for them as chosen agents. The underlying issue at stake is: Will Job—or anyone else who suffers unjustly—trust God to overcome evil?[287] Ironically, the two beasts exemplify the fitting response God seeks before the suffering agent can be restored to faithful service: Like Behemoth, we must be "tamed" to submit only to God's direction; but like Leviathan, our pride must first be subordinated to God's sovereign will. Thus, when Job finally acknowledges his self-righteous pride, his repentance releases him to fulfill his preordained purpose as God's chosen agent (42:1-6)—he can finally mediate the redemption of his friends and in turn be restored to full vitality[288] (42:7-17). The self-righteous reader is invited to follow suit.

1. God Confronts Job's Self-Righteous Presumption (40:6–14)

The second speech is set apart by the same opening marker as the first (40:6).[289] One last time God calls on Job to *answer* Him (40:7, cf. 38:3, 4b, 18b; 40:2b) and He identifies Job's self-righteous presumption: that he would *discredit* God's *justice* and *condemn* God in order to *justify* himself

---

[286] Job's hypocrisy was overtly demonstrated in his summary appeal before God (cf. nn. 168, 171). Whereas Elihu was more discreet in apprising Job of his need and of the role of suffering in getting his attention (33:14-30; 36:8-21), now the "gloves are off." The reader who bristles at the ostensible insensitivity, even cruelty, of YHWH's sarcastic confrontation would probably not blush nearly as much at the vehemence of Christ's excoriation of the Pharisees, whose hypocrisy was so much more obvious (cf. Matt 15:1-20; 23:1-33; and n. 174).

[287] From God's initial wager with Satan the main thread of dramatic irony has consisted of repeated literary insinuations of human and angelic collusion with Satan's subversive agenda (cf. nn. 19, 20, 38, 40, 41, 60, 65, 84, 90, 108, 137, 152, 182, 209). YHWH's second speech, with its sarcastic invitation for Job to exercise power and authority over the *proud* and *wicked* (40:11-12), now exposes how easily Satan has been able to suborn Job's complicity with his subversive agenda and unmasks such collusion as a flagrant counterfeit of the human coregency God originally intended (n. 20).

[288] *See* nn. 20, 23, 27. Elihu had predicted such restoration in very explicit terms (33:25-30; 36:11, 16).

[289] *Then the LORD answered Job out of the whirlwind, and said…* (cf. 38:1; n. 266).

(40:8, NIV).[290] God's second challenge naturally follows: Job must clearly possess his own power to execute judgment against evil (40:9-13) if he refuses to trust in God's power to *save* him from the powers of evil that afflict him (40:14), which was God's clear intention.[291] Job is therefore derisively challenged to *adorn* himself like God *with majesty and splendor* (40:10)[292] and judge the *proud* and the *wicked* (40:11-13); only then would YHWH concede that Job's righteous power could *save* him (40:14). The following section then proves that Job's miniscule power is absolutely incapable of backing up his judgments (40:15-41:34).

God's suggestion that Job *look down on everyone who is proud and bring him low* (40:12a) ironically skewers Job with his own arrogant claim to possess a righteousness that surpasses God's (cf. 33:8-12). The inference that Job needs saving (40:14) thus validates Elihu's contention that this pride would lead inexorably to self-destruction and that Job could be rescued only by accepting God's redemptive initiative (cf. 33:14-30; 36:8-15). However, since Job's demand for vindication *adds rebellion* in that he *multiplies his words against God* (34:37), he himself would first have to be "tamed"; thus, the two beasts exemplify how the headstrong Job could comply as the Creator's agent only by yielding his self-righteous pride to the Creator's sovereign rule (40:15-42:6).

2. God Challenges Job's Power to Control Evil (40:15–41:34)

To substantiate the implausibility of Job's ludicrous presumption that he could ever deliver himself from affliction by his own righteousness (40:9-14), God cites His relationship as Creator with two monstrous creatures. Job's opportunity to respond to God's satirical challenge is mercifully pre-empted by the ensuing object lesson of these two prototypes of earthly

---

[290] Elihu had already identified Job's presumption in justifying himself at God's expense (n. 223); YHWH now openly indicts Job for the bold arrogance of having in effect answered the central question of the debate "Can a man be righteous before God?" (cf. n. 22) by simply declaring *God* guilty before *man* (40:8).

[291] Elihu had already made it clear that Job was on his own with no hope if he did not accept God's overture to *deliver* him (36:15, Heb. *ḥālaṣ*) from the wicked who afflict him (36:5-16); with dripping sarcasm, YHWH now confirms the futility of Job's attempt to *deliver* himself (40:14, Heb. *yāšaʻ*) from the forces of evil. See n. 25. The rhetorical question *Have you an arm like God? Or can you thunder with a voice like His?* (40:9) also echoes Elihu's earlier imagery (cf. 37:5) in portraying God's sovereign power and prerogative as Creator to execute judgment.

[292] Cf. "splendor" and "majesty," 37:22. In alluding to Satan's aspiration to "be the Most High" (cf. Isa 14:14-17), God's sarcastic proposal compares Job's arrogant denigration of God's justice (40:8) with Satan's own pride (n. 19).

might and defiance.[293] It is a powerful *a fortiori* argument that finally strips Job of his self-righteous defiance: Behemoth is so massive that it could only be tamed by its Creator (40:15-24); Leviathan represents such malevolent pride that it is indomitable by anyone other than YHWH Himself (41:1-34). If even the mightiest and proudest of all God's creatures readily submit to Him **much more** should Job admit his own obstinate pride and presumption and also submit to God (42:1-6).

Behemoth is presented as a creature *which I made along with you* (40:15a), so it is explicitly clear that the intended point of comparison in Job's object lesson will be *the Creator-creature relationship*. The remark that Behemoth *eats grass like an ox* (40:15b) recalls the prior figure of the *wild ox* (cf. 39:9-12) to suggest the implausibility of taming such a beast. In the following description Behemoth is a quintessential example of the absurdity of trying to domesticate such a beast to serve one's own purposes: Its enormous structure and great momentum (40:16-18) as *the first of the great acts of God* demonstrate why *only its Maker can approach it with the sword* (40:19, NRSV); Job thus has no hope of subduing it in his own strength. If all Creation is subservient to such a creature and it can't be intimidated, even though *the river may rage* (40:20-23), much less could Job tame the beast into meek submission (40:24).[294]

---

[293] YHWH's defeat of the sea monster in Ps 74:14 and Leviathan in Isa 27:1 supports the idea that these beasts embody "the chaotic forces of evil" (Hartley, *The Book of Job*, 530). Note also Rev 12:7-9, where Satan is depicted as just such a dragon in his final defeat by God. The view that Behemoth and Leviathan refer to the hippopotamus and crocodile (Zuck, *Job*, 177-83) does not account sufficiently for the overtones of evil (cf. n. 287). Carson (*How Long, O Lord?* 172) agrees that Behemoth and Leviathan likely

> represent primordial cosmic powers that...break out against God. The argument, then, is that if Job is to charge God with injustice, he must do so from the secure stance of his own superior justice; and if he cannot subdue these beasts, let alone the cosmic forces they represent, he does not enjoy such a stance and he therefore displays extraordinary arrogance to call God's justice into question.

[294] The Heb. imagery sheds light on the point YHWH intended to make with the prospect of Behemoth's domestication, lit. "By his eyes could one take control of him; with a lure could one pierce his nose?" The idea is that of conscripting such a beast into service by luring him, rather than forcing him against his will. NKJV obscures the sense by rendering 40:24 as concessive rather than inferential: The rhetorical questions (so NASB, NIV, NRSV) infer from the foregoing evidence (40:15-23) that since Job cannot hope to subdue Behemoth he will never be able to subdue *everyone who is proud* (40:11-12). Job's comparison to Behemoth (cf. 40:15a) ironically portrays his own massive resistance and self-will and thus the difficult prospect YHWH faced of redirecting Job's attention to his created role as agent of God's purposes.

Leviathan is then introduced as the extreme prototype of violently hostile pride.[295] The same imagery of snaring and taming is again invoked to depict the equally absurd prospect of domesticating Leviathan (41:1-7, cf. 40:24).[296] Since Job thus has no *hope of subduing him*, how absurd to presume he could then *stand against* God, demanding restitution from Him to whom *everything under heaven belongs* (41:8-11, NIV)![297] YHWH then forecloses any further hope of prevailing against the beast, by showing off how extravagantly He had fashioned Leviathan's bold defenses and by pointing out his fierce hostility (41:12-32).[298] The speech closes with a final ironic insinuation that Job's own pride subjects him to Satan's dominion (41:33-34).[299]

While YHWH's speeches certainly extinguish all hope of suing God for restitution, the imagery projected by the two beasts functions as a sub-text intended to embarrass Job by reflecting his own determined resistance and aggressive pride: Whereas God **designed** the beasts to exhibit these traits, Job displays the traits **at cross-purposes** to his Creator's intent and ends up serving Satan. Job is therefore challenged to further emulate the beasts by similarly granting his Creator the sole prerogative to tame him and regain his allegiance. It thus becomes clear how God will secure His victory over Satan: Job will openly confess and forsake the self-reliant wisdom and self-righteousness (42:1-6) that Satan has been exploiting to fuel his own insurrection. So, hopefully, will the reader.[300]

---

[295] The large volume of text devoted to the description of Leviathan seems designed to address the remarkable intransigence of Job's own pride (cf. n. 283).

[296] The figures depicting Leviathan's domestication are especially ludicrous: God asks mockingly whether Job can turn Leviathan into an obsequious servant (41:3-4) or a docile pet that little girls could play with (41:5), or sell him as cuts of beef (41:6-7); it would be like taming *T. rex* into Puff the Magic Dragon wearing a tutu.

[297] Job's charge of injustice is based on the allegation that God has robbed him of title to his estate (cf. n. 155). God briefly acknowledges Job's claim in 41:10-11 (best conveyed in NIV), setting aside his blistering sarcasm to simply drive the point home and gut Job's claim of any legitimacy at all (cf. n 268).

[298] Leviathan's defenses in 41:12-17 are very daunting like those of Behemoth, but in 41:18-32 Leviathan is further characterized as downright hostile and defiant, just like Job: Smoke and flashes emanate from his nostrils, and sparks and flames shoot out of his mouth, too reminiscent of Satan to be coincidental.

[299] As *king over all the children of pride* (41:34), Leviathan exemplifies Satan's dominion over other proud creatures (cf. 28:8). Since Job's self-righteousness qualifies him as a "child of pride," Satan is therefore ironically presumed to have dominion over Job as well. Cf. also n. 292 and related text.

[300] Cf. nn. 19, 20, 38 and related text.

3. Job Confesses His Presumption and Repents (42:1–6)

Now that God has thoroughly undermined Job's case against Him, Job responds to the entire discourse[301] by prostrating his soul before God. He humbly acknowledges God's absolute sovereignty, affirming that *no purpose of* God *can be thwarted* (42:1-2, NASB). Recalling God's opening rhetorical question (38:2), Job now readily accepts God's appraisal of his ignorance in presuming to identify God's inscrutable purposes behind his suffering (42:3).[302] Job is now willing to speak to God and receive instruction as a faithful agent of His Creator, thus reversing his earlier petulant vow of silence (42:4 cf. 40:4-5).[303] He acknowledges that he *heard* such instruction (from Elihu's speeches) but had stubbornly resisted until his *eye* had *seen* God (42:5, NIV). Accordingly, he now speaks, *Therefore I retract* [my case], *And I repent in dust and ashes* (42:6).[304]

It is critical to note that when Job retracted his case and repented he still had no inkling that God would restore him or doubly bless him—any confidence of ultimate restoration was based only on the truth of redemption he had heard from Elihu.[305] Job repented when he was confronted by God's absolute power to judge evil and convicted of self-righteous

---

[301] Since Job proceeds to cite YHWH's opening challenge to his legal claim (42:3-4; cf. 38:2-3; cf. also 40:7b), it is apparent that Job's response is to the entirety of YHWH's speeches.

[302] Job's admission of ignorance also implies his willingness to submit, even when God's purposes remain inscrutable, so he responds to Elihu's concluding rebuke (37:15-24, nn. 253, 256) by forfeiting his presumptuous claim to wisdom.

[303] Job pleads with God to *Listen, please, and let me speak* (42:4a). He then quotes *verbatim* YHWH's opening sarcastic challenge (38:3b; cf. also 37:19), ironically reversing roles with YHWH and placing these words in his own mouth (42:4b), *"I will question you, and you shall answer Me."* The verb "answer me" is the Hifil *hôdî'ēnî*, lit. "bring me to know" (i.e., that which God knows). Job's acquiescence in humbly asking God to instruct him finally paves the way for God's commission (indicated in 42:8) for Job to intercede on behalf of his three former friends, thus fulfilling his redemptive purpose in the eyes of God (see exposition of 42:7-9).

[304] So NASB. NKJV *I abhor myself* is misleading. Scholnick ("The Meaning of *Mišpāṭ*," 356-7) argues that the verbs *mā'as* and *naḥam* (Nifal) are more accurately translated "withdraw" and "retract," respectively: *"Therefore, being but dust and ashes, I withdraw and retract* [my case]*"* (ibid., 357). In accordance with the forensic theme of YHWH's speeches (cf. nn. 172, 206, 215, 263, 264, 268, 301), the fitting response is indeed for Job to *retract* his case; however, this sense may be assigned to *mā'as*. Since the figure *dust and ashes* denotes repentance (Zuck, *Job*, 185), *naḥam* is best rendered "repent," as in NASB, with the additional nuance of "relenting" from his demands upon YHWH.

[305] Cf. 33:14-30; 36:5-11.

sin.[306] When he submitted to God's sovereign control (42:2), confessing his sinful presumption in light of God's truth (42:3), Satan was forced to forfeit his claim on Job's allegiance since he could no longer use deception to enlist Job's complicity in attacking God's sovereignty. When Job repented he opened the door to restoration of fellowship with God[307] with a revitalized, obedient service.[308] God could now freely display His redemptive activity through Job, who—though still afflicted—was finally released from his own slavish demand for vindication[309] to intercede on behalf of others in a state of fully restored righteous agency for his Creator (42:7-9).[310] His obedient service would in turn unleash God's abundant blessing (42:10-17).

---

[306] Isaiah likewise immediately recognized his own uncleanness when he was confronted by the unmasked majesty of God's holiness (Isa 6:1-4); like Isaiah, Job recognized his sinfulness as manifested in his speech (Isa 6:5), as Elihu had appropriately pointed out in perhaps his most explicit indictment of Job (34:37, n. 221).

[307] The restoration of full fellowship between sinful man and a holy God is linked to repentance (cf. n. 240). Job's bitterness and pride had effectively nullified his stewardship, as was evident in his defiant climactic speech (Job 27-31). Elihu's gracious response apprised Job of his need to propitiate God's displeasure and emulated Christ's own advocacy (cf. nn. 190, 199). Mankind's ongoing need for propitiation (cf. n. 204) is also evident in passages like Heb 2:10-18 and it dominates the entire Levitical system of sacrifices, in which the truth of propitiation is graphically played out (cf. n. 34 and Heb 9) as effecting reconciliation for mankind whenever one acknowledges and repents of his sin and rebellion (cf. Job 34:37). Job's repentance involved the confession and forgiveness of sin (1 John 1:9) in response to the convicting light of God's truth, which in turn enabled restoration of fellowship with God (1 John 1:7) on the basis of propitiation (1 John 2:2), just as Elihu taught in 33:23-27 (n. 201). This in turn would restore Job's righteous agency (33:26), which had been preempted by Job's vindictive anger (cf. Jas 1:20).

[308] Cf. nn. 19, 20, 264. Although Job still did not understand the reason for his calamities he finally did understand the redemptive character of God, so that this section in a sense fully reverses the existential despair that he displayed in chap. 3 (see the OVERVIEW OF JOB, the final paragraph of "LITERARY STRUCTURE IN THE ARGUMENT OF JOB"). Job's outlook was transformed by his confrontation with God from nihilistic expectation of impending death to (eager?) anticipation of the new work of his redemptive God.

[309] See nn. 11, 15, 84, 95, 102, 127, 170, 172, and related exposition.

[310] Just as Isaiah's repentance and consequent cleansing (n. 306) launched his ministry to Israel, calling a tenth of her inhabitants to repentance (Isa 6:9-13), so Job's own conviction of sin instilled in him a keen sensitivity to the deceitfulness of self-righteousness and reversed his prior vindictiveness (cf. n. 143), thus softening him to the same desperate need among his former friends.

Epilogue

SATAN'S DEFEAT

Mankind's Agency Vindicated

Job's Integrity Restored (Job 42:7-17)

*By describing the reconciliation that followed Job's repentance and the abundant blessing that followed his intercession for his friends, **the author associates intimacy with God and eternal reward with submissive service to God**, so that his readers might aspire to be faithful agents of God's redemptive blessing to others in all circumstances.*

The text of this final section mirrors the prologue with the style of prose narrative and relates the dramatic resolution of the wager with Satan and Job's calamitous affliction.[311] Careful attention to the sequence of events helps to avoid confusing the author's message:[312] Job is still destitute and afflicted in the first scene in which YHWH addresses Job's three friends (42:7-9). Only when Job obeys God's commission and intercedes for his friends **while still suffering** does God finally *accept Job* (42:9),[313] so Satan must concede that he has lost the wager (cf. 1:6-2:10). Job's fellowship is hence restored and his obedience rewarded (42:10-17).

The reader must keep an eye on the central issue at stake in the drama: Will Job remain faithful as God's chosen servant (1:8; 2:3) in spite of suffering? Having learned from Elihu that God sends a *mediator* to *deliver* man *from going down to the Pit* by propitiating God's wrath with a *ransom* (33:23-26), Job emulated Elihu's priestly advocacy by propitiating God's anger toward his former friends (42:7-9),[314] thus serving God faithfully through suffering and thereby defeating

---

[311] *See* the Overview of Job, "Literary Structure in the Argument of Job."

[312] Cf. n. 305. Carson (*How Long, O Lord?* 175) cites a common misperception:

> If some critics are displeased with God's answer to Job out of the storm, even more are incensed by this "happy ending." The story, they argue[,] should have ended with Job's repentance. Whether he was restored is irrelevant; in any case it is untrue to the experience of many, who suffer at length without reprieve. To end the story this way makes the doctrine of retribution basically right after all. The conclusion is therefore anticlimactic at best, contradictory at worst.

The main flaw in this reasoning is that the dramatic climax is not Job's repentance but rather his intercession.

[313] The three *waw* consecutive impf. (preterite) verbs in 42:9 convey a crucial chronological sequence of events (cf. Arnold and Choi, *Guide to Hebrew Syntax*, 84-85) that is not reflected in NKJV. Thus, after Job's repentance (42:6) YHWH commanded his friends to offer sacrifices that Job was to mediate (42:8), *so they went and* then *did as the Lord told them; and* [then] *the Lord accepted Job* (42:9, cf. NASB). This "acceptance" initiates the restoration of full fellowship (n. 307), as confirmed by the immediately ensuing abundant blessing (42:10-17).

[314] *See* nn. 9, 12, 23-27, and 201.

Satan (cf. 1:9-11; 2:4-5). But Job's resulting inheritance (42:10-17) represents more than his reward for obedient service[315]—it prefigures the eventual restoration of God's dominion over Creation.[316]

Job's multiplied blessings offer the reader tangible hope of an analogous future in God's kingdom in return for faithful service as an agent of the Creator. An archetypical patriarch (1:1-5), Job epitomizes the ultimate fulfillment of God's mandates to Abraham and his seed:[317] The reader whom God calls to serve Him is to become a faithful agent of God's redemptive blessing to others.[318] Though one may suffer present loss he is promised greater inheritance in God's kingdom. This

---

[315] While Carson (*How Long, O Lord?* 176) asserts that "the blessings that Job experiences at the end are not cast as rewards that he has earned by his faithfulness under suffering [but] as the Lord's free gift," the text clearly attests that Job's losses were *restored...when he prayed for his friends* (42:10), so that Job was rewarded for obeying the call to bless his unworthy friends. This notion of reward inheres in NT theology (e.g., Rom 8:16-25; 1 Cor 3:11-15; 2 Cor 4:16-5:10; Phil 2:12-13; Col 1:22-23; 2 Tim 2:12; Heb 2:5; 3:1, 6, 14; 4:14; 6:11-12; 9:11-12, 15; 10:19-27, 35-36; 11:6, 26; 12:22-23; 1 Pet 1:6-9; 1 John 2:28, Rev 2:26-27). See further Zane C. Hodges, *Grace in Eclipse—A Study on Eternal Rewards* (Irving, TX: Grace Evangelical Society, 2003); Joe L. Wall, *Going for the Gold: Reward and Loss at the Judgment of Believers* (Chicago: Moody Press, 1991); and Joseph Dillow, *Reign of the Servant Kings* (Hayesville, NC: Schoettle, 2002).

[316] As Yancey affirms,

the best way to view the ending in Job is to see it...as a sign of what is to come...the happiness of Job's old age was a mere sampling of what he would enjoy after death. The good news at the end of Job and the good news of Easter at the end of the Gospels are previews of the good news described at the end of Revelation. We dare not lose sight of the world God wants. [*Disappointment with God*, 295-6]

The Bible stakes God's reputation on his ability to conquer evil and restore heaven and earth to their original perfection. Apart from that future...God could be judged less-than-powerful, or less-than-loving....Evil, not good, appears to be winning. But the Bible calls us to see beyond the grim reality of history to the view of all eternity, when God's reign will fill the earth with light and truth. [ibid., 297]

God has intended all along that this reign should be mediated through a perfected human co-regency (n. 20).

[317] Note the striking parallel between Job's commission and blessing (42:7-17) and that of Abraham (Gen 12:1-3) as patriarchs within their respective domains. When Abraham fulfilled his covenant imperative to "be a blessing," God could then bless "all the families of the earth" through him (Allen Ross, "Genesis," in Walvoord & Zuck [eds.], *BKC*, OT [Wheaton: Victor Books, 1985], 47).

[318] Job's intercession for his friends reflected the intended connection between one's reconciliation **to** God and his transformed agency **for** God, as Elihu had explained (33:26-27) and as David testifies in Ps 51:13-15.

reward so far exceeds any blessing one could hope for in this life that it wholly overcomes and transcends the initial dread of encountering a sovereign God who would dare to postpone blessing just to flaunt a faithful servant's steadfast obedience amid suffering (1:6-2:10).[319]

A. Reconciled to God, Job Mediates Redemption (42:7–9)

By describing Job's intercession for his unworthy friends in the midst of suffering, **the author illustrates God's high priority of reconciling all men to Himself,** *so that his readers might see the supreme value of mediating the reconciliation of others to God.*

It may well strike the reader as a bit odd that God would attend to Job's unfeeling and critical friends before relieving Job's suffering, yet this sequence of events plays a crucial role in resolving the drama and unfolding God's sovereign intention in Job's suffering. Elihu had made it clear as God's representative[320] that he was also angry with the three friends, *because they had found no answer, and yet had condemned Job* (32:3). As men created in God's image they had *not spoken of* God *what is right* (42:7-8) and had thus colluded in Satan's subversive purposes[321] so they needed a credible mediator to reconcile them to God.[322] If God had first restored Job to his former wealth, it would have conveyed the wrong message.[323]

God's *wrath* was *aroused against* Job's *friends,* because they continued to misrepresent God (42:7-8), while Job—who had been depicted as one *who darkens counsel by words without knowledge* (38:2)—now gained God's favor by confessing *what is right* (42:7c, 8c; cf. 42:1-5).[324]

---

[319] Central to God's intent from the time of His commission to Adam to the present has been the abundant blessing of his agents, through whose faithfulness His creative design is ultimately realized. The problem, of course, as Christ Himself attested (Luke 16:1-9), is that God's stewards are all too prone to dismiss the wisdom of forfeiting present material blessing to gain greater eternal reward. The exceeding incomparability of this reward makes all the suffering worthwhile (cf. n. 333, below).

[320] *See* nn. 176, 183 and related exposition.

[321] Cf. n. 20.

[322] Cf. nn. 24, 27.

[323] Cf. nn. 312, 315. If God had restored Job immediately following his repentance (42:6) but prior to his intercession, it would have falsely validated the retribution theology implicit in the repeated suggestion of Job's comforters that all Job had to do in order to be restored was repent (cf. 5:8-27; 8:5-7, 19-22; 11:13-19; 22:21-30).

Consequently, Job was restored to vital agency through suffering, just as Elihu had predicted,[325] thereby earning the credentials he needed to mediate God's redemptive grace.[326] Now fully reinstated as God's exemplary *servant* (42:7-8),[327] Job was commissioned by God to intercede for his unworthy friends, who stood to gain infinitely more than just a corrected understanding of God's character (42:7-8):[328] Having been estranged from God—even hated—they were fully reconciled to God by Job's mediation.[329]

---

[324] What did Job speak "right" of God (42:7c, 8c)? Hartley asserts (*The Book of Job*, 539 [fn. 2]) that "this statement...must encompass more than his final words." However, YHWH had affirmed in 38:2 that Job's previous words had been spoken out of ignorance, and both Elihu and Job himself corroborated this assessment (34:37; 35:16; 42:3). Job's "right speaking" was in confessing that he should accept God's purposes behind his suffering and that those purposes had been inscrutable (n. 302). Job's comforters had not yet spoken likewise.

[325] Elihu had explicitly described God's intentional use of suffering to deliver man from self-destruction and restore him as a vital agent of God's redemptive purposes (cf. 33:14-30; 36:5-21; nn. 181, 201, 202, 204, 221, 236-256 and related exposition; also Christ's own teaching, cf. nn. 55, 253).

[326] Like Christ, Job *learned obedience* through suffering (Heb 5:8, cf. n. 29) and now—like Christ—he was truly qualified to mediate that grace by interceding on behalf of others (Heb 5:7).

[327] Cf. 1:8; 2:3. Zuck (*Job*, 187) duly notes that Job is called *My servant* four times in only two verses, thus underscoring his newly restored status, which qualified him to intercede before God on behalf of his friends, just as he had previously interceded on behalf of his children (1:5). There is no mistaking Job's role as restored High Priest, mediating the burnt offerings of his friends to propitiate God's wrath (cf. 33:23-30).

[328] Since God's *wrath* was *aroused against* the *friends, for* they had *not spoken of Me what is right, as Job* had (42:7, cf. n. 324), they were completely alienated from God. They remained mute, even though Elihu had corrected their flawed reasoning (cf. 32:2) and Job had modeled the confession of his own pride and presumption (42:1-6). When they offered the prescribed sacrifices (42:8), God's wrath was propitiated through Job's intercession and they were delivered, as Elihu had anticipated and Eliphaz ironically predicted (cf. nn. 126, 201).

[329] It is here that the full significance of the lineage of Job's friends finally emerges. As God testify, *Jacob I have loved, but Esau I have hated* (Mal 1:2-3), so Eliphaz the Temanite bore a heavy burden of alienation from God's promises to Abraham and his seed, and the other two friends were similarly alienated by virtue of their own lineages (n. 45). It would have been shocking to any Jew who was aware of their origins that God would now condescend to instruct Job, who had found favor in God's eyes, to intercede for those who were so completely estranged from God. In this light, the ending of Job is consistent with the ending of Malachi, where the prophet predicts that Elijah, like Job, would *turn the hearts of the fathers to the children, And the hearts of the children to their fathers* (Mal 4:6). Such reconciliation in the case of Job's three friends attests most powerfully to God's unbounded grace.

Job's intercession blessed his friends, in striking contrast to his prior vindictiveness and contempt. To condescend and pray on their behalf was clear testimony to the total transformation in Job's attitude that must have occurred when he was reconciled to God.[330] This should motivate the reader to replace self-righteous pride with a new openness to ministry as an agent like Job, who "learned obedience through the things which he suffered."[331] Job's keen awareness of the destructiveness of self-righteous

---

[330] Like Jonah, Job was called to intercede for his friends when they were completely unlovable. The natural human aversion to such intercession is graphically depicted in Jonah's bitterness and contempt on being chosen to mediate Nineveh's repentance (Jon 3-4; cf. n. 221). Job's disposition displayed the same contempt and hatred toward his former friends (cf. Job 27:7-23; n. 143) and had to be reversed before Job could pray to God on their behalf. This is the final stroke of irony in Job's determined quest for a mediator: This same man—himself once unable to find a mediator to adjudicate his dispute with God (9:33)—is the very one God chose to mediate His redemptive purposes toward the very antagonists Job found most unlovable. Job's intercession testifies to the authenticity of his transformation as God's chosen agent and portrays the power of restored fellowship (42:9c, cf. n. 307). Edith Schaeffer captures the key significance of his transformation (*Affliction*, 55-6):

> There is an amazing forgiveness shown in Job's willingness to pray for his friends, rather than to gloat over them. It would do us good...to recognize the opportunities that we have time after time to pray for people who have hurt us. We should pray with a desire that others may come to an understanding of the truth...rather than with a desire that they be proven wrong. The difference is in an inner attitude which God knows about as we pray for those who have in some form "railed against us." The friends did do as God told them, which meant a humbling kind of acknowledgment on their part that they had been wrong. Job did pray for them, and God must have been pleased with the motive and inner attitude of Job as he prayed.

Crabb is thus precisely on target when he notes that "recovery from terrible mistreatment is never meaningful until the victim hungers for the restoration of the abuser and is even willing to be an instrument of that restoration" (*Finding God*, 201). This is exactly the point of Luke 6:37-38—God will reward those who defer judging their persecutors and bless them instead (cf. 6:27-36). Such lip-biting blessing is enjoined of believers elsewhere in the NT (cf. Matt 5:43-48; 6:14-15; 18:21-35; Eph 4:32), and the promised reward reflects the great value God places on sacrificial service by heroes of faith in the midst of suffering (cf. Heb 11).

[331] Cf. n. 326. Job's experience of suffering prepared him—like Christ (Heb 2:17-18; 5:7-9)—to mediate God's redemptive purposes by propitiating His anger towards his friends (cf. n. 307). Perhaps the most important aspect of this "preparation" is to forge servants who can empathize with and comfort others in their need, in striking contrast to the lack of empathy manifested by Job's friends (Job 12:5; 13:4; 16:1-5; 19:21-22):

> Blessed be the God and Father of our Lord Jesus Christ...who comforts us in all our tribulation, that we may be able to comfort those who are in any trouble,

sin[332] should alert the reader to the need of others to be reconciled to God and motivate him to persevere in faith as a blessing to them in spite of present suffering. Besides teaching that suffering can qualify God's servant to intercede on behalf of others, Job's intercession would also exemplify how God intends to reward obedient service with abundant blessing (42:10-17)—a rich inheritance that should further motivate the reader to serve faithfully as God's chosen agent in spite of present suffering.[333]

B. Job Blessed with Double Inheritance (42:10–17)

By recounting the full measure and extravagance of Job's restored estate, **the author bases man's hope for a rich inheritance in God's kingdom on serving faithfully and with integrity as His agent,** *so that his readers might be motivated to persevere in faith as a blessing to others, even in the midst of suffering.*

The final section of the book is governed by the main verbs of the initial summary verse—*restored* and *increased* (42:10, NASB). These two verbs are separated by the phrase *when he prayed for his friends,* which suggests that Job's long-awaited blessing was logically conferred in two

---

with the comfort with which we ourselves are comforted by God. For as the sufferings of Christ abound in us, so our consolation also abounds through Christ. Now if we are afflicted, it is for your consolation and salvation, which is effective for enduring the same sufferings which we also suffer. Or if we are comforted, it is for your consolation and salvation. (2 Cor 1:3-6)
Job could empathize with his friends only after he "learned obedience" (Heb 5:8)—only then could he know firsthand what they needed. Job thereby serves as a model for the reader's own mediation of God's grace amid suffering (cf. Schaeffer, *Affliction*, 167-87; Carson, *How Long, O Lord?* 122-3). He exemplified a key tenet of the NT emphasis on suffering, *let those who suffer according to the will of God commit their souls to Him in doing good, as to a faithful Creator* (1 Pet 4:19). The specific ways that the Creator's servants will "do good" have been preordained (cf. Eph 2:10); however, the reader cannot know beforehand which of his works God will bless (cf. Eccl 8:16-17; 11:1-6; Ps 90:13-18). The confidence of God's agents is rooted in the firm hope that God will accomplish His works most powerfully through their humility and weakness—forged in the crucible of suffering (cf. 2 Cor 4:7-12; 12: 9-10; Phil 1:6; 2:5-13).

[332] *See* n. 310.

[333] We can be confident that *our light affliction, which is but for a moment, is working for us a far more exceeding and eternal weight of glory* (2 Cor 4:17, cf. n. 319). The "exceeding glory" of Job's restoration (see below) prefigures the promise to all who serve faithfully in spite of present suffering (cf. Rom 8:8-25; 1 Cor 9:24-27; 2 Cor 4:16-5:8; 2 Tim 2:10; 4:6-8; Heb 11:39-12:2; Jas 1:12; 5:11; 1 Pet 4:12-13).

stages.[334] Job's blessing therefore signifies much more than the simple restitution of all the losses he was obliged to endure as a consequence of God's wager with Satan: When Job relented from demanding vindication and calmly accepted his commission to be a blessing to his former friends, his faithful intercessory agency on their behalf (42:7-9) multiplied his blessing and restored a deeper fellowship with God and those in his community (42:10-17).

This understanding follows from certain unexpected elements that comprise Job's restoration and blessing. The first detail regards the restoration of Job's relationship with his friends and extended family members (42:11), implying that up to that point he had been alienated from them.[335] The meals he shared and his gifts of gold and silver (42:11a, c) thus represent the restoration of full fellowship and the "payout" of blessing that Job won from God's high-stakes wager[336] (42:10) when he finally "saw" God (42:5) and obediently blessed his unworthy friends with the same compassion and long-suffering that God had shown him (42:7-9).[337]

Other details of Job's restoration are vested with a symbolism that attests to the transcendent significance of his abundant blessing. Job's blessing in livestock—exactly twice what he had before (42:10b, 12, cf. 1:3)—implies special favor.[338] Double blessing is also exemplified in

---

[334] The first of the two main verbs šûb ("return, restore") coincides with Job's praying (Hithpael infinitive construct of pālal, "intercede")—lit. "in his praying." The second verb yāsaph (Hifil, "add, increase") is a waw consecutive preterite, implying logical or chronological sequence. Thus, with Job's prayer God first **repays** and then **exceeds** the loss sustained as a result of the wager with Satan (n. 336, below).

[335] Although Job's affliction could not help but alienate him (cf. 6:21-23), he was progressively hardened by contempt for his three friends (cf. nn. 102, 142, 221) and his sense of entitlement (cf. nn. 84, 152, 268); his bitterness disrupted even his closest relationships and forestalled God's full blessing (cf. Heb 12:14-15, 17). His fresh acceptance of consolation and comfort (42:11b) implies that his bitterness and contempt were fully reversed before he interceded for his friends (cf. n. 330).

[336] A modern analogy would be a high stakes poker game in which the last "player" to bet (in this case, YHWH) looks at the "pot" so far (all the consequences of Job's affliction that were "bet" by Satan) and bids in two stages (cf. n. 334): "I call you [restore Job's fortunes] and **raise** you double [increase Job's estate twofold]." God could safely "call Satan's bluff" and raise the stakes, then give Job all the "winnings" he had redeemed from Satan's stronghold, because Job came through (n. 334) as God's faithful servant "in his praying" (42:10; cf. 1:8; 2:3).

[337] Recall Elihu's point about God's persistence in 33:29.

[338] In the eyes of Job's ancient near eastern audience, his blessing here may well signify his "adoption" by God as a "firstborn" to whom special honor is due: the "double portion" reserved for the firstborn (cf. Deut 21:17; s.v. "Firstborn" and "Inheritance," in *Wycliffe Bible Encyclopedia*, Chicago: Moody Press, 1975). If so, Job's adoption and inheritance typify Christ's adoption and inheritance at His

Job's progeny: Exactly the same number of sons and daughters were added to those he had lost (cf. 1:18-19).[339] Moreover, Job's new daughters imply special favor: Their names (42:14) bespeak their exceeding beauty,[340] which was unmatched *in all the land* (42:15a), and they gain *an inheritance among their brothers* (42:15b), an unmistakable sign of favor among Job's contemporaries.[341] Finally, Job himself is singled out to live 140 years, seeing four generations of his progeny and dying *full of days* (42:16-17), thus prefiguring the fullest possible fellowship with God that is reserved for those who persevere in faithful service.

The nature and circumstances of Job's final blessing convey the object lesson that knowing God and fellowship with Him are of infinitely greater value than to avoid suffering at all cost.[342] Moreover, the children of Abraham who diligently pursue God as faithful agents in spite of suffering and obey His commission to be a blessing[343] will receive rich blessing

---

resurrection (cf. Ps 2:7-9; Rom 1:4; see David MacLeod, "Eternal Son, Davidic Son, Messianic Son: An Exposition of Romans 1:1-7," *BSac* 162:76-94 [2005], at 85-88).

[339] Schaeffer explains how Job's new children reflected double inheritance, in that his original ten children would be restored by resurrection from death (*Affliction*, 59):

> It is interesting to find [at] the end of Job's story, that he had three new daughters and seven sons born to him....Yet they did not "replace" the other ten who had died...A child who is in heaven is still your child and has not gone out of existence. One day (if they were all believers) the "double family," that is, the *twenty* children of Job, will receive their new bodies and demonstrate that God who is a God of detail did indeed give double of everything which Job had lost. [author's emphasis]

Cf. also n. 102; Heb 11:19.

[340] *Jemimah* means "dove;" *Keziah* means "perfume" (cassia is a bark used as a perfume); *Keren-Happuch* means "horn of eyepaint" (i.e., a bottle of dye used as "make-up" for the eyes) (Zuck, *Job*, 188).

[341] Inheritance by daughters was unusual in ancient near-eastern culture (Hartley, *The Book of Job*, 542-3 [fn. 5]), so this "extra" inheritance also reinforces the sense of superabundance (cf. n. 317)

[342] Job's blessing exemplifies the supreme value of knowing God in spite of suffering (cf. Phil 3:7-11; John 17:3; 1 John 2:3-6) and constitutes the main reward for the believer who faithfully perseveres through suffering (n. 315). Such obedient service stems from a faith brought to maturity, as displayed in the life of Abraham, and it merited him the title "friend of God" (cf. Jas 1:3-4; 2:22-23; Ezek 14:14, 20). Such intimacy with God far exceeded the value of mere restoration that was accomplished by reconciliation alone (n. 333).

[343] *See* n. 317. After God told Abraham to *go to the land I will show you* He promised to *bless* him, then told him to *be a blessing* (Gen 12:1-2, NIV). Job's mediation exemplified God's great generosity (n. 333), extending the promised blessing even to those who were originally excluded from His covenant with Abraham (notes 45, 119, 157). Cf. Rom 9:6-8; Gal 4:28.

themselves.[344] Readers who aspire to such valuable Agency will align their desires with God's redemptive purposes though they may not see how their obedience will fulfill those purposes, even as death approaches.[345] It is the confidence of knowing such a redemptive God and the hope of future blessing that fuel their incentive to persevere like Job in serving Him amid present suffering.[346]

---

[344] The obedience manifested in Abraham's sacrificial service yielded even more abundant blessing from God than was initially promised (Gen 22:15-18); Abraham and his seed obeyed, knowing that their promised blessing would be delayed, yet confident in their present suffering that they *would receive an inheritance...something better* (Heb 11:8, 16, 35, 40).

[345] The issue of existential uncertainty in the face of impending death (cf. Job 14:18-22; 17:6-16; n. 117) is also one of the principal themes of Ecclesiastes, and the prospect of God's blessing for wise stewardship amid uncertainty plays an equally important role in the argument of Ecclesiastes (cf. e.g., Eccl 8:16-9:10; 11:1-12:14). It sets up the main tension to be resolved in the second half of the argument, which charges the reader with accountability for wise decision-making as an agent of God despite uncertainty (see Reitman, *Structure and Unity of Ecclesiastes*, 302-3, 311-12). Illness and debility in life often force the issue; for further analysis of wise decision-making based on the arguments of Job and Ecclesiastes in common medical settings of intractable suffering, see the present author's "The Debate on Assisted Suicide," *ILM* 11 (1995), 299-329; "Wise Advocacy;" (cf. n. 91); "A 'Wisdom' perspective on Advocacy for the Suicidal" (cf. n. 66); "The Dilemma of Medical Futility," *ILM* 12 (1996), 231-64; and "Perinatal Hospice: A Response to Early Termination for Severe Congenital Anomalies," in TJ Demy & GP Stewart, eds., *Genetic Engineering: A Christian Response* (Grand Rapids: Kregel, 1999), 197-211.

[346] According to James, the main object lesson conveyed by Job's ultimate blessing in persevering through suffering is to underscore God's redemptive character, "the end intended by the Lord" (Jas 5:11). Job's ultimate reward is a type of the Kingdom blessing promised by Christ himself to those who responded with initial sacrifice of all worldly possessions in response to His own invitation to suffering servanthood (cf. Luke 9:57-62; 14:25-33; 18:28-30).

Selected Bibliography

Allender, Dan B. and Tremper Longman. *The Cry of the Soul*. Colorado Springs: Navpress, 1994.

Carson, Donald A. *How Long, O Lord? Reflections on Suffering and Evil*. Grand Rapids: Baker, 1990.

Crabb, Larry B. *Finding God*. Grand Rapids: Zondervan, 1993.

_____. *Inside Out*. Colorado Springs: Navpress, 1988.

Hartley, John E. *The Book of Job*. New International Commentary on the Old Testament. Grand Rapids: Eerdmans, 1988.

Hauerwas, Stanley. *Naming the Silences: God, Medicine, and the Problem of Suffering*. Grand Rapids: Eerdmans, 1990.

Kreeft, Peter. *Making Sense Out of Suffering*. Ann Arbor, MI: Servant, 1986.

_____. "Job: Life as Suffering." In *Three Philosophies of Life*. San Francisco: Ignatius, 1989.

Parsons, Greg W. "The Structure and Purpose of the Book of Job." *Bibliotheca Sacra* 138 (1981): 139-57.

_____. "Guidelines for Understanding and Proclaiming the Book of Job." *Bibliotheca Sacra* 151 (1994): 393-413.

Reitman, James S. "A 'Wisdom' Perspective on Advocacy for the Suicidal." In *Suicide: A Christian Response,* ed. Timothy J. Demy & Gary P. Stewart, 369-85. Grand Rapids: Kregel, 1998.

Schaeffer, Edith. *Affliction: A Compassionate Look at the Reality of Pain and Suffering*. Grand Rapids: Baker, 1978.

Tournier, Paul. "The Enigma of Suffering." In *A Listening Ear*. Minneapolis: Augsburg, 1987.

Waters, Larry J. "Reflections on Suffering from the Book of Job." *Bibliotheca Sacra* 154 (1997): 436-51.

_____. "The Authenticity of the Elihu Speeches in Job 32-37." *Bibliotheca Sacra* 156 (1999): 28-41.

_____. "Elihu's Theology and His View of Suffering." *Bibliotheca Sacra* 156 (1999): 143-59.

Yancey, Philip. *Disappointment with God: Three Questions No One Asks Aloud*. Grand Rapids: Zondervan, 1988.

Zuck, Roy B. *Job*. Everyman's Bible Commentary. Chicago: Moody Press, 1978.

_____. "Job." In *The Bible Knowledge Commentary*. Old Testament, ed. John F. Walvoord and Roy B. Zuck. Wheaton, IL: Victor Books, 1985.

_____, ed. *Sitting with Job: Selected Studies on the Book of Job*. Grand Rapids: Baker, 1992.

ECCLESIASTES: WISDOM IN SEARCH OF A LEGACY

*Enjoying Our Portion in God's
Inscrutable Work*

EXPOSITORY OUTLINE OF ECCLESIASTES

LITERARY STRUCTURE OF ECCLESIASTES

WISDOM'S FRUSTRATION: THE ILLUSIVE PROMISE OF SELF-SUFFICIENCY

WISDOM'S ADVANTAGE: ACCOUNTABLE STEWARDSHIP FOR THE WORK OF GOD

Section Titles

- **PROLOG** — Qoheleth's Futile Search for an Earthly Legacy (1:1-11)
- **Man's Futile Quest for Advantage** — The Futility of Prescribing a Heavenly Legacy (1:12-2:26)
- **The Futility of Forging His Own Advantage**
  - The Pervasive Oppression of Selfish Ambition (3:1-22)
  - The Foolish Presumption of Selfish Ambition (4:1-16)
  - The Ultimate Futility of Selfish Ambition (5:1-20)
  - Selfish Ambition (6:1-12)
- **ADVERSITY AT THE CROSS-ROADS**
  - The Instruction of Mourning (7:1-12)
  - The Inheritance of Wisdom (7:1-7)
  - The Depravity of Man—Wisdom's Advantage Preempted (7:8-14)
  - The Fear of God—Man's Only Confidence in Judgment (7:15-29)
- **Gaining Wisdom's Advantage**
  - The Work of God—Hope of His Favor for All the Living (8:1-15)
  - Wisdom's Success versus Self-Sufficient Failure (8:16-9:10)
- **Bringing Wisdom's Success**
  - Wisdom's Success amid the Hazards of Folly (9:11-18)
  - Wisdom's Success in Light of "Time and Chance" (10:1-20)
- **EPILOG** — Authoritative Words of Truth (11:1-12:7)

STRUCTURE (verse ranges)

1:12 – | 3:22 – | 4:1 – | 6:12 | 7:1 – 14 | 7:15 | 9:10 | 9:11 – | 12:7

MAN'S SELF-RELIANT SCHEMES: "Much dreaming and many words" (5:3,7; cf. 6:11); "he cannot contend with Him who is mightier" (6:10)

IN THE HOUSE OF MOURNING (7:1-4)

GOD'S INSCRUTABLE WORK: "...it will go well for those who fear God" (8:12); "Remember your creator before you find no more purpose" (12:1)

AUTHOR'S PERSPECTIVE / MAN'S QUEST FOR AN ADVANTAGE

- "What profit has a man?"
- "...who can...see what will happen afterward?" (3:22)
- "...who knows what is good for man...?" (6:12; cf. 5:11,16; 6:8)
- "Wisdom is good" (7:11-12)
- "Wisdom strengthens the wise" (7:19; cf. 8:1)
- "Wisdom brings success" (10:10b; cf. 9:16, 18)
- Fear God; Obey His Word

THE LEGACY OF MAN'S LABOR

- "What profit has the worker from that in which he labors?" (3:9); "All the labor of man is for his mouth, And yet the soul is not satisfied" (6:7; cf. 2:22; 4:8; 5:16-17)
- "Consider the work of God" (7:13-14)
- "God already favors your works...whatever you find to do, do with your might" (9:7,10); "Cast your bread...Give your portion...Sow your seed...all to come is vanity" (11:1-8)
- God will judge every work

ENJOYMENT

2:24-26 | 3:12-13, 22 | 5:18-20 | 8:15 | 9:7-10 | 11:9-12:7

FEAR OF GOD

3:14 | 5:7 | 7:18 | 8:12-13 | 12:13

OVERVIEW OF ECCLESIASTES[1]

By reflecting with unprecedented wisdom on his futile search for lasting satisfaction in life and conveying his conclusions with carefully selected proverbs, **Qoheleth traces all disillusionment and despair in life to our natural penchant for self-sufficiency and the constraints of our innate human depravity, uncertainty, and mortality**, *so that we might mourn our inability and find lasting fulfillment in our God-given "portion" by fearing God and enjoying His favor as valued agents of His inscrutable work.*

If we dare to reflect deeply on the events of life and the deeds of men in the world, life often seems unfair and unpredictable with no obvious meaning. Self-sufficient humans try in vain to mitigate this sense of futility by striving to succeed in endeavors that would seem to afford them the most control and lasting meaning in life. This quandary is the point of departure for the arguments of both Job and Ecclesiastes, both compelling the reader to reflect on the "seeming inequalities of divine providence."[2] However, while Job has a discrete literary structure, dramatic progression, and resolution,[3] Ecclesiastes seems fragmented or poorly organized, leading some expositors to infer that "in general no progression of thought from one section to another is discernible."[4] If in fact:

---

[1] This overview is adapted from the author's previous article, "The Structure and Unity of Ecclesiastes," *BSac* 154 (1997): 297-319.

[2] "The Scope and Plan of Ecclesiastes," in *The Biblical Repertory and Princeton Review*, July 1857, reprinted in Roy B. Zuck, ed., *Reflecting with Solomon: Selected Studies on the Book of Ecclesiastes* (Grand Rapids: Baker, 1994), 119. "It is...interesting to observe the harmony of the grand lessons inculcated by Job and by Ecclesiastes. No two books could well be more unlike in their style and method of discussion. The problem upon which they are engaged is one of the most perplexing of human life. They approach it, too, from quarters the most diverse...yet the principles which underlie their solutions are identical" (ibid.). See also J. Stafford Wright, "Introduction to Ecclesiastes," reprinted in Zuck (ed.), ibid., 167-8.

[3] *See* Gregory W. Parsons, "Guidelines for Understanding and Proclaiming the Book of Job," *BSac* 151 (1994): 395-98; and idem., "The Structure and Purpose of the Book of Job," *BSac* 138 (1981): 139-57, reprinted in Roy B. Zuck (ed.), *Sitting with Job: Selected Studies on the Book of Job* (Grand Rapids: Baker, 1992), 17-33.

[4] R.N. Whybray, *Ecclesiastes*, NCBC (Grand Rapids: Eerdmans, 1989), 17. Roland Murphy discusses the marked variability of proposed outlines (*Ecclesiastes*, WBC [Dallas: Word, 1992], xxxv-xli), and Eaton notes the tendency of most commentators to see "the Preacher's work as a string of unrelated meditations. A.G. Wright lists twenty-three commentators who virtually abandon the task of seeking coherence in the book....This list could easily be enlarged" (*Ecclesiastes*, 48).

Ecclesiastes is...not a single systematic treatise in which there is a progression from a set of premises to a logical conclusion, it remains to be considered in what other sense it might be a unified composition....[I]t deals with a number of distinct, though related, topics. If it could be shown that these have been arranged in some kind of logical order by Qoheleth himself, this would greatly assist the understanding of his thought.[5]

Adding to the difficulty of tracing the thread of Qoheleth's argument, the uniqueness of the Hebrew poses a serious challenge to the task of identifying the historical setting.[6] And who is Qoheleth? The peculiar quasi-autobiographical literary style has led many to question the book's purported authorship and purpose.[7]

---

[5] Whybray, *Ecclesiastes*, 19.

[6] C-L. Seow's convincing review of comparative orthography and diction (*Ecclesiastes*, AB [New York: Doubleday, 1997], 11-21) concludes that Ecclesiastes predates Postbiblical Hebrew (ibid., 20) and has "greatest affinities with the postexilic works of Chronicles, Ezra, Nehemiah, and Esther" (ibid., 19). However, "[t]he language of the book reflects not the standard literary Hebrew of the postexilic period....[I]t is the literary deposit of a vernacular...everyday language of the Persian period, with its large number of Aramaisms and whatever jargons and dialectical elements one may find in the marketplace" (ibid., 20-21).

[7] One must distinguish between the "frame narrator," who emerges as an editor-author in 1:1-11, 7:27, and 12:8-14, and Qoheleth himself, who is quoted by this editor in 1:12-12:7 (Tremper Longman, *The Book of Ecclesiastes*, NICOT [Grand Rapids: Eerdmans, 1998], 2-9). Whybray properly notes that "the implicit claim to be Solomon is a fiction; and indeed, the fact that it is made only indirectly...may suggest that Qoheleth never intended his readers to take it seriously" (*Ecclesiastes*, 4). However, Longman makes the implausible claim that Qoheleth's entire contribution can be summarized as "Life is full of trouble and then you die" (*Ecclesiastes*, 34). He sides with those who "view Qoheleth as a prime representative of skepticism in Israel," arguing that Qoheleth's teaching is only a **foil** for the frame narrator's theology and restricting the normative instruction to vv. 12:13-14 "that point away from skeptical thinking" (ibid., 36-39). See Iain Provan's persuasive rebuttal (*Ecclesiastes, Song of Songs*, NIVAC [Grand Rapids: Zondervan], 33, fn. 13). It is more plausible and internally consistent to view Qoheleth's reflections as evolving out of cynicism to *build* the frame-narrator's theology. Thus, we agree with Eaton that "the author is...an editor-author...writing up the lessons of Solomon's life in the tradition of the wisdom for which Solomon was famous....[He] portrays his material as coming from [Qoheleth], who has all the characteristics of Solomon except his name...an actual historical character: a wise man, a collector of proverbs, a teacher and writer....Avoidance of the name must stem from the fact that the editor-author puts things in his own way and declines to foist a work directly on Solomon. Yet he thinks of the material as Solomon's" (Michael A. Eaton, *Ecclesiastes*, TOTC [Downers Grove, IL: InterVarsity, 1983], 23-24).

This is only compounded by the generally skeptical tone and the dominant theme of *futility* ("vanity," KJV),[8] which strikes some as more consistent with aspects of existentialism than with the rest of Scripture.[9] The apparently contradictory reflections encountered in both near and remote context[10] only seem to confirm Qoheleth's profound cynicism. All this leads some students of the book to contend that "the bulk of the book" is so contrary to traditional wisdom it should hardly be viewed as prescriptive of godly living.[11]

Yet, the author himself clearly affirms that Qoheleth *pondered and searched out and set in order many proverbs....just the right words, and what he wrote was upright and true* (12:9-10, NIV). If we accept the premise of the basic perspicuity of Scripture we should be able to identifying a unified, coherent message in the text: Is there in fact a logical argument woven into the textual design, or is it only a literary "patchwork quilt" of assorted proverbs, reflections, and exhortations?[12] If the former is true, the expositor will discover how the argument reflects such intentional

---

[8] The precise meaning of the word *vanity* (*hebel*, lit. "breath") is widely debated (Murphy, *Ecclesiastes*, lviii-lix). Of the thirty-seven (or thirty-eight, ibid., 89, fn. 9b) occurrences in Eccl, twenty-nine are found in the first half plus the inclusion "vanity of vanities" at 12:8 (cf. 1:2). The oft-associated construction *grasping for the wind* supports a sense of frantic but completely empty effort in life. Context best supports rendering "futile," while recognizing other relevant nuances, such as "absurd" (ibid., lix), "empty," "fleeting," or "enigmatic."

[9] Notably, however, C. Stephen Evans has proposed legitimate parallels between biblical Christianity and certain aspects of existentialism (*Existentialism, The Philosophy of Despair and the Quest for Hope* [Dallas: Word, 1984]). Cf. also Peter Kreeft, *Three Philosophies of Life* (San Francisco, CA: Ignatius, 1989), 13-58; Ardel B. Caneday, "Qoheleth—Enigmatic Pessimist or Godly Sage?" reprinted in Zuck (ed.), *Reflecting with Solomon*, 81-113; and Philip Yancey, *The Bible Jesus Read* (Grand Rapids: Zondervan, 1999), 141-67.

[10] *See*, e.g., 8:12b-13 and cp. 9:4-6 with 2:17; 4:1-3; and 6:3-6.

[11] Cf. Longman (*Ecclesiastes*, 32-39, n. 7 above); also Gordon D. Fee and Douglas Stuart: "[E]verything but [the] two final verses, represents a brilliant, artful argument for the way one would look at life—*if* God did *not* play a direct, intervening role in life and *if* there were no life after death....[It] ought to leave you unsatisfied, for it is hardly the truth. It is the secular, fatalistic wisdom that a *practical*...atheism produces. When one relegates God to a position way out there..., then Ecclesiastes is the result. The book thus serves as a reverse apologetic for cynical wisdom; it drives its readers to look further because the answers...are so discouraging" (*How to Read the Bible for All It's Worth* [Grand Rapids: Zondervan, 1993], 214, emphasis theirs).

[12] Derek Kidner, *The Wisdom of Proverbs, Job, & Ecclesiastes* (Downers Grove: InterVarsity, 1985), 106.

and accurate design:[13] It must reconcile the seemingly contradictory reflections,[14] elucidate Qoheleth's apparent "attack on conventional wisdom,"[15] and account for the frequent exceptions to his otherwise pervasive cynicism: his allusions to *good/goodness* in life and his repeated exhortation to *fear God* and enjoy one's allotted portion in life.

This overview is designed to trace Qoheleth's argument by identifying the characteristic lexical/semantic, grammatical, structural, and literary elements of textual design that attest to a sequential, coherent line of reasoning. Perhaps the most straightforward way to begin is to pay careful attention to Qoheleth's distinctive use of key constructions in the argument.[16] Some of these constructions typically serve as structural markers to divide the argument into discrete paragraphic units, each with a unifying thought, and help the reader identify logical transitions in the argument. Some transitions, however, can only be inferred from major shifts in thematic emphasis or the tone of Qoheleth's reflections, often imbued with profound disillusionment and apparent resignation.[17]

By examining the contextual arrangement of repeated constructions it is possible to determine the semantic range most likely intended by the editor-author: whether the use is "technical" (referring in every case to one specific concept) or in fact more flexible.[18] These terms are often rendered differently in various

---

[13] *See* Christopher Bartholomew's persuasive argument for the logical coherence and design of Ecclesiastes and specifically the role of the frame narrator in validating the integrity and design of the book (*Reading Ecclesiastes: Old Testament Exegesis and Hermeneutical Theory* [Rome: Pontifical Biblical Institute, 1998], 212-70). Cf. also James Reitman, "Words of Truth and Words of Purpose—Exegetical Insights into Authorial Intent from Eccl 12:9-14," presented at the 58th annual meeting of the Evangelical Theological Society (www.21stcenturypress.com/wisdom.htm), arguing that the epilogue supplies both a logically coherent design and a strategic intent for the book; and Gregory W. Parsons, "Guidelines for Understanding and Proclaiming the Book of Ecclesiastes, Part I" (*BSac* 160:159-72, 2003), 162-3.

[14] Parsons, ibid., 171.

[15] Murphy, *Ecclesiastes*, lxi-lxiv, cf. esp. lxii.

[16] *See* Parsons, "Proclaiming the Book of Ecclesiastes, Part 1," 170-71.

[17] "Some statements must be viewed as having a negative contribution and other[s]...as contributing positively....Such considerations are particularly important in the interpretation of Job and Ecclesiastes" (Johnson, *Expository Hermeneutics*, 208). See also nn. 7, 11 (above) on the author's vantage point.

[18] *See* Grant R. Osborne's discussion of *sense* and *reference*, structural linguistics, and guidelines for the study of key words in *The Hermeneutical Spiral* (Downers Grove: InterVarsity, 1991), 76-78, 89-92.

translations and even in different verses within the same translation,[19] which can obscure the author's intended sense. Although some of this variability may be ascribed to uncertainty over the book's authorship and historical setting, the author clearly intended for certain constructions to denote the same referent each time they appear in the text.

Such inconsistencies do not preclude a proper understanding, as it is not difficult to identify recurring constructions and then to examine carefully how they are used in each context in which they occur.[20] The next section therefore traces Qoheleth's distinctive semantic and structural use of such terms, and how these constructions help to clarify the literary genre and textual design of Ecclesiastes and develop Qohelth's argument as it was most likely intended by the author.

QOHELETH'S USE OF TERMS IN THE ARGUMENT

The governing literary genre of reflection features a series of observations compiled from Qoheleth's experience, from which he draws inferences about life in general. The Commentary assumes that these inferences are arranged sequentially to construct the logic of argument, so we expect key terms to be used consistently throughout. We will thus anticipate this logical sequence as we explore the meanings of the key terms.

Given the apparently meaningless events that typify life *under the sun*,[21] Qoheleth could find no *profit* or *advantage*[22] to all

---

[19] Examples of such mistranslation will be cited in the exposition, as the intended contextual relationship between recurring constructions is developed.

[20] This task is feasible, even without advanced knowledge of biblical Hebrew (Johnson, *Expository Hermeneutics*, 80, n. 16). Every occurrence of a given construction in the text can easily be located with resources in currently available Bible software, including Hebrew interlinears, dictionaries, and lexicons to determine the best contextual fit of the different renditions of the construction in various translations. Technical commentaries can help with rare terms and difficult syntax. See "The Unity of Job and Ecclesiastes" in the Preface to the Commentary.

[21] The phrase *under the sun* occurs twenty-nine times and projects the perspective of mankind, using his own wisdom and senses within the apparently futile realm of "this world" (cf. also *on earth*, 5:2; 7:20, 8:14, 16; 11:2). The phrase *under heaven* seems to acknowledge by contrast (cf. esp. 1:13-14) that God's meaningful though inscrutable purposes are indeed worked out in this world (cf. 3:1; 5:2b). Eaton treats the two phrases as identical (*Ecclesiastes*, 44).

[22] Qoheleth uses the Heb. word-group *yôthēr/yithrôn/môthār* to convey the notion of *advantage* or *profit* in 1:3; 2:11, 13; 3:9, 19; 5:9, 16; 6:8, 11; 7:11, 12; 10:10, 11

mankind's *labor* or *toil*[23] (1:3, 13; 3:9-10; 7:25; 8:16). Life seems invariably tainted with *evil (adversity* or *misery)*,[24] so he searched for some evidence of *good* or *goodness* in life that might afford humanity some *satisfaction* or *fulfillment*.[25] Although we toil all our lives for some lasting meaning in our labor *under the sun* we cannot predict how things will turn out (3:21-22; 6:12; 7:14b). Qoheleth emphasizes the paradoxical nature of his observations by typically juxtaposing contrasting terms like *good(ness)* or *advantage* with *bad(ness)* or *futility*[26] and *darkness* with *light*.[27] The ultimate significance of our *works* is found only in the inscrutable *work* of God[28]—we don't know which of our efforts will turn out

---

(cf. Whybray, *Ecclesiastes*, 36-37). Exceptions to this are the occasional adverbial uses ("extremely" or "besides," 2:15; 7:16; 12:9, 12). Closely related are the words *kāšēr, kišrôn* ("succeed; success, profit," 2:21; 4:4; 5:11; 10:10b) and Qoheleth's frequent *better than* sayings, clustered conspicuously in three pericopae: 4:6-13; 7:1-10; 9:16-18.

[23] Qoheleth uses two virtually interchangeable word-groups for mankind's labor, *toil* (*'āmāl, 'āmēl*, 34 times) and *task* (*'ānâ, 'inyān*, 8 times, only in Eccl), as illustrated by their parallel use in 2:22-23 and 3:9-10. The sense conveyed is that of human striving with great trouble but diminishing return; it reflects the same kind of *toil* with which mankind was cursed in Gen 3:17b (Heb. *'iṣṣabôn*, cf. also Gen 5:29).

[24] The Heb. (*rā'â*, lit. "evil" or "bad") usually connotes *adversity* or *misery* in Eccl (cf. 2:21; 5:13, 16; 6:1; 7:14; 8:6; 9:12; 10:5, 13; 11:10; 12:1), rather than *moral* evil. However, several words derived from the same root (*rā'*) are used in Eccl with a predominantly moral connotation and clustered in 7:15-9:3 (esp. 8:2-15), where Qoheleth deals more explicitly with the nature and consequences of human depravity.

[25] The word *good* or *better* (*ṭôb*) occurs as an adjective or substantive 44 times, usually (but not always) with a non-moral, existential connotation. The noun *goodness* (*ṭôbâ*) occurs seven times (4:8; 5:11, 18; 6:3, 6; 7:14; 9:18) with the sense of "lasting satisfaction" or "fulfillment" (except in 5:11, "material goods"). This is obscured in 6:3, 6 by NASB, "good things;" the intended meaning of *ṭôbâ* in 6:3, 6 is elucidated by the contextually parallel *sābea'* ("to be satisfied," 1:8; 4:8; 5:10; 6:3) and *mālē'* ("to be full," 1:8; 6:7). Two other words—*yāṭab* ("to be good/well" or "to make glad," 7:3; 11:9) and *māthōq* ("sweet," 5:12; 11:7)—can also be rendered, respectively, "to be satisfied" (or "satisfy") and "satisfying."

[26] Cf. e.g., 1:2-3; 2:11; 5:16; 5:18-6:6; 6:11; 7:14.

[27] "Light" and "darkness" are often OT figures of life and death (Whybray, *Ecclesiastes*, 58). In Eccl the phrase *see light* denotes *satisfaction* or *meaning* in life, while "darkness" signifies *misery, adversity*, or meaninglessness (cf. 2:13-14; 5:17; 6:4; [8:1]; 11:7-8; 12:2); *see the sun* means "be alive" (6:5; 7:11).

[28] The same word (*ma'ăśeh*) is used to denote the achievements of mankind and the "work" of God. The word occurs 21 times. When used in reference to man *ma'ăśeh* differs from *task* or *toil* (n. 23) in that it reflects the tangible results of mankind's labor (cf. 2:17; 3:17, 22; 5:6; 9:7, 10). In referring to God's work, it

for good (6:12a; 8:16-17; 11:1-6) but we can find lasting satisfaction in our God-given *portion (lot* or *heritage)*.[29]

However, humans are predictably dissatisfied with their portion from God and prone to contend for a better lot in life (6:1-11), so Qoheleth repeatedly exhorts his readers to *enjoy*[30] their portion. When he turns to investigate the source of such "existential discontent" he discovers that it is attributable to three inherent human limitations—our invariable uncertainty, mortality, and depravity. The theme of *uncertainty* emerges early in the book, most often expressed as the rhetorical questions *Who knows...?* or *Who can tell...?*[31] or their declarative equivalents (i.e., man *does not know..., cannot find out...*).[32] In the first half of the argument we find that our uncertainty over what advantage we can gain in our labor precludes any lasting satisfaction. In the second half we find that satisfaction attends the opportune investment of our God-given *portion* (9:7-10; 11:1-8).

Mankind's inevitable *mortality* imposes an equally serious constraint on our capacity to find satisfaction in our labor. Qoheleth laments the finality and impartiality of death[33] and frequently alludes to the limited number of days we have to live.[34] In the first

---

denotes the ultimate fulfillment of His sovereign purposes (cf. 3:11; 7:13; 8:17; 11:5). It is the key term in Eccl 8:16-9:10, along with the single occurrence of the synonym *'ābad* in 9:1.

[29] Mankind's *portion* (*ḥēleq*, 2:10, 21; 3:22; 5:18, 19; 9:6, 9; 11:2) denotes his "lot," "share," or "heritage" in life. The closely related *inheritance* (*naḥălâ*) occurs only in 7:11 (they are synonymous in Job 27:13; 31:2). One can be truly satisfied only if he accepts his God-given *portion* and invests his labor in it.

[30] These so-called "enjoyment" pericopae are found in 2:24-26; 3:12-13; 3:22; 5:18-20; 8:15; 9:7-10; and 11:9-12:7, and each features the occurrence of either *śimḥâ* (*gladness, joy*; 2:26; 5:20; 9:7) or *śāmaḥ* (*be happy, rejoice*; 3:12, 22; 5:19; 8:15; 11:9); cp. also *ḥûš* (*enjoy*) in 2:25. A similar sense is conveyed by the constructions "see good[ness]" (2:1; 5:18; 6:6; cf. n. 25) and "see life" (9:9).

[31] These questions appear, respectively, in 2:19; 3:21; 6:12a; 8:1; and 6:12b; 8:7; 10:14. Analogous constructions occur in 7:24 (*Who can find out...?*) and 3:22 (*Who can bring him to see...?*).

[32] These are found, respectively, in 5:1; 8:7; 9:1, 5, 12; 10:15; 11:2, 5 (twice), 11:6; and in 3:11; 7:14, 28 (twice); 8:17 (three times). The Heb. verbs for *know* (*yada'*) and *find out* or *discover* (*māṣā'*) express in the negative the disappointing failure of the author's attempt to *seek* (*bāqaš* or *dāraš*, 1:13; 7:25; 8:17) or *search out* (*tûr*, 1:13; 2:3; 7:25) the meaning of things.

[33] The concept of death is communicated by the Heb. word-groups *mûth/māweth* (*die, death*, cf. 2:16; 3:2, 19; 4:2; 5:16; 7:1, 17, 26; 8:8; 9:3-5), and *qārā/miqreh* (*befall, fate*, cf. 2:14-15; 3:19 [three times]; 9:2, 3, 11). These terms serve, respectively, to underscore death's *finality* and *impartiality*.

[34] Cf. 2:16, 23; 5:17, 18, 20; 7:10; 8:13, 15; 9:9; 11:1, 8, 9; 12:1.

half of the argument mankind's mortality promotes disillusionment with self-sufficiency, but in the second half awareness of our mortality is emphasized (7:1-4) in order to compel us to invest expediently in the work of God (11:9-12:7). But this seems threatened both by our limited *time* to invest and by the inscrutable *timing* of God's purposes.[35] The closing sequence of figures in the body of the argument (12:1-7) symbolizes our inexorable incapacitation and loss of all remaining opportunity to serve as agents of our Creator.

Only later in the argument does Qoheleth reflect on the most devastating human limitation, our *depravity* or *sin*.[36] Self-sufficient people are not at all inclined to reflect on the harm caused by their own depravity (7:15-29) or accept accountability before God for the consequences of their sin (8:1-15) until they exhaust all hope of enjoying lasting satisfaction in their own strength (1:12-6:12). Our proclivity for sin is both **intensive** (it influences every aspect of one's being, 7:16-18, 20-21; 8:11; 9:3) and **extensive** (it is evident throughout all mankind, 7:20, 27-29) and most often manifested as "folly."[37] Even *a little folly* can nullify wisdom's advantage (10:1), from a trivial indiscretion to all-consuming self-indulgence; its potent influence is aptly conveyed in a sequence of word pictures portraying the disproportionately ruinous consequences (10:4-20).[38]

---

35 *Time* ('*ēt*) in Eccl often conveys the sense of inscrutable *timing* of God's sovereign purposes (thirty-one times in chap. 3, twice in 8:5-6); note the chiastic parallel in 3:1 with *z^emān* (*appropriate occasion* or *season*). In 9:11-12 '*ēt* (three times) denotes both one's appointed *time* to die and his consequently limited *opportunity* to achieve success.

36 The Heb. for *sin/sinner* (*ḥāṭā'*, *ḥôṭe'*) occurs five of seven times (2:26; 5:6; 7:20, 26; 8:12; 9:2, 18) in the second half of Eccl in close context with those words for "evil" having a predominantly moral connotation (n. 24). In 8:2-13 it serves as the focal point of mankind's moral accountability before God.

37 The *fool* in Eccl is clearly identified with *sin*. Note, e.g., the parallel in 9:17-18 between a *ruler of fools* (9:17b) and *one sinner* (9:18b). The usual word for "fool" in the OT (*k^esîl*) occurs sixteen times in Eccl; the related *kesel* (*folly, foolishness*) occurs in 7:25. Another word-group for *fool* or *folly* (*sākāl, sekel, siklûth*) is almost exclusive to Eccl, appearing in the book thirteen times. R.N. Whybray plausibly ascribes such dual use to Qoheleth's selective quotation of ancient proverbs ("The Identification and Use of Quotations in Ecclesiastes," reprinted in Zuck [ed.], *Reflecting with Solomon*, 185-99).

38 The intricate textual design of 10:1-20 is discussed in detail in the Commentary. Each word picture portrays the potent destructiveness of folly, from the perilous "pitfalls" of seemingly trivial oversights (10:4-10) to the total ruin of the self-indulgent fool (10:11-20).The whole sequence collectively illustrates the object lesson of the transitional verse (9:18), *wisdom's vulnerability*. For a capable discussion of this unifying theme in the passage, see Graham S. Ogden,

These inherent obstacles to lasting satisfaction in mankind's search for meaning lead invariably to a growing *vexation*,[39] so we typically strive all the more in our ambition to forge our own advantage in life (4:1-6:12). Our selfish ambition is characterized by grasping *envy* (4:4-6, cf. 6:9) and by bold presumption before God, exemplified in our *dreams and many words* (5:2-3, 7; 6:11) and our *vows* (5:4-6).[40] It is just this vain conceit that falsely justifies the ubiquitous *oppression*[41] of the powerless in life (4:1-3; 5:8). However, such oppression ironically returns to haunt the oppressor: Rather than affording satisfaction, it only multiplies fruitless strife and alienation (4:7-16, cf. 4:4). The selfishly ambitious inevitably forfeit all that they gained at others' expense, suffer profound disillusionment (5:10-17; 7:9-10), and wind up in the same state of existential despair[42] as those who were oppressed by

---

"Variations on the Theme of Wisdom's Strength and Vulnerability—Ecclesiastes 9:17-10:20," reprinted in Zuck (ed.), *Reflecting with Solomon*, 331-40.

[39] The word *vexation* (*ka'as*) appears seven times (1:18; 2:23; 5:17; 7:3, 9 [twice]; 11:10) and characterizes the typical human response to life's inexorable adversity. While it is rendered variably in most translations (*grief, sorrow, frustration, provocation, anger, anxiety* [NIV]; *grief, vexation, sorrow, anger* [NASB]; *grief, sorrow, anger* [NKJV], there is evidence for a more consistent sense of *frustration* or *disillusionment*. Most notably, the same profound disillusionment depicted in 5:17 is meant to be echoed in 7:3, 9 and 11:10. Such "vexation" is resolved by *authentic mourning* (7:2-4) but can become entrenched as bitterness (7:9-10).

[40] The repeated figure *dreams and many words* (5:3, 7) conveys the foolish presumption of a person announcing their selfish aspirations to God without considering God's purposes (5:1-3). With our *vows* we try to manipulate God into blessing our ambition (5:4-6) but only risks losing all we have worked for (5:6c-7). When the figure *many words* recurs (6:11; 10:14), it conveys the same sense of presumption and vain conceit. Elihu also reproved Job for his presumption in *multiplying words* before God (Job 34:37; 35:16).

[41] The notion of *oppression* or *oppressor* (*'āšaq, 'ōšeq, 'ăšûkîm*) appears in Eccl 4:1 (three times); 5:8; and 7:7. Those who oppress others (4:1-3) in their quest for meaning only compound the futility manifested *under the sun*. The blatant injustice of such oppression (3:16) leads Qoheleth to discover that all oppression stems from selfish ambition (4:4-6; 5:8). Such *oppression* adversely affects one's reasoning (7:7a, although the word is misconstrued by NIV as "extortion" in order to parallel "bribe" in 7:7b; so also Longman, *Ecclesiastes*, 186-7). This effect of *oppression* is also acknowledged by Job (Job 6:24, 26) and later by Elihu, when he challenged the faulty reasoning that emerged from Job's "victim's complex" (Job 35:9, cf. 10:3).

[42] The word *despair* (*yā'aš*) occurs only in Eccl 2:20 and Job 6:26, but the concept is more fully developed in both books with figurative imagery: The agonized preference for death or non-existence voiced in Job 3 and in Eccl 4:2-3 and 6:3-6 very effectively projects for the reader the intended sense of profound despair.

their selfish ambition (6:3-6, cf. 4:2-3).

Qoheleth responds to such self-consuming vexation by extolling the life-giving advantages of self-effacing *wisdom*;[43] after all, *a wise heart knows time and judgment* (8:5 [NASB], cf. 3:15): We are aware that there is a *time for every purpose*[44] in every choice we make (3:1, 17; 8:6) and that our stewardship of these purposes is subject to God's *judgment* [45] (3:17; 8:6), just as one's service to the *king* is subject to judgment (8:2-5a; 10:4, 20).[46] But this creates a seemingly unsolvable dilemma: If God gives such wisdom only *to a man who is good in His sight* (2:26),[47] yet all men

---

[43] The topic of *wisdom* (*ḥākām, ḥokmâ*) pervades the book, appearing 51 times. It appears twice as often in the second half (7:1-12:14), where the focus is on *wisdom's advantage* in bringing success to mankind's labor (7:11-12, 19; 8:1). Wisdom's strength is realized in humility but nullified by self-sufficiency played out as folly (9:13-18; 10:10b, cf. n. 38). Thus, wisdom's success depends critically on human disposition and by itself "is shown to be inadequate....Wisdom given by God...is allowed; autonomous, self-sufficient wisdom as a remedy to man's plight 'under the sun' is disallowed" (Eaton, *Ecclesiastes*, 47).

[44] The word *ḥēpheṣ* nearly always means "purpose" in Eccl. The construction *time for every purpose* (*ḥēpheṣ*) in 3:1, 17; 8:6 refers to the *appropriate timing* of God's preordained purposes (cf. n. 35). In 3:1-17 the phrases *under heaven* (3:1, cf. n. 21) and *God does* (or *makes*) (3:11, 14) occur in close connection with the terms *kol* (*everything, whatever*) and *'ôlām* (*eternity, forever*), implying that *ḥēpheṣ* in 3:1, 17 also refers to God's purposes. Although the wording is nearly identical in 8:6, NKJV and NASB miss the intended link and instead translate "delight" or "matter" (as in 5:8 where "matter" does make sense). The same nuance of *ḥēpheṣ* in 8:6 suggests an intended analogy in that context between God's purposes (8:6) and those of the king in 8:3 (NIV), *he does whatever he pleases* (*ḥaphēṣ*), i.e., whatever he "intends" or "purposes." The idea of "purpose" will also be argued for the final occurrences of *ḥēpheṣ* in 12:1 and 12:10.

[45] In all of its occurrences in Eccl (3:16-17; 8:5-6; 11:9; 12:14) the word-group *judge/judgment* (*šāphaṭ, mišpāṭ*) conveys the sense of mankind's ultimate accountability under sovereign authority. Again, the NASB is misleading: While the *mišpāṭ* word-group is appropriately translated "justice" and "judge" in 3:16 and 17, respectively, it is inexplicably rendered "procedure" in the comparable construction in 8:5-6. Given that it is associated in both contexts with the construction "time...for every purpose" (n. 44), the word *mišpāṭ* in 8:5-6 should be rendered as in 3:16 with exactly the same sense of "accountability under authority" (note esp. the immediately preceding phrase in 3:15, *God requires an account of what is past*).

[46] Even when men seem to escape judgment of their evil in this life (3:16; 7:15; 8:9-12a, 14; 9:2), God's judgment will prevail. His sure justice is only magnified by the failure of human justice; cp. 3:16-17 and 8:11-13.

[47] The label *good* in 2:26 probably conveys a moral sense, as also in 3:12; 7:20, 26b; 9:2 (twice); and 12:14 (cf. n. 25). The attribution of a a man's wisdom in 2:26 to his acceptability in God's sight anticipates and explains the otherwise cryptic association of *the righteous* and *the wise* in 7:16-18 and 9:1.

are tainted by depravity (see above), then how can anyone gain wisdom's advantage (8:1)? By thus preempting wisdom's advantage, our sin would seem to guarantee our failure as agents of God.

Qoheleth addresses this dilemma by proposing the *fear of God*[48] as the only solution to self-sufficiency that can reap wisdom's benefits and yield lasting meaning in life.[49] This is the interpretive crux of the book of Ecclesiastes:[50] Only in the *fear of God* can humanity acknowledge sin, become accountable as righteous and wise[51] stewards of God's purposes, and gain the confidence we need to flourish as God's chosen agents. Regrettably, we are not easily convinced that self-sufficiency will inevitably fail and we typically cling to it, even in the face of adversity—its strong counterfeit appeal only forestalls the decision to fear God, so we foolishly continue to forfeit wisdom's advantage in trying to fulfill our

---

[48] The *fear* (*yārē'*) of God is mentioned seven times in Eccl (3:14; 5:7; 7:18; 8:12-13 [three times]; 12:13), each in connection with some aspect of mankind's accountability before God. While the term does not appear *per se* in Eccl 7:13-14, these verses help to shape the concept as a crucial transition to the book's second half. Cf. also 5:18-20.

[49] Eaton suggests that Qoheleth "is the frontier-guard against *any* form of self-reliance. The fear of God which he recommends...is not only the beginning of wisdom; it is also the beginning of joy, of contentment and of an energetic and purposeful life. [He] wishes to deliver us from a rosy-coloured self-confident godless life, with its inevitable cynicism and bitterness, and from trusting in wisdom, pleasure, wealth, and human justice or integrity. He wishes to drive us to see that God is there, that He is good and generous, and that only such an outlook makes life coherent and fulfilling" (*Ecclesiastes*, 48, emphasis his).

[50] Note how the frame narrator's *conclusion of the whole matter* singles out the *fear of God* (12:13). This should prompt the reader to carefully mine every context in Eccl in which the *fear of God* is mentioned to determine the role that it plays in the argument. See Parsons, "Proclaiming the Book of Ecclesiastes," 164-5, 166.

[51] Although one may strive to be "righteous" and "wise" before God (7:16-17), only he who *fears God* will *come forth with both* (7:18, NASB), so that it is *well with him* before God (8:12b-13). See Wayne A. Brindle, "Righteousness and Wickedness in Ecclesiastes 7:15-18," reprinted in Zuck (ed.), *Reflecting with Solomon*, 301-13. Thus, *the righteous and the wise and their works are in the hand of God* (9:1; cf. 2:24), because God already *favors* their works (9:7b, NIV; n. 28). This accords with the common refrain *The fear of the Lord is the beginning of wisdom* (Job 28:28, Prov 1:7; 2:3-5; 3:5-7; 9:10; Ps 111:10) and it explains Qoheleth's apparent ambivalence toward wisdom (n. 15): Wisdom as a **source** of meaning in the first half of the book never ultimately satisfies (cf. 2:12-16; 6:8), whereas wisdom as the **path** to meaning in the second half of the book confers great advantage, because it is rooted in the fear of God (cf. 7:11-14; n. 50).

calling as chosen agents of God (9:11-18).[52]

Ironically, the one thing capable of displacing our infatuation with self-sufficiency is the same unassuaged *vexation* that can lead to despair. We ultimately have only two choices in response to such vexation: We can simply redouble our determination to be self-sufficient (6:10-11), so that vexation hardens into entrenched bitterness (5:16-17; 7:9-10), or we can endure the difficult but transforming process of authentic *mourning*[53] (7:1-4) and reap wisdom's inheritance (7:11-12). Mourning entails honest recognition of our inherent depravity, uncertainty, and mortality, and of the resulting futility of trying to forge our own advantage in life. Only then can we *fear* Him and prevail in righteousness and wisdom (7:16-18); only then do we gain enough confidence in His inscrutable purposes to become fruitful stewards of our God-given "portion" or "heritage" and capable of truly enjoying that heritage (7:13-14; 9:4-10; 11:9-12:1).

LITERARY STRUCTURE IN THE ARGUMENT OF ECCLESIASTES

While understanding the intended sense of recurring terms is essential to accurate interpretation of Ecclesiastes, this alone is not sufficient. Given the questions of authorship, historical context, distinctive

---

[52] The problem with self-sufficiency as mankind's chosen disposition is that it depends on sustaining the illusion that one can control the outcome of his toil in life. God has planted within human conscience an awareness of our accountability as stewards of a God-given "portion" within God's creative purposes (3:10-15). Though our consciences should attest to it, we refuse in our self-sufficiency to acknowledge our accountability or accept our portion and we resist God's repeated efforts to dispel the illusion that we can control our circumstances. This tenacious display of foolishness consequently dooms our quest for satisfaction to futility, in that we reject the fear of God (n. 51).

[53] The word *mourning* (*'ēbel*) appears only twice in the transitional passage (7:2, 4) but it delivers the key challenge to the disillusioned reader: Given the adverse effect of *oppression* on wisdom (7:7, n. 41), one cannot exploit wisdom's advantage without going through authentic mourning (7:3-6). Notably, LXX translates *'ēbel* as *penthous*, the same root as in Matt 5:4, *Blessed are those who mourn....* The spiritual intensity of this transition is graphically depicted in Job's final lament, expressing his grief with the same word, *'ēbel* (30:31). When we insist on remaining self-sufficient, our vexation only becomes entrenched and clouds the hope of any lasting meaning in life (5:16-17; 7:8-10, n. 39). Authentic *mourning* effectively resolves such vexation when it leads to brokenness—the acknowledgment of failure of self that releases our heart to accept our portion from God (5:18-20; 9:6-10; 11:9-12:1, n. 29).

Hebrew, significant variation in mood and tone, and the apparent internal contradictions, we will not be able to identify a logically coherent message and derive the author's intended purpose without a sense of the textual design and literary structure of the developing argument. Especially important in this regard are the structural markers and the author's versatile use of conjunctions in framing the logic of the argument.[54] The author's literary or "expressive" purpose gradually emerges as clues are incrementally recognized in the arrangement of the text.[55]

The book's dominant genre of "reflection"[56] is recognized in Qoheleth's distinctive use of constructions like *I have seen, I said in my heart,* and *I applied my heart.* In reflecting with blunt honesty on the events he sees *under the sun,* Qoheleth's inferences take on increasingly moral overtones in the *heart* as the "mirror" of conscience,[57] with an intended *a fortiori* impact: His cynical reflections on what **he** has seen and experienced in life are meant to convince his **readers** of their own existential and moral inadequacy; those who fear God and are convinced of their accountability before Him (7:15-8:15) can then be reassured that even though they cannot see how God will use their works they can still be confident He *has accepted their works* (8:16-9:10).

The author uses characteristic opening and closing constructions to delineate his thought units and help the reader track the evolving logic of the argument. Generally, the closing markers are easier to recognize. Qoheleth frequently uses the characteristic

---

[54] Osborne discusses the versatility of common Hebrew conjunctions (*Hermeneutical Spiral*, 57); in Eccl the intended force of *waw, kî, gam,* and *'ašer* is highly variable and depends on context.

[55] *See* the section entitled "Literal Composition" under the heading "The Unity of Job and Ecclesiastes" in the Preface to this Commentary.

[56] *See* Murphy, *Ecclesiastes*, xxxi-xxxii; and H. Carl Shank, "Qoheleth's World and Life View," reprinted in Zuck (ed.), *Reflecting with Solomon*, 76-77. The type-traits of "reflection" are characterized by the frequent mention of deliberative activity in the "heart" (*lēb,* forty-one times in Eccl, often translated "mind").

[57] For Qoheleth the heart is the seat of human conscience. While our conscience is intended to hold us morally accountable through awareness of God's sovereign design for life (3:11b, 14, cf. nn. 45, 52), the heart all too often sanctions evil (7:22; 8:11; 9:3). But as Qoheleth's reflections evolve in the second half of the argument, his inferences bear increasing witness to the positive influence of the *fear of God* on this "heart" awareness. See Shank, ibid., 77, and Caneday, "Enigmatic Pessimist or Godly Sage," 104-5.

expression *This also is vanity and grasping for the wind* (or the shorter *this too is vanity)* as a closing marker for thought units in the first half of the book.[58] There are also seven "enjoyment" pericopae that serve as closers in the first half of the book.[59] Finally, all three major sections that comprise 1:12-7:14 are each concluded by a variation of the same key repeating rhetorical question.[60] Some closing markers are also followed by a "summary appraisal" that recapitulates the "take home message" of the preceding thought unit.[61]

Typical opening markers include Qoheleth's repeated purpose statements (1:3, 12; 3:9) and some of the constructions indicative of reflection like *I have seen [*or *proved]* (3:16; 5:18; 7:15, 23; 8:9; 9:13), *I said in my heart* (1:16; 2:1; 8:16) and *I returned and saw [*or *considered]* (4:1, 7; 9:11).[62] While it is evident that these constructions are true "openers" when they are immediately preceded by recognized closing constructions, in other instances further textual evidence must be adduced to support such a structural role.[63] Some thought units can only be recognized by a distinctive shift in textual design or literary style, or

---

[58] Murphy, *Ecclesiastes*, 21. The full phrase occurs eight times (1:14, 17; 2:11, 17, 26; 4:4, 16; 6:9); the shorter expression is used many more times. These markers turn out to be extremely helpful guides to the subtle substructure of Eccl in the first half of the book, as pointed out in the Commentary.

[59] Murphy, *Ecclesiastes*, 25. See 2:24-26; 3:12-13, 22; 5:18-20; 8:15; 11:9-10. These pericopae also double as "oases of optimism" that balance Qoheleth's repeated inferences of futility and foreshadow the true basis for lasting satisfaction which Qoheleth will expound in the second half.

[60] Each of these asserts that a person cannot tell "what will happen afterwards" (3:22b; 6:12b; 7:14b).

[61] Wisdom instruction "often concludes with a pithy statement...a 'summary appraisal'" (Osborne, *The Hermeneutical Spiral*, 196). Such statements in Eccl often seem to dangle with no connection to what precedes or follows (cf. 1:15, 18; 4:5-6; 6:10-11; 7:7); they are probably earlier traditional wisdom sayings quoted by Qoheleth to corroborate the wisdom of the preceding reflections (R.N. Whybray, "The Identification and Use of Quotations in Ecclesiastes," reprinted in Zuck [ed.], *Reflecting with Solomon*, 198).

[62] The construction *I returned and saw* predictably signals a major turning point in the course of Qoheleth's argument (4:1, 7; 9:11).

[63] "[I]t is clear that...any one of these literary devices is as liable to occur in the middle of an argument as at the beginning....They certainly cannot be regarded as a consistent system of markers" (Whybray, *Ecclesiastes*, 47).

a new thematic emphasis,[64] often introduced by transitional verse(s) in the preceding section. The rest of this Overview will outline the textual design of the argument and demonstrate the literary coherence of the composite subsections with the overarching logical unity of the argument.

TEXTUAL DESIGN AND THE BROAD UNITY OF QOHELETH'S ARGUMENT

The argument of Ecclesiastes is essentially symmetrical: Both the prologue (1:1-11) and epilogue (12:8-14) are marked by the distinctive construction *vanity of vanities* (1:2; 12:8) and written from the perspective of a "frame narrator" who quotes Qoheleth in the third person.[65] The prologue and epilogue thus enclose the body of the argument, consisting of a long string of observations and reflections made by Qoheleth (1:12-12:7, except for 7:27[66]). These reflections are arranged in two sequences (1:12-6:12 and 7:15-12:7) that are joined by a transitional passage (7:1-14); the logic of the argument flows from the sequential inferences that Qoheleth draws from his reflections.

The first half of the argument culminates in a repetition of four rhetorical questions asserting the lack of any *advantage*[67] to mankind's quest for satisfaction in life, notwithstanding Qoheleth's unprecedented wisdom and experience (1:12-6:12). The concluding summary appraisal (6:10-12)[68] epitomizes the utterly foolish

---

[64] *See* above text accompanying n. 17. Notably challenging are the transitions at 7:1, 9:13, 10:1, 11:1 and 11:9. For 7:1, 10:1, and 11:9, the preceding verses serve as important "hinges" to the major themes that characterize the subsequent paragraphic units: The collection of aphorisms and word pictures in chap. 10 is introduced by 9:18b, as previously noted (n. 38). The question *Who knows what is good...?* (6:12a) introduces 7:1-14, with its sequential *better than* proverbs (Murphy, *Ecclesiastes*, 62), and the prospect of *days of darkness...all to come is vanity* (11:8b) constitutes the point of departure for 11:9-12:7.

[65] *See* again n. 7.

[66] The brief return of the frame narrator in 7:27 is intended to underscore the importance of the conclusion in 7:26-29 concerning the universal inability of mankind, which sets up the challenge in 8:1 (n. 92, below).

[67] Cf. 5:11, 16; 6:8, 11b. Among commonly used English translations only the NASB identifies the common thread that links these questions by aptly translating *kišrôn* or *yôthēr, yithrôn* with the same word "advantage" in each case (n. 22).

[68] While the text of 6:10-11 seems to dangle between two closing constructions—one at 6:12 (n. 60) and the other at 6:9—this design sets the pericope 6:10-12 apart as both a "summary appraisal" (n. 58) for 1:12-6:9 and the point of departure for the main transition in the argument, 7:1-14.

presumption of human self-sufficiency. This disposition is implied by the repetition of the figure *many words*,[69] which depicts self-sufficient humans verbally contending with God for a different lot in life (6:10-11), even though they cannot possibly predetermine what choices will be good for them or what will happen after they get their own way (6:12).

We can surmise from the climax of despair (6:1-12) at the end of this first sequence of reflections that the following pericope forms the major transition of the argument (7:1-14): A distinctive textual design (below) alerts the reader to the evolving tone and thematic content of Qoheleth's reflections. The prevailing themes of futility and selfish ambition give way to a new governing theme—*wisdom's advantage* for the *work of God* (cf. 7:11-14). The dominant mood of cynicism and despair in 1:12-6:12 gradually thaws into a cautious optimism for the reader who would aspire to gain wisdom's advantage as a steward of the work of God. Caution is still warranted, for the man who would gain wisdom's advantage will still inevitably be confronted with his innate depravity, uncertainty, and mortality. In the second half of the argument Qoheleth thus explores these human limitations with a view to harnessing wisdom's advantage to overcome their constraints on effective agency in the work of God (7:15-12:7).

THE PIVOTAL TRANSITION IN QOHELETH'S ARGUMENT

The transitional passage (7:1-14) is set apart from the preceding text by its distinctive textual design and from the following text by a repeated closing marker (7:14b).[70] Its design is distinguished **structurally** by the chiastic arrangement[71] of *better than* proverbs and **thematically** by the conspicuous confluence of repeating terms: *good, better* (eleven times); *wise, wisdom* (six times); *heart* (five times); *fool(s)* (four times); *vexation* [*anger*] (three times);

---

[69] The *many words* construction (n. 40) in 6:11a is best rendered the same as in 5:2c-3, 7 (cf. NASB) and thus serves as *inclusio* for the text within 5:1-6:12. The argument bounded by this repeated phrase shows how the oppression and alienation depicted in 4:1-16 are rooted in foolish presumption (5:1-6:12), the hallmark of human self-sufficiency.

[70] Whybray, *Ecclesiastes*, 112. Cf. n. 60.

[71] The four pericopae comprising the transitional passage demonstrate topical chiasm: "wisdom" (7:1-4); "folly" (7:5-7); "folly" (7:8-10); "wisdom" (7:11-14). The more detailed parallelism occurring within each of these pericopae will be demonstrated in the exposition of the passage.

mourning (twice); *advantage* (twice, NASB); and *oppression* or *adversity* (once each). In contrast to chaps. 1-6 Qoheleth now sees *wisdom* as an *advantage*, and this notion will continue as the main focus of the second half of the argument.

To this point in the argument Qoheleth's reflections proved that even when guided by the greatest of natural wisdom (cf. 1:12-18), the self-sufficient quest for an advantage in one's labor would yield only disillusionment and despair. Consisting of a sequence of wise sayings that describe what is "better,"[72] the transitional passage contrasts the perspective of self-sufficiency depicted in the first half of the argument with a more edifying perspective that emerges when one reflects with painful honesty on life's apparent futility. The predominant *good, better* motif responds to the rhetorical question that concluded the preceding section (6:12a)[73] by explaining how wisdom is *better than* simply redoubling self-sufficient effort in response to life's inevitable adversity.

Wisdom bestows an advantage on those who allow their *vexation* or *disillusionment* (cf. 7:3, 9)[74] amid life's inevitable adversity and disappointment to promote authentic *mourning*[75] and not pleasure-seeking distraction (7:1-7). Only by mourning can man come to realize the true wisdom of willingly submitting to God's inscrutable purposes as an agent "named" by God (7:8-14, cf. 6:10).[76] In the second half of the argument Qoheleth then explores wisdom's

---

[72] Eaton, *Ecclesiastes*, 108-13. Such *better than* sayings also furnish the structural framework for the anecdotal reflections of 4:1-16 and 9:13-18 (cf. n. 22).

[73] Murphy, *Ecclesiastes*, 62.

[74] Virtually all the popular modern translations of 7:3 render *ka'as* as "sorrow" rather than "vexation" or "anger," as in 7:9 (cf. n. 39). While "sorrow" fits the morbid theme of 7:1-4 and parallels "sad face" in 7:3b, the argument's logic turns on one's response to the crisis provoked by the unremitting frustration of his self-sufficient disposition (5:17). This suggests a preferable sense that complements 7:9: *Vexation* (or *disillusionment*) is better than *laughter* because it can lead to mourning in response to life's adversity and instruct the heart with wisdom (7:1-4, cf. n. 53), rather than corrupting the heart with the false comfort of diversion (7:5-7, n. 52). Indeed, the proud person who harbors vexation in his bosom rejects the preferable disposition of patience in adversity (7:8-10) and forfeits wisdom's benefits by resisting God's inscrutable plan (7:11-14).

[75] Note 53.

[76] The main premise of the second half of the argument is based on the implied connection here between submitting to the inscrutable *work of God* (7:13-14, n. 28) and accepting one's calling as an *agent of God* (6:10). This "acceptance" is the essential component of the *fear of God* as the only way to gain wisdom's advantage (7:15-9:10, cf. 7:11b) and bring wisdom's success (9:11-12:7, cf. 7:11a).

advantage in one's stewardship of these purposes—but with cautious optimism—for he finds this to be extremely vulnerable to the pitfalls of mankind's inherent depravity, uncertainty, and mortality. Qoheleth thus arranges his reflections in light of these pitfalls to motivate the reader as chosen agent of the work of God to gain wisdom's advantage by *fearing God* and then sustaining that advantage to bring wisdom's success (7:15-12:7).

THE LITERARY INFRASTRUCTURE OF QOHELETH'S TWO-PART ARGUMENT
Once this structural and thematic transition between the two stages of Qoheleth's argument is recognized, we can begin to identify the subordinate structure within each of these stages. The first stage (1:12-6:12) consists of two major sections delineated by nearly identical closing markers (3:22b; 6:12b) and the introduction of a new theme at 4:1. These two sections are in turn linked by a transitional pericope (4:1-8).[77] While both sections reflect the futility of self-sufficiency in one's pursuit of lasting satisfaction, the focus shifts from the futility of trying to **find** an *advantage* in one's toil "under the sun" (1:12-3:22) to the oppressive outcome of **forging one's own** *advantage* at the expense of others (4:1-6:12). On further exploring the heart of self-sufficient man, Qoheleth finds a "Pandora's box" of selfish ambition when he opens it he discovers that this ambition is at the root of all human oppression, foolish presumption on God, and our inherent inability to be *satisfied with goodness* (4:1-6:12).[78]

The two major sections are each in turn subdivided into distinct yet closely related subsections. Within the first section (1:12-3:22) the main transition is easily recognized at 2:24-26 as the first distinctive enjoyment pericope.[79] The coherence of these two

---

[77] This transitional pericope is itself set apart by repeated opening and closing markers, *I returned and considered* (or *saw*) in 4:1, 7, and *This also is vanity* in 4:4, 8, respectively. When Qoheleth "returned" to consider injustice (cf. 3:16) he "saw" unjust oppression (4:1-3) that stems from ambitious envy (4:4-6). When he further "returned" to explore the heart of the ambitious oppressor he "saw" the oppressive outcome of all self-sufficient strategies for success (4:7-6:12).

[78] It is interesting to note that those constructions portraying ambitious *oppression, presumption*, and lack of *satisfaction with goodness* are not emphasized at all until 4:1-6:12 (cf. nn. 25, 40, 41).

[79] *See* n. 30. While this pericope concludes the preceding subsection with Qoheleth's classic closing lament (n. 58) it also reintroduces the topic of God's role in mankind's destiny and thus serves as a literary transition to 3:1-22, with its predominant themes of divine *timing, purpose*, and *judgment* (cf. nn. 35, 44, 45).

subsections is preserved by the repeated purpose statement (1:13, 3:9-10) and the same predominant theme: the elusive advantage of all human labor,[80] whether one toils for his own legacy (1:12-2:26) or tries to curry God's favor with good deeds (3:1-22). The minor transitions within 1:12-2:26 are marked by the repeating conclusion *this also is vanity.* Those within 3:1-22 are marked by the rhetorical question in 3:9 (cf. 1:3) and a repeated opening marker in 3:10, 15.[81]

The entire second section (4:1-6:12) coheres under the one dominant theme of the invariable *oppression* that results from unrestrained selfish ambition. Three subsections can be recognized by a shift in literary type trait at 5:1[82] and by the enjoyment pericope at 5:18-20.[83] These are in turn divided by minor transitions (4:7a, 5:10c, 6:6b) that link selfish ambition with its oppressive outcomes: The selfish ambition that so profoundly oppresses others (4:1-6) also eventually afflicts the oppressor himself (4:7-16).[84] The same arrogant presumption that falsely entitles the oppressor to exploit God and those under his authority for personal gain[85] (5:1-10)

---

[80] Cf. 1:3, 14, 17; 2:11, 15, 19; 3:9, 21, 22c.

[81] The rhetorical question of 3:9 is "answered" in two stages, 3:10-15 (*I have seen...*) and 3:16-22 (*Furthermore, I have seen...*), each of which includes an enjoyment pericope (3:12-13; 3:22a).

[82] Qoheleth abruptly shifts from anecdote (4:1-16) to direct exhortation (5:1, 4, 8).

[83] Verses 5:18-20 conclude 5:1-20 but also form a hinge to 6:1-12 in the obvious symmetry of paired constructions with 6:1-3: *I have seen...good* (5:18) **and** *evil ...I have seen* (6:1); *God has given riches and wealth, and...power to eat of it* (5:19) **and** *God has given riches and wealth...yet...not...the power to eat of it* (6:2); *the days of his life...busy with the joy of his heart* (5:20) **and** *the days of his years are many, but his soul is not satisfied* (6:3).

[84] The entire passage (4:1-16) features the type trait of *better than* sayings (4:3, 6, 9, 13, cf. n. 72) and coheres under the motif of "two, both, the second" (Murphy, *Ecclesiastes*, 41). Qoheleth's realization that oppression is rooted in selfish ambition (4:1-6) prompts him to explore its effect on the oppressor himself (4:7-8), and he finds that anyone, whether pauper or king, who oppresses others to move up in the world is inescapably alienated from others by his own ambition (4:9-16).

[85] The interpretive difficulties of 5:9 are widely acknowledged (Murphy, *Ecclesiastes*, 46 [fn. 8a]; Whybray, *Ecclesiastes*, 97-98; Eaton, *Ecclesiastes*, 101-102). The allusion to royal advantage in 5:9 seems to arise from the "insider" perspective of Solomon (n. 7) as a logical inference of the observation in 5:8 regarding societal "pecking order: "So the only advantage of the land in all this is that it ends up serving the king" (see also Longman *Ecclesiastes*, 158-9). Thus, while *oppression* "trickles down" from king to serf (5:8), *advantage* flows in the opposite direction (5:9), thereby propagating a classical socioeconomic "pyramid" to further explain to the reader the cause of unjust *oppression* (cf. 4:1-3).

leaves him ironically dissatisfied with all he gained or was given by God (5:11-20).[86] Even when God gives *a man* all he wants, his selfish ambition ultimately turns to restless despair (6:1-6), because contending with God can never yield a better lot in life than God has already ordained (6:7-12).

The literary infrastructure of the second half of Qoheleth's argument (7:15-12:7) is even more widely debated. The frequency of terms like *cannot find [know, tell]* or *do not know* in this phase of the argument has led some expositors to suggest that it is framed by such constructions.[87] However, "man's inability to know his future is an idea implicit in the earlier chapters of the book"[88] and carries over from the main transition (7:13-14) as a necessary constraint on *wisdom's advantage for the work of God*, the unifying theme for the second half of Qoheleth's argument.[89] Thus, each major transition in 7:15-12:7 introduces a new twist in Qoheleth's reflections on *wisdom's advantage.*

The main transition in this stage (9:11-12) opens with the same marker as 4:1, 7.[90] After Qoheleth traced the human inability to gain *wisdom's advantage* to innate depravity, uncertainty, and mortality and relegated the reader's hope to the *fear of God* (7:15-9:10),

---

[86] The unity of 5:11-17 centers on the transitory nature of all earthly gain (cf. 5:11, 16): Not even the riches that accrue to the throne (5:9) are spared from attrition (5:11-17, cf. 2:21). Thus, 5:11-17 mirrors 4:7-16 by portraying yet another facet of the eventual collapse of even royal advantage under the weighty oppression that inevitably attends selfish ambition. This accords with Qoheleth's governing literary device of *a fortiori* reflection (cf. 1:16; 2:9, 25): Not even the king's riches can be preserved, so Qoheleth must then suggest the only viable alternative for lasting satisfaction in life in the concluding enjoyment pericope (5:18-20).

[87] *See* Murphy, *Ecclesiastes*, 81-82, 89; A. G. Wright, "The Riddle of the Sphinx," in Zuck (ed.), *Reflecting with Solomon*, 55; and Donald R. Glenn, "Ecclesiastes," in John F. Walvoord and Roy B. Zuck, eds., *BKC*, OT (Wheaton, IL: Victor Books, 1985), 996-1002.

[88] Ogden, "Wisdom's Strength and Vulnerability," 332. Indeed, each of the three major sections comprising 1:12-7:14 culminates with such constructions (n. 60, cf. also nn. 31, 32).

[89] *See* above, "THE PIVOTAL TRANSITION IN QOHELETH'S ARGUMENT."

[90] *See* n. 77. Although verses 9:11-12 may seem at first to be contextually isolated, the prominent marker at 9:11, *I returned and saw* (or *considered*), signals a major transition in reflection—just as at 4:1 and 7 (n. 62). Moreover, the absence of any typical opening markers between 9:13 and 12:7 supports viewing the entire section as a cohesive unit. Therefore, even though a minor transitional marker appears at 9:13, attempts to assign 9:11-12 to the preceding text (so Murphy, *Ecclesiastes*, 88-95) are unconvincing.

he *returned and saw* (9:11a) that wisdom's advantage is still elusive: When the man who fears God tries to succeed as an agent of God, he is tempted to revert to self-sufficiency, and these same limitations conspire to subvert the benefits of wisdom (9:11-12:7). Once we recognize how *wisdom's advantage* is reintroduced in 9:11-18[91] we can then see that Qoheleth designed his concluding exhortations to equip the agent of God for *wisdom's success* by alerting him to the pitfalls he is sure to encounter (10:1-12:7).

The first major section of this stage centers on our natural frustration in attempting to gain wisdom's advantage and please God: Since righteous works are apparently not rewarded in this life, the one who wants to please God can never be certain of having gained God's favor (7:15-9:10). Qoheleth first marshals incontrovertible evidence of universal human depravity (7:15-29), which relegates the reader's only hope of being righteous or wise to the *fear of God* (8:1-15, cf. 7:18). The transition at 8:1 is thus best seen as an invitation to respond:[92] Qoheleth advises the reader to submit to authority out of loyalty to God, because wickedness will inevitably incur judgment and death (8:1-8)[93]—even though evil may prosper in this life, in the final analysis *it will be well with those who fear God* (8:9-15).

The recurring lament (8:14) in the closing enjoyment pericope (8:14-15)[94] serves as the transition to the last subsection (8:16-9:10) and broaches the most difficult dilemma facing the reader who has chosen to fear God in response to Qoheleth's argument: The *righteous* who fear God still can't tell how their works fit into

---

[91] Of the five natural abilities listed in 9:11 that one might expect to yield an advantage, the last three are virtual synonyms for *wisdom*, which Qoheleth proceeds to depict in the object lesson of 9:13-18.

[92] Verse 8:1 is either a cynical closing synopsis of the hopeless estate of depraved humanity (Longman, *Ecclesiastes*, 208) or a hopeful invitation to those who still seek wisdom's benefits, while remaining fully cognizant of their own depravity (8:2-15, cf. 7:16-17). The latter alternative affords a more logical connection between 7:15-29 and 8:2-15, as Qoheleth had already intimated in 7:18-20 that *he who fears God* could still benefit from wisdom. Thus, 8:1 reintroduces into 8:1-15 the hope of *wisdom's advantage* in light of mankind's total inability.

[93] The affirmation of 8:8b, *wickedness will not release those who practice it* (NIV), prompts Qoheleth to cite an egregious apparent counterexample in 8:9 that elicits the long-term remedy in 8:12b-13.

[94] The observations in 7:15b, 8:14 are essentially identical and thus unite this section by *inclusio*.

the work of God (8:16-17).[95] This compels Qoheleth to test whether in fact the *righteous and the wise and their works are in the hand of God*, as he had presumed[96] (9:1a): Even though all we can see when we seek His favor is our common mortality and depravity, there is still hope for all the living—only the dead have no further opportunity to inherit a lasting legacy (9:1b-6). The section thus concludes with another enjoyment pericope (9:7-10), for *God* already *favors* our works (cf. 9:7b, NIV). This is the pivotal assertion for the following section.

The logic of the last major section (9:11-12:7) has eluded most expositors.[97] However, once the reader who seeks God's favor is recast as the chosen agent of His work on earth (9:7-10), the following injunctions cohere best as Qoheleth's advice to preserve *wisdom's advantage* in order to maximize success in the work of God: After presenting wisdom's hedge against mankind's inherent inability (9:11-18), Qoheleth addresses the limitations most likely to subvert wisdom's success—the pitfalls of *folly*[98] (10:1-20) and the constraints of *time and chance* (11:1-12:7, cf. 9:11b).[99] He advises the reader to submit to authority in view of mankind's recurring natural proclivity for folly (i.e., moral stupidity) (10:1-20)[100] and then encourages opportune stewardship of our God-given portion in the face of uncertainty over God's purposes (11:1-8)[101] and our impending debility or

---

[95] Qoheleth's nagging uncertainty over whether the *works* of the righteous do in fact count for God thus becomes the central focus of 8:16-9:10 (n. 28).

[96] *See* 7:16-18, 8:12b, and nn. 47, 51.

[97] Ogden's review of previously proposed outlines attests to the notorious difficulty of "determining some thematic arrangement of the material" in this passage ("Wisdom's Strength and Vulnerability," 331-35).

[98] The preceding transition (9:16-18) identifies *folly* as the main threat to wisdom's success (cf. n. 43).

[99] The notion of *time and chance* (9:11b) is formally taken up in 11:1-12:7 but also underlies the logic of 1:15, 7:14, and 8:6b-7. "Chance" denotes unpredictable fortune that limits mankind's opportunities to achieve success—the very dilemma behind 11:1-8. "Time" (cf. n. 35) is the main concern of 11:9-12:7 and refers to the limited *time* that a person has to serve God's purposes before they die (cf. 8:5b-6a) but also to the inscrutable *timing* of events on earth to fulfill those purposes (cf. 3:1, 17; 11:1-6).

[100] The apparent lack of cohesion of the anecdotes comprising chapter 10 resolves when we recognize that these figures collectively substantiate the reasoning of 9:18b, illustrating the disproportionate power of folly to nullify wisdom's benefits (cf. n. 38 and related text).

[101] The phrase *you do not know* is repeated four times in 11:1-6.

death as accountable and valued agents of the Creator (11:9-12:7).[102]

This section is subdivided by several subtle literary transitions. The assertion *one sinner destroys much good* (9:18b) serves as the point of departure for 10:1-20, which in turn is set apart from 11:1-8 by the device of *inclusio*.[103] The pericope 11:1-8 is distinguished from 11:9-12:7 by the closing marker *all to come is vanity* (11:8c) and by a shift in address at 11:9 to the *young man*. The *days of darkness* (11:8b) portend the futility of impending disability and death in 12:2-7 and the two verb forms also introduced in 11:8b serve as a point of departure for the sequence of imperatives in 11:9-12:1.[104]

These transitions dictate the flow of the argument: One cannot excel out of self-sufficiency for humans are limited by *time and chance* (9:11-12). Indeed, our greatest success comes from self-effacing wisdom (9:13-15a), yet we are all too prone to dismiss wisdom's advantage and undermine our success by foolishly reverting to self-sufficiency (9:15b-18). If we are to harness such wisdom and bring success in the work of God we must first remain accountable under authority to avoid the pitfalls of self-sufficient folly (10:1-20). In order to maximize our success in light of our unpredictable fortune and impending mortality, we should therefore squander no *time* or *chance* to invest our portion from God (11:1-8) and "remember" our Creator before we lose the strength and vitality to serve as His valued agents (11:9-12:7).

With the repeated opening lament *vanity of vanities* (12:8, cf. 1:2) the epilogue concludes Qoheleth's reflections by reintroducing

---

[102] This passage coheres around the repeated constructions *childhood and youth* (11:9, 11:10b, 12:1) and *before* (12:1, 2, 6). It is introduced by similar constructions in 11:8 advocating present fulfillment in view of imminent futility: *years* or *days* (11:8, 12:1); *rejoice* (11:8b, 9); *remember* (11:8b, 12:1); *darkness*, *darken* (11:8b, 12:2); and *vanity* (11:8b, 11:10b). See Murphy, *Ecclesiastes*, 114-15.

[103] The imperative in 10:4 is mirrored by a similar "book-end" counterpart in 10:20, forming an inclusion: Both verses directly urge the reader to remain accountable under authority when tempted to succeed in life by indulging in *folly* (cf. 10:1-3).

[104] The two verbs are imperfect in form but have jussive function, thus *let them rejoice*...and *let them remember*. These verbs are "answered" by the corresponding imperatives *Rejoice* and *remember*, which in turn encompass the sequence of imperatives in 11:9-12:1 urging joyful yet accountable service to God.

the frame narrator, who delivers a decisive two-stage authentication[105] of Qoheleth's wisdom: Qoheleth's teaching of the people was reliable, inspired wisdom of God, so it could be known well enough to guide and direct those who desire to succeed in life (12:8-11).[106] The student of wisdom is therefore well advised to diligently heed wisdom such as that which Qoheleth taught above all other sources of knowledge (12:12-14).

---

[105] Both 12:9 and 12:12 begin with the opening marker *weyōthēr*, and 12:12 is also marked by a conspicuous shift to direct address ("my son").

[106] *See* n. 13.

Prologue

PROPOSITION

I Can't Get No Satisfaction

"What Advantage Has a Man?" (Eccl 1:1-11)

In reflecting on the apparently futile cycles of nature and human history, **the frame narrator laments humanity's apparent inability to experience lasting satisfaction in anything under the sun,** *in order to challenge the reader to reflect with Qoheleth on whether there is any advantage at all to human labor in life.*

The "frame-narrator" introduces the book's major theme in the words of Qoheleth (1:1-2), whose Solomonic self-portrayal[107] provides the author with the unprecedented wisdom he will need in his exhaustive search for lasting satisfaction in life. The author uses the catch-phrase *vanity of vanities* to mark his primary concern[108]—the question of whether there can be any *advantage*[109] to human labor (1:3), since all evidence *under the sun*[110] only points to life's utter futility (1:1-2). The remainder of the prologue (1:4-11) then reflects on this futility from a cosmic perspective in anticipation of Qoheleth's personal reflections throughout the rest of the book.

The argument of the prologue is framed by its textual design. To substantiate Qoheleth's claim of futility in all things (1:1-3) the frame narrator cites his own observations of the repeating cycles that have characterized life since the beginning of time (1:4-11). With mirror-image symmetry[111] he introduces the central premise (1:8) of the first half of his argument, supported by his observations of the equally futile cycles in the realms of nature (1:4-7) and human history (1:9-11). A conspicuous change of narrator (1:12a) sets the prologue apart from the text that follows.

Thus, the argument: The author's sense of the futility in all

---

[107] *See* n. 7.

[108] Since the phrase *vanity of vanities* marks the beginning of both the prologue (1:1-11) and the epilogue (12:8-14) it functions as an inclusion for the entire book (cf. n. 8). The question in 1:3 immediately follows this phrase in the prologue but is distinguished from the rest of the prologue by the inclusion of 1:4-11 (n. 111), thereby marking 1:3 as the author's principal concern for the entire book.

[109] *See* n 22. The concept of "advantage" in the face of apparent futility is clearly woven into the first half of the argument (cf. n. 67) as Qoheleth's principal—almost obsessive—quest, which culminates inexorably in utter frustration by the end of this portion of the argument.

[110] *See* n. 21.

[111] NRSV best reflects the similarity of 1:4 (*A generation goes...a generation comes*) and 1:11 (*the people of long ago...people yet to come*) in forming an inclusion (Seow, *Ecclesiastes*, 111).

things and the resulting inference that there is therefore no advantage to all human labor (1:1-3) is prompted by the monotony observed in the repeating cycles of nature (1:4-7)[112] and human history (1:9-11).[113] He epitomizes his findings by asserting that *All things are full of labor…The eye is not satisfied with seeing, Nor the ear filled with hearing* (1:8).[114] He then goes on to prove his assertion *a fortiori* by enlisting Qoheleth's matchless wisdom and resources (1:12ff) to maximize the chances of finding some advantage for humans in all their labor that can escape life's futile cycles and gain them an enduring legacy (1:3, 11).

Thus, Qoheleth will reflect in the first half of the book (1:12-6:12) on the results of his own auspicious attempts to achieve something new that could bring lasting *remembrance*[115] (1:11). As the reader experiences the vicarious failure of each of Qoheleth's successive schemes to gain any advantage in all his labor (1:12-3:22, cf. 1:3), the author intends to progressively disabuse the reader of the hope that comparable strategies of one's own can satisfy. Having thus identified with Qoheleth in his stylized perspective, the reader will then be co-opted into exploring with him the pervasive harm done by selfish ambition (4:1-6:12), with the attendant implication that no self-sufficient strategy for one's own labor is capable of bringing lasting satisfaction (cf. 1:8).

---

[112] The editor-author's observation of the earth's monotonous cycles in the sun, wind, and rivers is directly at odds with mankind's aspiration to achieve new precedents and order with all his effort (cp. Gen 3:17b-19). This is remarkably consistent with the Second Law of Thermodynamics, which states that entropy (randomness, disorder) in the world is always increasing.

[113] Nothing that humans do is new (1:9-10) so they can do nothing to leave behind a unique and lasting legacy (1:11). The term *ri'šonim* in 1:11 can be read *former things* (so NKJV), but the symmetry with *generations* in 1:4 suggests that it is former *people* in view (n. 111). Greek mythology adeptly portrays this lack of progress in the myths of Sisyphus, who was condemned to repeatedly roll a huge stone up to a mountain top, only to have it roll back down again; and the daughters of Danaüs, who were condemned to repeatedly fill leaky vessels from the river with water that always drained out before they could reach the cistern.

[114] The "eye" and "ear" in 1:8 are the hyperbolic conduits that fill one's soul, and the same verbs "satisfy" and "fill" are used in 6:3 and 7, where the first half of the argument ends with emptiness of soul as the futile outcome of mankind's laborious and monotonous existence.

[115] The boundary verses (1:4, 11) both mention the monotony of passing *generations* (notes 112, 113) to establish the lack of any precedent for which to be remembered. The idea of *remembrance* (*zikkārôn*) will play a key role in Qoheleth's negative precedent for the reader; note esp. 2:16 and 9:5.

Part I

EXPLORATION

Trying to Find an Angle

The Futility of Toiling for a Lasting Legacy
(Eccl 1:12-3:22)

*By reflecting on the futility of either unprecedented earthly achievement in this life or trying to discern which works God will favor in the life to come, **Qoheleth proclaims the futility of all human effort to gain lasting satisfaction, whether empirically by the greatest earthly achievements or morally by prescribing good works**, so that his readers might be quickly disillusioned in any similar quest for some advantage in their labor.*

This section is comprised of two reflections with divergent literary styles, but both describe aspects of Qoheleth's quest for some advantage in human labor (1:13; 2:22; 3:9-10; cf. 1:3). The first of these recapitulates his unprecedented yet futile attempts to find lasting satisfaction in great earthly achievement (1:12-2:26); the other recounts the futility of trying to determine which works will gain God's favor (3:1-22). The logical link between the two reflections is found in the transitional passage (2:24-26): The dismal outcome of Qoheleth's **empirical** approach to a lasting legacy for his labor (1:12-2:23) forced him to acknowledge God's necessary role in granting ultimate satisfaction (2:24-26). But this only portended the equally futile **prescriptive** strategy of trying to anticipate which deeds gain God's favor, for we cannot tell in this life how these deeds serve God's purposes or how God will judge them afterwards (3:1-22). The same closing marker (3:22b) also concludes the first half of the book (6:12b) and the transitional passage (7:14b).

Qoheleth's unequivocal failure to find any advantage to his labor—whether in great earthly achievement (1:12-2:23) or in moral behavior God would deem worthy (3:1-22, cf. 2:26)—should assure readers of their own inevitable failure. Qoheleth's negative precedent was intended to thoroughly undercut the readers' own quest for advantage (1:3) and thereby abolish any false hope in self-sufficient strategies to achieve lasting satisfaction (1:8), so that they might *fear God* instead (cf. 3:14-15). However, the strong appeal of self-sufficiency required Qoheleth to delve even farther into the self-sufficient soul and expose the destructive ambition that exploits God and others for personal gain before the typical reader would be disillusioned enough to honestly mourn the failure of self-sufficiency (4:1-6:12).

— 15 —

A. The Futility of Empirically Searching for an Earthly Legacy (1:12-2:26)

In reflecting on the failure of his unprecedented wisdom, power, and wealth to find lasting satisfaction in earthly achievement, **Qoheleth establishes the lack of any advantage in toiling for an earthly legacy,** *so that his readers might not waste their effort pursuing lasting satisfaction in earthly achievement.*

The passage has a well-defined structure delineated by the five-fold use of the closing marker *this is vanity and grasping for the wind.*[116] Qoheleth's parallel introduction (1:12-15; 16-18)[117] twice expresses his qualifications and intent to investigate the meaning of human labor and twice lamented that all was futile. Each pericope that follows then develops a different strategy to pursue lasting satisfaction, quickly advancing from one strategy to the next (2:1-26), as if to goad the reader along quickly to arrive at the same inference of futility.[118] The closing enjoyment pericope (2:24-26) serves as a literary transition to the equally futile endeavor of trying to determine how human works may elicit God's favor (3:1-22).

Qoheleth realized that his readers would share his great capacity for self-deception in their own search for lasting satisfaction through self-sufficient achievement.[119] By recounting his progressive disillusionment over even the greatest of his own achievements, Qoheleth

---

[116] Cf. 1:14, 17; 2:11, 17, 26; n. 58. This marker even punctuates the closing enjoyment pericope (2:24-26), so the latter must be interpreted in light of the pessimism projected (see exposition of 2:24-26 below).

[117] Wright, "The Riddle of the Sphinx," in Zuck (ed.), *Reflecting with Solomon*, 52, 57. The two pericopae both close with the "vanity" marker and are both adorned with a summary appraisal (1:15, 18, cf. n. 61) that foretells the subsequent key conclusions within the first half of the argument (2:23; 5:17; 7:13).

[118] The progressive sense of futility in this section is transparently projected by an accelerating frequency of the phrase *this* (or *all*) *is vanity* (2:1, 11, 15, 17, 19, 21, 23, 26; cf. n. 58).

[119] Over half of Qoheleth's first person references ("I ", "my", "myself ", "me") are found in 1:12-2:26. God is viewed only as a grudging benefactor (1:13; 2:24-26), reflecting the mindset of Gen 3:5; others are seen only as tools to be used in the self-sufficient pursuit of earthly achievement (2:1-11, 19).

hoped to preempt any expectation his readers might have of succeeding in comparable exploits of their own. He wanted them to waste as little toil as possible emulating such efforts before going on to consider God's role in securing lasting human satisfaction in life (2:24-26).

1. Introduction: Qoheleth's Futile Quest (1:12-18)

Qoheleth—the "Assembler"[120] (1:12)—introduced his quest: *to seek and search out by wisdom...all that is done under heaven; this burdensome task God has given to the sons of man* (1:13).[121] However, he promptly concluded he could find no meaning in *all the works that are done under the sun*[122] (1:14)—we cannot change or fathom those things that just don't seem to fit (1:15).[123] A parallel introduction (1:16-18) then explains how Qoheleth had used his unprecedented wisdom (1:16)[124] to distinguish *wise* from *stupid* strategies[125] for human labor to achieve anything of lasting significance (1:17a). Again, he preemptively concluded *this also is grasping for the*

---

[120] The root verb *qhl*, from which *Qoheleth* is derived, "is never used of gathering inanimate objects but always of an assembly of people" (Whybray, *Ecclesiastes*, 2), just like Solomon himself in 1 Kgs 8 (Longman, *Ecclesiastes*, 2). However, the Qal feminine participle with the definite article in 12:8 may well serve as an occupational title (ibid., 1) for a "gatherer" or "collector" of wise proverbs (Seow, *Ecclesiastes*, 97, 99; cf. Eaton, as quoted in n. 7 above). This accords with the frame narrator's description of Qoheleth's role as "compiler" of collected proverbs to "teach the people" (12:9-10). Recently, the title has more often been defended as referring exclusively to one who assembles the people to teach them (so Whybray; Longman; Murphy; NET fns. on 12:1, 8)—thus "Preacher" or "Teacher."

[121] Both the noun and verb here come from the same root, *'anâ* (n. 23), i.e., "this burdensome *task*...by which they may be *tasked* "—it seems to echo the frustration of mankind's work after the fall (Gen 3:17-19).

[122] There is an intended parallel between 1:13 and 14: When Qoheleth tried to discover how God assigns mankind his work *under heaven* (1:13), all the *works* done *under the sun* seemed futile (1:14, cf. n. 21).

[123] The phrasing of this summary appraisal is echoed in subsequent closing pericopae (cf. 6:10b; 7:13b).

[124] This *a fortiori* emphasis in the introduction (1:12-18) is transparently preemptive. "[I]f even Solomon, who possessed everything...a man can possess, nevertheless found all his efforts to achieve happiness and contentment profoundly unsatisfactory, how much more would lesser persons be likely to fail in that attempt!" (Whybray, *Ecclesiastes*, 48).

[125] NKJV follows MT *to know wisdom and to know madness and folly* (1:17a), but the repeated infinitive construct *da'at* (*to know*) may read better as a noun, "to know wisdom and knowledge" (*so* LXX), and thus echo *wisdom and knowledge* from 1:16 to balance the phrase *madness and folly* in 1:17 (Murphy, *Ecclesiastes*, 12 [fn. 17.b]). Moreover, the parallel phrasing suggests that the word *madness* (*hôlēlôth*) should be translated "stupidity" to reflect the opposite of wisdom: It is not an intellectual deficiency but rather **moral** stupidity, as indicated by its connection with *folly*

wind (1:17b, cf. 1:14b) for as he increased in wisdom and knowledge to find the best way for us to invest our labor, it only intensified his *vexation* and *grief* (1:18).[126]

The frame narrator's objective in citing Qoheleth's wisdom and perspective in this passage emerges directly from the literary device of quoting an extended narrative in the first person. The "pen name" and indirect allusion to Solomon as referent[127] serve to introduce the reader to a "thought experiment": What would happen if we found the wisest, most experienced person in history and charged that person with reflecting on their experiences and observations of life to answer the question *What profit has a man from all his labor In which he toils under the sun?* (1:3)? The answer is summarized in 1:12-18, thus portending Qoheleth's progressive disillusionment in the first half of the book: After relating his own personal failure to find lasting satisfaction (2:1-23), Qoheleth will recount his cumulative observations of all the futile results of every kind of self-sufficient labor in life (chapters 3-6).

2. The Empty Legacy of Pleasure (2:1-11)

Starting with the pursuit of pleasure, Qoheleth proceeded to relate the outcome of his quest to find meaning in human labor yet again concluded preemptively that *this also was vanity* (2:1-2). He sought to *gratify* his *flesh with wine*—yet still retain his wisdom—and to indulge in all kinds of *folly* to find out what would be worth pursuing (2:3).[128] He *made* his *works*

(n. 37, cf. 2:12; 7:25; 9:3; 10:13)—Qoheleth tried "to distinguish *wisdom and knowledge* from *stupidity and folly.*" This might in fact be a double hendiadys—"to distinguish *full wisdom* from *utter stupidity*" (Longman, *Ecclesiastes*, 84).

[126] The words *ka'as* ("vexation," *so* NRSV) and *mak'ôb* ("sorrow " or "grief," as in NIV) also culminate Qoheleth's reflections on earthly achievement in 2:23, but in reverse order: Whether in self-centered pursuit of pleasure (2:1-11) or in the ostensibly more altruistic pursuit of wisdom (2:12-17), mankind's quest for an advantage in his labor invariably yields only *mak'ôb* and *ka'as* (2:23). While *mak'ôb* occurs only in 1:18 and 2:23, *ka'as* goes on to play a key role in the argument (5:16-17; 7:3, 9; 11:10; cf. n. 39).

[127] *See* n. 7.

[128] While expositors have tried to avoid the apparent contradiction between Qoheleth's wisdom and his unrestrained pursuit of wine and folly, the sense is dictated the context of Qoheleth's quest (see Longman, *Ecclesiastes*, 88-90): He viewed himself as a pioneer on behalf of all mankind (cf. n. 124), one who would do all the "work" needed to find out rationally (n. 132) what is worthwhile for *a man* (1:3). A reasonable yet literal translation might therefore read, "I sought in my heart to gratify my flesh with wine—still guiding my heart by wisdom—and to embrace folly, in order to see what good this [is] for the sons of man to do under the sun all the days of their lives."

great (2:4-7),[129] acquired great wealth and entertainment (2:8a),[130] and had every kind of woman in his unbridled pursuit of sexual pleasure[131] (2:8b). Qoheleth reconfirmed that he excelled in all these exploits while still retaining his great wisdom[132] so that he might accurately evaluate whether he could gain lasting satisfaction in any of these great pleasures pursued by men (2:9-10).

Although all his labor was indeed rewarded with pleasure (2:10b), Qoheleth could only conclude that there was no advantage to the self-sufficient pursuit of pleasure—the gratification was ephemeral and thus an empty legacy for all his toil (2:11, cf. 1:3). Again, his claim to have excelled more than anyone else in all these endeavors (2:9a) was meant to deter the reader from trying to emulate his unprecedented achievements. The realization that pleasure brought only fleeting satisfaction—as epitomized by great sex

---

[129] The key phrase "for myself" (NASB) is repeated three times in 2:4-7, a list that included *houses; vineyards; gardens and orchards* with *all kinds of fruit trees* and the waterworks to support them (cp. Gen 2:8-14); and abundant *slaves, herds and flocks*. Qoheleth concluded this list with the phrase "greater than all who were in Jerusalem before me" to emphasize how unprecedented these achievements were—just as in 1:12-18 (n. 124), such *a fortiori* reasoning continues to pervade this section (cf. 2:9a, 12b, 25).

[130] The allusion to *male and female singers* may well be hyperbole for all forms of entertainment.

[131] Longman argues that the hapax *šiddâ wešiddôt* most plausibly alludes to "breasts" (not *musical instruments*, NKJV) and is "thus a crude reference to women who are used for sexual pleasure only," lit. "concubine after concubine" (ibid., 92). By combining singular and plural forms of the same word, this construction seems to denote both variety and plurality (cf. Seow, *Ecclesiastes*, 131-2)—thus, "all kinds of women, the [greatest] pleasure of mankind" (i.e., the best imaginable sex), a fitting culmination of Qoheleth's efforts to preempt similar endeavors among his readers and, sadly, a fitting precedent for the current widespread accessibility of pornography.

[132] Qoheleth found it necessary to affirm twice (2:3, 9) that his wisdom stayed with him. His affirmation in 2:9b is especially emphatic, "*indeed*, my wisdom stood...." To be sure, the reader could claim Solomon was so jaded after his unrestrained indulgence in wine and pursuit of foreign women and gods (cf. 1 Kgs 4:29-34) that he lost the great wisdom he was given, and there is no evidence that Solomon ever returned to orthodox faith by the end of his life (Longman, *Ecclesiastes*, 3). Moreover, his use of the pen name *Qoheleth* may well have been designed to protect his own reputation (12:9-10) from the corruption of wisdom one would expect from Solomon's sin (see 7:7). It therefore stands to reason that Qoheleth would assiduously reaffirm that his wisdom remained to the end of his "experiment" with pleasure (2:3, 9), thus substantiating his resulting conclusion (2:11) for the benefit of the reader (n. 128).

(2:8b)—led Qoheleth to consider the prospect of a more enduring legacy (2:12-26). The repeated affirmation that Qoheleth's *wisdom remained with* him (2:3, 9b) appears to have prompted Qoheleth to reflect on the value of pursuing wisdom on its own merits as a means of achieving such a legacy (2:12-17).

3. The Empty Legacy of Wisdom (2:12-17)

After *embracing folly* to no avail (2:3, NIV), Qoheleth returned to compare *wisdom and madness and folly* (2:12a, cf. 1:17) to see if pursuing wisdom in its own right would yield a greater advantage for his labor than folly (cf. 1:3), again citing his own unprecedented experience as paradigmatic for all humanity (2:12b).[133] And he saw that wisdom in this life affords the wise one the advantage[134] of *eyes in his head* ("insight") over the fool who *walks in darkness* (2:13-14a). Yet he also realized[135] that death is impartial to the wise and the fool alike, thus precluding wisdom from conferring any lasting advantage on the wise (2:14b-15a). So he lamented his superior wisdom (2:15b), for the legacy of the wise lasts no longer than that of the fool, as both are soon forgotten after they die (2:16a, b),[136] ironically making them peers

---

[133] Lit. "For what [can] the man [do] who comes after the king?—that which they have already done." Note the similar construction in 6:8, and cp. the point made in 2:25 (cf. nn. 124, 129).

[134] Most translations obscure the point of Qoheleth's comparison of *wisdom* and *folly* in that they miss the technical sense intended for *yithrôn* (n. 22) in 2:13-15: "And I saw that wisdom is an *advantage* over folly, just as light is an *advantage* over darkness—the wise man has eyes in his head, but the fool walks in darkness. Yet I also knew that the same fate befalls them both. So I said in my heart, 'As the fate of the fool will also befall me, why then did I become so wise?'" See also Longman, *Ecclesiastes*, 95 (fn. 43), 97-98. Qoheleth will later argue from greater to lesser that if wisdom confers no lasting advantage, then one can gain no lasting advantage in any self-sufficient endeavor to satisfy the soul (6:7-9).

[135] The opening *wᵉyāda'tî gam–'ānî* (lit. "And I knew, even I...") in 2:14b is clearly adversative in context—"Yet I also knew...".

[136] The notion of "remembrance" is pivotal to Qoheleth's quest (n. 115). He sought not just a **temporary** advantage (cf. 2:13) but a **lasting** (*'ôlām*) legacy. However, NKJV translates *'ôlām* adverbially ("forever"), not attributively ("lasting, enduring," so NASB, NIV, NRSV) and renders *kōl* as "all" rather than "both" (so NIV), thereby obscuring the intended parallel with *kᵉbār* ("soon"): "For there is no *lasting remembrance* of the wise man, just like the fool, in that both are *soon forgotten* in the days to come" (my translation). In sum, the pursuit of wisdom as an end in itself affords no more lasting legacy (cf. 9:5-6) for all one's labor than his monuments of material achievement (2:1-11)—any meager advantage dissipates all too soon; though ironically, Solomon's reputation for wisdom continues in perpetuity in the form of Qoheleth's reflections.

(2:16c).[137]

Although Qoheleth had set out "to distinguish wisdom and knowledge from stupidity and folly"[138] he could find no meaningful distinction under the sun. Consequently,[139] he was deeply disillusioned; he *hated life, because* his great effort to achieve unprecedented wisdom also failed to give him any lasting satisfaction (2:17). Such intensity of emotion was meant to deter readers from trying the same exploits, for though they had not yet reached the same level of disillusionment[140] they would surely fail to achieve any more satisfaction, having far less wisdom than Qoheleth. Since great wisdom signified the pinnacle of human achievement for Qoheleth (1:16), he went on to draw the logical inference that *all* toil done under the sun is therefore futile then cited the vexing outcome of his own toil to warrant his complete disillusionment (2:18-23).

4. The Empty Legacy of All Toil Under the Sun (2:18-23)

Distraught that death would rob his unprecedented wisdom of any lasting meaning (2:16), Qoheleth was painfully aware that none of his other great achievements would last. So[141] he deemed *all* his *labor* in life equally futile and *hated* it (2:18a), anticipating the inexorable collapse of the magnificent legacy he had worked his entire life to build (2:18b-23, cf. 2:16). The text is arranged in three couplets to track Qoheleth's progressive disillusionment—each couplet closes with the familiar *This also is vanity*. The ultimate prospect of losing his entire estate only accelerated his disillusionment to *despair* (2:20a),[142] and

---

[137] NKJV best reflects Qoheleth's bitter irony, *And how does* the *wise man die? As the fool!* Qoheleth will later cite the ironic parity of *the wise* and *the poor* (6:8; n. 247) to similarly epitomize the lack of advantage in self-sufficiency to yield soul-satisfaction (cf. n. 134).

[138] *See* 1:17, cf. n. 125.

[139] The consequential force of the opening *waw* ("therefore") in 2:17 is reflected in most translations.

[140] While Qoheleth does not actually use the word *vexation*, his obvious disillusionment in 2:17 anticipates the more explicit all-encompassing frustration of his conclusion in 2:23 (cf. n. 126).

[141] The opening *waw* is inferential ("so," as in NIV), since the preceding reflection *I hated life* (2:17) argues *a fortiori* to the conclusion *I hated all my labor* (2:18a; cf. Seow, *Ecclesiastes*, 155).

[142] Qoheleth *despaired* to the point that he *hated life* (2:17) and *all* his *labor* (2:18)—just like Job when he lost his entire estate (Job 3; 6:26, cf. n. 42). Qoheleth's estate was quite comparable (Eccl 2:4-9), and his emotional response in anticipation of total loss (2:17-23) appropriately echoes Job's despair. Qoheleth will go on to show that such despair clearly extends beyond the material realm—it afflicts anyone whose *soul is not satisfied by goodness* (6:3, cf. 4:2-3; 6:6, 7).

this in turn led to the resigned conclusion in 2:24-26.

In the first couplet (2:18-19) Qoheleth deeply resented having to forfeit the fruit of his labor when he couldn't tell whether his heir would turn out to be a wise steward or a fool who would squander his heritage.[143] The second couplet (2:20-21) further explains his disillusionment as deep chagrin over the travesty of having toiled with great *wisdom, knowledge and* success[144] only to enrich his successor, who did nothing to deserve it. Now Qoheleth could fully substantiate his opening premise (2:22-23, cf. 1:3, 12-18):[145] In fact, there is no advantage to all human labor *under the sun* (2:22), for it only results in *grief* and *vexation* (2:23).[146] Qoheleth is therefore left with no hope that he can build his own enduring legacy for all his labor and can only surmise that human legacies are apportioned by God (2:24-26).

5. An Enduring Legacy from the Hand of God (2:24-26)
This initial sequence of reflections on Qoheleth's personal experience is now concluded[147] with the book's first "enjoyment pericope;" but it sounds more like a grudging concession[148] than a

---

[143] The reader should note the irony of how promptly Rehoboam squandered the entire northern portion of Solomon's kingdom as a result of his foolish management (1 Kgs 12). Qoheleth will further develop the implications of such imprudent stewardship in 10:1-20.

[144] The word "success" (*kišrôn*) is rendered *skill* by NKJV, NASB, NIV, however "equity" (KJV) is closer to the mark—the sense is that of accumulated wealth or success that affords one an advantage (cf. n. 22). In Qoheleth's self-sufficient view *under the sun*, to have to surrender one's hard-earned wealth to another who didn't work for it makes so little sense, that only God could be responsible (cf. 2:26).

[145] The opening *kî* (2:22) echoes 1:3 as a rhetorical inference, "*So* what does a man get for all his labor...?" (nothing), which is then substantiated by 2:23. Repeated verb-forms for "toil" in 2:22 (*'āmāl, 'āmēl*) mirror synonymous forms in 1:13 (*'ānâ, 'inyān*, cf. nn. 23, 121), and *God* is finally mentioned again in 2:24-26 after first being mentioned in 1:13, which probably serves as *inclusio* for 1:12-2:26.

[146] The terms *mak'ôb* and *ka'as* (2:23) echo from the opening conclusion (1:18, cf. n. 126).

[147] *See* n. 119. Hereinafter, allusions to Qoheleth's own experience are indirect but still often invoke the perspective of royalty, with which Qoheleth naturally identifies (cf., e.g., nn. 84-86).

[148] Longman appropriately points out Qoheleth's "lack of enthusiasm" in beginning with the phrase "There is nothing better for a man..." (*Ecclesiastes*, 107). Nevertheless, this assertion establishes the foundation for subsequent enjoyment passages (n. 30) that will further elaborate how God intended to favor humanity from the beginning (cf. n 155, below).

commendation of joy, in light of Qoheleth's despair of ever gaining an enduring legacy for his labor (cf. 2:16-23). The pericope is comprised of a principal assertion (2:24), followed by two corroborating motive clauses (2:25-26).[149] The first of these parenthetically reaffirms Qoheleth's negative precedent, lest the reader try to replicate what Qoheleth had already achieved but to no avail (2:25).[150] The second motive clause (2:26) then validates the claim of 2:24 and thereby explains why Qoheleth could not find lasting satisfaction (2:1-23), thus concluding the argument and again justifying the repeated closing sentiment, *this too is vanity*[151] (2:26c, NASB).

Qoheleth continues to voice the perspective of one who seeks an advantage in his own strength[152] but must now concede that any lasting satisfaction in human toil comes only *from the hand of God* (2:24).[153] Thus, his advice to enjoy whatever good God may provide in our labor (2:24a) serves mainly to protect the ambitious reader from wasting any further effort seeking a legacy in earthly achievement, for Qoheleth had already definitively exhausted all promising strategies (2:25, cf. 2:20).[154] The concluding verse then explains **how** the "hand of God" trumps the best human efforts to

---

[149] Both 2:25 and 2:26 begin with *kî* ("for"), as they substantiate in tandem the principal assertion in 2:24.

[150] There are two textual variants for the rhetorical question in 2:25. LXX reads "who...without Him" (so NASB), whereas MT can read either "who...more than I" (so NKJV) or "who...apart from me" (cf. Murphy, *Ecclesiastes*, 25 [fn. 25.b]). However, LXX proves too much by casting God as the source of any enjoyment in life (cf. n. 153). MT more plausibly renders 2:25 as yet another parenthetical reminder designed to preempt the reader from replicating Qoheleth's futile quest (cf. 1:16; 2:9, 12; and n. 129), which conforms with Qoheleth's overarching strategy of citing his own experience as a negative precedent for the reader (ibid., 26). It also helps elucidate the otherwise confusing refrain of *vanity* (2:26c): If the LXX reading of 2:25 were correct, it would **not** be "vanity" to seek God's favor.

[151] *See* n. 118.

[152] This is the mindset of selfish ambition (nn. 119, 129) and it is further elaborated for the reader in 4:4-8.

[153] Qoheleth does not assert that the *hand of God* is the source of **all** enjoyment in life (cf. n. 150) for he clearly did enjoy many achievements apart from God (cf. 2:10). Rather, it is only by God's favor "that his *soul* should enjoy good" (2:24)— this is what had invariably eluded Qoheleth throughout his quest for an advantage in his labor (cf. n. 142). The phrase *hand of God* recurs only once in the book with a similar sense—it is the only source of lasting reward for *the righteous and the wise* (9:1).

[154] Cf. 2:12b and nn. 133, 150.

build their own legacy and **why** it is therefore futile for them to continue trying: Regardless of how ambitiously humans may strive, *God gives wisdom and knowledge and joy to a man who is good in His sight; but to the sinner He gives the work of gathering and collecting, that he may give it to him who is good before God* (2:26).[155]

If God indeed favors those who are *good in His sight*, then, logically, Qoheleth and his readers must alter their strategy if they are to secure an enduring legacy.[156] Those who perform the deeds that God deems to be *good* (2:26) should logically become the recipients of God's redistributed blessing. Yet the hidden premise—that we are indeed capable of prescribing works that can fulfill God's inscrutable purposes and thus be judged "good"—only portends

---

[155] While it strikes Qoheleth as terribly unfair to have to forfeit his fortune to someone who did not deserve it (2:21, cf. n. 144), his concession here that God "plays favorites" opens the door to the possibility of pleasing God with good works, rather than finding satisfaction in empirical achievement: The beneficiary of God's favor—here manifested as *wisdom and knowledge and joy* (2:26a)—is the one *who is good before God* and receives the blessings that God confiscates from *the sinner* (2:26b). The terms "good" and "sinner" clearly have a moral connotation here, just as in 7:26 (cf. n. 47; *contra* Longman, *Ecclesiastes*, 109-110). Qoheleth will later affirm the irrelevance of present material prosperity to true satisfaction of the soul (5:18-20, cf. 2:24) by showing that a man can despair even when he possesses every material thing he could conceivably desire (6:1-6).

[156] Qoheleth's change of strategy foresees mankind's natural quest for some legacy in life that will outlast the ephemeral satisfaction of "aesthetic" pleasure (cf. 2:1-11), as so well described by Kirkegaard:

> The aesthetic view takes account of the personality in its relation to the environment, and [its] expression…upon the individual is pleasure. But…he who lives aesthetically seeks as far as possible to be absorbed in mood, he seeks to hide himself entirely in it, so that there remains nothing in him which cannot be inflected into it; …such a reminder has always a disturbing effect….The more the personality disappears in the twilight of mood, so much the more is the individual in the moment, and this, again, is the most adequate expression for the aesthetic existence: it is in the moment….He, too, who lives ethically experiences mood, but for him this is not the highest experience; …he sees the mood below him. The remainder which will not "go into" mood is precisely **the continuity** which is to him the highest thing. He who lives ethically has memory of his life—and he who lives aesthetically has not. [*The Living Thoughts of Kirkegaard*, presented by W.H. Auden (Bloomington, IN: Indiana Univ. Press, 1966), 77]

Qoheleth will seek such a "memory" (n. 136) in morally acceptable behavior (3:1ff) but he will show—and Kirkegaard would surely agree—that while an "ethical" existence may afford meaningful "continuity" in this life it is ultimately no more capable than mere aesthetic pleasure of securing a legacy that will outlast death (3:18-22, cf. 2:16).

further disillusionment in the next phase of the argument (3:1-22):[157] The prospect of gaining God's favor with these prescribed moral deeds will prove to be totally elusive and doomed to the same vexation that attended the empirical approach to a lasting legacy (cf. 2:1-23)[158]—it too will turn out to be *vanity and grasping for the wind* (2:26c).[159]

---

[157] Qoheleth assumes in 2:24-26 that the frustrated reader will adopt a strategy of religious moralism and thus prepares him for yet further disillusionment, the main objective of the first half of the argument: While Qoheleth recognizes that moral character has lasting value (n. 156) he anticipates that readers are prone to use their moral behavior to exploit *the hand of God* in yet another ploy for some advantage in their labor—the one who believes he can somehow be *good in His sight* thus presumes that God is obligated to bless him with *wisdom and knowledge and joy* and material prosperity (cf. 2:26). Unless readers are fully convinced that even the best of prescribed moral behavior is just as futile as other self-sufficient strategies to gain a lasting legacy they will not accept the wisdom in chapters 7-12 concerning the advantage of *fearing God*. Qoheleth will therefore preempt all "prescriptive" strategies to gain God's favor, by proving that God's inscrutable purposes can never be tied *a priori* to any specific human deeds in this life (3:1-22).

[158] This perspective by which one imagines that he can rescue himself from a life of futility by "bartering" his good works for God's favor will be further exemplified in 5:1-7 and shown to incur the same oppressive consequences to oneself and others as raw selfish ambition (5:8-17, cf. 4:1-8).

[159] This final inference of futility looks both backward and forward. Not only does it culminate the empty quest for an enduring legacy in empirical achievement (1:12-2:26) but it also heralds the outcome in 3:1-22 of mankind's futile attempt to secure his legacy in God's inscrutable plan with predetermined good deeds.

B. The Futility of Prescribing Good Deeds for a Heavenly Legacy (3:1-22)

By declaring that God's purposes are accomplished by His inscrutable timing, design, and judgment of all the deeds of men on earth, **Qoheleth shows that prescribed moral behavior can neither satisfy God's sovereign will nor guarantee His favor**, *so that we would not try to gain a heavenly legacy by currying God's favor with a list of preconceived "good" deeds.*

The realization that only God bestows lasting satisfaction in human labor (2:24-26) led Qoheleth to explore how best to invest one's labor to please God with the promising strategies now presupposed in these three reflections.[160] The first of these is a poem distinguished by repeating pairs of "opposites" that illustrate merism,[161] implying that any effort to please God by prescribing good deeds will be confounded by God's inscrutable **timing** for those deeds (3:1-8). After restating his quest (3:9, cf. 1:3) Qoheleth responds with two more reflections on the implausibility of predicting God's favor from His inscrutable **design** (3:10-15) and **judgment** (3:16-21). The concluding enjoyment pericope thus concedes the inscrutable outcome of any specific works designed to curry God's favor (3:22).

The argument logically follows this three-step textual design. Given the presumption that God rewards those who are *good in His sight* (2:26), Qoheleth set out to discover which deeds would be good enough to earn God's favor and thereby gain him a legacy for his labor. Yet this very premise was immediately challenged by his observation that every deed on earth has an appropriate *time* that fits God's purposes (3:1), so that even deeds at opposite moral extremes have suitable *times* (3:2-8). How then can we predict the

---

[160] Whereas Qoheleth explicitly introduced his **empirical** strategies in 1:13-18 (cf. n. 124), the **prescriptive** strategies anticipated by 2:24-26 (n. 157) are implied in 3:1-22 by the phrasing of the opening markers of each reflection (3:1, 10, 16) and how each of these markers is "answered" by the text.

[161] The literary device of *merismus* in 3:2-8 demonstrates the universal applicability of the point made in 3:1 by affirming its truth at opposite "moral" extremes in each of 14 different categories of human activity. The intricate literary substructure of these pairs of opposite extremes is beyond the scope of this exposition but nicely reviewed by Loader ("The Grip of Time"), 257-61.

"right" deeds in which to invest our labor at any given time (3:9, cf. 1:3)? When Qoheleth tried to discover the specific deeds God favors he could neither discern God's intent (3:10-15) nor anticipate who would be judged good (3:16-22).

Qoheleth saw that while God has given humanity a task within His eternal creative plan and made them aware of His design, they still cannot see how their labor will fit into that plan (3:10-11). He realized that God does this so that we will have to rely on Him to do good, enjoy our labor, and account for the works that God has preordained for us (3:12-15). When he tried to predict how humans might earn God's favor by observing how they are judged for their deeds he saw that justice on earth was corrupt and unreliable, and though he was confident that God would judge fairly he could not discern this from the way people die (3:16-20). Since no one can tell what will happen afterwards, Qoheleth advised his readers to simply enjoy their God-given portion (3:21-22).

Compared to the self-sufficient pursuit of a legacy in pleasure or achievement (cf. 2:1-23), the attempt to prescribe how we can please God may at first seem noble or high-minded. However, all such effort is just as self-sufficient: Humans try to wrest for themselves what *God* only *gives...to a man who is good in his sight* (2:26)—we connive with our good deeds to cajole God into granting us the legacy we want, because we just can't seem to pull it off ourselves.[162] The notion that God thus keeps His plan veiled and immutable (3:11, 14) so that we might *fear* God (3:14) and *enjoy* our portion (3:12-13, 22) portends for the reader how one may finally gain a lasting legacy: We must come to the end of ourselves, thoroughly disillusioned with self-sufficiency,[163] before we can

---

[162] This flawed notion that we must wrest favor out of God's grudging hand will become the dominant undercurrent of 4:1-6:12, as portrayed by manipulative vows (5:4-5) and contentious bargaining (6:10-11). Such a pursuit is as old as Cain's frustrated quest to curry God's favor (Gen 4:3-7) and only boils down to trying to fulfill God's law in one's own strength; it is doomed to failure, just like any other works-based philosophy of human fulfillment (n. 158). Qoheleth will go on to trace the root of this failure in Eccl 7:15-29.

[163] Qoheleth wisely perceives that we do not readily give up self-sufficient strategies to achieve lasting satisfaction in life. If the reader can finally be convinced that *he cannot contend with him who is mightier* (6:10, cf. 1:15; 7:13) he will give up his attempts to manipulate God into blessing him (6:11). This allows us to shift our focus from **working** to earn God's favor (cf. nn. 158, 157) to **grace** in receiving the favor already granted us in our portion from God—He preordains the works that He wants us to enjoy in that portion (9:7-10, cf. 3:10-15). One's enjoyment of his portion can thereby evolve from mere consolation (cf. 2:24, 3:22; n. 148) into genuine *lasting satisfaction*.

truly fear God and enjoy our portion from God (4:1-7:14).

1. God's Inscrutable Timing for Every Deed (3:1-8)

When Qoheleth deduced that God favors those who are *good in his sight* (2:26), it prompted him to find which deeds would render one "good" before God, but he saw at once that every event on earth has a suitable occasion[164] and matches the timing of some purpose of God (3:1).[165] This connection was demonstrated with a list of events arrayed in 14 pairs (3:2-8)—each pair spans opposite extremes in a given category of effort, so the list is virtually all-inclusive.[166] While it might dismay the "moral" reader that both "good" and "bad" deeds may be equally appropriate,[167] depending on the timing of God's purposes, this only reflects the fact that the limited human perspective *under the sun* falls hopelessly short of God's sovereign view *under heaven*.[168]

---

[164] The phrase "suitable (or *appropriate*) occasion" translates Heb. $z^e m\bar{a}n$ and indicates the sense intended for "time" (*'ēt*) in 3:1 and throughout the ensuing poem (3:2-8, cf. n. 35):

> The word can in fact mean "occasion"....For everything under heaven (everything that happens) there is a specific occasion. When the occasion arrives, the event that fits it occurs....[T]here is nothing anyone can do about it. In harmony with this view is the regular repetition of the word *time* that occurs 28 more times; it sounds like a clock that, inexorably and independent of the wishes of people, keeps ticking....Whatever happens happens, and there is nothing you can do about it. (J.A. Loader, "The Grip of Time: Ecclesiastes 3:1-9," reprinted in Zuck [ed.], *Reflecting with Solomon*, 257-61, 259)

[165] The verse demonstrates chiastic parallelism, lit. "To everything an appointed time, and a time to every purpose under heaven." This seems to affirm that the timing of every deed done on earth corresponds to a purpose served *under heaven*. The sense of "purpose" intended for *ḥēpheṣ* in 3:1 is conveyed well by NKJV but obscured by most other popular English translations (cf. n. 44).

[166] *See* n. 161.

[167] This is the inference Qoheleth intended the reader to draw from 3:1 (cf. n. 164) as illustrated by 3:2-8.

[168] The phrase *under heaven* probably denotes the realm of God's inscrutable *purposes* (cp. 1:13, cf. nn. 21, 122), as is strongly implied by repeated references to God's activity in the near context (3:10-22). An example of the dichotomy between the perspectives *under the sun* and *under heaven* is seen in Habakkuk's response to God's plan to use the evil Chaldeans (Hab 1:5-17, cf. also Job 1:12-17). The dichotomy can be reconciled only by acknowledging the direct, if inscrutable, correspondence between heaven's purposes and what happens on earth (n. 165; cf. Eccl 8:16-9:1).

In affirming that every deed on earth has an appropriate occasion that corresponds to the timing of God's inscrutable purposes, Qoheleth sought to deter the reader from attempting to elicit God's favor by prescribing good works. His observation that God's purposes encompass both "good" and "bad" deeds was meant to provoke an "existential crisis": Any reader who adopts a morally prescriptive strategy to curry God's favor will be unable to predict which "good" deeds suit God's timing and is thereby doomed to frustration in the pursuit of some advantage to one's labor (3:9, cf. 1:3). This is now proved in Qoheleth's own frustrated attempt to decipher which works might gain God's favor by observing His eternal plan (3:10-15) or His judgment of the deeds of men (3:16-22).

2. God's Inscrutable Design for Every Deed (3:9-15)

Since humans cannot predict which deeds will suit God's timing (3:1-8), what advantage can a laborer gain from all his toil (3:9)? In reply, Qoheleth recalled the *God-given task with which men are to be occupied* (3:10, cf. 1:13b) and that God *has made everything* they do *appropriate*[169] *in its time* (3:11a, cf. 3:1). Moreover,[170] He placed an awareness of His eternal plan *in their hearts* (3:11b),[171] *except that*[172] *no one can find out the work that God does from beginning to end* (3:11c).[173] Thus, while we are intuitively aware

---

[169] NASB correctly translates *yāpheh* as "appropriate" (cf. Longman, *Ecclesiastes*, 112 [fn. 6]) rather than "beautiful" (NKJV). This parallels the sense of "fitting occasion" for *season* and *time* in 3:1-8 (n. 164); the only other occurrence of *yāpheh* in Eccl is in 5:18, where even NKJV translates "fitting."

[170] The *gam* that initiates 3:11b is more emphatic than the sense conveyed by *also* (so NKJV, NASB, NIV)—the idea is to communicate the *extra* trouble God has taken to inform man; thus, *moreover* (NRSV) is better.

[171] The term *'ōlām* ("eternity") has a wide range of potential meanings (Brian Gault, "A Reexamination of 'Eternity' in Ecclesiastes 3:11," *BSac* 154 [Jan–Mar, 2008]: 39-57). In this context it continues the sense from the preceding construction of *everything appropriate in its time*, and is most likely a circumlocution for the notion of "God's preordained and immutable eternal plan" that will be elaborated in 3:14-15 (n. 173). The sense is that God has informed the human *heart* (i.e., "conscience," n. 57) that He has preordained an eternal plan, and the conscience should remind people of that reality when contemplating how best to invest their labor (3:9-10).

[172] The compound negative conjunction *mibbᵉlî 'ᵃšer* ("from without that") conveys the adversative sense *except that* (NKJV) or *yet so that* (NASB) in this context. Thus, God intentionally withholds from mankind the details of his purposes, as Qoheleth immediately explains (3:12-15, cf. 7:14, n. 299).

[173] The construction *the work that God does from beginning to end* refers to God's sovereign decree. Several related constructions in 3:11—*everything...eternity...God does*—are repeated in 3:14, so the reader will more fully absorb this sense of God's sovereign purpose for his labor (cf. n. 165).

that God has assigned us tasks in His eternal plan we cannot predict the detailed purposes of that plan or what specific works will
suitably contribute to those purposes (cf. 8:16-17).

So what's the point of knowing that God has a plan for our labor
when we can't discover the specific details (3: 9-11)? Qoheleth's conclusion is twofold:[174] First, God wants people to *do good* and *enjoy
good* in all the labor that God has given them (3:12-13).[175] Second,
whatever *God does*[176] endures *forever* (3:14a) and can't be altered
whenever our aspirations vary from what He has ordained (3:14b)—
God does it that men should fear before Him (3:14c).[177] That is, God
preordains *whatever* happens[178] (3:15a) and *seeks what is past*[179]

---

[174] Both 3:12-13 and 3:14-15 begin with *I know...* to denote Qoheleth's conclusion to the question raised in 3:9. However, the enjoyment pericope 3:12-13
seems misplaced in that it doesn't seem to conclude the passage, as do the other
enjoyment pericopae (n. 30). This is resolved if we view 3:12-13 as concluding
3:10-13, while 3:14-15 serves as the summary appraisal for all of 3:1-15 (with
3:15 explaining Qoheleth's allusion to the *fear of God* in 3:14c). Moreover, a second conclusion to 3:9 follows in 3:22, including another enjoyment pericope
(3:22a) as a summary appraisal of Qoheleth's further disillusionment in 3:16-21
(n. 81).

[175] The injunction for us to *do good* clearly has moral overtones (n. 47), but
Qoheleth redefines "good" here in terms of what *God does* (3:11a; n. 176) and
not what we imagine **we** can do. This should only demoralize those who set out
to gain an advantage by "doing good" (3:9), for one *cannot find out the work
that God does* (3:11c). Since one's labor is the *gift of God* (3:13; cf. 2:24), he
will realize what it means to *enjoy good* in his labor only after he accepts what
God gives him (5:18-20), instead of continuing to strive for something better on
his own (6:1-12).

[176] The phrase "God does" occurs four times (3:11, 14). By associating this
phrase with *'ōlâm* ("eternity" [3:11]; "forever" [3:14]), Qoheleth implies that
God's *inscrutable* decree (n. 173) is also *immutable*.

[177] Whenever we presume to know what deeds will gain God's favor, God
reverses the presumption by doing whatever He has immutably preordained
(3:14a, b), so the only logical alternative is to *fear* Him (n. 48).

[178] Both present and future events have *already been* (3:15a, twice). This
notion of recurring cycles is a transparent allusion back to the prologue (especially 1:9), but there is now a sense of *purpose* (cf. 3:1) to these repeating events—
God has preordained them on the basis of His unchanging eternal design (3:14a,
b; cf. 3:11a).

[179] The participle *nirdāp* is best rendered "what is past" (see lexical discussions
by Whybray, *Ecclesiastes*, 75-6; Murphy, *Ecclesiastes*, 30 [fn. 15a], 36). The idea
is that God seeks *an account of* the works He has preordained for men to accomplish (cf. 3:15a), so that they may *fear Him* in order to *do good* (cf. 3:12; 14c, n.
177).

(3:15b) in order to hold us accountable for all the works He has preordained at their appropriate times (cf. 3:1). Thus, while humanity is to *do good in all his labor* (3:12-13), we are called to do works not as a "moral audition" before God (as implied in 2:26) but rather as a preordained commission[180] from Him.

"Moral man" is therefore pinned on the horns of a dilemma, accountable as stewards for specific preordained works within God's eternal plan (3:9-15) yet unable to tell in advance which works would render us "good" enough to gain God's favor. Realizing he could not tell which works God would bless, Qoheleth exploited his insight that *God requires an account of what is past* (3:15b, NKJV) to try out another strategy for gaining God's favor: Perhaps God's *judgment* of the deeds of others could shed some light on what deeds God might expect of him (3:16-22). The hidden presumption is that one can rank the value of certain deeds in God's eyes by observing the earthly fate of those who do them,[181] thereby guiding the prudent investment of one's labor in works that are most likely to merit God's favor.

3. God's Inscrutable Judgment of Every Deed (3:16-22)

When Qoheleth further observed[182] *under the sun* how people are judged so he could find out which deeds would yield an advantage for human labor (cf. 3:9) all he saw *in the place of judgment* was justice corrupted by *wickedness* (3:16). So, why toil so hard to gain God's favor when one's works will not be properly judged as righteous? Qoheleth therefore tried to rationalize present injustice by affirming that *God will* eventually *judge the righteous and the wicked* (3:17a), since[183] *there is a time for every work* to be judged that accords with *every purpose* of God (3:17b).[184] Such

---

[180] The details of this commission are not fully revealed until 9:7-12:1, after readers have hopefully been convinced that they cannot alter God's preordained creative purposes for them (see exposition of 6:10-12).

[181] Christ anticipated this very presumption in Luke 13:1-5 in response to His promise of judgment (Luke 12:42-59) when His followers questioned the untimely fate of some of their contemporaries.

[182] The pericope begins with $w^{e'}\hat{o}d$ ("and further," 3:16a) to introduce Qoheleth's second observation (note the repetition of "I have seen" [NASB], cf. 3:10) in response to the question *What profit has the worker from that in which he labors?* (3:9; cf. n. 81).

[183] The introductory $k\hat{i}$ in 3:17b is corroborative ("since"); it recalls the assertion in 3:1 (n. 44) in order to substantiate Qoheleth's confidence in 3:17a.

[184] The syntax is difficult, but the text is not corrupt (Murphy, *Ecclesiastes*, 30 [fn. 17.a]). Qoheleth simply modified the assertion in 3:1 to make his point in context,

is the confidence moral people need to assure them of God's favor, given the flagrant disregard of justice in this life (3:16).[185] However, the ensuing reflection suggests that Qoheleth's hope of seeing good rewarded was anything but a settled conviction (3:18-22).[186]

In order to bolster his hope that God would eventually favor the righteous, Qoheleth thus tried to discern the ultimate fate of those who do good deeds. But his hidden presumption that one's earthly fate can attest to God's ultimate justice was immediately refuted when he realized that we all die just like animals (3:18-19a),[187] so that the "moral man" has no apparent advantage (3:19b, cf. 3:9):[188] *All* have the same fate in this life in that they *all* return to dust (3:20), so no one can tell from the way one dies whether the soul will go *upward* to God after they die

---

that *there is a time **there** for every purpose and for every work.* The adverb *there* (*šām*) was added to recall the *place of judgment* in 3:16 (ibid.), and the term *everything* (3:1) was replaced by *every work* to encompass all the works that had been ignored *in the place of judgment* (3:16); that is, it is **there** that *God will judge the righteous and the wicked* (3:17a), but it will happen at the *time* God has appointed *for every purpose and...work* (3:17b, cf. 3:1, 15c; n. 179).

[185] God's favor seems totally arbitrary (cf. 2:26) unless *wickedness* is *called to account* (3:15c-16, NIV).

[186] Qoheleth's deep uncertainty over the ultimate fate of mankind (3:18-21) goes on to pervade the argument until he realizes that *all* of us are sinners (7:15-29) and that God will judge *all* wickedness (8:6-8); ironically, at that point in the argument "moral man" will lose *all* confidence in his own righteous works, leaving his only hope of God's favor to *fear before God* (8:12b-13, cf. 3:14c).

[187] The threefold mention of "fate" (or "befall") in 3:19 transparently alludes to one's indiscriminate death (n. 33) and thus explains the assertion in 3:18b (lit.) that "God tests them so that they might see for themselves that they are [but] animals." This parallels the preceding assertion that whatever God does lasts forever and can't be changed, so that men might fear Him (3:14). For a discussion of various views regarding the peculiar syntax of 3:18b and the probable sense of "test" for the verb *bārar*, see Whybray, *Ecclesiastes*, 78; Murphy, *Ecclesiastes*, 30 (fn. 18.b); and Longman, *Ecclesiastes*, 128.

[188] To underscore Qoheleth's conclusion to his question in 3:9, the *waw* that initiates 3:19b is asseverative: *indeed...there is no advantage for men over beasts* (NASB). The final *kî* in 3:19 is inferential ("*so* all is vanity") in concluding all of 3:9-19: The stark realization that death is completely indiscriminate precludes any attempt to predict God's favor from the way men die, thus foreclosing all prescriptive strategies to secure God's favor (n. 157), as substantiated in 3:20-21, leading in turn to a consolatory enjoyment pericope (3:22a) and summary appraisal for all of chap. 3 (3:22b).

(3:21).[189] Qoheleth was thus again forced to concede[190] that we should just enjoy whatever work comes with our lot in life (3:22a),[191] for[192] no one can *bring* us *to see what will happen* afterwards[193] as a consequence of deeds we do now (3:22b).

The upshot of Qoheleth's investigation on our behalf is that we are left with no viable strategy to determine how—or even whether—we can gain favor in God's eyes (cf. 2:24-26). Readers must therefore relinquish the prospect of prescribing specific deeds

---

[189] The intended meaning of this verse is controversial. It either reads after MT (so NKJV, NASB), "Who knows the spirit of man, **which** goes upward, and the spirit of the animal, **which** goes down to earth?" or after LXX (so NIV), "Who knows **if** the spirit of man goes…and **if** the spirit of the animal goes…?" Some dismiss the MT pointing as a reflection of the effort of later scribes to mitigate Qoheleth's apparent lack of distinction in 3:18-20 between the fate of men and animals after death (cf. Whybray, *Ecclesiastes*, 80). Others favor MT because of biblically unattested grammar in LXX and the apparent contradiction in 12:7 (cf. Eaton, *Ecclesiastes*, 88-89). However, lexical arguments based on comparing Eccl with the rest of the OT are weak at best (see OVERVIEW OF ECCLESIASTES), and the alternative reading accords better with the pessimistic context of 3:18-22. Moreover, the apparent contradiction should be understood as a consequence of Qoheleth's different objectives in the two passages: From the perspective of "moral man" who trusts in his good works to gain God's favor there is no evidence in this life from the deaths of men and animals to reassure him that God rewards good men (3:16-20) or that their destiny after death is any different (3:21). The uncertainty in the rhetorical question of 3:21 is better reflected in LXX than MT and harmonizes better with 3:22b. In contrast, the context of 12:7 is addressed not to the self-sufficient person but to the one who fears God and is assured that the soul will return to its rightful Owner. The goal of 12:7 is therefore not, as in 3:16-21, to provoke further disillusionment but rather optimistic, to prepare God's created agents to serve God faithfully in light of our limited opportunity in this life.

[190] The conclusion in 3:22a furnishes a second answer to 3:9 (cf. 3:12-13; n. 174); thus, the opening *waw* is again inferential ("so", cf. 3:19c, n. 188).

[191] The phrase *there is nothing better than* imbues the enjoyment pericopae in the first half of Qoheleth's argument with a sense of resignation (cf. 2:24, 3:12; Longman, *Ecclesiastes*, 122). However, the phrase is conspicuously absent from 5:18-20, perhaps to signal for the reader that Qoheleth had finally emerged from his self-sufficient perspective to "see the light": Humanity's portion from God is far more than mere consolation in this life—it is a much greater source of enjoyment and advantage in life than we could ever possibly forge for ourselves (cf. 2:24-26; n. 175).

[192] The opening *kî* (3:22b) introduces a rhetorical question (*For who can bring him…?*) to substantiate the consolatory call to enjoyment in 3:22a (cf. n. 188).

[193] The construction *after him* in 3:22b is more appropriately rendered "afterwards" (cf. 6:12; n. 257). This summary appraisal derives from the rhetorical inference in 3:21 that we cannot determine from present events what reward awaits us *afterwards* for the deeds we have done in this life.

to gain an advantage for their labor, for such a strategy is no less self-sufficient than Qoheleth's more transparent empirical attempts to gain an advantage (2:1-23).[194] By demonstrating conclusively that people cannot gain a lasting legacy for themselves—either in unprecedented achievement or by prescribing moral behavior— Qoheleth tried to disabuse his readers of the idea that they could rely on natural ingenuity (1:16-18) to find lasting satisfaction in life (cf. 1:8). Yet he also knew that people in their stubborn pride typically cling so tenaciously to self-sufficiency they will still try to realize their own ambitions—even at the expense of God and others[195]—before they will ever fear God and accept their God-given portion (4:1-6:12).[196]

---

[194] Cp. Mark 2:18-3:6; 7:1ff; Rom 2:1, 14-15; 14:3; Col 2:16, 23; 1 Tim 4:2-4, 8; Heb 9:9-10.

[195] The disillusionment experienced by the moralist who finally comes to the realization that people cannot find meaning in an "ethical" existence alone (n. 156) may provoke rage at God for rejecting an "offering" of good works. Like Cain, they may so envy those who receive God's favor (cf. 2:26) that they takes matters into their own hands (Gen 4:3-8). This helps to explain the otherwise unfathomable oppression that results from selfish ambition—**no one** is spared when they try to find satisfaction by forging their own advantage apart from God (Eccl 4:1-6; 5:8; cf. Gen 4:9-24, esp. vv. 23-24).

[196] The human conscience has to be seared by selfish ambition in order to ignore the instinctive sense of God's sovereign control over the events of life *from beginning to end* (3:11, cf. n. 173) and perpetrate the grievous injustices Qoheleth had observed (3:16). Qoheleth thus aims in the next section to convince self-sufficient readers of their desperate need to *fear God* in order to avoid perpetrating such injustices themselves: Until and unless our conscience is penetrated with full awareness of the profound consequences of shamelessly exploiting God and others to further selfish ambitions (Eccl 4-6), our soul will never enjoy the lasting satisfaction that God intended for us in his God-given heritage (5:18-20).

Part II

VEXATION

*If It Doesn't Work, **Force** It*

The Futility of Selfish Ambition (Eccl 4–6)

*In reflecting on all the oppression, alienation, and despair that inevitably attends the self-sufficient pursuit of ambitious dreams, **Qoheleth proclaims the invariably futile outcome of demanding a better lot in life than God has given**, so that his readers might be thoroughly disillusioned with the false promise of selfish ambition and instead seek satisfaction in their God-given portion.*

Qoheleth's lingering concern over observed injustice (3:16) led him to interrupt his quest for an advantage in human labor to trace the roots of such injustice to the relentless pursuit of selfish ambition (4:1-8).[197] His investigation exposed the invariable damage that results from selfish ambition, which thus serves as the unifying theme for the three reflections that comprise this section. Qoheleth again drew from his experiences and perspective as king[198] to expose the pernicious chain of oppression that is typically propagated[199] by unbridled human determination to realize selfish aspirations. With proverb, vignette, and direct imperative he showed that all selfish ambition is rooted in human contention for a better lot than God has given but only yields alienation, vexation, and despair, even when supported by royal power and charisma.

Qoheleth's argument thus tracks the tragic consequences of forging one's own advantage to satisfy selfish aspirations. The same ambition that grievously oppresses others also isolates one from the protective benefits of community (4:1-16). Such oppression stems from the vain conceit that falsely justifies exploiting God and others for personal gain, yet the same foolish presumption eventually leaves that person utterly destitute and disillusioned (5:1-20). Their final state of despair can only be ascribed to rejecting their God-given portion in life (6:1-12). The concluding pericope (6:10-12) epitomizes the utter failure of selfish ambition and infers that **all** self-sufficiency in the human quest for satisfaction is therefore futile (1:12-6:12, cf. 1:8).

---

[197] *See* n. 77.

[198] Cf. 4:7-8, 13-16; 5:10-17. Qoheleth's stylized experience as king (n. 7) again affords ample *a fortiori* substantiation of the lack of advantage of selfish ambition in achieving lasting satisfaction (n. 124).

[199] *See* nn. 82-86 and the accompanying textual discussion of how these cause-effect relationships contribute to the literary structure of Eccl 4-6.

By apprising his readers of the oppressive outcomes of selfish ambition, Qoheleth intended to provoke reflection on its role and influence in their own quest for satisfaction. If readers were fully aware that the only lasting result of selfish ambition would be their own alienation, vexation, and despair they might be disillusioned enough to abandon the false promise of selfish ambition, mourn the utter failure of self-sufficiency, and embrace God's wisdom as their only hope for an advantage in their labor (7:1-14). Yet our only hope of benefiting from such wisdom is to *fear God*, and we have no incentive to fear God until we fully accepts our complete depravity and accountability before God (7:15-8:15).[200] Only readers who walk this pathway from self-sufficiency to the fear of God can go on to transcend the limitations of their folly, uncertainty, and mortality and bring wisdom's success as agents of God's inscrutable purposes (8:16-12:7).

---

[200] This is the essence of *brokenness* (cf. n. 53); without it the logic of 8:16ff is pointless (cf. n. 52).

— 17 —

A. The Pervasive Oppression of Selfish-Ambition (4:1-16)

In reflecting from his royal perspective on the unjust oppression suffered by all those who lack power in life, **Qoheleth discovers that selfish ambition is at the root of all oppression and even alienates the oppressor from the benefits of community,** *so that his readers might realize their own vulnerability to the pernicious effects of selfish ambition.*

Qoheleth's observation of human injustice (3:16) compelled him to interrupt his reflection on the quest for an advantage in human labor in order to further explore the root of such injustice (4:1a). The passage seems at first to have no consistent textual design or unifying theme; however, on closer study a framework of four *better than* sayings can be identified which is governed by the motif of *two* (or *the second*).[201] This framework supports the argument in two reflective sequences each punctuated with variants of Qoheleth's familiar lament; it is *vanity and grasping for the wind* (4:6c, 16c). Qoheleth first finds selfish ambition at the root of all oppression (4:1-6); but even for the *oppressor*, his ambition only alienates him from the benefits of community (4:7-8, illustrated by the two ensuing object lessons, 4:9-16).

The argument can now be traced: Oppression of the powerless is so grievous that death seems preferable (4:1-3); it can all be traced to one man's envy of the successful work of another, rooted in his grasping, selfish ambition (4:4-6). The violent oppression generated by such selfish ambition led Qoheleth to explore further how this might affect the oppressor himself. With insight from Solomon's royal experience[202] he realized that the oppressor invariably becomes a victim of his own ambition, completely isolated from loved ones (4:7-8):[203]

---

[201] *See* n. 84. "Two" or "both" (same word) occurs in 4:3, 6, 9, 11, 12; "the second" occurs in 4:8, 10, 15.

[202] *See* n. 7.

[203] These transitional verses serve to conclude 4:1-6 but also introduce 4:9-16. Thus, the insatiable ambition portrayed in this "cameo" of the oppressor (4:7-8) explains why he envies and oppresses others (4:1-6), but the alienation that his ambition inevitably incurs (4:8) is then further explored in the anecdotes that follow (4:9-16).

Even the king's ambition precludes the advantages of community by eventually alienating him from all those over whom he rules (4:9-16). The repeating inference is that selfish ambition is inevitably futile (4:4, 7, 8, 16).

By subtly shifting the focus of reflection from the suffering of the oppressed to the oppressor's alienation by his own selfish ambition, Qoheleth draws the reader into identifying with the oppressor. By viewing life from the common perspective of alienation that the readers have surely also experienced in their own lives, Qoheleth hoped to provoke them to reflect on the oppressive outcomes of their own ambition. If their consciences convict them of their own role in promoting the oppression of others, they will be suitably disposed to accept the ensuing admonition: Qoheleth will unmask and discredit the foolish presumption that falsely justifies one's ambitious exploitation of God and others in order to realize their selfish aspirations (5:1-20).

1. Mankind's Extensive Affliction by Selfish Ambition (4:1-6)

With the marker *Then I returned and considered* (4:1a) Qoheleth signals his intent to reflect more thoroughly on the cause of injustice (3:16) and he immediately observed that the poor are invariably oppressed by those who are more powerful (4:1-3). The extent of "man's inhumanity to man" so overwhelmed him (4:1b), that all he could see was the hopeless estate of the oppressed, vicariously expressed in his desire to extinguish their suffering through death or non-existence (4:2-3, cf. 6:3-6).[204] When Qoheleth saw *the evil work that is done under the sun* (4:3b), it provoked him to explore the root of all this oppression. He promptly observed (*Again, I saw*) that it all stems from one man's envy of another man's success (4:4a),[205] the hallmark of selfish

---

[204] Qoheleth's emotion here only reflects his natural perspective "under the sun." This same sentiment is used to justify eugenics or actively ending the lives of the terminally ill, when prolonging life only seems to prolong unmitigated suffering. However, Qoheleth later views even the bleakest circumstances in life from God's perspective and clearly affirms that there is hope for *all* the living (9:4-10). See further the author's exposition of Eccl 4:1-3 as applied to requests for assisted suicide or to the abortion of genetically abnormal preborn children in "Wise Advocacy," in JF Kilner et al, eds, *Dignity and Dying: A Christian Appraisal* (Grand Rapids, MI: Eerdmans, 1996), 208-222; and "Perinatal Hospice: A Response to Early Termination for Severe Congenital Anomalies," in TJ Demy and GP Stewart, eds, *Genetic Engineering: A Christian Response* (Grand Rapids, MI: Kregel, 1999), 197-211.

ambition. All such striving is thus only *vanity and grasping for the wind* (4:4b).

A summary appraisal then graphically depicts how this *vanity* results from *grasping* self-destructive extremes (4:5-6):[206] One extreme is inert resignation, when the hope of selfish ambition is extinguished by the vanishing prospect that one's labor will ever yield any advantage (4:5, cf. 2:20-23).[207] The opposite extreme is a tenacious determination to fulfill one's ambition at the expense of others (4:6b).[208] Both extremes are rooted in selfish ambition but only amount to *grasping for the wind* (4:6c, cf. 4:4b)—both preclude the satisfied rest that God intended for humanity to enjoy in labor (4:6a, cf. 3:12-13, 22). Deeply disturbed by these observations Qoheleth proceeded to explore this lack of rest within the mindset of the ambitious oppressor (4:7-8).

---

[205] There is a logical connection between "evil work" (4:3) and "successful work" (4:4a, lit. "success [*kišrôn*] of work") (cf. n. 144, and Whybray, *Ecclesiastes*, 83). The phrasing of 4:4a, lit. "And I considered all toil and all success of work, that it [is] man's envy of another," can mean that success results **from** envy (NASB) or results **in** envy (NIV). The context supports the latter reading: One man's success will inflame another's envy, and this envy leads to the "evil work" of oppression (4:3), as exemplified by Cain (n. 195); Jacob's sons (Gen 37:4ff); Saul (1 Sam 18-19, 22); Ahab (1 Kgs 21); and many other kings.

[206] The oppressor's ambition can result in two extremes, symbolized by a proverb constructed around the imagery of human hands: The first extreme is represented by the figure of folded hands—it is a resigned disposition that vows to eschew all labor if one cannot quickly and easily achieve the same "success" as his neighbor. The second extreme is represented by "two fistfuls with toil," an all-out attempt to grab all that can be acquired by ambitious effort, regardless of the unjust oppression such strife may cause. This contrasts directly with the balanced figure of "one handful with rest"—a calm confidence in one's allotted portion that may at first appear to be inferior to that of others but is to be accepted with joy (cf. 5:19). Similar imagery in which a third alternative avoids destructive extremes is seen in 7:16-18.

[207] One might not immediately connect the oppression observed in 4:1-3 with the resignation depicted in the imagery of "folded hands." However, alcoholism, drug or gambling addictions, pornography or other sexual addiction, and suicide are just a few of the "resigned" yet oppressive behaviors that are rooted in frustrated ambition. One can readily observe the oppressive consequences of such addictive behaviors on those who remain related to the addict. Qoheleth will further explore the self-destructive foolishness symbolized by "folded hands" in 10:11-19 (cf. Prov 6:10; 24:30-34).

[208] This dynamic is further described in 5:8-9 and exemplified by Cain's progeny (Gen 4:16ff). However, for Qoheleth such exploitation was best exemplified by the kings (1, 2 Sam; 1, 2 Kgs), most explicitly Solomon and his progeny (cf. 1 Kgs 12:4-17 and nn. 85, 198).

2. Mankind's Eventual Alienation by Selfish Ambition (4:7-16)

Qoheleth's intent to investigate the oppressor's futile motivation is indicated by the repeated transitional marker "Then I returned and considered..." (4:7): Even after selfish ambition had left the oppressor *alone, without companion* (4:8a), he continued to grasp for more because he was never satisfied (4:8b, cp. 1:8; 2:18; 5:10). The concluding rhetorical lament *For whom do I toil and deprive myself of good?* [209] expresses the restlessness and grievous isolation that necessarily attends the oppressor's indulgence in selfish ambition (4:8c), so his lament is punctuated with Qoheleth's expected inference of futility (4:8d). That the oppressor's frantic labor was indeed futile is then illustrated in two vignettes depicting how selfish ambition invariably excludes one from the benefits of community by alienating him from others (4:9-16).

While 4:9-12 and 4:13-16 at first seem unrelated, the two pericopae are structurally parallel—each begins with a *better than* proverb that echoes the term "a second" from the transitional verse, 4:8.[210] The passage logically substantiates the futility of the preceding cameo (4:7-8) by demonstrating how the benefits of community (4:9-12) are forfeited when others are alienated by selfish ambition (4:13-16). Qoheleth again drew from his royal perspective to depict *a fortiori* this inevitable outcome and thus deter his readers from pursuing selfish ambition: Even if a king's charisma initially endears him to his subjects it will not keep him from eventually alienating them (4:13-16, cf. 4:1-3)—hence the passage ends again with Qoheleth's standard *vanity* refrain.

Thus unfolds the argument: People who rely on one another enjoy the fruit of their labor better than the self-sufficient (4:9) for they derive greater protection from accidental harm (4:10), exposure (4:11), or oppression (4:12). However, these advantages of

---

[209] The sense is totally confused when the editorial phrase *But he never asks* is inserted (NKJV, NASB) before the rhetorical question *For whom do I toil and deprive myself of good?* It is because the oppressor indeed **does** lament his total alienation from others that the conclusion of futility is justified—his genuine disillusionment underscores how high a price selfish ambition is willing to pay. Larry Crabb well describes how such alienation will invariably afflict one who is thoroughly committed to self-sufficiency (*Connecting: Healing for Ourselves and Our Relationships* [Nashville, TN: Word Publishing, 1997], 75-76).

[210] While "a second" (4:8, lit.) may be rendered *companion* (NKJV) or *dependent* (NASB) it clearly introduces the theme that unifies 4:9-16 (n. 201): "The occurrence of 'the second' in verse 15 serves as a catch word that ties vv 13-16 with vv 9-12, in which 'two' occurs so frequently" (Murphy, *Ecclesiastes*, 42).

community are inevitably forfeited by selfish ambition (cf. 4:7-8): Wisdom may initially afford an advantage to a popular king (4:13-14), but not even royal charisma can keep his ambitious rule from eventually disaffecting his subjects (4:15-16).[211] The implied object lesson? If even powerful kings can't sustain their ambitious rule, much less will the readers profit from **their** ambition—again, it *is vanity and grasping for the wind* (4:16c). Qoheleth now raises the stakes by exposing the foolish presumption behind ambitious gain and the high price paid by acting on that presumption (5:1-20).

---

[211] The sequence of events involves three kings who rule successively over a particular kingdom: An old but foolish king is deposed by a poor but wise youth who ascends the throne from prison (4:13-14), yet the loyalty of his countless subjects inevitably shifts to a *second youth* who deposes him (4:15-16a), but again their loyalty is short-lived (4:16b). Although the royal referents in 4:13-16 are ambiguous (Murphy, ibid., 41 [fns. 14-16]), *the second youth* "cannot be taken to mean merely that the first youth was the second king after the foolish one"—thus *three* kings must be in view (ibid., 43). As to their historical identity, some elements of the vignette suggest seeing Saul-David-Solomon (or Absalom) or Solomon-Rehoboam-Abijah (cf. 2 Chr 9-13), but neither sequence fits all the details. Murphy concludes, "the case is typical and need not refer to any specific historical incident" (ibid., 41). See also n. 208.

18

B. The Foolish Presumption of Selfish Ambition (5:1-20)

By declaring the grievous consequences of seeking personal gain at the expense of God and others, **Qoheleth exposes the foolish presumption that falsely justifies exploiting God or others to fulfill ambitious dreams***, so that his readers might forsake their selfish ambition, fear God, and joyfully accept their God-given portion.*

Qoheleth now abruptly shifts to direct exhortation (5:1ff). The literary link with the previous passage is not immediately apparent, but Qoheleth yet again observed man's widespread inhumanity to man (5:8-10, cf. 4:1-3). The connection emerges when we recognize that one's willingness to exploit others for personal gain (5:8-10, cf. 4:1-8) is rooted in the same presumption that would drive one to exploit God (5:1-7), even to their own eventual detriment (5:11-17, cf. 4:9-16). This is the foolish presumption of selfish ambition which Qoheleth exposes in a sequence of warnings to the reader, culminating with the appraisal *this too is vanity* (5:1-10). He then corroborates this futility by describing the unrelenting vexation that inevitably attends ambitious gain (5:11-17), contrasting it with the joy and fulfillment of accepting one's portion from God (5:18-20).

The hidden presumption that first led Qoheleth to try to find out which deeds might curry God's favor (3:12-22) is finally exposed. It is the vain conceit of selfish ambition, signified in this passage by the notion of *dreams* (5:3, 7), that we would think our good works entitled us to fulfill our *dreams:* When we can't realize our ambitious aspirations on our own we typically cajole God with *many words* (5:2, 7) to return His favor for our good works—this is the pretext of the rash *vows* (5:4-5). However, it is utterly futile for us to thus presume on God, for we incur great personal liability (5:6-7): the inevitable dispossession of all we have gained (5:11-17).[212] Our only hope of

---

[212] The loss implied by the repeated construction *nothing in his hand* (5:14b, 15b) is foreshadowed by the rhetorical question *Why should God...destroy the work of your hands?* (5:6)—it portends God's eventual confiscation of all the riches accumulated at the expense of others. The imagery of *hands* (cp. 4:4-6; n. 206) plays a central role in the unity of the whole section.

satisfaction is thus to simply accept our portion from God (5:18-20, cf. 2:24; 3:22; 4:6a).

Qoheleth's exposure of this foolish presumption that fuels selfish ambition is meant to provoke the readers' disillusionment with such ambition in their own lives. By seeing through Qoheleth's eyes the pervasive oppression that results from selfish ambition (4:1-8), self-sufficient readers should more readily recognize their own presumption on God and others for ambitious gain (5:1-10). By warning us that this only incurs the liability of ultimately forfeiting such gain, as it leaves us with great vexation our entire lives (5:11-17), Qoheleth hopes to loosen our tenacious grip on ambitious aspirations, so that we might accept our God-given portion with an open hand (5:18-20, cf. 4:4-6).

1. Mankind's False Entitlement: to Exploit God or Others (5:1-10)

Qoheleth's exposition of the pernicious influence of selfish ambition now escalated to abrupt admonition as he sought to unmask the hypocrisy of such ambition. The text is framed by three warnings[213] aimed at the person who would foolishly presume to cajole God into fulfilling their ambitious aspirations. Each warning is qualified by the circumstance of such exploitation—*when you go to the house of God* (5:1); *when you make a vow to God* (5:4); *if you see...oppression* (5:8); and each is justified by motive clauses[214] that should supply the reader with sufficient incentive to heed Qoheleth's admonition.

The warnings are designed to discredit the allure of self-sufficiency by exposing the hypocrisy of exploiting God (5:1-7) and others (5:8-10) to satisfy ambitious *dreams*. Qoheleth first warns the reader to approach God *prudently...to hear* (5:1a), with *few words* (5:2c) rather than presumptuous *dreams* and *many words* (5:2a, 3);[215]

---

[213] Each admonition centers on a primary imperative, *draw near to hear...* (5:1ff); *do not delay to pay...* (5:4ff); *Do not marvel...* (5:8). The first two imperatives are clarified and expanded by associated *secondary* imperatives (5:2a, c, 4c-5, 6a, b); the third then justifies the conclusion *This also is vanity* (5:10).

[214] Each clause is initiated by a causal *For...* (5:1c, 2b, 3, 4b, 7a; 8b) or rhetorical *Why...?* (5:6c).

[215] Lit. "Don't be hasty with *your mouth* or let *your heart* hasten to bring something up to God [5:2a]...for the dream [only] comes through great effort, and a fool's voice through many words [5:3]." Thus, when a fool sees that he can't realize his *dream* on his own he presents it to God with a positive "spin" using *many words*. His *dreams* and *many words* thus portray his foolish presumption before God (n. 40).

the latter is only *the sacrifice of fools,*[216] *for they do not know that they do evil* (5:1b): They sinfully ignore God's purposes *in heaven* in their ambitious plans *on earth* (5:2b, cf. 3:1, 10). Such foolish presumption is exemplified when a self-sufficient person offers a rash *vow*[217] (5:4-5) in return for God's complicity in blessing their ambitious *dreams.*[218] Such a vow is best avoided, because the hypocritical sense of entitlement that compels it (5:5-6a)[219] will incur God's retribution (5:6b).[220] Thus, it is utterly futile for humans to promote their ambitious *dreams* by cajoling God with *many words* (5:7a);[221]

---

[216] The *sacrifice of fools* (5:1b) consists of "offering" *many words* to God (cf. *voice of fools*, 5:3b).

[217] It appears that the fool's words are directed at God in the setting of worship (5:1-2) and take the form of rash vows (5:4-5) intended to manipulate God into blessing his *dreams*. However, not all vows are rash (cf. Deut 23:21-23). The difference is in the motivation of the one making the vow: Is the vow made out of a sincere desire to serve God or only to gain an advantage in gratifying selfish ambition? The latter motive is revealed in his lack of sincerity in keeping the promise (5:6, see below).

[218] The presumption inherent in the *sacrifice of fools* (5:1b) consists in the fact that the fool's *many words* are only designed to exploit God. A self-sufficient fool dares to approach God only because 1) it takes too much effort to realize his "dream" (5:3a; n. 215); and 2) this ambitious dream ignores the purposes of God (5:2b). The vain conceit that God will surely comply is antithetical to the fear of God (5:7, cf. n. 177); this false sense of entitlement only reflects the evil allure (cf. 5:1b) of Satan's original offer (Gen 3:4-5; cf. Larry Crabb, *SoulTalk: The Language God Longs for Us to Speak* [Nashville, TN: Integrity, 2003], 77-81).

[219] The command in 5:6a clearly substantiates the immediately preceding advice (5:4-5) by exposing the duplicitous motivation behind failing to keep a vow, lit. "Don't let your mouth make your body sin or say before the messenger [of God] that it was an inadvertent error"; thus, a false vow in one's mouth before God will trigger a false excuse before God's witnesses (cf. Longman, *Ecclesiastes*, 154-55). The vow will *cause your flesh to sin* (5:6a), in that reneging on the duplicitous vow forces the prevarication that it was an unintended oversight, like Saul's false excuse before Samuel for reneging on his vow to God (cf. 1 Sam 15:15, 20-21). The warning of Eccl 5:4-6 is echoed in the Sermon on the Mount (Matt 5:33-37), and Christ later exposed such hypocrisy when gifts vowed to God were flagrantly intended for personal gain (Matt 15:3-6).

[220] The pretense of inadvertent error before others only compounds the foolish presumption of attempting to manipulate God (n. 218), thus provoking God's wrath (Longman, ibid., 155; cf. Acts 5:1-10).

[221] This clause reads lit. "for in a multitude of dreams and vanities and many words." The opening *kî* probably infers ("So") the futility of verbally manipulating God into blessing ambitious aspirations, as conveyed by the recurring *dreams* and *many words* (cf. 5:3; n. 40). The last two *waw* could be rendered "both...and..." and give us "So, in many dreams *both* vanities *and* words are multiplied." Or, we could read a *waw* associative "also" plus a hendiadys, "many vain words" (cf. Longman, *Ecclesiastes*, 156), yielding "So, in many dreams are *also* many vain words." The meaning is similar in either case (cf. also 6:11).

rather,[222] Qoheleth advises, *fear God* [223] (5:7b, NASB).

Qoheleth then explains how such ambitious presumption is logically related to all the oppression he had observed (cf. 3:16; 4:1-16): Whenever we see *oppression* and injustice *in a province* we shouldn't be surprised[224] (5:8a): Those in authority[225] rely on the same false sense of entitlement to exploit others below them[226] for personal gain (5:8b),[227] so the only *profit* in *all* this is that the *king is served by* those who till *the field* (5:9).[228] As a result, *He who loves* gain is never *satisfied with* gain (5:10a);[229] *this too is vanity*

---

[222] The *kî* that initiates 5:7b is strongly adversative (Longman, ibid.): *rather* (or *instead*).

[223] Contextually, this connotes deference to God's preordained and immutable purposes in heaven (cf. 5:2b, 3:14; n. 177).

[224] NKJV *do not marvel at the matter* [*ḥēpheṣ*]. The context suggests a preferable sense for *ḥēpheṣ* (n. 44): the "purpose" or "reason" behind the observed oppression and injustice. The final clause should thus read "do not wonder about the reason..."

[225] The substantive *gābōah* ("high one") is usually rendered "official," which certainly fits the context of a bureaucratic "pyramid" that converges on the king at the top of the "food chain" (5:9, cf. n. 85). But Seow argues well for the sense of "haughty" or "arrogant" and cites support that "the word may...be used of people who are ambitious" (*Ecclesiastes*, 203-4, 218)—the exact sense implied in context (n. 227).

[226] The contextual nuance of ambition suggests that the verb *šāmar* ("watch, observe") bears a negative sense akin to "micromanagement," that is, exercising authority to the detriment of those being "watched" (cf. 8:9b). Qoheleth will later develop the further implications of such injustice and oppression, for when it is not promptly judged it may create a crisis of confidence for *those who fear God* (cf. 8:10-15).

[227] That is, the same arrogant conceit and sense of entitlement that falsely justifies bartering with a sovereign God for personal gain (5:1-7, n. 218) also drives "man's inhumanity to man" (5:8; cf. 4:1-6).

[228] Expositors are overly pessimistic about making good sense of 5:9 (cf. Longman *Ecclesiastes*, 158-9), lit. "and the land['s] advantage in all it [is] the king to the field is served." The phrase *leśādeh* ("to the field") should be construed with the passive Nifal of *'ābad* as signifying *agency* ("is served *by* the field," s.v. "*le*—", BDB, 514a). Moreover, the initial *waw* should be taken as inferential, as the phrase "in all it" alludes to Qoheleth's previous observation (5:8), so that 5:9 is the ironic conclusion (n. 85): "So the [only] advantage of the land in all this [is that] the king is served by the field." See, e.g., 2 Sam 8:9-18; 1 Kgs 12:1-15; cf. 21:1-11). The reader now finally understands why even a popular king is also inevitably alienated from his subjects (4:13-16).

[229] This summary appraisal echoes the prior closing sentiment *his eye is not satisfied with riches* (4:8) and serves as a transition to the following section, which substantiates this lack of satisfaction.

(5:10b): Selfish ambition is destined to fail. Qoheleth then substantiated his appraisal with wise axioms attesting the fleeting nature of ambitious gain.

2. Mankind's Fitting End: to Accept One's God-Given Portion (5:11-20)

This text validates the prior warning against presuming on God—i.e., how God will *destroy the work of your hands* (5:11-17, cf. 5:6b)—but it also explains why it suits God to reapportion the fruits of our labor (5:18-20, cf. 2:26). Qoheleth first substantiated the futility of ambitious gain (cf. 5:10) by explaining why it never affords any lasting satisfaction: The selfishly ambitious person multiplies wealth only to find that others will multiply who consume it, so the only *profit* is but *to see* it briefly (5:11, cf. 5:8-10)—the continual preoccupation of trying to preserve one's wealth deprives them of hoped-for rest (5:12). It is a *severe evil* that he returns as naked as he came, keeping *nothing in his hand*[230] (5:13-15)—not only is he deprived of any lasting advantage (5:16)[231] but *all his days he* sees no meaning in life[232] and is greatly vexed in his *sickness and anger* (5:17).[233]

---

[230] The same construction appears in both 5:14 and 15, but this is poorly reflected in NASB. The imagery of *hands* in 5:13-15 links its message to 4:5-6 and 5:6 (cf. n. 212). Cp. Job 1:21.

[231] The interposed text in 5:16 is an echo of 5:15 (plus a parenthetical rhetorical inference) that should be read in apposition to $w^e gam$–$z\bar{o}h$ in 5:16a, and this *gam* should in turn be linked to the *gam* in 5:17a and rendered "both...and...". Stated **negatively**, "And *not only* is *this* a miserable evil—that just as a man is born so will he die (so what advantage has he who toils for the wind?)—*but also* all his days he eats in darkness...[5:16-17a]."

[232] The clause *all his days he eats in darkness* connotes mere day-to-day survival with no insight into life (cf. 2:14). The ultimate desolation of this "darkness" of self-sufficiency is elaborated in 6:1-6.

[233] The abbreviated syntax of 5:17 is similar to 5:7a (n. 221). The *waw* consecutive perfect form of "to be vexed" (*ka'as*) should be read as a "habitual" imperfect to parallel *all his days*, and the ensuing *waw* distributes the force of the prepositional prefix on $b^e h\bar{o}\check{s}ek$ (*in darkness*) to the phrase *his sickness and anger*. This gives us "...all his days he eats **in** darkness and is greatly vexed **in** his sickness and anger" (cf. Murphy, *Ecclesiastes*, 47 [fn. 16.b]). This sense of *disillusionment, ill health*, and *anger* echoes the conclusion of 2:23 (n. 145) and will again be recalled in Qoheleth's use of *ka'as* (n. 39) in 7:8-10 and 11:10a.

In stark contrast to this *evil* (cf. 5:16) Qoheleth had seen what is *good* and *fitting:*[234] One's portion is to *enjoy the good of all his labor all the days God gives him*—even the one *whom God has given riches* and enabled him to enjoy them—and to accept[235] one's portion and enjoy the *labor* that *God* gives him (5:18-19),[236] so that he is not constantly preoccupied with making a living, because God fulfills the *joy of his heart* (5:20).[237] This is truly preferable ("better and fitting") to the vexing legacy of selfish ambition (cf. 4:4-8; 5:6-7, 11-17), because one is truly satisfied only when he freely accepts what God has given: It is the only way one can avoid the ultimate futility of insisting on a different lot in life than God has ordained to suit our created nature (6:1-12).

---

[234] The word *good* (*ṭôb*) can be read as comparative ("better," cf. 7:1) in that it introduces all of 5:18-20 as the **preferable** alternative to 5:11-17; thus, there is no full stop before the *gam* that begins 5:19 or the *kî* that initiates 5:20 (see nn. 236, 237). The coupled adjective *fitting* (*yāpheh*, cf. 3:11; n. 169) refers to the preferable *portion* (*ḥēleq*, 5:18, 19; n. 29) God designed for humanity in lieu of the futile legacy of selfish ambition (5:16-17).

[235] It is misleading to construe *nāśāʿ* ("take, bear," cf. 5:15) as *receive* (5:19, NKJV, NASB). Both a man who is satisfied with his lot in life (5:19) and one who is not (6:2) may "receive" *riches and wealth*, but only the former is fulfilled because he "takes" (or "accepts," *so* NIV) his *portion* (Whybray, *Ecclesiastes*, 102-3).

[236] Qoheleth's preferable alternative (5:18-19, cf. n. 234) to the ambitious man's vexatious obsession with riches (5:10-17) is ironic, in that God intends to satisfy even those whom He has given riches. The *gam* that introduces 5:19 is thus asseverative, lit. "Look what I have seen is good, what is fitting: to eat and drink and to see goodness in all the labor that one does under the sun [for] the days that God has given him, for that is his portion—**even** every man whom God has given riches and possessions and enabled him to partake of them—and to accept his portion and enjoy his labor; it is God's gift" (5:18-19). The sense is that if even a rich man could be satisfied by accepting his portion, much more could those with fewer possessions (cf. 5:12).

[237] The opening *kî* explains why the alternative presented in 5:18-19 is *good and fitting*, as substantiated by the following *kî:* "**For** he does not greatly remember [is not unduly preoccupied with] the days of his life, **for** God keeps him busy with the joy of his heart." This is God's answer to the ambitious man's sleepless obsession with gain (5:11-17): God created mankind to freely enjoy the desires that God has placed in our hearts (cf. 11:8, NIV; cp. Ps 37:1, 4). This is the fundamental premise of Larry Crabb's *The Pressure's Off* (Colorado Springs, CO: Waterbrook, 2002); cf. also John Eldredge, *Wild at Heart* (Nashville, TN: Thomas Nelson, 2001).

19

C. The Existential Despair of Selfish Ambition (6:1-12)

*By attributing the eventual despair of even the most successful of self-sufficient humans to vain contention with God over their portion in life, **Qoheleth establishes the ultimate futility of selfish ambition for all mankind in light of their preordained calling of God**, so that ambitious, self-sufficient readers might acknowledge their contention with God and be entirely disillusioned by the false promise of lasting satisfaction in self-sufficiency.*

By immediately following the scenario in 5:18-20 with that in 6:1-3, Qoheleth meant to compare two radically divergent responses to the same abundant lot in life (cp. 5:19, 6:2):[238] Having observed that we were meant to be fully satisfied with our portion from God (5:18-20), Qoheleth described the final state of a man who is completely dissatisfied with his bountiful portion (6:1-3). This in turn compels the question of what it is that determines these dichotomous outcomes from the same lot in life, so the argument now traces the final restless despair of a self-sufficient man (6:1-6, cf. 5:16-17) to a problem far worse than losing all he gained through selfish ambition (cf. 5:11-15): His insatiable ambition is totally at cross-purposes with his original calling by God (6:7-12, cf. 5:18-20).

Ironically, the despair inflicted by the ambitious oppressor on the lives of those he oppressed (cf. 4:1-3; 5:8-9) now comes back to haunt him (6:1-6). This subjective portrayal of existential nihilism is meant to complete the disillusionment[239] of the reader who still clings to selfish ambition for lasting fulfillment: The illusion that humans can dictate their own legacy stems from the self-sufficient conceit that they can effectively contend with God for a different lot in life (6:10-11) even though they can't possibly know what is good for them or what the future holds (6:12, cf. 3:10-22). Those of us who recognize this as our own dilemma can foolishly

---

[238] *See* n. 83.

[239] The motif of *disillusionment* is conveyed in 6:1-12 by the negation of similar terms in 5:18-20 denoting satisfaction or enjoyment (cf. n. 83). This disillusionment culminates with Qoheleth's repeated harping on the total absence of any lasting advantage from ambitious self-sufficiency (6:8, 11b, cf. 5:11, 16, n. 67).

keep resisting our God-given heritage and nurture a legacy of bitterness or we can wisely mourn our broken dreams and accept the portion that God intended for us within His inscrutable plan (7:1-14).

1. The Self-Sufficient Soul Languishes in Restless Despair (6:1-6)

In stark contrast to what Qoheleth had *seen* to be *good and fitting* (5:18-20), *There* was *an evil* he had *seen* that *weighs heavily on* humanity:[240] It was the ironic instance of the man whom *God* also *gives wealth, possessions and honor, so that he lacks nothing his heart desires, but God does not enable him to enjoy them* (6:1-2b [NIV], cf. 5:19).[241] He then explained this *evil affliction*[242] (6:2c) by recalling the imagery of *light* and *darkness* to describe the futile and desolate destiny of the ambitious man who *all his days eats in darkness* (cf. 5:17a): Even a stillbirth is preferable to a long, prolific life, if a man is not *satisfied with goodness,* for the *stillborn* has more *rest—it has* never *seen the sun* and then had the hope of lasting satisfaction crushed in restless despair (6:3-6b).[243]

This first reflection concluded with a rhetorical question *Do not all go to one place?* (6:6c)—a final reminder that death will

---

[240] The opening construction in 5:18a "Look what I have seen is good, what is fitting" (n. 236) is paralleled by the converse scenario in 6:1, lit. "There is an evil I have seen...and it is great on mankind" (or better, "it weighs heavily on mankind," cf. NIV, 8:6b). The contrast is between the *good* God intended for humans to accept as their portion and the *evil* they bring upon themselves.

[241] Qoheleth does not yet explain why God permits one man to enjoy his bountiful heritage yet another is not allowed to enjoy the same heritage. One clue here is that one man "accepts his lot" (5:19, NIV; n. 235), but we see no such acceptance by the man in 6:2—the reason why is elaborated in 6:7-12 (cf. esp. 6:10b).

[242] This *affliction* is the same "sickness" (*ḥŏlî*) that typically culminates a life of selfish ambition (cf. 5:17).

[243] The intricate logic of this run-on sentence is governed by sequential conjunctions: "If ['im] a man has a hundred children and lives many years, so [waw] that many are the days of his years, but [waw] his soul is not satisfied with goodness, or indeed [wᵉgam] he has no burial, I say a stillborn child is better off than he [6:3], for [kî] it comes in futility and goes in darkness and its name is shrouded in darkness [6:4]; moreover [gam], it has not seen the sun ['lived'] or known ['had any awareness']—it has more rest than that man [6:5], even if [wᵉ'illû] he lives a thousand years twice but [waw] has seen no goodness [6:6a, b]." Thus, the stillborn is spared the **greater** futility of having lived an entire life with no "goodness." This same imagery pervades Job's opening soliloquy (Job 3), in which he also wished he had been stillborn and never "seen light": *"For* then *I would have been at rest...,* but *I have no rest"* (Job 3:13, 26).

ultimately dispossess all men (cf. 3:18-21; 5:11-17). Since not even an unprecedented lifespan with a hundred progeny can yield lasting satisfaction (6:3-6b), this should provoke the self-sufficient reader with even greater urgency to wonder, Could I also be one whom *God has not empowered* to enjoy his lot (6:2b, NASB)?[244] The grim prospect of unremitting restless discontent should motivate us to avoid this *evil affliction* (6:2c) by attending to Qoheleth's explanation of why God would deliberately prevent one's soul from being satisfied (6:7-12).

2. The Self-Sufficient Soul Labors for the Wrong Destiny (6:7-12)

The focus now shifts from mankind as victim of dissatisfaction (6:1-6) to mankind as perpetrator of his own dissatisfaction (6:7-12). The two pericopae (6:7-9, 10-12) are arranged in parallel (a:b:c/a':b':c') to culminate Qoheleth's reflections on the lack of advantage to self-sufficiency.[245] He first portrays mankind as so totally preoccupied (contrast 5:20a) with feeding his appetite ("mouth," 6:7a), that his soul remains completely unfulfilled (6:7b, cf. 6:3b).[246] This is substantiated by recalling that not even great wisdom can afford any advantage in filling his soul's appetite for lasting satisfaction (6:8).[247] He can

---

[244] The logic of 6:1-3 thus argues *a fortiori:* If a self-sufficient man has all the *riches and wealth and honor* he could desire yet he can still despair of life, how could anyone with **less** status expect to be satisfied by his own effort?

[245] Two primary assertions (6:7, 10) are both followed by the rhetorical inference "What then is the advantage?" (6:8, 11) and concluded in turn by a summary appraisal (6:9, 12). The second pericope (6:10-12) also serves as a summary appraisal for the first half of the argument (cf. nn. 68, 67 and related text).

[246] The aphorism *all man's labor [is] for his mouth* (6:7a) means that generally all of one's hard-earned resources are expended just to sustain life (cf. 5:11-15). The next two verses apply this principle to the frustrated attempt to "feed" the human "appetite" of selfish ambition (see below).

[247] The text of 6:8 is difficult (Murphy, *Ecclesiastes*, 48 [fns. 8.b, c]), lit. "For what [is the] advantage to a wise man over the fool? What [is it] for a poor man knowing to walk among the living?" The verse is a rhetorical inference from the observation of 6:7. The opening *kî* ("so") introduces two rhetorical questions in such a way that the second answers the first with a sardonic twist (6:8b): "So what advantage has a wise man over the fool?—no more than a poor man who knows how to survive." In other words, at most the wise man may live a little longer than the fool. This "advantage" of *mere survival* parallels the imagery in 6:7—that all one's labor is spent just to physically sustain him—and it echoes the results of Qoheleth's earlier quest for an advantage in wisdom (2:12-16): All he found was a mere survival advantage over folly (2:13-14a) but no lasting legacy, for both he **with** his wisdom and the fool **without** it would eventually die as peers, with no remembrance at all (cf. nn. 134, 136).

therefore only conclude that a person can gain nothing by ambitiously pursuing anything one has not already been given (6:9a).[248] This once again justifies the standard refrain of futility (6:9b).

The second pericope (6:10-12) explains why self-sufficiency is ultimately futile and thus warrants God's prerogative of letting one man enjoy *riches and wealth* (5:19) while depriving another from enjoying the same lot in life (6:2): Given that one's "calling" in life is preordained (6:10a),[249] it is utterly foolish for him to resist God's purposes in that calling (6:10b).[250] Such foolishness is again manifested in the utterly futile presumption of trying to cajole God with *many words* into fulfilling ambitious dreams (6:11, cf. 5:1-7).[251]

---

[248] To prove his point Qoheleth cites a proverb *Better is the sight of the eyes than the wandering of desire* like the saying "A bird in the hand is worth two in the bush." The *wandering of desire* (lit. "the roving of the soul") epitomizes the ambitious quest for satisfaction (cf. 1:8) that pervades the first half of the argument. The *sight of the eyes* represents the *lot* or *heritage* that one already has. Qoheleth's point is that the unfulfilled soul described in 6:7 would be better off accepting what he has been given (cf. 5:18-19; 6:2, n. 241) than seeking an advantage through ambitious self-effort.

[249] The opening saying lit. reads "Whatever has come to be has already been given his name, and it is known that he is man" (6:10a), implying that mankind's role or "calling" in life is pre-assigned by his Creator. The profound "finality" of the naming act is illustrated in the Creation narrative, *And whatever Adam called each living creature, that was its name* (Gen 2:19); the act of naming can't be separated from the purpose intended for the creature named (cf. Eph 2:10). The saying quoted in Eccl 6:10a thus naturally leads to the inference in 6:10b—one's "calling" should not be resisted (cf. 1 Cor 7:20-24).

[250] The logical thrust of the opening *waw* in 6:10b is best read as inferential, "*so* he cannot contend with him who is stronger than he." It is absurd for a mere human to contend with *him who is stronger* (NASB) for a different destiny than the one he was given, a clear allusion to God as Creator (Longman, *Ecclesiastes*, 176-7). This "contention" belies an arrogant claim to know better than God *what is good for a man* (6:12). Such arrogance is also implied in Job's brazen demand that God account for Job's unjust suffering and restore his lost estate (Job 29-31) and it elicits a rebuke from Elihu based on the same reasoning as Eccl 6:10b: *For God is greater than man. Why do you contend [rîb] with Him?* (Job 33:12b-13a). Sure enough, God Himself answers Job (*rîb*, cf. Job 40:2) by arguing from His indisputably greater creative knowledge and power (Job 38-41).

[251] Lit., "For there are many words multiplying vanity; [so] what [is] the advantage to a man?" The first line substantiates the assertion of 6:10b, while the second line draws the rhetorical inference, echoing the rhetorical question in 6:8a (cf. n. 247). Qoheleth again relates "many words" and "vanity" (cf. 5:7a; nn. 40, 215, 218) to underscore the futility of trying to co-opt God into fulfilling ambitious "dreams." The word *hebel* could also be rendered *vapor* or *breath* (n. 8), so the line might read "For many words are only so much vapor, so how do they help a man?" It does not bode well for one to plead with God for a different lot in life (6:10b, cf. 5:1-7) if he wants to gain lasting fulfillment in his labor (cf. 1:3; 3:9). Cf. also Job 34:35-37; 35:13-16; 38:2.

Thus, the restless dissatisfaction and ultimate despair of the man portrayed in 6:1-6 is directly attributable to his own rebellious contention for a destiny that is at total cross-purposes with his God-given heritage (6:10-11).[252]

Qoheleth then explained why it is so ludicrous for mankind to presume they can devise a better plan than God (6:10-11): *For who knows what is good for man* during his few numbered days[253] (6:12a)—indeed,[254] he spends them "in the dark,"[255] since[256] no one *can tell him what will happen* afterward[257] (6:12b). The crowning disillusionment that we can't conceive of a greater legacy than God has preordained for us (6:12) is meant to elicit a wiser response from the reader in adversity than to cling tenaciously to a self-determined destiny (7:1-14): As our ambitious dreams are finally shattered (cf. 5:3, 7; 16-17), we are well advised to abandon the false hope of self-sufficiency and accept our God-given calling.[258]

---

[252] This is captured well by Larry Crabb (*Inside Out* [Colorado Springs: NavPress, 1988]), 133:

> Can you imagine an army where new recruits give orders…? And yet mere people shout orders to the universe. Such foolishness is the inevitable result of taking responsibility for securing our own happiness, a burden that's simply too heavy….When we assume responsibility for what we desperately need but cannot control, we irrationally demand that our efforts succeed.

[253] The construction is most likely prepositional, "[during] the numbered days of his vain life."

[254] The introductory particle we^- in 6:12b is probably intended as asseverative ("yea" or "indeed"), since the logic of 6:12b emphatically substantiates the truth affirmed in 6:12a.

[255] Expositors often take MT "like a shadow" as a redundant expression of life's brevity (cf. "numbered days," n. 253), but Qoheleth's only other use of "shadow" in reference to time (8:13) signifies **long** life. However, LXX "in a shadow" is more logical (*contra* Longman, *Ecclesiastes*, 176 [fn. 3], 178): It adds to human disillusionment over life's brevity with the further notion that humanity spends that short life "in a fog" (cf. 5:17a, "in darkness"), unable to see clearly what will happen. This in turn decisively refutes the implicit claim of self-sufficiency to *know* better than God *what is good for* a *man* (6:12a, n. 250).

[256] The conjunction *'ašer* introduces the rhetorical question in 6:12b as the main reason **why** man spends his days "in a shadow" so it should read "because" or "since" (cf. also 8:12b, 13; n. 365 below).

[257] Most translations read "after him" in spite of the feminine suffix, yet the same construction in 9:3c is adverbial, not prepositional (cp. 3:22, n. 193; cf. Seow, *Ecclesiastes*, 234); moreover, it cannot refer to the afterlife when used in conjunction with the phrase *under the sun* (ibid.). Thus, "Qoheleth does not have in mind…'life after death,' but rather how things will turn out…on earth" (Murphy, *Ecclesiastes*, 59).

[258] Cf. 6:10a, n. 249. This is the premise of Larry Crabb's *Shattered Dreams—God's Unexpected Pathway to Joy* (Colorado Springs: WaterBrook Press, 2001). God allows the frustration of our dreams and our attendant disillusionment to promote mourning and patient confidence in God's creative design for us; exactly the point of Qoheleth's transitional passage (7:1-14). The utter failure of self-sufficiency to achieve lasting satisfaction in life (cf. 1:3) forces the reader to make a choice: We can wisely mourn the failure of our self-sufficiency and submit to God's inscrutable purposes (7:1-4, 11-14) or we can ignore wise counsel and try foolishly to appease the inevitable despair of broken dreams by seeking diversionary pleasure (7:5-10).

Part III

TRANSITION

Wisdom through Brokenness

Adversity at the Crossroads of Wisdom
(Eccl 7:1-14)

By comparing wise and foolish responses to disillusionment in adversity, **Qoheleth shows how we gain wisdom's benefits in adversity only when we mourn the failure of self-sufficiency and consider the work of God,** *so that his readers might wisely forsake selfish ambition and patiently submit to God's inscrutable purposes.*

Thus far Qoheleth has utilized proverbs, vignettes, and injunctions to show how selfish ambition in the human quest for an advantage in our labor will only result in oppression and disillusionment (4:1-6:12). Although this section initially appears to lack any logical coherence or obvious relationship to the preceding context, it provides the key logical transition in the flow of Qoheleth's argument[259] from *total disillusionment* to *lasting satisfaction*. Closer inspection of the textual design reveals an intricate chiastic arrangement of the themes of *wisdom* and *folly*[260] that "answers" the immediately preceding rhetorical question, *who knows what is good?* (6:12a). A series of *better than* proverbs is arranged in two clusters, each introduced by an analogy,[261] to explain why one disposition in response to disillusionment in life is *wise* but the other *foolish*. This short but critical transitional section concludes with a variant of the same literary marker (7:14d) as the previous two major sections (3:22b, 6:12b).[262]

The communicative intent of this logical transition in Qoheleth's argument is to introduce a preferable alternative to the obvious futility of selfish ambition (cf. 4:1-6:12). By comparing

---

[259] Although the passage is set apart from the surrounding text by conspicuous literary markers and a different textual style, Whybray abandons the task of finding any "logical progression of thought" (*Ecclesiastes*, 112); Murphy is more adept here at identifying the logical flow (*Ecclesiastes*, 61-63). See the section entitled "THE PIVOTAL TRANSITION IN QOHELETH'S ARGUMENT" in the OVERVIEW OF ECCLESIASTES.

[260] *See* n. 71.

[261] The two steps of the argument are each initiated by an implied analogy (*As..., so...*) comparing *wise* and *foolish* responses in adversity (7:1a; 7:8a). The "better than" construction occurs five times in the first cluster (7:1-7) and three times in the second, along with two other affirmations of "advantage" (7:8-14, NASB, cf. vv. 11-12), thus balancing the chiastic symmetry (n. 71) with an equal number of allusions that address *what is good* (6:12a).

[262] See n. 60.

wise with *foolish* responses to disillusionment, Qoheleth expounds the critical importance of *brokenness* in response to life's inevitable disillusionment in adversity. Whereas our natural, self-reliant tendency would be to stubbornly cling to our ambitious dreams (7:8-10), Qoheleth recommends a broken willingness to *mourn* our inadequacy and *consider the work of God* (7:1-4, 13-14). While self-reliance seeks pleasure to placate impending despair, it only fosters angry impatience and corrupts the heart with entrenched bitterness (7:5-10). But authentic *mourning* edifies the *heart* with *wisdom,* which *gives life* in adversity by patiently considering *the work of God* (7:1-4, 11-14). In sum, we are well-advised to release our grip on ambitious dreams amid life's inevitable adversity and accept both the "bad" and the "good" in the work of God.

Qoheleth aimed to transform foolish, self-sufficient readers into wise and confident stewards of their God-given portion. However, in order to stop contending with God for a better lot in life (cf. 6:10-11), we would have to truly mourn and give up our emotional investment in selfish aspirations—only then could we patiently accept our God-given portion and enjoy the fruit of our labor in the work of God (cf. 3:10-15; 5:18-20). The second half of the argument thus describes what we must mourn in order to preserve wisdom's advantage and bring success in the work of God: Qoheleth's reflections warn of our inherent depravity, mortality, and uncertainty, so that wise readers might fear God in order to enjoy their portion and remain alert and responsive to opportunities to participate in the inscrutable work of God (7:15-12:7).

— 20 —

A. Authentic Mourning is better than False Optimism (7:1-7)

With proverbs that commend mourning over mirth in response to disillusionment, **Qoheleth affirms that authentic mourning edifies the heart with wisdom, while false optimism only debases the heart by promising empty pleasure,** *so that readers might not foolishly try to placate their despair amid adversity but rather genuinely mourn their own inadequacy.*

The logic of this section revolves around two comparisons that encourage the self-sufficient reader to respond differently than usual when vexed by adversity (7:1b, 5, cf. 5:16-17).[263] First, Qoheleth favored *mourning* one's inadequacy in adversity, rather than trying to fend off despair with pleasant diversion, because the heart is more edified by mourning (7:1-4). Then, in order to foster such *mourning* in response to disillusionment, Qoheleth favored listening to the *rebuke of the wise* and not the cheery but false optimism of *the fool* which only *debases the heart* (7:5-7). Qoheleth thus urged the disillusioned reader to embrace *mourning* rather than *pleasure* by appealing to their respective effects on the *heart:* to be edified by wisdom (7:2-5a) or corrupted by folly (7:5b-7).

Qoheleth intended to convince the reader as a prospective steward that one cannot remain neutral when vexed by life's inevitable adversity. When fully disillusioned over our inability to gain any advantage in our labor (cf. 1:12-6:12) we have a choice: We can wisely mourn the failure of our ambitious attempt to contend for a better lot than God has given us (7:1-4, cf. 6:10-12) or foolishly seek pleasure in order to appease impending despair in the false reassurance that we can secure our own dreams (7:5-7, cf. 6:1-6). By then

---

[263] Each comparison is a somewhat unsettling *better than* proverb that is clarified by additional sayings. The first (7:1) asserts an advantage of *mourning* over pleasure-seeking, as clarified by two additional *better than* proverbs (7:2, 3) and a summary appraisal (7:4). The second (7:5) favors *wise rebuke* over the *song of fools*, which is unmasked by a parenthetical analogy as a futile attempt at false reassurance (7:6); another summary appraisal (7:7) in turn specifies the nature of the negative outcome of the fool's advice implied by the comparison in 7:5 (n. 271, below).

comparing the opposite outcomes of either choice (7:8-14), Qoheleth aimed to elicit from his readers the *better* response to disillusionment, when we are forced in adversity to honestly ask "What **is** good...?" (cf. 6:12a).

1. A Heart Built Up: The Wise Enter their Disillusionment (7:1-4)

This pericope begins with an unsettling analogy (7:1)[264] that addresses the preceding uncertainty over *what is good* (6:12a). The point of the analogy is elucidated by the two ensuing proverbs (7:2-3):[265] For those truly disillusioned over the abject failure of self-sufficiency (cf. 6:1-12), mourning is far preferable to pleasure-seeking. Given this advantage, a summary appraisal encourages the wise reader to choose *mourning* over *mirth* (7:4). There is no formal closing marker, since the following pericope just substantiates the message of 7:1-4: It encourages the same choice by warning of the **disadvantages** of pursuing mirth over mourning in response to adversity (7:5-7).

Qoheleth thus answered the rhetorical question *who knows what is good for man?* (6:12) by recommending a funeral over a birthday party (7:1);[266] that is, mourning is better than pleasure-seeking (7:2a), because reflecting on our mortality informs our disillusionment over self-sufficiency—we will *take it to heart* (7:2b).[267] Thus, *vexation*[268] is to be preferred over *laughter* (7:3a, cf. 7:2a), because

---

[264] Using an intricate wordplay (Eaton, *Ecclesiastes*, 109), the author crafted an implied analogy (n. 261) between the proverb cited in 7:1a and the truism affirmed in 7:1b: The rhyming of "ointment" (*šēm*) with "name" (*šemen*) in 7:1a is paralleled by the repetition of "day" (*yôm*) in 7:1b.

[265] These proverbs are arranged in alternate parallel (a:b/a':b') to explain why the *day of death* is better than the *day of birth* (7:1b). The second (7:3) expands on the first (7:2), and each is substantiated by a motive clause ("for..."), so that "mourning" and "feasting" (7:2a) are linked, respectively, to "vexation" (*ka'as*, n. 268) and "laughter" (*śeḥōq*) (7:3a). But mourning is *better*, because the living "take it to heart" (7:2b) and the heart is "made better" (7:3b).

[266] Lit. "the day of death [is better] than the day to be born," implying that the living derive greater benefit from the **occasion** of death than that of birth, not that one's **own** death is preferable to his **own** birth (so NASB, cf. NKJV), as was inferred in Job 3 and Eccl. 4:1-3; 6:3-6. In this context it is mourning over death's inevitability that edifies the heart of those who are still *living* (7:2b), as reflected in NIV, NRSV.

[267] The intended sense of this verse is perfectly reflected in Ps 90:12, *Teach me to number my days, that I may gain a heart of wisdom.* Consequently, the construction "the heart of the wise" implies an awareness of one's mortality as a requisite of skillful living (7:4; 8:5, cf. also 7:22).

it promotes mourning and can gladden *the heart* with wisdom[269] (7:3b, cf. 7:2b). Accordingly, those who would be *wise* dwell *in the house of mourning* (7:4a), while fools remain *in the house of mirth* (7:4b).[270] This counsel is then further supported by explaining the disadvantages of pursuing pleasure (7:5-7).

2. A Heart Debased: The Fool Tries to Appease Despair (7:5-7)

The preceding context made it clear why dwelling in *the house of mourning* is wise, but it remained unclear why choosing *the house of mirth* was foolish (7:4), so Qoheleth cited another arresting *better than* proverb (7:5) to warn of the great risk of succumbing to the false appeal of pleasure in an attempt to ward off impending despair. The parallel arrangement of 7:5 and 7:7[271] explains how one incurs this risk by listening to the *song of fools* (7:5b), the futility of which is depicted by an interposed analogy (7:6).[272] The now standard

---

[268] Longman (*Ecclesiastes*, 183-4) and Seow (*Ecclesiastes*, 229) appropriately translate *ka'as* as "anger" or "vexation" (i.e., *disillusionment*) in 7:3 to match its sense in 5:17 and 7:9 (n. 74).

[269] The clause lit. reads "for in a sad face the heart is glad." The parallelism with 7:3a suggests that "a sad face" here projects not so much the tears of *grief* as the frown of *vexation* (n. 268, cf. Longman, *Ecclesiastes*, 184) when life will not cooperate with one's own ambitions. The point is that by honestly facing one's disillusionment over the failure of self-sufficiency, he is enabled to mourn that failure and humbly assimilate the wisdom that a good steward will need to be effective (cf. nn. 53, 267; 11:9-10).

[270] The natural human tendency to avert disillusionment in life by seeking diversion is captured well by Larry Crabb (*Inside Out*, 213):

> The illusion that life in a fallen world is really not too bad must be shattered. When even the best parts of life are exposed as pathetic counterfeits of how things should be, the reality drives us to a level of distress that threatens to undo us….When hints of sadness creep into our soul, we must not flee into happy or distracting thoughts.

[271] Expositors struggle over an apparent lack of logical connection between 7:7 and the preceding or following verses (cf. Eaton, *Ecclesiastes*, 110-11; Whybray, *Ecclesiastes*, 115-16; Murphy, *Ecclesiastes*, 63-65). However, there are two key interpretive clues: (1) Qoheleth parenthetically substantiates in 7:6 what he means by the *song of fools* in 7:5b (n. 272 below); and (2) the causal force of the opening *kî* ("for") in 7:7a distributes to 7:7b, so that **both** are logically connected to corresponding clauses in 7:5; that is, *the rebuke of the wise* in 7:5a is called for by the negative effect of *oppression* on rational thought described in 7:7a (n. 273 below) and *the song of fools* in 7:5b only ends up being a *bribe* in 7:7b. Thus, 7:5-7 has an alternate parallel structure a:b:c:a':b', where *a* = 7:5a; *b* = 7:5b; *c* = 7:6; *a'* = 7:7a; and *b'* = 7:7b. While Longman recognizes this link between 7:7 and 7:5 he misconstrues the intended sense of *oppression* in 7:7a (*Ecclesiastes*, 184-87; so NIV, cf. n. 41), which serves as the thematic point of departure for 7:8-10.

[272] The analogy between the fool's *laughter* and the *crackling of thorns* serves to explain why the *song of fools* is not worth heeding (7:5b), so that it *too is vanity* (7:6c). The conspicuously alliterative wordplay in 7:5b-6 (Seow, *Ecclesiastes*, 236-37) associates *song* (*šîr*) with both *pot* (*sîr*) and *thorns* (*sîrîm*). The sense

refrain *this too is vanity* (7:6c) isolates 7:7—which thus serves as a summary appraisal parallel to 7:4. The concluding phrase *debases the heart* (7:7b) serves in turn as the thematic point of departure for the exposition of 7:8-10.

The argument explains the risk one incurs in adversity when enticed by the *house of mirth* with the false promise of warding off impending despair over the abject failure of selfish ambition (7:4b, cf. 6:1-6): *It is* far *better to hear the rebuke of the wise* (7:5a) than succumb to this *song of fools* (7:5b). The former restores wisdom in adversity, because *oppression destroys a wise man's reason* (7:7a).[273] However, the *song of fools* is only a desperate attempt to placate his despair with the empty promise of pleasure (7:6);[274] it is merely a *bribe*[275] that *debases the heart* (7:7b). Qoheleth goes on to elaborate what this entails when we stubbornly resist disillusionment in adversity (7:8-10), rather than patiently submitting to *the work of God* (7:11-14).

---

intended is that the fool's promising *song* "goes up in smoke" amid adversity just as quickly as *thorns crackling* in the fire. Note the comparable analogies of such false cheer to the futility of fresh streams that only vanish in the heat (Job 6:15-20), or of *songs* sung *to a heavy heart* to a garment *removed* in cold weather and *vinegar* neutralized by *lye* (NRSV) (Prov 25:20).

[273] The verb *yᵉhôlēl* ("make foolish") is related to *hôlēlôth*, "stupidity" (n. 125), thus "oppression makes the wise stupid." Job recognized his own need for the "rebuke of the wise" in the face of oppression when he pleaded with his friends to "Teach me, and I will hold my tongue; Cause me to understand wherein I have erred. How forceful are right words!" (Job 6:24-25a). For practical application of these texts to the experience of adversity in physical illness, see the present author's "A Wisdom Perspective on Advocacy for the Suicidal," in Demy and Stewart (eds.), *Suicide—A Christian Response* (Grand Rapids, MI: Kregel, 1998), 369-85; and "The Dilemma of 'Medical Futility'—A 'Wisdom Model' for Decisionmaking," *Issues in Law & Medicine* 12:231-64 (1996), 253-55.

[274] Although Qoheleth did not spell out exactly what he meant by the *song of fools* (7:5b) or *laughter of the fool* (7:6), the imagery conjures up the figure of a court jester who tries to placate the king's melancholy and thereby avert his displeasure. Thus, Nehemiah risked his life when he appeared before the king with a sad face (Neh 2:1-3), and the natural urge to placate impending despair is indeed powerful (cf. Eccl 4:1-3; 6:3-6); however, wisdom is truly at stake (7:7a).

[275] From the parallelism of 7:5 and 7:7 (n. 271) we can see that this *bribe* is the counterpart of the *song of fools*, an attempt at false cheer with a detrimental effect on the heart—the antithesis of the edifying *rebuke of the wise* (7:5a, cf. 7:3). Job readily recognized this kind of "bribe" when his friends tried to appease his distress by promising prompt restoration in return for his repentance: *"Did I ever say, 'Bring something to me'? Or, 'Offer a bribe for me from your wealth'? Or, 'Deliver me from the enemy's hand'? Or, 'Redeem me from the hand of oppressors'?"* (Job 6:22-23). For examples of such a "bribe" promising relief amid suffering in the world of medicine, see the references cited in n. 273.

— 21 —

B. Patient Submission is better than Stubborn Pride (7:8-14)

*By comparing the broken dreams of proud self-sufficiency with wisdom's life-giving inheritance in the work of God, **Qoheleth affirms it is better to face disillusionment in adversity by patiently accepting the inscrutable work of God, not by stubbornly clinging to broken dreams,** so that his readers might forsake selfish ambition in favor of a preferable, though uncertain, destiny in the work of God.*

This passage is distinguished from the preceding text by the closing marker *this too is vanity* (7:6c) and the transitional summary appraisal in 7:7.[276] The author continues to compare wise and foolish responses to disillusionment in adversity but in reverse order,[277] and there is a shift to the imperative mood.[278] The opening *better than* proverb again begins with an analogy (cf. 7:1)[279] affirming that the wise and preferable response in adversity is to wait for *the end of a thing* and not cling to *its beginning* (7:8a). This *end* is only realized "afterward,"[280] not by the immediate gratification of selfish ambition (7:8b-10) but in *wisdom's inheritance* in the *work of God* (7:11-14). The final couplet thus reintroduces God's inscrutable role in determining humanity's destiny (7:13-14)[281] and

---

[276] The theme of *oppression* is reintroduced in 7:7 as the point of departure for Qoheleth's discussion of *vexation* in 7:8-10 (n. 271), and 7:11-14 concludes with the construction *day of adversity* in 7:14a, so that the whole pericope 7:8-14 is framed by the concept of *adversity* as Qoheleth compares the radically different outcomes of two dichotomous dispositions in adversity—*stubborn pride* (7:8-10) and *patient submission* (7:11-14).

[277] The themes of *folly* and *wisdom* in 7:1-14 are chiastically arranged (n. 71). Just as in 7:1-7, there is no formal textual marker in the present passage to signal the thematic shift between *folly* (7:8-10) and *wisdom* (7:11-14).

[278] The **negative** injunctions of 7:9-10 *Do not hasten...to be angry...* and *Do not say...* stand in contrast to the **positive** commands of 7:13-14 *Consider the work of God* and *...be joyful, But...consider....* cf. n. 261.

[279] Cf. n. 261.

[280] The terms "end" (7:8a) and "afterward" (7:14d, cf. n. 193 below) thus comprise an inclusion for 7:8-14. Regarding the literary framing of this passage, see also n. 276.

[281] By recalling God's unchangeable and inscrutable purposes for the work of mankind (cf. 3:10-15), this couplet invites readers to patiently submit to their preordained calling as a response to disillusionment that is far preferable to stubborn contention with God for a different lot in life (cf. 6:10-11).

closes with the same marker as the preceding major sections[282] to set the stage for the second half of the argument.

Having affirmed the value of *mourning* over *laughter* in response to disillusionment in adversity (cf. 7:1-7), Qoheleth now compares the opposing dispositions behind each response. He first warns his readers not to react to disillusionment with stubborn pride, for one will only harbor bitterness in persistently pining over shattered dreams (7:8-10, cf. 5:16-17). Qoheleth then presents a better alternative: the life-giving advantage of wisdom when one faces disillusionment with patient acceptance of an uncertain destiny in *the work of God* (7:11-14). By comparing the radically divergent outcomes of patient submission and stubborn pride, Qoheleth aimed to elicit the wise alternative from God's agents, so they may realize their portion in *the work of God* (7:15-12:7).[283]

1. Shattered Dreams: The Fool's Legacy of Angry Self-Determination (7:8-10)

The passage begins by citing a *better than* proverb that favors patient submission over stubborn pride (7:8) and closes by quoting a lament that exemplifies how foolish it is to stubbornly cling to the broken dreams of selfish ambition (7:10).[284] Qoheleth had warned the reader not to appease his despair by yielding to the false appeal of pleasure (7:5b-7a) but he had not explained why this *debases the heart* (7:7b). The present pericope thus describes how the heart is affected when a disillusionment person steadfastly resists the mourning and wise rebuke one needs to avail the benefits of wisdom (cf. 7:1-5a). The *wisdom* motif is reintroduced in the transitional inference of 7:10b, as Qoheleth goes on to explain these benefits in 7:11-14.

The destiny of the "heart" thus depends on whether vexation is **replaced** by patient submission or **entrenched** in stubborn pride (7:8):[285] To be *patient in spirit* in this context amounts to mourning

---

[282] *See* n. 60.

[283] *See* n. 76.

[284] Qoheleth switches to the second person in 7:10 to quote the stereotyped lament of the vexed but self-determined reader. Here he depicts the mindset that never benefits from *the end of a thing* (7:8a) because it responds to disillusionment in adversity not with patience (7:8b) but by angrily insisting that things should revert to the way they used to be (7:9-10), which only blinds one to God's ultimate intent in the end (7:13-14, cf. James 5:11).

[285] As in 7:1, this comparison relies on an analogy that may best be rendered "*Just as* the end of a matter is better than its beginning, *So is* the patient in spirit better than the proud in spirit."

(7:2) and patiently accepting wise rebuke (7:5) in order to appropriate the threatened benefits of wisdom (7:7a). The heart is *debased* when proud self-sufficiency resists authentic mourning (7:7b, cf. 7:2-4), thus allowing vexation to fester (7:8b) and breed long-term bitterness (7:9).[286] Qoheleth cites evidence for such bitterness by quoting an imagined self-sufficient reader who clings tenaciously to shattered dreams (7:10a).[287] Stubborn pride is *not wise* (7:10b), for it will not permit us to embrace the preferable *end of a thing* (7:8a)—a destiny in *the work of God* (7:13)—as the fitting end to life's labor.[288] Qoheleth thus goes on to explain how the advantage of being *patient in spirit* consists in an *inheritance* that wisdom confers on the one who patiently accepts his God-given lot, whether in *prosperity* or *adversity* (7:11-14).

2. Wisdom's Inheritance: A Preferable Legacy in the Work of God (7:11-14)

Following the implication that wisdom is what humans desperately need in response to disillusionment in adversity (7:2-7, 10b), this pericope finally explains why *Wisdom is good and an advantage* (7:11, NASB). Qoheleth had discovered that one finds lasting satisfaction only when he accepts his God-given *portion* or *heritage* (5:18-20)—now he affirms that *wisdom* is the means by which we avail ourselves of this heritage (7:11-12). His prior pessimism about wisdom thus yields to the hope that wisdom affords in forsaking our own ambition to *consider* the the inscrutable *work of God* (7:13-14). It is just this prospect that in turn occupies the rest of Qoheleth's argument (7:15-12:7).

---

[286] Verse 7:9 lit. reads "Do not be hasty in your spirit to be vexed, for vexation settles in the bosom of fools." Ironically, the same vexation that can lead to beneficial mourning (cf. 7:3) can "settle in the bosom" as smoldering bitterness (cf. n. 39) and preempt the satisfaction one would otherwise enjoy if he patiently accepted his portion in the work of God (7:11-14). Thus, one who is *proud in spirit* (7:8b) harbors resentment when disillusioned over the failure of his selfish ambition to yield lasting satisfaction in life (4:1-6:12). The potential for the prospective steward to harbor such bitterness in response to adversity is exemplified in Job's final defense before God (Job 30) and warned against in Heb 12:15. Consequently, it would behoove such a steward to *remove vexation* from the heart (11:9).

[287] The change to the second person (n. 284) is transparently intended to personalize the object lesson of stubborn pride—the same device is used in 7:16-22, esp. vv. 21-22. A prime example of this disposition of stubborn pride can be found in Job 29, where Job also pines over the passing of his own "former days."

[288] Cf. 5:18-20, n. 241.

So then, *what is good for man* (6:12)? *Wisdom is good with an inheritance,*[289] *and* an *advantage*[290] *to those who see the sun*[291] (7:11), *for wisdom*—just like *money*—will afford one *protection*[292] from the ravages of adversity (7:12a) and *gives life*[293] *to those who have it* [wisdom] (7:12b). This s sharply with radical self-sufficiency, which only ends in death-like despair by dissuading one from accepting his portion from God (cf. 5:18-6:6). At this point Qoheleth again reverts to the imperative to impress upon his readers how they should avail themselves of wisdom's advantage in adversity: We are to *consider the work of God* (7:13a) and see that

---

[289] The word *inheritance* used in 7:11 (*naḥălâ*) is not the same as that which Qoheleth typically uses to denote one's *portion* from God (n. 29). However, in context this *inheritance* of wisdom is parallel to *life* (7:12b), and the following verses strongly imply that it is indeed closely related (if not identical) to man's *portion* in the *work of God* (7:13-14).

[290] The translation *advantage* (NASB) better reflects the technical sense of *yôthēr* (nn. 22, 67) than *profitable* (NKJV). For the reader who has followed Qoheleth's pessimistic quest for advantage under the sun, this assertion should come as a surprise: *Wisdom* was heretofore disappointing (Eccl 2:13-16; 6:8, cf. n. 247), but now apparently has a lasting *advantage* after all. This advantage will be found to depend on one's disposition in adversity: patient acceptance (7:13-14) rather than stubborn pride.

[291] The construction *see the sun* carries over from 6:5, where it clearly signifies to "be alive." Thus, Qoheleth intended with the phrase to introduce a dramatic contrast: Whereas one who never *sees the sun* has an advantage over one who has no rest in a self-sufficient existence (6:1-6, cf. n. 243), wisdom **is** an advantage *to those who see the sun* (7:11-12), as long as they *consider the work of God* (7:13).

[292] So NASB. Heb. *ṣēl* means "shade" in the sense of *protection* against the sun—wisdom affords analogous protection from the adverse effects of life's disappointment and adversity (7:5-7). There is an irony intended in equating the "shelter" of wisdom to that of having *money* (7:12a, NIV; cf. Longman, *Ecclesiastes*, 190-1): Whereas even plentiful "riches and wealth" were of no avail in fending off despair for one who is dissatisfied with his "portion" from God (6:2-3), it is now evident that wisdom is as "protective" as riches for the one who patiently **accepts** his portion (7:11-14, cf. 5:18-19). This same protective sense is clearly also conveyed by the allusion to money in 10:19b (n. 449).

[293] The parallel between the construction *gives life* (7:12b) and the *protection* of shade (7:12a, n. 292) suggests that this construction denotes a "survival advantage" to wisdom. Whereas Qoheleth had been thoroughly pessimistic about this advantage in 2:12-16 and 6:8, where he perceived it to be only temporary and unsatisfying, in this context it suggests a vitalizing effect that can transcend mere survival when applied not out of self-sufficiency (as in the previous passages) but out of patient acceptance of God's purposes. Wisdom's life-giving benefit is also implied in 8:1b where it *makes* a man's *face shine*.

God often permits adversity in life to frustrate our own ambitions,[294] so that we might realize a preferable, albeit uncertain,[295] destiny in His inscrutable plan (7:13b-14, cf. 6:10).

Qoheleth's aim is for the reader to accept life's inevitable adversity as essential to the fulfillment of transcendent purposes—the inscrutable *work of God*. Accordingly, if God's chosen agents are to serve these purposes, they must *consider the work of God:* Only by acquiescing to His sovereign but inscrutable orchestration of life's events can they joyfully and successfully invest their labor in His work.[296] The reader is to accept the good along with the bad (7:14a)[297] so that we might not be preoccupied about the future and thus be enabled to enjoy our labor.[298] This acquiescence to *what He has made crooked* (7:13) is predicated on adopting and sustaining the new disposition of *fearing God*,

---

[294] The explanatory clause *For who is able to straighten what he has bent* (7:13b, NASB) virtually echoes 1:15 (cf. n. 123), where it is used to preempt Qoheleth's quest before it ever begins. In the present context the phrase *what he has bent* refers to God's deliberate permission of certain events in life to frustrate our own aspirations (7:7-10), so *the day of adversity* (7:14a) is figurative for those obstacles to self-determination we encounter on a daily basis.

[295] The steward of God is to *consider* (lit. *see*) that *God has appointed* adversity as well as prosperity, "so that [*'al-dibrat*] man may not find anything afterward" (7:14b, cf. n. 193). God thus deliberately keeps mankind in the dark for their own good. The implication is that since one cannot predict the outcome of his own plans (cf. 3:22; 6:12) he is far wiser to submit to the inscrutable *work of God*.

[296] Cf. especially 8:5-6, 16-17, and 11:1-12:1.

[297] The *day of prosperity* and *day of adversity* are lit. "day of goodness" and "day of badness"—the same as *goodness* in 6:3, 6 and *evil* ("badness") in 5:13, 16; 6:1.

[298] The fact that both good and bad are taken in stride by the one who *considers the work of God* (7:13) explains why he he can *rejoice in his labor* and does *not dwell unduly on the days of his life* (5:19-20): By accepting (cf. 5:19, n. 241) the inscrutable vagaries of the work of God, the steward ironically frees himself from contending for a destiny **apart from** what God has ordained (6:10-12) that he may gain wisdom's advantage **in accord with** what God ordained (7:11-14). His advice is reminiscent of Paul's own testimony of acceptance (Phil 4:9-11), in the context of his exhortation to always rejoice and not worry, being confident of God's control over all things (Phil 4:4-8). The impact that these dichotomous "days" should have on mankind's choices in life is expounded in Eccl 11:1-8: Given the unpredictable "bad" (11:1-2) and "good" (11:6) in life, Qoheleth encouraged his reader to invest their resources whenever feasible in order to maximize their joy for however long life will last (11:8).

which thus becomes the transparent strategic intent of the second half of Qoheleth's argument in light of the inscrutability of His purposes for us (7:15-12:7, cf. 7:14b).[299]

---

[299] The purpose clause "so that man may not find anything afterward" (7:14b, cf. n. 295) accords with Qoheleth's prior admonition concerning mankind's proper place within God's preordained but inscrutable will: One cannot fathom all the work in life that *God does* (3:11), and *God does it that man should fear...Him* (3:14), so the fear of God involves patiently accepting *adversity* along with *prosperity* in humble acquiescence to of God's inscrutable purposes. The message of the second half of the argument thus aims to elicit and sustain the fear of God (cf. n. 48), so that the reader may exploit wisdom's advantage and succeed as a steward of His inscrutable purposes. Regarding the hermeneutic notion of "strategic intent," see the Preface to the Commentary, "The Unity of Job and Ecclesiastes— A 'Canonical Linguistic' Approach."

Part IV

RESOLUTION

Fear of God & Hope of His Favor

Gaining Wisdom's Advantage for the Work of God
(Eccl 7:15-9:10)

In reflecting on the confusing lack of evidence that God favors the righteous in this life, **Qoheleth affirms that all men are sinners accountable to God in judgment and can therefore do well only by fearing God,** *so that his readers might not rely on self-righteousness or earthly wisdom but rather fear God and enjoy His favor in their God-given portion.*

Although the hope of wisdom's *inheritance* in *the work of God* (7:11-14) now holds the promise of fulfilling humanity's pursuit of a lasting legacy (cf. chaps 1-6), Qoheleth still hasn't solved the problem of how one can be assured of God's favor (cf. 2:24-3:22). Therefore, several conspicuous constructions now reappear:[300] *the hand of God* (9:1; cf. 2:24); the *work of God* (8:17, cf. 7:14); *time* and *judgment* for every *purpose* (8:5-6; cf. 3:1, 11, 16-17); the *fear of God* (7:18; 8:12b-13; cf. 3:14; 5:7b); mankind's *portion* from God (9:6, 9; cf. 3:13, 22); and God's *favor* on mankind (7:26; 9:7; cf. 2:26). The first two sections argue logically and sequentially[301] that since mankind's confidence as steward is categorically pre-empted by human depravity, all promise of God's favor is thus redirected to the *fear of God* (7:15-8:15). Conceding that God's favor is not apparent in this life, Qoheleth rooted his readers' incentive to serve God in their hope of realizing God's *favor* in their God-given *portion* (8:16-9:10).

The argument removes depravity's constraint on the prospective servant of God after warning that human righteousness and wisdom can never please God or fulfill one's calling as God's chosen agent (7:15-29). Since the wise steward is aware of humanity's inability and that we are subject to God's judgment, the reader is encouraged to submit to authority out of allegiance to God, for even though the wicked prosper, it will be well for those who fear God (8:1-15). Indeed, even when all we can see is our own depravity and mortality when we seek God's favor, we still have hope of lasting satisfaction in our God-given portion, for God has already accepted our works; so we should enjoy our portion and labor in it

---

[300] Cf. nn. 28, 29, 44, 45, 47, 48, 51.
[301] Cf. nn. 24, 94.

as long as we are still alive (8:16-9:10).

After discrediting all human hope of gaining a self-sufficient advantage in life's labor (1:1-6:12), Qoheleth now aims to substantiate his claim that *mourning* can "gladden" the heart with *wisdom's advantage* and the hope of *inheritance* in the *work of God* (7:1-14). If he can convince his readers that universal depravity excludes all humanity from meriting God's favor and that their only hope is in the *fear of God* (7:15-8:15), they may be persuaded to wisely mourn their inability, fear God, and enjoy their God-given portion, even though His favor is inapparent in this life (8:16-9:10, cf. 5:18-20; 6:10). For those who respond, however, a final warning is necessary: Since wisdom remains vulnerable to even casual folly and life is fleeting, they must take advantage of every opportunity to invest their portion and bring success in the work of God (9:11-12:7).

— 22 —

A. The Depravity of Mankind—Wisdom's Advantage Excluded (7:15-29)

In recounting his extensive observations of mankind's totally inadequate righteousness before God, **Qoheleth discounts the value of any effort to seek God's favor by making oneself righteous or wise,** *so that prospective stewards might acknowledge their sinfulness and refrain from trying to to earn God's favor by perfecting their own righteousness or wisdom.*

The marker *I have seen everything in my days of vanity* (7:15a) indicates that Qoheleth again tapped his unprecedented experience, this time to draw inferences about human *righteousness* and *wisdom*. The apparent disconnect between merit and reward is so unsettling (7:15b) that it becomes the pretext for an extended discourse on human depravity.[302] The first section is a direct three-part admonition[303] for his readers not to rely on their own righteousness (7:16-22). The second section substantiates this admonition by citing the evidence Qoheleth found in his investigations of life that human righteousness is completely inadequate (7:23-29). There is no closing marker,[304] because Qoheleth immediately proceeds to explore how mankind might mitigate the preemptive effect of human depravity on wisdom's advantage (8:1-15).

We can now trace Qoheleth's logic. Having disabused his readers of any expectation of finding lasting meaning through selfish ambition (4:1-6:12), Qoheleth addresses those who are convinced that they should seek an inheritance in the *work of God* (7:1-14). He immediately warns them that they are unable to impress God by depending on their own righteousness and wisdom, for all such effort is totally preempted by the pernicious influence of the sin they know they have (7:15-22). To substantiate his warnings Qoheleth cited the results of his exhaustive search for righteousness among men and concluded that no one since creation—with a single exception—has

---

[302] The observed disparity between *righteousness* and *reward* (7:15b) recalls the previous lament over the lack of justice for the wicked (3:16) but now serves ironically to challenge the premise that man is even **capable** of righteousness before God.

[303] The admonition consists of three warnings, each of which begins with "Do not…" (7:16a, 17a, 21a) and is followed by a motive clause that discloses in turn the negative consequences of failing to heed that warning (7:16b, 17b, 21b).

[304] Cf. n. 92.

been able to please God with their own righteousness (7:23-29).[305]

The goal is now clear. When Qoheleth had affirmed that *God gives wisdom and joy to a man who is good in His sight* (2:26) and that *wisdom,* like an *inheritance, gives life* (7:11-12) he anticipated that his readers would naturally seek to be "good in His sight" by their own effort and thereby secure wisdom's "inheritance"—a long life of prosperity and joy. By confounding their expectation that such righteousness will be rewarded in this life (7:15), Qoheleth dashed any lingering hope in self-sufficient righteousness and wisdom (7:16-29) and thus triggered a crisis of accountability: How can sinful humanity be wise enough to be deemed worthy of God's favor (8:1-15, cf. 3:15)? In dismantling the illusion that they could possibly earn God's favor, Qoheleth left them a single ray of hope—the *fear of God* (7:18, cf. 8:12-13).

1. Mankind's Hopelessly Inadequate Righteousness (7:15-22)

The structure of the passage is dictated by Qoheleth's response to his disappointing observation that human lifespan bears no relation to evidence that one is *righteous* (7:15): Three warnings (7:16-17; 21) immediately expose as an illusion the false premise that we can earn God's favor **at all** (7:15). The first two warnings are coupled in the form of a dual analogy, asserting that perfecting one's own *righteousness* and *wisdom* is no more effective than overindulging in *wickedness* and *folly* (7:16-17).[306] The following verses (7:18-20) then

---

[305] This immediately raises the question of how Qoheleth could have asserted in 2:26 that "God gives...to those who are good in His sight when in fact he has now clearly affirmed that **no one** is "good in His sight" (7:20). The solution comes with the recognition that Qoheleth's strategic intent in 2:24-26 was to discourage the reader from replicating Qoheleth's own failure to please God and achieve a lasting legacy. Without clarifying at that point **how** man could be "good in His sight," Qoheleth intended to redirect the reader's attention to the "hand of God" as the only source of lasting satisfaction, thus anticipating the clear NT message that *righteousness* (2 Cor 5:17-21) and *wisdom* (1 Cor 1:18-2:16) avail nothing unless **conferred by God**, as Qoheleth himself will infer in 7:16-20 (see exposition below).

[306] Brindle ("Righteousness and Wickedness," cf. n. 51) explains that the textual design of these difficult verses anticipates extreme self-reliant responses to the disillusionment expressed in 7:15 (ibid., 312-13): Arranged in alternate parallel, "extremely wicked" (7:17a) is paired with "extremely righteous" (7:16a) and "being foolish" (7:17b) with "being extremely wise" (7:16b). Thus, trying to perfect one's own *righteousness* and *wisdom* to gain God's favor is ironically no more helpful than *wicked self-indulgence* and *being a fool*, respectively: *Both* extremes will result in self-destruction (7:16c, 17c), so Qoheleth is warning the reader in light of the disconnect between *righteousness* and *reward* in 7:15 not to become self-righteous or overly wise to gain God's favor (7:16) or self-indulgent out of utter resignation (7:17).

explain why *righteousness* is still important in order to retain *wisdom's advantage* for the work of God (7:11-14), but in a way that is not possible **on one's own**.[307] Qoheleth's blunt assertion that no one is righteous (7:20) in turn supplies the pretext for the third warning, which cynically convicts the reader of sin in the very act of trying to affirm his or her own righteousness (7:21-22).[308]

The argument anticipates reader concern that one's reward may be jeopardized by God's unpredictablity (7:13-14). Qoheleth realized that lifespan does not correlate with righteousness (7:15) so he warned his readers not to try to earn God's favor by perfecting their own righteousness (7:16a) or making themselves very wise (7:16b)[309], for this

---

[307] The meaning of 7:18-20 has been extensively debated (cf., e.g., NET fns. on 7:16-20), lit. "It is good that you grasp the one and not let go of the other, for the one who fears God will come forth with *both of them*; Wisdom strengthens the wise..., for there is no righteous one on earth who does good and does not sin." At first glance, the term *both of them* in 7:18 seems to include the moral extremes in 7:17, yet it is hard to see how *wickedness* or *folly* could possibly promote *wisdom's advantage* (7:19). On the other hand, the motive clauses in 7:18-20 seem ideally suited to answer the implied question that emerges from 7:15-17, Then what kind of wisdom and righteousness **is** able to secure an advantage in God's eyes? Thus, both 7:18b and 20 begin with an adversative *kî* to qualify exactly how man should go about acquiring both righteousness and wisdom to secure this advantage: "It is good to aspire to both (wisdom and righteousness), *but* (only) the one who fears God will come forth with both; (for) wisdom does strengthen the wise, *but* there is no one who is righteous by nature (and can thus avail wisdom's benefits)." That is, given the extent of human depravity (7:20), only by the *fear of God* (7:18), and no self-effort of any kind (7:16-17), can we gain the righteousness necessary to sustain wisdom's advantage (7:19, cf. n. 51).

[308] The scenario in 7:21-22 depicts someone who overhears the gossip of others who are unaware of that one's presence. The implied motive for listening so attentively is that this person seeks validation from others of his or her own righteous character and works. Although Qoheleth is ostensibly protecting the reader from the disillusionment of overhearing himself being disparaged (7:21b, "lest you hear...;" cf. n. 313), a genuine concern that the ego may be bruised seems completely foreign to the argument. The warning begins with a textual link "moreover" (*gam*, 7:21a) that clearly establishes continuity of the logic with the preceding observation (7:20). Given this connection, the warning is sarcastic as suggested by the wordplay on "heart" and "curse": If the reader "takes to heart" the "cursing" of others (7:21), then his own "heart" (i.e., "conscience," cf. n. 57) will realize that he himself has "cursed" others (7:22), thus implying that one should **not** try to avoid disillusionment (7:21b) over adverse criticism (7:21a), for it confirms the validity of 7:20.

[309] Brindle (ibid., 312) argues convincingly from the verb form that "be very wise" (7:16b) should be "make yourself very wise" (implying self-sufficiency), which is no better than to *be a fool* (7:17b, n. 306; cp. 2:15).

is as self-defeating (7:16c, 17c) as self-indulgence (7:17a) or being a fool (7:17b), which no one would pursue to try to gain God's favor. To be sure, one should seek both *righteousness* and *wisdom*, but they are attainable only by the one *who fears God* (7:18);[310] yes, wisdom's advantage is great (7:19) but it requires a righteousness that no one can claim (7:20).[311] Qoheleth proves his contention in the life of the reader with an ironic appeal to subjective experience: "Indeed,[312] don't take to heart what others say, lest you overhear your servant scorning[313] you (7:21); for many times even your own conscience has convicted you of scorning others (7:22)."[314]

In order to dissuade the reader from trying to gain wisdom's "inheritance" (7:11-12) by becoming wise in their own eyes, Qoheleth aimed to disabuse him of the illusion that he could thereby curry God's favor. By asserting that self-sufficient righteousness and wisdom is as futile as self-indulgence, Qoheleth would draw the reader's attention to the pivotal imperative of fearing God (7:18) as the only way to meet God's expectations for worthy stewardship. If the reader did not accept Qoheleth's warnings against self-sufficient effort to please God, Qoheleth would now justify his

---

[310] The sense depends on whether the verb *yāṣā'* reads *escape* the consequences warned against in both 7:16c and 7:17c (so NKJV) or *follow* the warnings of both 7:16 and 7:17 (so NET), or *go forth* ("prevail") in both righteousness and wisdom (cf. 7:16, the position adopted herein). The latter option is the most consistent with the context of *grasping* (7:18a) and wisdom's advantage (n. 307); thus, "he who fears God will prevail in both of them."

[311] *See* n. 307. Unless a man *fears God* (7:18) he is incapable of the *righteousness* needed to gain wisdom's advantage (cf. 1 Cor 1:20-30 and Rom 3:10-23 [Seow, *Ecclesiastes*, 269]; cf. also Job 33:23-26).

[312] To personalize the truth of 7:20 the opening *gam* (7:21) is asseverative, not copulative ("also," NKJV).

[313] "Cursing" is too strong here for *qillēl* (Whybray, *Ecclesiastes*, 122-3); "scorning" fits better (so also 7:22).

[314] *See* NIV, NRSV, lit. "for also (*kî gam–*) many times your heart has known that also (*gam–*) you have cursed others." With Nathanic irony (cf. 2 Sam 12:5-14) Qoheleth again convicts the self-righteous reader with the testimony of his own conscience ("your heart," cf. nn. 287, 308). Larry Crabb (*Inside Out*, 221) explains the role of this heightened sensitivity to one's own sin:

> If we limit our awareness of sin to such things as obvious moral failure and undisciplined living, we will tend to become a rigidly good person whose best relationships remain stiff. We will not learn to love. But when we become sensitive to the subtle violations...involved in our self-protective style of relating, we'll feel overwhelmed with personal sinfulness.

warnings by pointing out the empty results of his own exhaustive search for human righteousness (7:23-29).

2. The Hopelessly Elusive "Scheme of Things" (7:23-29)

To eradicate any vestige of hope in self-sufficient *wisdom* or *righteousness* among his readers, Qoheleth asserted that he had *proved all this*[315] from personal observation (7:23a, cf. 7:15a): He first cited his effort to profit from his own great wisdom, but it had proved quite elusive (7:23b)[316]—what happens in life is completely unfathomable (7:24). When he redirected his great wisdom[317] *to discover the scheme of things* (7:25a, NIV)[318]—that is, to fathom[319] mankind's stupid penchant for *evil* and *folly* (7:25b)[320]—all he

---

[315] "All this" refers to the preceding assertion that there is no advantage to perfecting one's righteousness or wisdom, because there is no one who is truly righteous (7:16-22). This assertion is proven in 7:23b-24 with respect to being *wise* and in 7:25-29 with respect to being *righteous*.

[316] Lit. "I said 'I will be wise,' but it was far from me—far, what happens, and very very deep—who can find it?" The implication is that anyone less capable than Qoheleth of "making himself wise" (cf. 7:16a) would have no more success than he did, thus foreclosing any lesser attempt to gain a similar advantage.

[317] The verse begins awkwardly, lit. "I turned and my heart to know…" The construction indicates a change of strategy (cp. the constructions in 4:1, 7; 9:11) for Qoheleth's great wisdom—from seeking even greater wisdom to investigating the problem of human righteousness (cf. n. 315).

[318] Lit. "to know and to search out and try to find wisdom and an explanation…" Although the phrasing seems to indicate that wisdom is the object of Qoheleth's search, the wording of 7:23a ("to search and to seek out *by* wisdom…," cf. also 1:13) suggests that wisdom is playing an instrumental role; thus, the construction "wisdom and an explanation" may read best as a *hendiadys*, "a wise explanation," prefiguring a similar construction in 8:1 (n. 339, below). The sense of 7:25a is that Qoheleth redirected all his intellectual energy toward finding a "wise explanation," to be specified in 7:25b (see below).

[319] The fact that the initial complementary infinitive *lāda'at* ("to know, fathom") in 7:25 is repeated at the beginning of the second clause suggests that the second clause is in apposition to the first: The second infinitive is prefixed by a non-consecutive *waw* to **specify** that Qoheleth's objective, "to know" a *wise explanation* (7:25a, n. 318), was in fact "to fathom" *evil* and *folly* (7:25b, n. 320).

[320] The notion of human depravity is conveyed in 7:25b with an unusual construction comprised of four nouns, arrayed in two pairs joined by a single copulative *waw*. The simplest explanation is that it is a double *hendiadys* (cf. 1:17, n. 125), so the clause could be rendered "to understand *foolish evil and stupid folly*." In this way the construction echoes the prior verbal construction in 7:17 "do not be very wicked and do not be a fool," as if to validate Qoheleth's warnings in 7:16-17 with the results of his own extensive investigation into human depravity.

could infer[321] was that people are completely incapacitated by sin (7:26), and that this sin has pervaded mankind ever since the prototype first sought to be self-sufficient (7:27-29).

To inform his first inference (7:26) Qoheleth drew from the jaded experience of Solomon, who found his own besetting sin—the deadly allure of women—to be *more bitter than death* (7:26a).[322] Except for the elusive man who is *good* in God's eyes,[323] there is no escape for mankind from the same kind of entrapment by sin in general (7:26b). Qoheleth then drew from the frustrating observations of his empirical search for righteousness to summarize what he had discovered about human depravity (7:27-28a):[324] Having found only *one* righteous *man*[325] and not a single

---

[321] The threefold "I have found…" (7:26a, 27a, 29a) seems to designate three different inferences; however the last one only traces the second inference to its origin.

[322] *The woman who is a snare, whose heart is a trap* (NIV) is "the *femme fatale*…the principal figure representing the deadly seductive power of evil" (Seow, *Ecclesiastes*, 263). For Qoheleth nothing depicted the disabling influence of sin better than the women who drew Solomon away from his commitment to YHWH (1 Kgs 11:1-10). Ironically, these totaled one thousand, so Qoheleth (in the persona of Solomon, cf. n. 7) could infer that an upright *woman among these* [thousand] *I have not found* (7:28).

[323] In 2:26 the identical construction *he who pleases God* (lit. "he that is good before the face of God") is likewise contrasted with *the sinner* to clarify how a man receives *wisdom and knowledge and joy*. In the present context, however, no man *does good* (7:20) so presumably no man can enjoy the benefits of wisdom.

[324] This second conclusion (7:27) repeats the phrase in 7:25a, "to try to find an explanation," to denote his attempt to explain human depravity (n. 320). Since he could not find this "explanation" (7:28a) he reported what he **did** find, but with a heightened emphasis ("*Look…*", cp. 7:26a) and quoted by the frame narrator (n. 66) to underscore the universal relevance of Qoheleth's important conclusion: Man's depravity is **universal**, having spread to all since the fall of mankind (7:27-29, cf. Gen 8:21; 1 Kgs 8:46; Ps 14:2-3; 143:2; Prov 20:9; Eccl 9:3; Jer 17:9; Rom 5:12).

[325] The phrase "one man among a thousand" seems to suggest that at least *a few* men are naturally "upright." But the phrase clearly denotes **singularity**—there is **one** and **only one** who fits the description. The only other occurrences of this construction are in Job 9:3; 33:23, where it transparently projects this same sense of uniqueness. Note esp. the wording of Job 33:23-24: "If there is a messenger for him, A mediator, *one among a thousand*, To show man His uprightness…Then He…says, '…I have found a ransom'." The context for this remarkable statement is Elihu's speech to Job concerning God's unique redemptive initiative to save mankind's soul from destruction (33:14-30, cf. n. 310). The correspondence of terms between these two texts is unlikely to be coincidental: The term "uprightness" in Job 33:23 is the noun form of the same word used in *God made man upright* (Eccl 7:29), an unequivocal reference to man's prototype *Adam* before his fall. Considering the parallelism between 7:28 and 29, Qoheleth's use of *'ādām* is a transparent play on words: The one and only upright *'ādām* ("man," 7:28) was *Adam* before his fall (7:29).

righteous woman (7:28b),[326] he could only infer[327] that human depravity has existed since the Fall when *God made mankind upright, but they have sought out many schemes*[328] (7:29). With this summary appraisal on human depravity Qoheleth conclusively validates his assertions in 7:18-20, but this provokes an imminent crisis of confidence over the consequent possibility of any advantage to wisdom (8:1).[329]

---

[326] There is great debate about the significance of Qoheleth's inability to find a single "upright" woman "among a thousand." Longman (ibid., 206-7) joins others who conclude that Qoheleth harbored misogynistic bitterness (cf. 7:26a). However, if we understand "one man" (7:28) to refer only to Adam in his unfallen state (n. 325), then the bias disappears: There is now none righteous, male **or** female, so that Qoheleth's stylized negative experience with a thousand women exactly paralleled his findings among all men (n. 322).

[327] The critical importance of Qoheleth's summary finding is attested by his adding "only" to the repeated announcement, "*Only* look, this have I found..." (7:29, cf. 7:27), to emphasize the unifying principle behind all his findings (7:25-28; cf. n. 321 and Longman, ibid.).

[328] Longman (ibid., 207) asserts that the term for "schemes" (lit. "devices") is a "verbal echo" from Genesis 6:5, "every inclination of the thoughts of his heart was only evil...." The word translated "thoughts" and the word "devices" both derive from the same root meaning "to think, to calculate" (ibid.). In the context of Eccl the notion of "seeking out schemes" is reminiscent of the ambitious self-sufficiency conveyed by the construction "dreams and many words" (Eccl 5:1-7, n. 40). The point of the allusion seems clear: Since mankind's uprightness was permanently lost through such "calculating" self-sufficiency, the same tactic would still hold no promise of rendering the present reader "good in the eyes of God" (cf. 7:26b).

[329] If all men since Adam are depraved, then none of them has the righteousness it takes to profit from wisdom's advantage (7:18-20; cf. nn. 307, 315); therefore, "Who can be wise...?" (8:1).

— 23 —

B. The Fear of God—Mankind's only Confidence in Judgment (8:1-15)

By advising those who would be wise to submit to human authority out of loyalty to God, even though the wicked often escape present judgment, **Qoheleth reaffirms the final accountability of all sinners before God and that it will be well only with those who fear God***, so that prospective stewards might confidently fear God and enjoy life in their labor for all the days God has given them.*

In focusing on judgment of evil,[330] this section continues the emphasis on human depravity and further develops the governing theme of the second half of the argument, *wisdom's advantage* (8:1b).[331] The textual design follows that of the prior passage,[332] where Qoheleth had planted a seed of hope that in spite of his pervasive depravity one could benefit from wisdom in the fear of God (cf. 7:18-19). In light of that depravity, Qoheleth now explains how one can harness wisdom's advantage as an accountable steward of God. The passage models wise accountability after submission to the king (8:1-8) and assures the reader that it will go well with those who submit likewise to God,[333] even when the wicked prosper in this life (8:9-13); this in turn warrants the concluding call to rejoice in one's labor in spite of present disillusionment (8:14-15, cf. 7:15).

The opening question *Who is like a wise man and who knows...?* (8:1a) acknowledges the formidable dilemma of how one can gain wisdom's advantage in view of the preemptive effect of human

---

[330] References to *evil* or *wickedness* occur 12 times in the passage (cf. n. 24).

[331] The governing theme is reintroduced parenthetically in 8:1b (cf. n. 92): to equip the prospective steward with the previously affirmed life-giving benefits of wisdom (cf. 7:11-12; 7:19, n. 293).

[332] In both passages, an initial dilemma is posed for the reader (8:1, cf. 7:15b) and immediately followed by a set of warnings plus the consequences for failure to obey them (8:2-8, cf. 7:16, 17, 21, n. 303). The warnings are validated by Qoheleth's extensive empirical observations of human nature and his awareness of God's attitude toward mankind's sinfulness (8:9-14, cf. 7:23-29, n. 315).

[333] This relationship between the two pericopae is clarified by the comparable constructions *he who keeps his command will experience no evil thing* in 8:5a and *it will be well with those who fear God* in 8:12b.

depravity (cf. 7:15-29). Qoheleth asserts that a wise steward will submit to authority, because he *knows* we have limited *time* to serve God's purposes and that our *wickedness* will surely incur God's *judgment* (8:1-8). Indeed, while *the wicked* often seem to escape judgment in this life (8:9-12a), *it will* go *well* only for *those who fear God* when they face God's ultimate judgment (8:12b-13, cf. 7:18). However, Qoheleth again conceded that the *work of the righteous* often goes unrewarded in this life (8:14, cf. 7:15), *so* he *commended* the *enjoyment* of life, for at least *this* would *remain with* one *in his labor* during his allotted days *under the sun* (8:15).

Given that the sinner's only hope of gaining God's favor is to *fear God* (7:18-19), Qoheleth now aimed to convince the prospective steward that he was still limited by the constraints of sin: his finite *time* to serve God's purposes and his continued liability to God's *judgment* of evil. He would gain wisdom's advantage in serving those purposes as an accountable steward only by submitting to authority in the fear of God. Anticipating discouragement whenever evil flourished and knowing that only those who fear God would do well before Him, Qoheleth advised his readers to enjoy their God-given lot; he then went on to assure those who fear God that though they might not see it now, their works are indeed accepted by God (8:16-9:10).

1. Wise Accountability in Light of *Time and Judgment* (8:1-8)
The key to this passage is to identify the intended sense and relationship of certain distinctive constructions. The opening two-part question *Who is like the wise man and who knows...?* (8:1a, NASB) is answered in two steps: *Obey the king's command...* [334] (8:2-5a) and *a wise heart knows...* (8:5b-8, NASB). The overall sense derives from the phrase *for the sake of your oath to God* (8:2b), which denotes one's oath of allegiance to God.[335] That is, those

---

[334] So NIV; lit. "I..., watch the king's mouth..." (8:2a). While "I" (MT *'ani*) may be a confusion of letters for the accusative marker *'eth–* (so LXX, cf. NET fn. on 8:2a), context supports the MT reading as Qoheleth's answer to the problem posed in 8:1—how to gain wisdom's advantage in light of mankind's universal depravity (7:15-29)—from his assumed royal perspective (cf. 1:16; 2:9, 25; 4:13-16; 5:8-17; nn. 7, 86, 124): The imperative "you watch" following the isolated "I" can reasonably be rendered "I *advise you to* watch the king's mouth" (cf. Longman, *Ecclesiastes*, 211).

[335] Longman (*Ecclesiastes*, 211) asserts that "oath" *(šebû'â)* here is a synonym for "vow" *(neder)* in 5:1-4, implying a rash promise to God, independent of one's obedience to the king. However, in the present context "the king's command" and "oath to God" are logically connected, and "oath" clearly conveys a sense of allegiance or loyalty to God that warrants submission to human authority. Cp. Job 34:10-30; Rom 13:1-7.

who are loyal to *God* should not hesitate to submit to the *king* (8:2a, 3-5a), whose authority is ordained and overridden by God (8:2b).[336] This reflects the broader contextual emphasis on the *fear of God* (cf. 7:18; 8:12b-13) and it also explains why mankind is still liable for wickedness (8:3-8), even when it remains unjudged by human courts in this life (8:9-14, cf. 3:16).[337] The pivotal construction—*for every purpose there is time and judgment* (8:6a, my translation)—relates this message to the dilemma of chap. 3;[338] that is, how to gain God's favor as His intended servant.

This, then, is Qoheleth's logic: Given that wisdom's advantage is completely pre-empted by human depravity (7:16-29), Qoheleth invites the reader to consider how man might then gain this advantage and be able to explain things (8:1).[339] Qoheleth's counsel is to obey the king (8:2a) because of his allegiance to God (8:2b) as a would-be steward who is accountable for wickedness: It is prudent to submit to the king (8:3a, b), *for he does whatever he pleases* and can enforce his will (8:3c-4),[340] so that the one who obeys him is most likely to avoid evil and escape punishment

---

[336] The *waw* between 8:2a and 8:2b seems superfluous; the idea may be "...*and* [obey him] because of your oath to God."

[337] Obedience to the *king* only makes sense because of the steward's awareness of "judgment" regarding the purposes of *God*, as implied in 8:5b-8. Thus, the obedient steward tolerates the apparent prospering of evil in this life only because he fears God's judgment above that of human authority (8:9b-14).

[338] The association of the same words in 8:5b-6a as in 3:1, 16-17—"purpose," "time," "judgment"—is meant to denote the same sense in the latter passage: *Purpose* refers to God's sovereign purpose (n. 44); *time* signifies both the appropriate timing of events within God's inscrutable plan and mankind's limited opportunity to serve as an agent of God (n. 35); and *judgment* refers to mankind's accountability for his intended stewardship as God's agent (n. 45).

[339] Verse 8:1a illustrates standard Hebrew parallelism—the second predicate "knows the interpretation of a thing" is intended to sharpen the first "[is] like the wise." The two lines can therefore be conflated to give "Who [then] can be wise and know how to explain things?" (cf. 7:25, n. 318; cf. also 1 Cor 1:20, n. 311).

[340] The warnings "Don't be hasty to leave his presence" (8:3a) and "Don't take your stand for an evil thing" (8:3b) merely expand on the governing imperative in 8:2a ("watch his mouth"); i.e., prudence dictates diligently attending to the king's words. The motive for these warnings, *he does whatever pleases him* (8:3c), reflects the king's unpredictable *purposes* (the verb is *ḥaphēṣ*, cf. n. 44). Since the king's purposes are backed by the power to punish (8:4a), it is wise not to resist them. The rhetorical question "...who may say to him, 'What are you doing?'" (8:4b) is meant to be applied as much to the sovereignty of God as to that of the king (8:2; cf. Dan 4:35).

(8:5a).[341] Indeed,[342] in order to gain wisdom's advantage (cf. 8:1a) *a wise man's heart* will *know*[343] *time and judgment* (8:5b,), as Qoheleth proceeds to explain in 8:6-8.

The *wise* steward remains aware that his service to God is constrained by *time and judgment* (8:5b), because[344] *for every* purpose[345] *there is a time and judgment*[346] (8:6a): Mankind is bound by *time*, because[347] adversity will inevitably take its toll on him

[341] This protection afforded by obeying the king is linked to the injunctions of 8:2-3 by the same verb "to observe" in 8:2a and by a play on the words *dābār rā'*—i.e., he who obeys does not stand for an "evil thing" (8:3b) so he will not experience ("know") an "evil thing" (8:5a) (cf. Longman, *Ecclesiastes*, 212-13). That it is *wise* to *keep his command [miṣvâ]* (8:5a, cf. 12:13) refers not to obeying known law but rather the king's unpredictable whim (8:3c, cf. n. 340), as also reflected in the analogous injunction of 10:4 (Eaton, *Ecclesiastes*, 118-9).

[342] The *waw* initiating 8:5b is asseverative, the emphatic answer to the question asked in 8:1a (n. 329).

[343] The Qal impf. verb *yēda'* may be rendered as future ("will know") or modal ("would know"), which fits well in this context of potentially gaining wisdom's advantage (8:1). Cf. also 7:4, regarding the construction *the heart of the wise*.

[344] The eight clauses in 8:6-8 are initiated by a causal *kî* (8:6a, "for") to explain why the wise man would *know* (or be aware of) *time and judgment* (8:5b): The first four of these (8:6-7) are consecutive *kî* clauses (Whybray, *Ecclesiastes*, 132), with the logic probably best conveyed as "for..., for..., but..., so...." to substantiate mankind's need for wisdom regarding *time* (n. 347). The last four clauses (8:8) are also logically related, each beginning with "[there is] *no...*" or "*not...*" (ibid., 133), and they substantiate the need for wisdom regarding *judgment*.

[345] Again, many English translations and commentaries only confuse Qoheleth's logic by rendering *ḥēpheṣ* in 8:6a as "delight" or "matter" (n. 44). The sense is dictated by an associated construction (*time and judgment*) that is repeated in immediate context: The *wise* man will "know" *time and judgment* (8:5b), because his obedience to the *king* (8:2-5a, n. 336) logically depends on his allegiance to *God* (8:2b; n. 335). That is, *time and judgment* holds mankind accountable for obeying *whatever the king pleases* or "purposes" (*ḥaphēṣ*, 8:3c; n. 340) because it ultimately serves *every purpose* or "pleasure" (*ḥēpheṣ*, 8:6a) of God. Awareness of this connection constitutes the "wisdom" of obedience.

[346] Unfortunately, NASB, NIV, and many commentators (cf. Longman, *Ecclesiastes*, 213; Eaton, *Ecclesiastes*, 119; Whybray, *Ecclesiastes*, 131-2) all translate the word *mišpāṭ* (8:5b, 6) as "procedure" or "way," rather than the standard meaning "judgment" (n. 45). The wisdom of "knowing" *time* and *judgment* (8:5b) depends critically on what Qoheleth means by "time and judgment," and this is made clear by his use of these same terms in 3:1, 16-17 (n. 338) and by the theme of accountability reintroduced in 8:2 (cf. 3:15; nn. 335, 345).

[347] The opening *kî* in 8:6b is best taken as **causal** ("for," *contra* NKJV, NIV, NASB, NRSV), so that all three clauses in 8:6b-7 are read as explaining why one's *time* to serve God is limited (8:6a, n. 344). The *kî* in 8:7a qualifies the explanation by posing a "double bind" of unpredictability so it has **concessive** force ("although"). The final *kî* (8:7b) presents the fitting inference of this unpredictability and should thus be read as **inferential** ("so"). This gives us "*For* man's adversity will increase upon him, *although* he does not know what will happen, *so* who can tell him when it [adversity] will occur?" This is a typical rhetorical inference characteristic of Qoheleth's style.

(8:6b),[348] although *he does not know what will happen, so* no one *can tell him when* such adversity *will* cut short his opportunity to serve God's purposes (8:7).[349] Mankind is also constrained by *judgment,* for death inevitably terminates all opportunity for productive stewardship (8:8):[350] When we die (8:8a) we cannot escape the judgment incurred by our wickedness (8:8b, cf. 8:3b). Since a wise sinner *knows* these constraints of *obeying the king,* he will also *fear God* (cf. 8:2b) in light of His **ultimate** *judgment,*[351] even though at **this** *time* evil may seem to prosper (8:9-15, cf. 8:5-6).

2. Confident Stewardship in Light of Prevailing Evil (8:9-15)

Qoheleth now anticipates a logical concern on the part of the prospective steward: Given the obvious widespread injustice under the sun (cf. 3:16, 7:15b), how can God's servant be assured that mankind will ultimately be held accountable for evil (8:8b)? The opening marker *all this I have seen and [I] applied my heart* (8:9a) echoes 7:15a to build on Qoheleth's argument from 7:15 through 8:15.[352] The logic of 8:9-15 turns on the grammatical transitions at 8:9b and 12b.[353] At 8:9b Qoheleth cites an example of such extreme injustice under human authority, that to him it seemed to belie any accountability for evil at all. He then abruptly reverses this misgiving at 8:12b with the firm conviction that all such injustice will ultimately be recompensed *before God,* as all mankind is

---

[348] Lit. "man's *rā'â* [adversity, misery] is great to him." Cp. the similar expression in 6:1b (cf. 7:14a).

[349] Since a wise man remains fully aware of the unpredictability of the *timing* (8:5b) of adversity (8:6-7) and ultimately of death itself (8:8) he will not procrastinate in serving God's purposes before it is too late. The notion of opportune investment in the work of God is further developed in 11:1-12:8.

[350] The logic of 8:8 is governed by the opening *kî* in 8:6 and explains why man is constrained by *judgment* (n. 344). The four clauses of 8:8 cohere best as paired analogies (cf. 7:1a; n. 264): "*As* no man has power over the wind to restrain it, *so* no man has power in the day of death; and *as* [there is] no release from war, *so* evil will not release those who are given to it" (cf. Longman, *Ecclesiastes,* 210, 214-5). Thus paired, these clauses affirm that all men are ultimately held accountable for their wickedness; a wise man remains fully aware of this *judgment* (8:5b).

[351] See n. 340; cf. also 10:4, 20; 11:9; 12:1, 14.

[352] Qoheleth continues to draw logical inferences from "all he has seen" (cp. 7:15a; 7:23a, 29; 8:9a).

[353] If Qoheleth could decisively justify continuing to submit to human authority (cf. 8:2-8), given the egregious miscarriage of justice cited in 8:9b-12a, then *a fortiori* it should resolve the reader's skepticism in **any** situation where there is perceived injustice.

finally called to account for wickedness.

Qoheleth thus argues from a worst-case scenario of unjudged present wickedness to prove the point in general that mankind is still ultimately accountable for sin:[354] Of *all* the deeds Qoheleth had *seen under the sun*, he reflected on the *time* when[355] *one man* ruled *over another to harm him*[356] (8:9), and *then*[357] he had even seen *the wicked buried* honorably, the same ones *who had* faked *holiness* in the temple—they got away with their wickedness *in the city where they had so done* (8:10a, b),[358] which struck him as utterly futile (8:10c): When *the sentence against an evil work is not executed* quickly, mankind's proclivity for evil is unchecked (8:11),[359] so that[360] a sinner may prosper in his evil for many years

---

[354] This is the main premise of the preceding pericope, summarized in 8:8b (cf. n. 93).

[355] Longman points out that 8:9b "is dependent (marked by *'ašer*) and not an independent sentence" (*Ecclesiastes*, 215), so that *'et* ("time") should be recognized as an accusative of time (ibid.); it has occasional force, lit. "All this I saw and I applied my heart to every deed done under the sun, a *time when*...." Cp. NASB.

[356] My translation of 8:9b. The phrase "to his harm" could refer to either the victim (so NRSV) or the perpetrator ("to his *own* harm," so NIV, NKJV), but the ensuing context strongly suggests that the victim is in view. The verb "rule over" is perfect, denoting that the occasion was prior to Qoheleth's reflection.

[357] The initial compound conjunction *ûbᵉkēn* ("and then") distributes the occasional force of "a time when" (8:9b, n. 355) to 8:10, so that Qoheleth's offended sense of justice in 8:9 also extends to the events of 8:10.

[358] Qoheleth was outraged that the wicked were honored by the "rest" of burial (cf. 6:3, n. 243) after "they had gone in and out of the holy place." That is, he had seen those who were guilty of wicked deeds (as in 8:9b) flourish behind a veneer of piety, only to be *forgotten in the city where they had so done.* Although it may seem that justice was vindicated when the perpetrators were *forgotten,* their burials were in fact honorable and their wickedness was unjudged by those who later "forgot" them. By contrast those who aspire to *wisdom* and *righteousness* **want** to be remembered (2:16).

[359] This reflection recalls Qoheleth's previous conclusion regarding mankind's inherent lack of righteousness (7:20, 29) and clarifies why the wise steward should submit to royal authority (8:1-5): One's accountability under *human* rule is designed to restrain his proclivity to sin but also to alert him to his greater accountability under *divine* rule (n. 337), so that even when human justice fails (8:11-12a) it should remind him that he remains liable *before God* (8:12b-13).

[360] Most translations construe 8:12a as disjunctive, assigning a poorly attested concessive sense to *'ašer* ("though" or "although") because of the obvious contrast with 8:12b (Whybray, 137; Longman, *Ecclesiastes*, 217).However, there should be no break between 8:11 and 8:12a; the conjunction is intended to convey consequence, "When the sentence for an evil deed is not executed quickly, thus the heart of the sons of men is fully set in them to do evil, *so that* a sinner may do evil a hundred times and [still] prolong [his days]."

(8:12a). Qoheleth's preceding advice on submission to authority would thus seem ridiculous and confirm the worst fears of any steward in pursuit of God's favor who might lack confidence in serving Him.[361]

How could such a disconcerting travesty of justice be reconciled with the preceding bold assertion that *wickedness will not release those who practice it* (8:8b)? In spite of the apparent contradiction over whether or not the wicked will indeed *prolong his days* (cf. 8:12a, 13), Qoheleth nevertheless reassures the reader[362] by introducing a system of justice that views human lifespan from an eternal perspective:[363] It will go well for sinners *who fear God,*[364] because[365] they *fear before Him* (8:12b), but *it will not be well with the wicked...because he does not fear before God*

---

[361] Qoheleth's advice (8:2-5a) had come from the perspective of a king (n. 7) charged with administering justice fairly. What cruel irony it would be for a faithful servant to heed his advice and live dutifully beyond reproach, only to be cut down in his prime, while a wicked man lives a long life (8:11-12a, cf. 7:15b; 8:14)! This was also a grievous concern for Job (cf. Job 21) and is the pretext for many of the Psalms. While it may seem hypocritical for Qoheleth to advise submission in the face of such gross inequity, his strategy is to show how the solution reconciles even the most egregious injustices in this life (n. 353).

[362] Although the opening *kî gam* ("for also") technically marks 8:12b as a subordinate clause (cf. Murphy, *Ecclesiastes*, 85) it is strongly adversative or even asseverative—"*however,* I know" or "*yet* I *surely* know" (so NKJV). The syntax of 8:12b-13 thus informs the reader of a preferable alternative.

[363] The apparent contradiction in Qoheleth's observations—"his days are prolonged" (8:12a) vs. "he will not prolong his days" (8:13)—simply reflects the difference between mankind's temporal perspective "under the sun" and God's eternal perspective. Qoheleth had previously affirmed that God "has put eternity in their hearts" (3:11), and it is this notion that informs the present context: The days of the wicked may be "prolonged" in this life (cf. 3:16; 7:15b; 8:14) but not in the inscrutable *work of God*, which extends beyond the grave *from beginning to end* and lasts *forever* (3:11c, 3:14). See Eaton, *Ecclesiastes*, 123.

[364] Since 8:12b-13 is subordinate to the preceding clause (n. 362), the logical antecedent of "those who fear God" in 8:12b is the "sinner" in 8:12a. If so, then the direct parallel between 8:12b and 8:13 implies that "the wicked [man]" in 8:13 is to be contrasted with sinners "who fear God" (see below).

[365] The final clauses in both 8:12 and 13 begin with the conjunction *'ašer*—this is usually translated "who" in 8:12b and "because" in 8:13. However, the parallelism strongly suggests that both of them should be read as causal (Longman, *Ecclesiastes*, 217); thus, "it will go well with those who fear God, *because they fear Him* (8:12b), but not so for the wicked, *because they don't fear Him* (8:13)."

(8:13).[366] Although the ultimate resolution of miscarried present human justice is not visible *under the sun* (8:9-12a), human accountability before God is nevertheless assured (8:12b-13).[367]

Although this confidence should console him, Qoheleth again laments his observation that the wicked so often enjoy an earthly fate that is better suited to the *work of the righteous* (8:14).[368] Consequently, his concluding advice is tinged with resignation: All he can do for now[369] is to *commend* joy, *for* at least *this will remain with* one *in his labor all the days of life*[370] *which God* has given *him* (8:15). His continued consternation that *the righteous* often see no reward for their labor (8:14, cf. 7:15b) reflects our natural human skepticism over the purported advantage in serving God: Those who fear God may still lack confidence that their works will ever gain His favor, so this becomes the pretext for further reassurance that Qoheleth provides in the next section (8:16-9:10).[371]

---

[366] Qoheleth already established that *there is* no *just man...who does not sin* (7:20). Now it appears that a sinner may fear God (n. 364) and "do well," whereas if he does not fear God he will incur the judgment of the wicked (8:13). The parallel is therefore completely inclusive of all mankind: Even when a man *seems* righteous from a human perspective, the fear of God is the only discriminator of one's well being in God's eyes (3:14, cf. n. 177). Not only does this belie the delusion that wickedness is shielded from punishment simply because that judgment is not apparent in this life (8:9-12a), it also belies the false assurance that a man is "safe" simply because his sin is not flagrant.

[367] Cp. Qoheleth's expression of confidence in 3:17 (n. 46). The difference is that he now expresses this confidence not as a self-sufficient moralist but as one who fears God. The doctrine that God will judge fairly—even when evil thrives among the human judges He has ordained—is also attested by Elihu (cf. Job 34:16-30) and the NT (cf. John 19:10-11; Rom 13:1-6; 1 Pet 2:13-19).

[368] Curiously, this lament immediately follows the affirmation that *it will be well with those who fear God* (8:12b), who are deemed righteous (cf. n. 307). Thus, even that conviction may not inspire the confidence to serve God, lacking any evidence in this life that the *work of the righteous* is actually **rewarded** (8:14, cp. Rev 6:9-11). This crisis in turn gives rise to the reassurance offered in the following section (9:4-10).

[369] Qoheleth's consolation (cf. n. 191) occurs from his perspective "under the sun," mentioned twice in 8:15. Cp. Phil 4:4ff.

[370] So NIV, NASB. The sense is that the number of one's days is preordained (cf. 3:15a; n. 178).

[371] The logic of 8:16-9:3 is clearly predicated on the inherent skepticism of 8:14. Cf. also n. 361.

C. The Work of God—Hope of His Favor for All the Living (8:16-9:10)

*By testing the premise that the righteous and the wise and their works are in the hand of God, **Qoheleth affirms that even though God's work is presently inscrutable and evil prevails, there is still hope of His favor for all the living in their portion from God**, so that readers who fear God might enjoy their portion and labor confidently in the work of God.*

Since 8:14-15 is a transitional pericope, there is some debate over where this section begins.[372] Qoheleth's concern that the *work of the righteous* is often not rewarded in this life (8:14) compelled him to search for some assurance that they would find favor in the inscrutable *work of God*.[373] This explains the abrupt shift in tone at 9:4,[374] where two sharply contrasting pericopae are juxtaposed: Qoheleth's continuing lament over God's inapparent favor and mankind's pervasive sin (8:16-9:3) is answered by the confidence that all the living can indeed enjoy God's favor before they die (9:4-10). The concluding enjoyment pericope (9:7-10) is thus the point of departure for the final hortatory sequence, which can at last invite the readers' full confidence in the possibility of joyful and opportune investment in the present work of God (11:1-12:7).

The key to Qoheleth's logic in this section is to see his communicative intent as bolstering the hope of those who *fear God* (8:12b; cf. 7:18) that in spite of present appearances to the contrary

---

[372] The sentiment of 8:15 seems almost parenthetical in the immediate context of the ensuing passage, with 8:14 serving as the specific point of departure for the concerns expressed in 8:16-9:3. Moreover, the lament of 8:14 echoes that of 7:15b, suggesting an *inclusio* for the entire preceding passage (n. 94). This therefore casts the enjoyment pericope (8:15) as a summary appraisal recalling Qoheleth's previous resignation (n. 191), so the following phrase "I applied my heart..." (8:16a) serves as an opening marker, as in the immediately preceding reflection (8:9a, cf. n. 352).

[373] The word "work" (n. 28) appears twice and "labor" (n. 23) once in the transitional pericope (8:14-15) leading to the present passage (8:16-9:10), where "work" occurs five times and "task/labor" or "do/done" occur another nine times.

[374] Expositors struggle with this abrupt transition (nn. 392, 394 below); moreover, there are two different major textual variants of 9:4 (n. 388 below).

they are indeed *the righteous and the wise* and thus firmly in *the hand of God* [375] (9:1-3): Given that *there is not a just man who does good* (7:20), Qoheleth had been forced to conclude that only *those who fear God* would *come forth* as *righteous* and *wise* (7:16-18, NASB), so he tentatively asserted his confidence that it would thus *be well with* them before God (8:12b, 15).[376] However, there is **still** no evidence *under the sun* that God indeed favors their works (8:16-17; cf. 8:14), so Qoheleth now anticipates reader skepticism:[377] Are *the righteous and the wise* **truly** *in the hand of God*— can they ever **really** find joy in His favor for *their works*—in the face of conspicuous and persistent human depravity in this present life (9:1-3)? The final segment of the argument provides the reader with a resounding affirmative answer (9:4-10).

These constructions indicate that Qoheleth identifies with *those who fear God* yet lack the confidence they need to serve His inscrutable purposes because they are not sure He will reward them, since they cannot see how their works connect with God's work (8:16-17) and they still manifest sin in this life (9:1-3). However, even though Qoheleth cannot confirm from all that he sees *under the sun* that God favors *those who fear God*—that they will indeed "come forth" as *both righteous and wise* and that *their works* are *in his hand* (9:1, cf. 7:18; 8:12b)—he can nevertheless assure the living that they have hope of reward, for God already

---

[375] This construction is repeated from 2:24 and denotes God's favor as destined only for those who are *good in His sight* (2:26). Though Qoheleth had first assumed that works could gain God's favor (n. 158) he still sees true satisfaction as coming only from *the hand of God* (n. 153), his view of who is *good in His sight* is completely different.

[376] Qoheleth's presumption is based on the implications in 7:18 and 8:12b that God favors those who fear Him, which is the crux of the argument in 7:15-8:15 (cf. nn. 50, 307, 310, 364, 365) and should alert his readers to their need: Unless they first *fear* God they have no hope of being *good in His sight* (cf. n. 155) and no assurance of the favor that awaits them in their God-given heritage. Thus, the present section draws on this anthropology inferred from Qoheleth's reflections in 7:15-8:15 to build a foundation of hope for laboring in the work of God (9:4-10).

[377] Qoheleth's thorough investigation of God's work on earth (8:16-17) had turned up no evidence at all that God truly favors the righteous and the wise (cf. 8:14). In expressing this disappointment he continued his strategy of anticipating reader skepticism in order to answer it decisively (cf. n. 353), so on their behalf he now challenges (9:1) his previous presumption regarding the ultimate fate of those who fear God (8:12) in order to instill in them a more durable confidence that God does indeed favor them (9:4-10), despite how it may presently appear (9:1c-3).

favors their works when they receive their God-given *portion* in joy (9:4-10). This in turn frees them to become confident stewards: In spite of their continued depraved tendency to revert to self-sufficient *folly*, they can wisely resist that temptation in their pursuit of success (9:11-10:20) and confidently invest their God-given portion whenever the opportunity presents itself, thus maximizing their joy while also fulfilling their stewardship of His inscrutable purposes (11:1-12:7).

1. God's Inscrutable Work and Inapparent Favor (8:16-9:3)

The flow of the argument critically depends on how we view the logical transition at 9:1. Most translations give the impression that despite being unable to discover the work of God on earth (8:16-17), Qoheleth was confident that *the righteous and the wise and their works are in the hand of God* (9:1a, b). Yet the immediate context (8:14-9:3) suggests that this is anything but a settled conviction. There is a frustrating lack of evidence for God's favor on the righteous in this life; in fact, people can never tell whether God "loves" or "hates" them from anything *they see before them* (9:1c).[378] Thus, Qoheleth relates how he tried in this distressing uncertainty to **verify** that it will indeed go well with those who fear God (9:1a, cf. 8:12b)—*that the righteous and the wise and their works are* in fact *in the hand of God* (9:1b, cf. 2:24-26).

Thus follows the argument: Given the observed disparity between the *work of the righteous* and their lifespan (8:14), not

---

378 The fragment 9:1c reads lit. "Man knows neither love nor hate...all ["both"] before them." It is not readily apparent whether this love or hate is human or divine and whether *all* looks back to the antecedent "love or hate" or forward to the common fate of man (9:2-3). One can infer from the preceding mention of the "hand of God" that it refers to **divine** love or hate (cf. Longman, *Ecclesiastes*, 227; Murphy, *Ecclesiastes*, 90; cf. Mal 1:2-3, "Jacob I have loved, but Esau I have hated"). Similarly, the contextual wordplay on "all" in 9:2-3 (n. 384) suggests that *all* in 9:1c looks **prospectively** to one's indiscriminate fate in this life, "mankind can predict neither love nor hate [from] all [that lies] before them." On the other hand, if we read "both," the sense is that God's *love* and *hate* seem **presently** to be indiscriminate, "mankind can perceive neither love nor hate; both are before them." Either reading expresses an unsatisfied longing to see God's favor outwardly manifested on the individual for his works. This links 9:1 with both 8:16-17 and 9:2-3, as Murphy so well expresses, "one cannot know from experience, from the way things turn out, whom God truly loves since the same treatment is dealt out to the just and the wicked alike (vv 2-3). The customary signs of blessing or curse have been displaced, since there is no comprehension of what God is about (8:17)" (*Ecclesiastes*, 90).

even Qoheleth's most thorough investigation[379] could find out how human work *done on earth* contributes the *work of God* (8:16-17).[380] Therefore,[381] he reflected on all this to try to prove[382] that God in fact **does** favor *the righteous and the wise*[383] *and their works* (9:1a, b), but what he found only reinforced his skepticism: Mankind can never determine empirically whether God favors him, since neither *love* nor *hatred* are discernible from *all* that men can

---

[379] Qoheleth's dedication is depicted in 8:16c by the phrase "in day and in night not seeing sleep in his eyes" (Longman, *Ecclesiastes*, 222). The clause is introduced by *kî gam*, which in context is best read as concessive (*contra* Longman, ibid., 223), "*even though* a man gets no sleep, day or night," to justify the *a fortiori* conclusion in 8:17b (n. 380). That conclusion is therefore introduced by *beˀšel ˀᵃšer*, a compound conjunction with inferential force "*so that when* a man strives to discover [it] he will not find [it]…"

[380] A typical *a fortiori* comparison is framed by an alternate parallel array of clauses (a:b:c/a':b':c'): When Qoheleth (a) tried "to know wisdom and see the task that is done on earth" (8:16a), (b) "even though one gets no sleep" (8:16b), (c) then he "saw all the work of God, that man cannot find out the work that is done under the sun" (8:17a), (a') "so that when a man strives to discover it he will not find it" (8:17b); (b') "even if the wise were to say 'I know,'" (c') he would not be able to find it" (8:17c). Thus, if Qoheleth with all his wisdom—even if he never slept—could not find out how mankind's work on earth fits into the work of God, much less would any other man succeed.

[381] The thrust of the opening *kî* governs Qoheleth's communicative intent in 9:1, but the standard causal sense ("for") is awkward (so NKJV, NASB) and fits the context poorly. Given the versatile role of *kî* in Eccl (Longman, *Ecclesiastes*, 155-56, cf. n. 347), Longman (ibid., 224), Murphy (*Ecclesiastes*, 88, 90), Whybray (*Ecclesiastes*, 139), and Eaton (*Ecclesiastes*, 124), all prefer an asseverative sense that is essentially **disjunctive** at 9:1. By contrast, reading "so" (as in NIV) naturally construes 9:1-3 as the logical **consequence** of Qoheleth's frustrating conclusions in 8:14-17 and introduces his resolve to verify that those who fear God will indeed find God's favor, given that they cannot presently see it *under the sun* (9:1a, cf. 8:12b, n. 377).

[382] The infinitive construct *lābûr* is often construed as "explain" or "declare," yet it is hard to see how such confidence would fit with the skepticism conveyed in 9:1c-3 (n. 378). If the *hapax bûr* is a cognate of *bārar* (3:18, n. 187) then it may mean "test" or "sift" (Longman, *Ecclesiastes*, 224 [fn. 3]; Murphy, *Ecclesiastes*, 88 [fn. 1c]; Whybray, *Ecclesiastes*, 140). It is more plausible that God's inscrutable work on earth (8:16-17) led Qoheleth to reconsider his assertion in 8:12b in order to verify its premise (9:1a,b; cf. n. 377); thus, *lābûr* is most logically a construct of purpose: "So I took all this to heart *in order to prove* it—that the righteous and the wise and their works are in the hand of God."

[383] Since Qoheleth had already disproved the notion that man can ever merit God's favor ("the hand of God") in his own righteousness or wisdom (7:20-22), the "righteous and the wise" can only refer to *those who fear God* (cf. 7:18, nn. 307, 310, 376). The real issue to be "confirmed" is in the subtext: whether it is still worth fearing God and serving Him when His favor is so inapparent.

see (9:1c). The same thing happens to *all*[384]—one fate (that is, mankind's common mortality, cf. 3:18ff), regardless of moral status, at least from a human standpoint (9:2).[385] The worst *evil* in *all* that happens is this:[386] Not only is there one fate to *all* mankind (9:3a), but they all fully embrace *evil*, which makes them stupid *while they live* and then they die (9:3b).[387] Since this would hardly inspire the confidence that God favors *the righteous and the wise and their works*, Qoheleth goes on to draw his assurance from logic based on other than outward appearances (9:4-10).

2. God's Inherent Favor in Mankind's God-given Portion (9:4-10)

Although an abrupt transition is obvious at 9:4,[388] this pericope is

---

[384] The phrase lit. reads "All is as to all" (Whybray, *Ecclesiastes*, 141). Qoheleth uses the word *kol* ("all") seven times in 9:1-3 to universalize the sense of futility when trying to discern God's favor from the way things turn out in life. The *kol* in 9:4 thus serves as a literary fulcrum to move from the skepticism that anyone can ever be assured of God's favor (8:16-9:3) to a true hope *for all the living* that their works indeed find favor in their *portion* from God (9:4-10).

[385] Reflecting the transparent merism in 3:2-8 (n. 161), the ten behaviors in this verse are arrayed in pairs of moral "opposites," effectively eliminating **any** category of moral behavior as an indicator of God's favor (cf. 9:1c). The extra *ṭôb* ("good") included in MT between the first two pairs is likely "a later intrusion into the text" (Graham Ogden, as quoted by Longman, *Ecclesiastes*, 225 [fn. 7]) and should therefore be omitted (ibid.). Note that the first behavior listed in each pair is assigned the "good" sense; thus, for example, a "good" behavior like "sacrificing" or "taking an oath" (of devotion to God; cf. 8:2; n. 335) is of no avail in seeking to secure God's favor in this life.

[386] In one of the few non-moral uses of *rā'* ("evil") within this major section (cf. n. 24), the literal phrase "This [is] an evil..." in 9:3a probably has the force of the superlative (Longman, *Ecclesiastes*, 227): "This is the *worst* in all that is done...."

[387] Lit. "and moreover the heart of the sons of men is full of evil, and madness [is] in their heart in their lives, and afterwards to the dead." The word "madness" (*hôlēlôth*) can mean "insanity," but in this context it denotes "stupidity," the absence of wisdom (n. 125, cf. also 1:17; 2:12; 7:25 [n. 320]). That is, mankind's common depravity leads first to stupid choices and then to death, as was so evident in Solomon's own life (cf. n. 132). This allusion to *moral stupidity* anticipates 9:16-10:20, which warns of the devastating effect of such stupidity on mankind's productivity as a chosen agent of God.

[388] The sense of the opening *kî* depends on which text is followed in reading 9:4. If the Qere is original, it is assumed that two consonants were transposed in Ketib from *hbr* ("join") to *bhr* ("choose") (Longman, *Ecclesiastes*, 228). Thus, in Qere the opening *kî* is strongly **adversative** in response to the pessimism of 9:2-3, "*But* for him who is joined to all the living there is hope...," whereas in Ketib it is an **inferential** reply to the dilemma initially posed of how to discern God's favor (8:16-9:1; cf. nn. 378, 382), "*So* who is chosen [to receive His favor]? For all the living there is hope..." Either alternative fits the context as a plausible explanation for the abrupt transition from 8:16-9:3 to 9:4-10 (n. 374).

linked to 8:16-9:3 by the common themes of *love* and *hate*[389] (9:6, cf. 9:1c) and textual indications of lingering reader concern over whether God will favor our *works* (9:7, 10, cf. 8:16-9:1b). Qoheleth surprisingly asserts that there is genuine *hope for the living*, thus sharply reversing his previous skepticism. The focus of this hope is the assurance that one can indeed experience God's favor—it is realized in our present *portion* of the lasting *reward* or inheritance that God has designed for maximum human satisfaction in this life (9:5-6, 9).[390] Thus, those who fear God can have confidence[391] of enjoying His *favor* in a lasting heritage (9:4-6) but they will realize that heritage only when they accept the *portion* God has already ordained for them to enjoy now (9:7-10).

The argument is thus meant to allay any lingering skepticism[392] over whether it truly "pays" to fear God. Since God's favor cannot be perceived *under the sun*—all we can see is our inevitable, indiscriminate mortality (9:1-3)—our awareness of death's finality should impart a sense of purpose and urgency to the life that

---

[389] In 9:1 *love* and *hate* clearly refer to God's positive or negative disposition toward mankind (*hā'ādām*). The issue is whether his works can elicit God's favor (cf. nn. 163, 378). In 9:6 *love* and *hate* constitute a merism that covers the full range of human passion that is evident in life.

[390] Qoheleth aligns the words *śākār* ("reward") and *ḥēleq* ("portion," cf. n. 29) in alternate parallel (9:5b, 6b; NASB) to denote a "lasting share" in life. The use of *śākār* (lit. "wages") as a parallel for *ḥēleq* may be an allusion to Qoheleth's prior illustration of *wisdom's advantage* with a monetary simile: Since *wisdom is protection just as money is protection* (7:12a, n. 292) it yields "wages" as an *inheritance* (7:11, n. 29). A subsequent play on the word *ḥēleq* suggests that this **lasting** *portion* or "share" (9:6, n. 399 below) is realized when one invests his labor in his **present** *portion* from God (9:9). Thus, one's *reward* or "wages" (9:5-6) becomes a *lasting share* in God's inscrutable purposes when one accepts his God-given *lot* in this life (9:9, cf. 5:18-19). Cp. Gk *klēronomeō* ("inherit") and *meros* ("portion") in Rev 21:7-8 (cf. John 13:8; Rev 20:6). Beginning at 9:4, then, the text clearly attests to real hope in an enduring legacy that completely reverses Qoheleth's previously expressed fatalism (n. 384).

[391] The unusual word *biṭṭāḥôn* ("hope," 9:4) is elsewhere translated "confidence" or "trust" (Whybray, *Ecclesiastes*, 142). In the present context it denotes the confidence—much like John's use of Gk *parrēsia* in 1 John 2:28—that those who fear God will indeed find God's favor (cf. 9:1, 7).

[392] The apparent confidence expressed by Qoheleth in this passage (nn. 390, 391) contrasts so sharply with his immediately preceding pessimism (9:2-3) and his previous portrayal of one's present lot as a mere consolation for the lack of any other advantage (cf. n. 191), that some expositors assume this is only jaded sarcasm (n. 394, below). However, *see* Whybray (*Ecclesiastes*, 142-3) and Eaton (*Ecclesiastes*, 126-9).

remains: There is hope for all the living, even for those of the lowest estate in life[393] (9:4), for they *know that they will die* (9:5a)[394] and still have the opportunity to gain a lasting legacy by investing their passions[395] in their God-given portion (9:6). *But*[396] *the dead know nothing and...have no more reward (for* all *memory of them* is gone).*[397] Since they no longer have passions to invest,[398] *they*

---

[393] The comparison of *a living dog* and *a dead lion* builds on the prior observation that even the poor have hope as long as they *walk* among *the living* (6:8, cf. n. 247). However, Qoheleth had already hinted that this hope is vested in more than present gain: Even though the poor can have an advantage and aspire to greatness (cf. 4:13ff), even the king's accumulated wealth affords no advantage in the face of death (5:9-17); so the hope of the living does not consist in one's "estate" in this life, as attested by the ironic despair of some men with bountiful material wealth (cf. 6:1-6). This newly introduced hope thus tempers Qoheleth's previously expressed disillusion over the fate of the oppressed (4:1-3) or those who lack satisfaction despite every material advantage (6:3-6).

[394] This is not the continued expression of jaded sarcasm regarding the meager benefits of being alive (as in 6:8, cf. also Murphy [*Ecclesiastes*, 92] and Longman [*Ecclesiastes*, 228]). Qoheleth's point here recalls his teaching that awareness of one's mortality can "edify the heart" (7:1-4) by enlisting wisdom's advantage to fulfill the purposes of God (7:11-14, cf. 8:5b-8). He is thus reminding his readers that they may "gain a heart of wisdom" by "numbering their days" (cf. Ps 90:12; nn. 267, 269).

[395] People manifest their hope of reward (n. 390) whenever they express the intense passions (9:6a) of *love, hate,* and *envy* (a yearning for something better). This expression of envy reflects a natural tension in one's pursuit of an enduring legacy between what **is** and what is **not yet** realized—such envy drives a man to seek fulfillment either in destructive rivalry (cf. 4:4-6) or in their potentially fulfilling portion from God (9:7-10). By lamenting that the dead have lost these vital attributes, Qoheleth underscores the urgency *for all the living* (9:4) to invest those same attributes in their God-given portion (9:5-6).

[396] The logic of 9:5b-6 depends on how one reads the sequential conjunctions: *waw..., waw..., kî..., gam..., waw....* The context supports reading the first *waw* as strongly adversative and the *kî* clause is parenthetical. The *gam* in 9:6 then further specifies the assertion of 9:5b, and the last *waw* is consequential. This understanding yields the logical sequence: "*But* the dead know nothing, *and* they have no more reward (*for* the remembrance of them is forgotten); *indeed,* their love, their hate, and their envy have already perished, *so* they have no more lasting portion in all that is done under the sun."

[397] The wordplay lit. "there is to them no more reward [*śākār*], for forgotten is their memory [*zēker*]" involves a *double entendre:* Since the *dead know nothing* they retain neither their own *memory* nor the *remembrance* of others; moreover, the rhymed words in brackets link the concept of *memory* to mankind's innate yearning for a *lasting legacy* or *inheritance* (cf. 2:16; nn. 115, 136, 390).

[398] *See* n. 395.

have no more opportunity to inherit a lasting *share*[399] *in anything done under the sun* (9:5b-6).[400]

The stark contrast between death's finality and life's continuing hope thus prompts a concluding string of exhortations that is meant to spur the would-be steward to action (9:7-10).[401] Those readers who embrace Qoheleth's promise of a lasting legacy in their portion from God (9:4-6, cf. 9:1) are urged to *Go...* (9:7a). However, this "action" is described in the ensuing imperatives in terms that indicate they are simply to accept and appropriate what God has already given (9:7-10).[402] We should labor confidently, because (1) *God has already accepted* our *works* (9:7b);[403] (2) it is our *portion* in life (9:9b); and (3) we have limited time to redeem the opportunities God

---

[399] The similar phrasing "no more *reward* to them" (9:5b) and "no more *portion* to them" (9:6b) supports the intended parallel between *reward* and *portion* (n. 390). The final *'ôlām* is best read with *ḥēleq* attributively ("no more *lasting* portion," cf. also 2:16, n. 136), rather than adverbially ("no more portion *forever*," so most translations).

[400] Longman (*Ecclesiastes*, 229) insists that Qoheleth had no concept of an afterlife or heavenly rewards. However, Qoheleth does not claim that the dead have no reward at all but that their reward is limited by the extent of their prior participation in life *under the sun* (9:6b)—it is the chance for **further** reward that ceases with death (9:4-6, 10), not the reward already gained. This should motivate the reader to labor now in the *portion* God has given him, because one's works will thereby gain God's favor (9:7-10; n. 401, below), even though he may not be able to tell what happens after death (9:10, cf. 3:19-22; 6:12; 7:14). See also 12:7; cf. n. 189.

[401] There are five direct imperatives ("go", "eat", "drink", "see life", "do") and two related jussives ("let your clothes be white;" "let your head lack no oil"). These imperatives are arranged in three groups (9:7a, 8-9a, 10a), each followed by a motive clause that emphasizes God's sovereign provision (9:7b, 9b, 10b). The steward is to enjoy his heritage from God now—any time wasted contending with God for a different heritage (cf. 6:10) will only further limit his present opportunity to gain a lasting reward (n. 400).

[402] Each of the activities in these verses is "receptive." Man is to joyfully accept (cf. 5:18-19; n. 241) his bread and wine (9:7a) and the wife he loves (9:9a) as God's provision to help him do his work on earth in his role as God's agent (9:10). Similarly, *wearing white* and *pouring oil* on the head (9:8) symbolize enjoying the favor God has already shown. Even the work that man is given by God is "accepted" as his preordained portion whenever he "finds" it (9:9b-10a), instead of selfishly contending for a different portion (cf. 4:1-6:12).

[403] The verb *rāṣâ* is Qal pf. ("has accepted with favor"), and the adverb *kĕbār* ("already") repeats from 9:6 to confirm this sense of "completed present." This is essential to a coherent understanding of 9:1-10 (Caneday, "Enigmatic Pessimist or Godly Sage?" in Zuck [ed.], *Reflecting with Solomon*, 86 [fn. 24]); that is, the works of the living are "*already* favored" (9:7), just as the passions of the dead have "*already* perished" (9:6). This should settle any remaining uncertainty over whether God truly favors *the righteous and the wise and their works* (9:1, cf. nn. 378-382), thus freeing the reader from the need for self-sufficient achievement: Man can do the work God has given him, confident that it is preordained (3:15, n. 178) and therefore "pre-approved."

has provided mankind to accomplish the work that He has already ordained (9:10b).[404] Thus, God's sovereign, creative initiative should become our primary incentive to realize our intended agency for God during the short time we have to live.[405]

The strategic intent behind this section is reflected in the closing sequence of imperatives (9:7-10): Readers who have "bought" the logic of Qoheleth's argument concerning the prospect of God's favor should thus be motivated to "go" as confident and faithful servants of God who know that their only hope of enjoying lasting significance in their work (9:4-6) is vested in God's presently inscrutable purposes on earth (8:16-9:3). From this point on Qoheleth will therefore address those readers who have embraced the hope he has offered of a *lasting portion* in God's preordained work and are thus motivated to partici-pate in that work as chosen agents of His purposes. If we count our-selves among them we will need God's wisdom to succeed, which thus constitutes the point of departure for the last major section: Given the necessary human constraints on our opportunities to accomplish the work of God,[406] we will need to sustain wisdom's advantage if we are to remain submitted to God's inscrutable purposes and *bring success* in the *work of God* (9:11-12:7).

---

[404] Death eliminates all opportunity for "work" (*ma'ăśeh*, n. 28), "explana-tion" (or "reckoning," *ḥešbôn*, as in 7:25, 27), or "knowledge and wisdom" (cf. 1:16-17). Qoheleth had tried to exploit these resources to little advantage in his earlier effort to realize his own ambition; the same resources are now deemed valuable when invested in the preordained work of God. This exhortation to wise and opportune investment of God-given resources in the work of God anticipates the more extensive exposition in 11:1-12:7.

[405] Only this incentive can properly motivate the prospective steward who fears God to "go" and do the work God has purposed (9:7-10). No commentary expresses this holy yearning to participate in the work of God better than Ps 90:13-17 (NIV):

Relent, O LORD! How long will it be? Have compassion on your servants. Satisfy us in the morning with your unfailing love, that we may sing for joy and be glad all our days. Make us glad for as many days as you have afflict-ed us, for as many years as we have seen trouble. May your deeds be shown to your servants, your splendor to their children. May the favor of the Lord our God rest upon us; establish the work of our hands for us—yes, establish the work of our hands.

The Psalm underscores the central role of God's creative initiative as the basis of His *favor* on the works of men. It reflects the exact sentiment and purpose behind the message of Eccl 9:7-10 and is also the key principle that animates the speech-es of Elihu (Job 32-37).

[406] Mankind's longing for God's glory to be realized in his own work (n. 405) presupposes a sober understanding of his mortal limitations (Ps 90:1-11)—they do not disappear when he fears God. It thus behooves the prospective steward to "know" *time and judgment* (8:5b), i.e., to remain aware of his inherent uncertain-ty, depravity, and mortality when challenged with the opportunities that God offers him to accomplish His work in the hope of a lasting reward—life's adversity will regularly remind the steward of these limitations (see exposition of 8:5b-8).

Part V

COMPLETION

The Way of Wisdom & the Work of God

Bringing Wisdom's Success in the Work of God
(Eccl 9:11-12:7)

*With a series of proverbs, aphorisms, and exhortations that relate wisdom's success to the topics of folly and "time and chance," **Qoheleth warns his readers as prospective stewards that wisdom is vulnerable to their inherent depravity, uncertainty, and mortality**, so that they might not revert to self-reliant effort but rather remember their created calling as God's valued agents, labor expediently in the work of God, and thereby bring wisdom's success.*

The last major section logically follows the preceding guidance on gaining God's favor. While Qoheleth longed for those who fear God to enjoy God's favor in their portion from God and labor with success in the work of God (9:7-10), his lingering concern over inherent human depravity, uncertainty, and mortality compelled him to "return and consider" (9:11a)[407] these natural constraints on *bringing success in the work of God*.[408] After confirming one's ultimate inability to succeed on his own (9:11-12), Qoheleth guides the reader around the ubiquitous and treacherous pitfalls to human *success*. The passage concludes with a final enjoyment pericope (11:9-12:7) and is distinguished from the epilogue by the recurring opening marker *"Vanity of vanities"* (12:8, cf. 1:2).

Few transitional markers occur within the body of this section. Instead, the textual design is developed along a sequence of prominent themes and related imperatives as they touch on Qoheleth's overall objective for his readers, to succeed in the work of God. The governing theme of the book's second half—*wisdom's advantage*—is reintroduced in the opening pericope (9:11-18) where it is portrayed as highly vulnerable to mankind's natural penchant for self-sufficiency. The most pernicious threat to wisdom's success is our proclivity to *folly* (9:16-18),[409] so it is the first to be

---

[407] This phrase marks a major transition in Qoheleth's argument (n. 90).

[408] The verb *kāšēr* ("succeed, bring success") occurs in this major section in 10:10b and 11:6b. The related noun occurs in 4:4 and 5:11 and is related to the key theme of *advantage* in Eccl (n. 22).

[409] This emphasis initially seems misplaced, since Qoheleth had already addressed sin extensively, and the reader should already know that successful stewardship requires fearing God (7:18; 8:12-13). However, the appeal of self-sufficient folly competes with the fear of God in every decision. Whether man will benefit from wisdom depends on how he invests his labor: He can either humbly accept his portion from God (cf. nn. 390, 405) or revert to proud self-sufficiency, which is destined for failure

addressed, considering its disproportionate consequences (10:1-20). Qoheleth then urges opportune labor in the work of God in view of *life's unpredictability* (11:1-8) and *death's finality* (11:9-12:7), the two pitfalls to success designated by the phrase *time and chance*.[410]

This supplies the framework for Qoheleth's argument. While even the greatest of natural human abilities are completely subverted by *time and chance* (9:11-12), self-effacing wisdom affords great advantage for success (9:13-15a). Even so, we typically dismiss wisdom's advantage in favor of self-sufficient folly (9:15b-18). The danger of such folly in the hands of even *one sinner* is so great (9:18b), that one can only avert it by remaining under submission to authority—only then can *wisdom bring success* in the work of God (10:1-20). Similarly, mankind's *unpredictable fortune* makes it expedient to invest our labor whenever feasible (11:1-8), and *death's finality* makes it wise to *rejoice in your youth* yet also *remember your Creator,* who deeply values mankind as the chosen agent of His inscrutable purposes (11:9-12:7).

Qoheleth aimed to persuade the ambitious steward not to revert to self-sufficiency but to remain mindful of his created calling and to avail himself fully of wisdom's advantage in order to bring maximum success in the work of God. To curb the reader's inclination to revert to self-sufficiency, Qoheleth portrayed the devastating outcome of self-sufficient folly (10:1-20). Yet, this alone would not persuade the prospective steward to invest his life fully in the work of God. Such motivation can only arise from the confidence that his work will in fact serve God's purposes, even when they remain inscrutable (11:1-8), and that he can truly enjoy his calling as a valued agent of those purposes, even though his days are limited (11:9-12:7). All that remained was to confirm that Qoheleth's wisdom is in fact inspired by God Himself (12:8-14).

---

[410] Some see the phrase *time and chance* (9:11) "as a *hendiadys*, probably expressing a single idea" (Whybray, *Ecclesiastes*, 146; cf. also Walter Kaiser, *Ecclesiastes: Total Life*, 103)—it is the notion of *limited and unpredictable opportunity* that is woven into the contexts of 9:11-12 and 11:1-12:7 and links the arguments of the beginning and concluding passages of this major section (cf. n. 99).

— 25 —

A. Wisdom's Success versus Self-Sufficient Failure (9:11–18)

In reflecting on a fable that depicts wisdom's superiority over great natural strength in the face of adversity, **Qoheleth affirms that wisdom prevails in humility but remains vulnerable to self-sufficient folly***, so that the reader might not try to bring success in the work of God by foolishly reverting to self-sufficiency.*

As soon as Qoheleth advised his readers to take opportune advantage of the portion God has given them to do His work (9:7-10) he realized that their success as agents of God would still be threatened by their natural tendency to revert to self-sufficiency. Even if the reader fears God and is fully motivated to do the work of God one still needs wisdom to succeed, so Qoheleth "returned to consider" (9:11a) how mankind's innate depravity, uncertainty, and mortality (cf. 8:16-9:3) naturally conspire to subvert wisdom's advantage in pursuit of success. The passage is thus designed to equip God's chosen agents to stay vigilant amid these pitfalls to success if we are indeed to preserve wisdom's advantage for the work of God.

The passage consists of three textually distinct pericopae: an initial disconcerting reflection on mankind's natural inability (9:11-12); a vignette that promotes wisdom's advantage over even the greatest of human strengths (9:13-15); and a sequence of three *better than* proverbs that affirm wisdom's advantage but warn of mankind's propensity to eschew that advantage in favor of self-sufficient folly (9:16-18).[411] As is so typical of Qoheleth's literary

---

[411] Expositors debate where this pericope ends (n. 97). Ogden concedes that the three proverbs in 9:16-18 share the same *better than* form ("Wisdom's Strength and Vulnerability," 335) but proposes that 9:17 initiates a new thought unit on the basis of literary figures in chap. 10 that are in common with 9:17-18 but not 9:16 and the thematic shift to *folly* at 9:17 (ibid., 335-7). However, the phrase "words…heard" in 9:16 is repeated in 9:17 to underscore the transparent folly of ignoring the words of the wise in 9:16. The entire pericope 9:16-18 thus comprises a literary transition to 10:1-20, and 9:18 serves as the point of departure, summarizing *wisdom's advantage* but also reintroducing the theme of *depravity* (*one sinner destroys much good*, cf. nn. 38, 100). This imbues *folly* with the disproportionately pernicious influence so colorfully depicted in 10:1-20.

style, the textual design of this section involves the strategic use of conjunctions to mark key transitions in his logic: The transition at 9:13 presents a contrast to the dilemma described in 9:11-12 by offering the self-effacing wisdom depicted in the fable of 9:14-15 as the logical solution.[412] The transition at 9:16a then marks the wisdom of 9:16-18 as the moral to be inferred from that same fable.[413]

Not even the utmost natural ability, including wisdom, can reliably bring success to mankind's labor (9:11a, b),[414] for [415] human ability is constrained by *time and chance* (9:11c).[416] Indeed,[417] *man does not know his time…. So…men are snared in an evil time* when they least expect it (9:12). However, Qoheleth was greatly impressed by the wisdom he saw depicted in a fable (9:13) whereby a *poor man by **his** wisdom delivered* a *little city* under *great* siege (9:14-15a),[418]

---

[412] Once Qoheleth realized that self-reliant success is subverted by *time and chance* (9:11-12) he was greatly impressed by *this wisdom* (9:13-18) as the answer to this existential dilemma (cf. 8:16-9:3). Most translations of 9:13 translate the opening *gam* as "also" or "moreover." However, this *gam* introduces the following vignette of wisdom's success (9:14-15) as a **contrast** to the failure of natural wisdom (9:11-12) so it should probably be construed as a strong adversative: "*However,* I saw this wisdom under the sun, and it was great to me." Qoheleth then illustrates *this wisdom* with a fable (9:14-15) whose object lesson is qualified by three proverbs (9:16-18), so the entire pericope 9:14-18 could be viewed as appositional to *this wisdom* (9:13).

[413] The opening *waw* is inferential, "*So* I said…" (9:16a, NASB, NIV); it introduces the three proverbs in 9:16-18 as a logical implication of the disappointing conclusion (9:15c) to the fable about the poor but wise man.

[414] As with the five supposed **moral virtues** in 9:2-3 (n. 385), Qoheleth now lists five **natural strengths** in 9:11 that he expected to bring success: speed, strength, wisdom, intelligence, and knowledge. The last three in the list are grouped together by a repeating *gam lō'* (*neither…, nor…, nor…*), as they are all constitutive of *natural wisdom* (n. 91), which Qoheleth himself had hoped (1:13-18) to parlay into *bread, riches,* and especially *favor* (9:11). His prior disillusionment over the lack of any advantage to his own natural wisdom (1:16, 18; 2:12-16; 6:8; cf. n. 247) now serves as a foil for the kind of wisdom that **does** bring success (9:13ff).

[415] The final clause of 9:11 is initiated by a causal *kî* (so NASB), confused by NKJV, NIV, and NRSV.

[416] Two related nuances of *time* are developed in 9:12 to explain what *time* means in 9:11 (cf. n. 99) and how it is related to the notion of *chance* (*pega'*, lit. "event," the only occurrence in Eccl).

[417] The opening *kî gam* in 9:12a marks emphatic *specification* ("for indeed") of the preceding assertion (9:11c): *Time and chance* deprive those who are naturally gifted of any reliably predictable advantage (9:11), *for indeed* adversity and death strike all men without warning or discrimination (9:12, cf. 7:14; 8:6b-7; 9:2-3).

yet no one remembered that poor man (9:15b). The fable illustrated a double moral (9:16-18):[419] Qoheleth saw that *Wisdom is better than* natural *strength* (9:16a), like the loud boasts of foolish
ruler (9:17b) or *weapons of war* (9:18a, cf. 7:19). Yet such *wisdom*
is *quiet*, self-effacing, and typically *despised*, so that the *words of
the wise are not heard* (9:16b, 17a; cf. 7:5a), and *one sinner* in his
self-sufficient folly *destroys much good* (9:18b).[420]

This sequence of proverbs thus reaffirms that humble wisdom
has great power, but it also warns that wisdom's advantage is nullified by self-sufficient pride and that sin lies at the root of that pernicious pride. Since the intended audience for this last phase of
Qoheleth's argument consists of those who fear God and want to
succeed in the work of God, the implication is that even **they** can
all too easily succumb to the powerful appeal of self-sufficiency.
When that happens, wisdom gives way to folly, and the steward's
choices are again dictated by pride and selfish ambition, which only
foils one's success. It is now clear why Qoheleth begins his concluding teaching on wise stewardship with an exposé of folly, the
most serious threat to wisdom's advantage (10:1-20).

---

[418] The poor man's specific stratagem is not mentioned nor is it relevant to
Qoheleth's point. While Qoheleth had just disqualified *self-reliant* wisdom as a
reliable means to success (9:11) he saw *self-effacing* wisdom prevail (cf. 7:11-12,
18-20; cf. n. 311).

[419] The *better than* proverbs of 9:16-18 comprise three couplets arrayed in
alternate parallel—the first line in each couplet exalts *wisdom's* great *strength*; the
other presents the *subversive* effect of *folly*. While the middle couplet (9:17) lacks
the opening "better," it can be inferred from the *min* ("than") that initiates the second line: "[Better are] the words of the wise heard in quiet *than* the shout of a ruler
of fools" (cf. 7:5-7).

[420] Folly is thus clearly associated with sin (n. 37); its great destructive potential derives from the sinner's failure to fear God (8:12-13, cf. nn. 364, 409).

— 26 —

B. Wisdom's Success amid the Hazards of Folly (10:1-20)

With a palistrophic sequence of word pictures that illustrate how even a little folly can thoroughly undermine a steward's success, **Qoheleth warns his readers to avoid self-sufficient folly by remaining accountable under authority,** *so that they might preserve wisdom's advantage in their labor and bring success in the work of God.*

The structure of this passage may be the least transparent in the whole book, as it presents a virtual potpourri of platitudes and aphorisms that at first seem to bear no obvious relation to each other. However, on further scrutiny of the text one can eventually identify a surprisingly intricate chiastic structure. The key to the textual design is to identify the palistrophic sequence of six repeating word pictures (10:4-20)[421] following a thematic introduction in 10:1-3 and highlighting wisdom's advantage over folly (cf. 9:18b):

"Ruler" (10:4) >
    "Princes" (10:5-7) >
            "Serpent" (10:8-10a) >
              "Wisdom brings success" (10:10b)
            "Serpent" (10:11-15) <
    "Princes" (10:16-19) <
"Ruler" (10:20) <

Each figure is the focus of a wise saying within its respective pericope and in some way epitomizes the foolishness of reverting to self-sufficiency in the pursuit of success. The two repeating sequences converge at the turning point of the palistrophe to highlight the main message of 10:4-20—*wisdom* is the advantage that *brings success* (10:10b).[422] The result is a series of object lessons, each illustrating

---

[421] Qoheleth seems to prefer figures of status and authority, as we would expect from having assumed Solomon's royal perspective (cf. nn. 7, 85, 86, 208, 322). Besides the figures of civil authority—"ruler" (*môšēl*) and "official" (*šallît*)—there are three references to "king" (*melek*), three to "princes" (*śārîm*), and two to "the rich."

[422] Cp. the central location and message of 1:8 within the prologue, 1:4-11.

in some way how easily *folly* can subvert *wisdom's success*, as 10:1 has affirmed. The imperatives in the boundary verses of the pal-istrophe (10:4, 20)[423] are designed to dissuade the reader from indulging in such folly by reminding him in both half-sequences of his accountability under authority.

This admonitory sequence underscores the ever-present danger of a lack of moral vigilance when the steward is tempted to bring success out of self-sufficiency, which invariably involves *folly*. In this respect, there is a subtle difference in emphasis between the two half-sequences of the palistrophe: The first (10:4-10) illustrates how even trivial lapses in vigilance can foolishly undermine the steward's success; the second (10:11-20) reveals how foolish self-indulgence completely subverts one's intended agency. The reader who remains morally sensitive to the treacherous pitfalls of folly is well equipped in light of "time and judgment" (cf. 8:5b-6a) to exploit wisdom's advantage for maximum success in the work of God (11:1-12:7).

Qoheleth intended to supply wisdom to guide the steward's choic-es in the face of *time and chance* (11:1-8, cf. 9:11c), but it made little sense to undertake that exposition when self-sufficient folly posed a more immediate threat to wisdom's advantage. The assertion that *one sinner destroys much good* (9:18b) should concern anyone who may question whether the assertion is in fact true and thus be tempted to dis-miss wisdom in favor of folly (cf. 9:16-18). Qoheleth therefore intro-duced a striking analogy that affirms the devastating influence of just *a little folly* (10:1) as a "wake up call" for the steward to remain moral-ly vigilant in his work, from the most banal activities (10:4-10) to his very commission from the throne itself (10:11-20).

1. "One Sinner Destroys Much Good" (10:1-3)

This pericope expands on point made in 9:18b and serves to introduce the whole chapter. The first verse recapitulates the theme of the first half-sequence in 10:4-20 by alerting the reader to the potent destructive influence of even *a little folly* (10:1).[424]

---

[423] The imperatives in 10:4 and 20 refer to analogous authority figures: The *ruler* in 10:4 has authority over those in his charge. Likewise, *the king* and *the rich* in 10:20 signify political and economic authority that should command respect. In effect both imperatives recall Qoheleth's advice in 8:1-8: The steward who would *bring wisdom's success* (10:10b) is to remain accountable under authority, no mat-ter how tempting it might be at times to indulge in folly.

Each figure in 10:4-10 thus portrays how even the most trivial imprudence in a steward's labor can seriously undermine his skill and honor and thereby thwart his purposes. Verses 10:2-3 then introduce the theme of the second half-sequence, asserting that the fool's very inclination is sinful, so that all his actions betray him as a fool.[425] Thus, each figure in 10:11-20 depicts how self-indulgence leads a fool under authority to shirk his responsibility and squander his resources, thereby nullifying his stewardship.

2. "A Little Folly Outweighs Wisdom or Honor" (10:4-10)

The first half-sequence (10:4-10) depicts how much is at stake when the steward is tempted to revert to self-sufficiency and engage in folly—he risks completely subverting his intended purpose. Thus follows the logic: When reproved by your boss for a mistake, don't foolishly seek to avoid exposure, for integrity under fire covers even great errors (10:4). By contrast, even a small lapse of integrity (cf. 10:1, *a little folly*) seriously jeopardizes the success of those with great reputed *honor* or *wisdom:* Folly can thoroughly humiliate even the most honored and highly placed steward (10:5-7); a minor indiscretion, like taking shortcuts on the job, can completely undermine the handiwork of even highly skilled craftsmen (10:8-10a). *But* the *advantage* that *brings success* to the steward's intended purpose is *wisdom* (10:10b).

a. "Ruler" (10:4)

The opening figure signals the potential danger of shirking one's duty under authority. The implied occasion is a situation in

---

[424] Like 7:1, verse 10:1 also takes the form of an understood analogy ("*As...*, *so...*," cf. NIV) and employs the imagery of perfumed ointment. The point of the analogy depends on the intended sense of *yāqār* in the second line. The usual sense of "precious" or "valued" seems misplaced; "heavy" or "weighty" seems to suit the context better (cf. Longman, *Ecclesiastes*, 238 [fn. 4]). By asserting that *folly* outweighs *wisdom*, just like "dead flies stink up and spoil a perfumer's oil," the analogy affirms *wisdom's vulnerability* (n. 38). The semantic range of *ḥokmâ* includes "technical skill," so we could read "a little folly is weightier than skill, than honor" (cf. NIV, NASB), such that 10:1 presents all the vignettes depicted in 10:4-10:10a as examples of *skilled* or *honored* servants whose stewardship is subverted by folly.

[425] Verse 10:2 lit. reads "A wise heart to his right but a fool's heart to his left" (cf. NASB). The phrase "wise heart" (cf. 7:4; 8:5) implies *prudence*, while "to his right" implies "upright" and "to his left" implies "shady" or "evil" (cp. Lat *sinister*). Thus, a fool's choices reflect his *moral inclination*, which is eventually obvious to everyone (10:3).

which a steward who is accountable under a supervisor fails his responsibility in a way that angers the boss.[426] The steward is tempted to escape the boss's wrath but is warned instead not to *leave* his *post* (10:4a).[427] Although the steward under authority may be tempted to avoid the exposure of his mistakes when held to account by his supervisor (cf. 3:15b), he is more likely to conciliate the boss's wrath[428] (and God's?) by remaining true to his calling under fire (10:4b). The object lesson: In the end faithfulness, not *folly*, prevails.

b. "Princes" (10:5-7)

The opening marker *There is an evil I have seen* (10:5a)[429] initiates the sequence of figures in 10:6-10 that illustrate the power of *folly* over *wisdom and honor* (cf. 10:1b). By contrast with the integrity that *allays **great** offenses* (10:4b, NASB), even the **smallest** lapse of integrity by a knowledgeable steward has disproportionate consequences—like a stupid error committed by the one in authority[430] (10:5). Folly has such great influence (lit. "is placed very highly"), that Qoheleth had seen *rich men* humiliated and *princes* replaced by slaves (10:6-7),[431] thus portraying the power of

---

[426] The object lesson of the *môšēl* figure ("ruler") here differs from that in 9:17 (cf. Ogden, "Wisdom's Strength and Vulnerability," 336). The *môšēl* figure in 9:17 is to be viewed as a fool, while the one in 10:4 commands respect and submission. Thus, the *folly* in 10:4 is focused not on the authority figure itself—as it is in 9:17 and 10:5—but on the steward who attempts to avoid accountability *under* that authority (cf. also the "mirror image" figure in 10:20).

[427] The imagery recalls 8:3, *Do not be in a hurry to leave him. Do not join in an evil matter, for he will do whatever he pleases* (NASB), thus illustrating the moral accountability of a servant under authority.

[428] The intended sense of the noun *marpē'* ("gentleness") is debated (Longman, *Ecclesiastes*, 241) but is aptly reflected by NASB, *composure allays great offenses*. The context invokes the sense of *maintaining integrity under fire*.

[429] Cp. 6:1. Most translations do not reflect the different word for "ruler" (*šallît*) in 10:5 (cf. n. 430). In contrast to *môšēl* in 10:4, the figure *šallît*—like the *môšēl* in 9:17 (n. 426)—is itself intended to exemplify the failed stewardship that stems from engaging in folly.

[430] Lit. "like a mistake that comes from the one in charge" (10:5b). From its use in 7:19 the term *šallît* suggests a person in high authority in the community. The simile highlights the disconcerting discrepancy (= "evil," 10:5a) between the boss's *error* and his *position of authority*.

[431] The alternate parallelism ("high," "low"/"high," "low") in 10:6-7 helps illustrate Qoheleth's point (Ogden, "Wisdom's Strength and Vulnerability," 337): Folly is very *highly* placed (10:6a) and can *promote* slaves (10:7a) while it utterly *humiliates* rich men (10:6b) and princes (10:7b).

folly over *honor* (cf.10:1b). The following figures (10:8-10) then depict folly's equally pernicious influence on *wisdom*.

c. "Serpent" (10:8-10a)

The serpent's bite epitomizes this deadly effect of foolish indiscretion in this pericope. Each figure illustrates the craftsman's skill and intended purpose subverted by the influence of folly.[432] The text highlights the tasks of four **different** craftsmen in a way that depicts the **same** subversion of intended purpose across a range of different trades and skills (10:8-9).[433] The concluding moral for these word pictures[434] is that even a small lapse in vigilance—like failing to sharpen an axe blade or a chisel—greatly jeopardizes the steward's success and in the end only increases the labor required (10:10a). Nevertheless, *wisdom* still *brings success* (10:10b).

d. "Wisdom Brings Success" (10:10b)

In concluding the logic of 10:8-10, this last clause[435] is strategically situated at the pivot of the palistrophe (10:4-20, see figure) to reinforce Qoheleth's opening point in this major section (9:11-18): Humble wisdom affords great success, when

---

[432] Some expositors assume *malicious* activity like digging a pit for a trap (so Eaton, *Ecclesiastes*, 135), but this is inconsistent with the overall thrust of 10:4-10. The sense is rather that they try to hurry the job by taking short cuts. The figures in 10:8-9 thus alert the steward to the peril of failing to exercise due vigilance in his labor. The figure of the *serpent* aptly illustrates the imprudence of such a lapse of integrity—the steward may be "bitten" by his folly: The scenario is that of a *vine-dresser* who tries to break through instead of going around a stone wall or hedge meant to protect the vineyards of two fields (cp. Matt 21:33) and inadvertently disturbs a snake lurking in the shelter of the normally undisrupted barrier.

[433] Each clause in 10:8-9 begins with a substantival participle: "the one digging," "the one breaking through," "the one quarrying," and "the one splitting."

[434] Even though 10:10a only alludes to splitting wood or rock (cf. 10:9) it introduces the moral that is to be inferred from all four figures in 10:8-9. The logic of 10:10 is thus best taken as "If..., *and...*, *then...*, *but...*" (the last three conjunctions are all *waw*).

[435] This clause is arguably the most difficult construction in the book (Longman, *Ecclesiastes*, 244-5), lit. "and advantage to give success wisdom" (cf. Murphy, *Ecclesiastes*, 98 [fn. 10h]). The opening particle *wᵉ⁻* is ignored by NASB yet rendered adversative ("but") in NKJV, NIV, NRSV. Since this construction serves as a contrast to 10:10a (n. 434), and Qoheleth's idiosyncratic syntax in other instances typically preserves the logic of his argument, the opening particle in this case is most likely adversative. Cp. 10:19c (n. 449 below).

it is not subverted by *folly*. This links the logic of 10:1-10 with 9:11-18 and brings the object lesson of the entire passage into focus: Although a little folly seems to afford an advantage in pursuit of success, it can foil the purposes of the most highly honored or skilled steward (10:4-10a, cf. 10:1), but (again) *wisdom* is *an* advantage that *brings success* (10:10b).[436] This serves in turn as the literary point of departure for the full-fledged folly illustrated in 10:11-20.

3. "The Heart of a Fool Inclines to the Left" (10:11-20)

Turning on the literary pivot of 10:10b, the same sequence of figures now repeats in reverse order, but the focus shifts from the imprudent error of a steward who only trifles in folly to the profound dereliction of all-consuming self-indulgence.[437] The fool's utter failure in his calling is traced to his evil inclination (cf. 10:2): As the serpent's bite depicts the deadly consequence of an uncontrolled "tongue," so do a fool's *many words* betray a stewardship "poisoned" by selfish ambition (10:11-15); fools in high places even devastate the whole land by squandering their resources in unrestrained self-indulgence (10:16-19). The closing injunction insinuates that a fool's failed stewardship stems from rebellion against authority (10:20):[438] If such insubordination can destroy one's stewardship under **human** authority, how much more under **God's** authority!

---

[436] The Hiphil infinitive construct of *kāšar* ("to bring success") is likely a genitive in construct with the noun *yitrôn*, "advantage *of* bringing success" (cf. Robert Chisholm, *From Exegesis to Exposition: A Practical Guide to Using Biblical Hebrew* [Grand Rapids: Baker, 1998], 78), most plausibly a genitive of *result* (cf. Arnold and Choi, *Hebrew Syntax*, 11); i.e., "advantage *that brings* success." Reading an adversative *wᵉ–* (n. 435), the clause would thus read "but *wisdom* is an advantage that brings success." The object lesson: Any steward tempted to cut corners in his work is reminded of his need for *wisdom* in order to bring success, which should redirect him to the wise injunctions of 10:4 and 20 that reaffirm the protection afforded against the pitfalls of folly by wise accountability under authority (n. 423).

[437] By echoing the word *yithrôn* ("advantage") from 10:10b, verse 10:11b serves as the thematic turning point to the second half-sequence (10:4-20): While the previous figures pointed *toward* wisdom's advantage in *bringing success* (10:10b), these figures now lead *away from* wisdom's advantage (10:11b), culminating in *complete nullification* of the fool's calling.

[438] Just as in 8:2-8 (cf. n. 337) the object lessons regarding submission to **human** authority in the opening and closing injunctions (10:4, 20) are to be applied to the readers as agents in submission to **God's** authority.

c'. "Serpent" (10:11-15)

The palistrophic structure of 10:4-20 is preserved by the repeating "serpent" figure in 10:11a (cf. 10:8b) and the parallel syntax of 10:10 and 11.[439] The deadliness of being bitten by an uncharmed serpent transparently depicts the "poisonous effect" of a fool's unbridled tongue:[440] In contrast to the gracious *words of a wise man*, the fool's ridiculous words are of utterly no avail (10:12-13).[441] Yet he still *multiplies words* (10:14a)[442] in pursuit of presumptuous schemes with no clue how they will turn out (10:14b).[443] The closing figure depicts how easily the fool loses his way (10:15), which in turn prefigures the main object lesson of 10:16-19.[444]

b'. "Princes" (10:16-19)

This pericope mirrors the previous figure of *princes* (10:5-7) with structurally parallel proverbs that depict the diametrically opposed outcomes of wise and foolish stewardship and illustrate how folly influences the final outcome (10:16-17):[445] The

---

[439] Besides sharing the word *yithrôn* (n. 437), both verses employ "If..., then..." logic (nn. 434, 441) consistent with the palistrophic structure of 10:4-20. Although Ogden cites this similarity to align 10:11 with 10:8-10 ("Wisdom's Strength and Vulnerability," 337), given that 10:10b parallels the concluding moral of 10:19b (cf. n. 449), it is more plausible that 10:10b is (like 10:19b) a **closing** construction for its half-sequence, while 10:11 **introduces** its half-sequence.

[440] "If the snake bites when not charmed, then [there is] no advantage to the *master of the tongue.*" The phrase "master [or *owner*] of the tongue" is likely a *double entender* for the snake charmer's control of the serpent's tongue and the steward's control of his words.

[441] The "oral" imagery continues, explaining the devastating effect of the fool's drivel on his intended purpose: Both the fool and his stewardship are ultimately *swallowed up* by his "lips" (10:12). The effect is insidious: Initial words of foolishness lead inexorably to overwhelming moral stupidity and ruin (10:13, cf. 9:3, n. 387; cp. Jas 3:8 in context).

[442] So NASB. An adversative opening *waw* recalls the inconsistency of a fool's brazen presumption (as conveyed by his *many words*, n. 40) with his calling as an agent of God (cf. 6:10-11, n. 251).

[443] The phrase lit. reads "Man does not know what will happen, and what will happen afterward who can tell him?" This is also the main thrust of 8:7; it recalls the sense of the closing constructions in 3:22, 6:12, and 7:14 (n. 299), thus foreclosing the possibility that a fool could ever control his own destiny.

[444] Verse 10:15 portrays a fool who intends to conduct business "in the city" to fulfill his stewardship, but this is too much work for him, and he loses his way. This becomes the metaphor for losing sight of his calling in 10:16-19.

land **suffers** when a weak king cannot control his princes but **prospers** when a king of noble birth commands their respect.[445] The former princes *feast in the morning* in their self-indulgence and deplete resources intended to fulfill their royal calling, but those who *feast at the proper time* have *strength* to realize that calling.[447] The insidious ruin that ensues from the dissipation of foolish princes is depicted by the imagery of a house in utter disrepair (10:18).[448] The closing moral thus highlights the advantage of diligent stewardship (the wise use of *money*) over foolish self-indulgence (10:19).[449]

---

[445] Verses 10:16 and 17 are identical in form (Ogden, ibid., 339) and use contrasting extremes to illustrate the ill effects of folly in high places, just as in 10:6-7 (n. 431). While the final result in 10:6-7 was "low," the analogous outcome in these verses is "woe." Such *woe* has spread from the **personal** consequences of "a little folly" (cf. 10:1-10) to the **nation-wide** calamity of a fool's self-indulgent lifestyle.

[446] The contrast in this anecdote is not intended to differentiate between wise and foolish *kings*. The point of the illustration is that faithful stewardship depends on respecting the authority—in this case *the king*—to whom one's stewardship is due. When such respect is absent, foolish stewards—in this case *princes*—are virtually free to indulge in dissipation (cp. 8:11). Seen in this light, the *king* figure thus serves as the appropriate object of respect in the ensuing final injunction to potential stewards (10:20).

[447] The closing clause *for strength and not for drunkenness* makes the point of the contrast between wise and foolish princes: The word *strength* echoes from 9:16 (cf. also 7:19) and thus recalls the association of *wisdom* with *success* (10:10b), while the word *drunkenness* conveys the strong sense of self-indulgence. The *foolish* princes are not just eating breakfast; rather, they are indulging their insatiable appetites (cf. 10:12, *the lips of a fool consume him* [NASB]).

[448] Expositors debate whether 10:18-19 is related to vv. 16-17. Neither Whybray (*Ecclesiastes*, 157) nor Longman (*Ecclesiastes*, 250) sees any connection at all, which undercuts the logical unity of the passage. However, by attributing a house in disrepair to laziness (10:18, cp. 4:5), Qoheleth highlights the logical consequences of the lazy self-indulgence exemplified by foolish princes in 10:16b. This in turn leads to the moral in 10:19 as the conclusion for the entire pericope, 10:11-19 (see below).

[449] The significance of *money* in 10:19 is debated, but the context conveys the superiority of *diligence* over *dissipation*, in which case the final *waw* is adversative, "A feast is for laughter and wine makes life happy, *but* money answers all." The pretext for this moral is the fool's lack of respect for money and his failure to exercise wise and diligent stewardship to preserve his "house" (10:16-18). Thus, the phrases *for laughter* and *makes happy* (10:19) do not denote that sense of joy conveyed in the enjoyment pericopae, but rather the foolish dissipation of self-indulgence (cf. 7:3). This casts *a feast* and *wine* (10:19a) in a negative light: Princes who *feast for drunkenness* (10:17) are foolish, because their merry indulgence results in the disintegration of the house over which they are stewards (cf. 10:18)—*but money answers all* (10:19b), just like *wisdom brings success* (10:10b). The term *kōl* ("all") alludes to the preceding warnings in chap. 10; thus, *money* exemplifies how *wisdom* (cf. 7:11; 10:10b) *answers* the root problem of *all* the vignettes in chap. 10: *a little folly destroys much good* (9:18b, cf. nn. 38, 100).

a'. "Ruler" (10:20)[450]

The opening and closing injunctions (10:4, 20) serve as "book-ends" for the text of 10:4-20 with obvious parallels that under-score the critical role of submission to authority in order to yield effective stewardship.[451] The mandate in 10:20 stems directly from the preceding concern over the deprivation that attends a fool's disrespect for authority or money (10:16-19).[452] When the steward is tempted to voice such disrespect by disparaging the king or the rich man he is warned not to do so, even in private (10:20a),[453] for "what goes around comes around" (10:20b).[454] This warning against imprudent disdain for authority and money sets the stage for Qoheleth's instruc-tions concerning opportune stewardship of the resources God provides to fulfill His purposes (11:1-12:7).

---

[450] I use the label "ruler" to match the parallel figure in 10:4; it is a suitable symbol for the authority exercised over the steward by both the *king* and *rich man*.

[451] *See* nn. 103, 423, and compare 8:2-5: While the initial injunction (10:4) addresses the impulse to *be in a hurry to leave* when one is held to account (cf. 8:3a, NASB), the closing injunction (10:20) addresses mankind's inherent tenden-cy to *stand for an evil thing* (cf. 8:3b). Both injunctions affirm that stewards who voluntarily submit to authority are less likely to suffer harm (8:5a).

[452] The logic of 10:20 relates directly to 10:16-19: If successful stewardship depends on submission to the king's authority (10:16-17, cf. n. 446), then the stew-ard who aspires to success will certainly resist the temptation to *curse* (n. 313) the king. Likewise, if *money answers everything* (10:18-19, cf. n. 449), then how stu-pid to denigrate a rich man! Such "cursing" echoes the fool's futile *multiplied words* (10:11-14) and the futile "verbal insurrection" against one's calling from God (6:10-11, cf. n. 250).

[453] The force of the opening emphatic *gam* "even" (cf. NKJV) distributes to the *waw* in the second, parallel clause: "Do not curse the king *even* (*gam*) in your thought, nor curse the rich *even* (*waw*) in your private chamber." The need to squelch any lack of respect for the *king* or *rich man* is directly linked to the con-cerns of 10:11-19 (cf. nn. 446, 449): The fool's disrespect for *authority* and *money* so nullifies effective stewardship, that the reader dare not disparage either of them, even in private. Cp. Titus 3:1-2.

[454] Words of contempt have a way of returning to haunt the perpetrator (cf. 7:21, n. 308), which could seriously jeopardize one's stewardship (cp. the fate of the unjust steward, Luke 16:1-2). Both the "bird of the air" and the "owner of wings" are transparent metaphors for the spread of malicious gossip. It is plausible that these "winged" figures in 10:20 are intended to parallel the "flies of death" in 10:1, thus enclosing 10:1-20 as the main boundary figures. Although I argue that the pal-istrophic arrangement bounded by the parallel injunctions in 10:4, 20 fits better (n. 450) I do acknowledge that both parallels may be literarily significant, since vv. 10:1-3 are integrally related to vv. 4-20 (see exposition above).

C. Wisdom's Success in Light of "Time and Chance" (11:1-12:7)

In a sequence of imperatives occasioned by the constraints of mankind's unpredictable fortune and limited time to do the work of God, **Qoheleth urges the "young man" to rejoice in his youth yet remember his Creator in opportune stewardship of his God-given portion,** *so that the readers might account well for their steward-ship as God's valued agents through expeditious investment in the work of God before all opportunity is gone.*

This section expands and concludes Qoheleth's previous con-tention that the steward's only hope of lasting satisfaction is to invest his portion in the work of God (9:7-10). Although there is no formal opening marker, the preceding emphases on *bringing suc-cess* and *money* (cf. 10:10b; 10:19b) carry over to the present text: Qoheleth's concern over squandering one's portion as a steward under authority (10:11-20) serves as the pretext for several clusters of imperatives that urge expedient investment in order to bring maximum success in the work of God. The key to the exposition is to recognize how the constraint of *time and chance* mentioned at the outset of this major section (9:11) compels these exhortations intended to equip stewards of God with wisdom to account well for their labor as valued agents of the Creator.[455]

The structure of the passage is dictated by the audience speci-fied in each section. While the opening injunctions are directed to the reader in general (11:1-8), the closing cluster of imperatives is addressed to the *young man*[456] (11:9-12:7). The transitional peri-cope is stylistically distinct (11:7-8).[457] While 11:8 introduces the

---

[455] Qoheleth thus prefigured Christ's own exhortations to expedient invest-ment of the resources God gave man to accomplish His work on earth (cf. e.g., Matt 24:42-25:30; Luke 16:1-13; 19:11-27; cf. also Jas 4:13-5:5).

[456] The *young man* is the prototype for the student of wisdom (cf. *my son*, 12:12; as also in Prov 2-7) and has the most to gain or lose, depending on how he responds to Qoheleth's instruction; he thus receives more explicit guidance on expedient stew-ardship. Cp. John's advice to his own "young men" (1 John 2:15-17).

[457] The volitives in these vv. switch to **jussive**, thus distinguishing them from the **imperative** in both the previous (Eccl 11:1-6) and following (11:9-12:1) pericopae.

themes that follow,[458] the logic of 11:7-8 is dictated by a sequence of conjunctions[459] that affirm the value of the preceding advice (11:1-6)[460] in view of future woe. Thus, the construction *all to come is vanity* (11:8b) serves as a closing marker, and the preceding verbs—*rejoice* and *remember*—anticipate the two imperatives that dominate 11:9-12:7, thus serving as the point of departure for the concluding exhortation.[461]

These textual clues shape the final phase of the argument. Deeply disturbed by the folly of ineffective and self-indulgent stewardship (10:1-20), Qoheleth expanded on his prior advice that the reader invest his God-given portion (cf. 9:7-10) to maximize his success in the work of God. Thus, the steward should invest his portion diversely and seize every opportunity to labor in the work of God in view of life's unpredictable fortune (11:1-8). The *young man* is encouraged to *rejoice* in his youth and pursue his heart's desires yet remain aware that he is accountable for all his works and so purge his heart of all vexation; and he is to *remember* his Creator before debility and death rob him of all further opportunity to glorify his Creator (11:9-12:7, cf. 9:4-6).

1. Opportune Investment in View of Life's Unpredictable Fortune (11:1–8)

The structure of this passage is governed by two sets of imperatives (11:1-2, 6)[462] that speak to unpredictable fortune,[463] given the prospect of both adversity (11:2b) and prosperity (11:6b) in

---

[458] The themes of joy, mankind's limited lifespan, the *days of darkness*, and the advice to *rejoice...* and *remember...* all carry over to the following passage (n. 102). See Whybray, *Ecclesiastes*, 161.

[459] The logical flow of 11:7-8 follows the sequence of conjunctions *waw...waw...kî 'im...waw...kî...* (see nn. 469-473).

[460] The *good* in 11:7b (so NASB) echoes the *good* in 11:6b of *sewing* ("investing") in spite of uncertainty.

[461] *See* n. 104. The imperative *rejoice* formally marks 11:9-12:7 as the last "enjoyment" pericope.

[462] These imperatives utilize commercial (11:1-2) and agricultural (11:6) imagery to express Qoheleth's instruction on *opportune* investment in the face of uncertainty. The agricultural imagery depicts the expedience of *timely* investment, while *bread on the waters* is most likely a *synecdoche* for marine commerce, symbolizing the expedience of *liberal* investment.

[463] The four-fold repeated phrase "you do not know" in 11:1-6 recalls the constraint of *time and chance* (9:11; n. 99), which may be viewed as a *hendiadys* for "limited and unpredictable opportunity" (n. 410).

life.[464] These imperatives are occasioned by the reader's implied hesitation to invest his resources in life because of the risk of failure, when such hesitation only curtails the opportunity for a harvest in the inscrutable *work of God* (11:5).[465] Thus, the two sets of imperatives set the priority for the entire section as successful stewardship in *the work of God* by the reader as an agent of God facing unpredictable circumstances. The summary appraisal (11:7-8) offers hope in the face of impending future adversity and thereby introduces 11:9-12:1.

This argument for opportune investment revolves around the uncertain fate of the steward's God-given portion:[466] He should invest his portion liberally in order to yield a maximum dividend for his efforts (11:1) and he should diversify his investment in view of life's unpredictable adversity (11:2). It is futile to wait for ideal circumstances before investing one's resources, since such circumstances cannot be controlled (11:3-4); *the work of God* is as inscrutable as *the wind* that drives the *clouds* and the *breath* that vitalizes the *bones* that form *in the womb* (11:4-5, NRSV).[467] The prospective steward should therefore seize every opportunity to *sow your seed* (11:6a) *for you do not know* which of your investments will turn out to *be good* and *succeed*[468] (11:6b, NASB)

---

[464] The words for "good" in 11:6 and "evil" in 11:2 are the same as in 7:14, where they are used with a non-moral connotation (cf. n. 298). This recalls the prior admonition that God's inscrutable *work* includes both *adversity* and *prosperity* (7:13-14), so that the imperatives in 11:1-2 relate to unpredictable *adversity* (11:2b), while those in 11:6 relate to equally unpredictable *prosperity* (11:6b).

[465] The focal point of this passage is the analogy in 11:5 between the vagaries of the wind's direction and the inscrutability of God's creative work, as depicted by the knitting together of an infant in the womb. Mankind can never be sure how God is working, but God controls the inscrutable circumstances of mankind's labor and determines whether it will *succeed* (11:6, cf. n. 468 below).

[466] Verse 11:1 and 2 involve alternate parallelism, such that the force of the pronominal suffix (*your bread*) in 11:1 distributes equally to the anarthrous term *portion* (*ḥēleq*) in 11:2 ("your" *portion*, so NASB). Qoheleth intends to denote the steward's own God-given *portion*, not "a serving" (so NKJV), so that *bread* and *portion* (NASB) are parallel and virtually synonymous, reflecting the previous consistent use of *ḥēleq* in Qoheleth's argument (cf. 3:22; 5:18; 9:6, 9; n. 29).

[467] Seow argues persuasively that only one comparison is intended (*Ecclesiastes*, 337) and not two, as in NIV, NKJV, or NASB: A contextual wordplay employs the imagery of the inscrutable *wind* (*rûaḥ*) in 11:4, as an appropriate and intended analogy for the *breath* of life (*rûaḥ*) in 11:5 (ibid.) to portray the inscrutable creative work of God.

[468] This recurrence of *kāšēr* ("succeed," cf. 10:10b; n. 436) links mankind's success in inscrutable the work of God with mankind's obedience in mediating

in *the work of God.* Yes,[469] the *light is sweet,* and it is *good* to experience life (11:7),[470] so *however*[471] *many years a man may live, let him enjoy them all but let him remember*[472] *the days of darkness* (11:8a, NIV), *for*[473] *they will be many—all that is* to come *is vanity*

God's creative activity (cf. 11:5) in the opportunities He provides:

> [I]t is God who sovereignly opens doors of opportunity for us. When we ask for wisdom, He gives it through the channels He has established for our benefit....He brings to successful completion those of our plans that are within His sovereign will....He utilizes the circumstances and the very process of decision making to change our character and bring us to maturity....He blesses our obedience...and produces His...fruit in our lives....He works through our decisions to accomplish His purposes.... [Garry Friesen, *Decision Making and the Will of God* (Portland: Multnomah Press, 1980), 253]

[469] The opening *waw* bears an affirmative sense in light of the preceding uncertainty over what will turn out to be *good* (11:6).

[470] Lit. "And *sweet* [is] the light and *good* for the eyes to see the sun." The phrase *see the sun* derives its meaning from 6:5, where it is a figure for "experiencing life." Qoheleth is affirming the *good* of enjoying life.

[471] Cf. NIV. The sense of this clause does not cohere very well in NKJV or NASB. The opening *kî 'im* (11:8a) cannot bear its usual **exceptive** sense ("unless"), as in 3:12b; 5:11b; and 8:15 (see Murphy, *Ecclesiastes*, 112 [fn. 8.a]). Since the jussives *let him enjoy* and *let him remember* in 11:8 follow logically from 11:7 (cf. n. 460), the opening *kî* is most likely **inferential** ("so" or "thus," ignored by NIV) and the interposed *'im* cannot be merely **contingent** ("if," so NKJV, NASB), but is more plausibly **concessive** (cf. NIV, NRSV): "So, however [whether, even if] many years a man may live...."

[472] The *waw* between *let him enjoy* and *let him remember* is clearly adversative, as the *days of darkness* allude to future adversity and disappointment (11:8, cf. 5:17, n. 233) in contrast to *light* and *sun* in 11:7. This clause is thus designed to warn the reader that full enjoyment of life depends on sobering disillusionment to refocus the soul's perspective in life. While these *days of darkness* may seem to threaten mankind's fulfillment, to honestly reckon with such "days" permits his heart to be edified by mourning (7:1-4; nn. 258, 269). Larry Crabb describes this "advantage" in honestly facing our disillusionment (*Shattered Dreams*, 35):

> Shattered dreams destroy false expectations....They help us discover true hope. We need the help of shattered dreams to put us in touch with what we most long for, to create a felt appetite for better dreams. And living for the better dreams generates a new, unfamiliar feeling that we eventually recognize as joy.

This notion of reckoning with the *days of darkness* serves to introduce the final pericope, which challenges the *young man* to *remember* God when he acts on the desires of his heart, *before* it is too late (11:9-12:7).

[473] The opening *kî* retains its standard causal sense ("for"): The urgency of enjoying *all* the *years* a man has to live (11:8a) is explained by impending adversity; that is, it is foolish to forgo present *good* (11:7) in favor of what is to come, which is *vanity,* **because** the *days of darkness will be many* (11:8b). This sense of futility in "holding back" one's investment for future opportunity provides a fitting summary appraisal for 11:1-6 but also supplies the pretext for the concluding

(11:8b).[474]

2. Opportune Investment in View of Death's Finality (11:9–12:7)

The prospect that *good* would be replaced by *vanity* during future *days of darkness* (11:7-8) was intended to underscore the urgency of investing in the work of God before it was too late. Consequently, Qoheleth's logic in this final pericope of the argument is addressed to the *young man:* The reader's success as an agent of God would depend on how soon he anticipated these *days of darkness.*[475] The sooner he frees his heart from disillusionment (11:10) over the failure of selfish ambition and finally views himself as an agent of the Creator the sooner he will enjoy life in the opportunities God provides to accomplish His work (11:1-8). If he realizes that God will judge **how** he pursues those opportunities (11:9) he will *remember* his *Creator* (12:1a) *before* the *difficult days* leave him in *darkness*, bereft of any further purpose in life (12:1b-7).

The textual design consists of a chain of seven volitives or commands (11:9-12:1a) followed by a cluster of word pictures that portray how physical debility and death foreclose all further opportunity to heed those commands (12:1b-7). The boundary imperatives *rejoice* and *remember* are repeated from 11:8b and tagged with the same literary marker to encompass all the other volitives in 11:9-12:1a.[476]

---

pericope, in which the same sense of foreboding is signified by the repeated "before" (12:1, 2, 6, cf. n. 479, below). Thus, maximum satisfaction in life depends on mankind's present enjoyment of the *good* and acceptance of the *bad* (n. 464): Since the "bad" days *will be many* (11:8b), the opportunity to be truly fulfilled will dry up sooner than we think. This accords with the ample NT teaching that encourages the reader to take full advantage of present resources and opportunity (cf. e.g., Luke 9:59-62; 16:1-13; 19:12-26).

[474] This warning refers to the eventual lack of any "good" (11:6b-7, n. 470) in the future *days of darkness*, when adversity will become insurmountable (11:8a), as described in detail in 12:1b-7. The *vanity* thus consists in the ultimate loss of all remaining opportunity to realize one's created *purpose* in the work of God (cf. 12:1b, n. 488 below).

[475] The logic turns on a subtle shift in the meaning of *darkness*. Expositions that read only a single nuance to *darkness* miss the *double entendre* meant to evoke a response from the young man: to reckon with his present "darkness" (disillusionment, vexation) before he is incapacitated by future "darkness" (infirmity and death) and can no longer *rejoice* (11:9). The *darkness* in 11:8b thus portends both the *darkness* of vexation over life's adversity in 11:10 (cf. 5:17) and the *darkness* of inexorable debility and death in 12:2.

[476] *See* n. 104. The marker *in the days of your youth* is repeated at the beginning and the end of the sequence (11:9a, 12:1a) and thus applies to all the enclosed imperatives.

While these commands are joined by the same repeating conjunction,[477] the intended force of each conjunction must be adduced from Qoheleth's logic.[478] The word pictures of 12:1b-7 are then grouped into three prepositional clauses[479] to emphasize for the *young man* the urgency of heeding the preceding commands.

This conclusion to the argument comprises the final enjoyment pericope, culminating the cumulative wisdom of his preceding reflections.[480] The series of commands is to be observed together as a logically related "set": The *young man* is encouraged to *rejoice in* his *youth* (11:9a)[481] *and* follow his heart's desires in whatever he sees (11:9b)[482] *but* he is to *know that for all these God will bring* him *into judgment* (11:9c).[483]

---

[477] Seven consecutive clauses are initiated by seven distinct volitives, joined in turn by the repeating particle w^{e-}: *Rejoice… let (…) gladden… walk… know… remove… purge… remember…* (11:9-12:1a).

[478] The sequence should read: *and… and… but…*[11:9]; *therefore… and… (for…)* [11:10]; *and…*[12:1]. The third conjunction ("but") introduces a qualification (Longman, *Ecclesiastes*, 259 [fn. 29]) which leads in turn to a **purpose** or **result** clause ("therefore…" or "so…") that governs the last three imperatives. A parenthetical **motive** clause ("for…," 11:10b) explains why the *young man* should heed these imperatives *in the days of* his *youth* (n. 476).

[479] The same construction '*ad 'ašer* ("until that" = *before*) introduces each of the main clauses of this last pericope (cf. NASB, NIV; Longman, *Ecclesiastes*, 262). The first of these (12:1b) reintroduces the theme of *darkness* to set the tone for 12:2-7 (cf. n. 475). The next (12:2-5) depicts an impending state of infirmity that is further characterized as *the day when* his vital functions inevitably wane. The last (12:6-7) includes four metaphors for death, depicting how it irrevocably forecloses all opportunity (cf. 8:8).

[480] This applies especially to the enjoyment pericopae 5:18-20; 7:8-10; 8:12-13; 9:4-10; and 11:1-8.

[481] The parallel volitives in 11:9a—*rejoice* and *let your heart make you glad* (cf. n. 25)—are realized by following the *ways of your heart* (11:9b), which is the seat of human passion (cf. 9:5-6; n. 395).

[482] The imperative *walk* (*halak*) governs two prepositional phrases—*in the ways of your heart* and *in the sight of your eyes,* in effect a *hendiadys*—yielding the sense "follow your heart's desires in whatever you see." The danger that this imperative will be read as a license to indulge in unrestrained hedonism is promptly mitigated by the ensuing qualification, introduced by an adversative *waw* (11:9c, n. 478).

[483] The *young man* is to "know" *that for all these God will bring…judgment* in the same sense that *a wise heart* "knows" *judgment* (8:5b): because *for every purpose there is…judgment* (8:6a, cf. nn. 338, 343). The antecedent of the construction *for all these* is *your heart's desires* (n. 482). The qualification introduced here thus reminds the would-be wise *young man* to remain aware as he pursues his *heart's desires* that his choices as a prospective agent of God will be *judged* by their conformity with *every purpose* of God: As long as he pursues *all these* passions

320

Therefore,[484] as he pursues his desires he should remove any *vexation* he may harbor in his *heart and* purge any *evil* from his *flesh* (11:10a)[485]—for youthful vitality is *fleeting*[486] (11:10b); and he should *remember*[487] his *Creator* (12:1a), *before* he is eventually "decommissioned" as an **agent** of the Creator, as depicted in metaphor by the concluding sequence of figures (12:1b-7).

Opportune stewardship of one's life from the Creator thus entails heeding all these imperatives (11:9-12:1a) as **early** in life as possible, *before* the *difficult days come when* we find no further

---

while remaining alert to the opportunities God provides to invest his God-given portion in the work of God (11:1-8, cf. n. 466 and related text) he should be confident that he will receive God's favor in the judgment of his works (cf. 9:1b, 4-10; nn. 390, 403). See also 1 Cor 3:11-15; 2 Cor 5:10. The same notion of judgment was implied by Qoheleth in Eccl 8:12b-13, where he associated a person's ultimate "well-being" with whether they *fear before God* (n. 366). In light of this *judgment*, the same sense of prudent "awareness" thus inheres in the ensuing mandate to *remember your Creator* (12:1, n. 487 below) and will also carry over into the frame narrator's recapitulation of *all* that *has been heard* in 12:12-14.

[484] The *waw* here conveys the force of intended purpose or result in light of the preceding three volitives (n. 478).

[485] The terms *remove vexation* (NASB) and *put away evil* are parallel. *Vexation* denotes disillusionment over ambitious dreams that have been frustrated by adversity (cf. 5:17; 7:8-10; nn. 39, 233, 286, 474); *evil* refers to the entrenched bitterness of selfish ambition (Eccl 4-6); and both must be "put away" (cf. Eph 4:26, 31) if God's agent is to *succeed* in the work of God (11:5-6, cf. n. 468).

[486] So NASB. This may be one instance of *hebel* that bears the primary nuance of *fleeting*, although there is also a sense in which youth is *futile*. The *hapax šaḥărûth* ("blackness") probably denotes youthful black hair, so the construction "childhood and blackness" may be a *hendiadys*, "youthful vitality," and the subsequent allusion to white hair in 12:5 in the metaphor of *almond blossoms* may refer to the inevitable loss of such vitality in old age. The young man is therefore urged to "put away" his vexation *in the days of your youth* and thereby release his heart's desires to align with the Creator's purposes (11:9, n. 483) as early as possible, i.e. while he still has the vitality to fulfill those purposes.

[487] When the *young man* "knows" that *God will bring* him *into judgment* (11:9c) and that he has precious little time (11:10, n. 486) to do works that God will judge favorably he will more likely *remember* ($z^e k\bar{o}r$, "consider" or "reckon with") his *Creator* (cf. 6:10). So the steward who *remembers* God (whose work allows both *prosperity* and *adversity*, cf. 7:13-14) will more readily *remove* vexation from his heart in the face of adversity and fulfill the purposes of God in pursuing his desires (n. 483): He will joyfully invest his portion in God-given opportunities (11:1-8) and thus reap lasting *remembrance* and *reward* in the work of God (cf. 9:5-6; n. 397), securing (ironically) the lasting legacy he has been seeking unsuccessfully in all his own labor (2:16; cf. n. 136).

purpose[488] in the gloomy life that remains (12:1b); *before* all sources of *light are darkened* and life no longer has any meaning (12:2).[489] These *difficult days* are further described as a time when[490] one is bereft of stamina and stature, teeth no longer chew, vision fails (12:3),[491] and sounds can no longer be distinguished (12:4)[492]—indeed, *when* one is totally incapacitated by aging (12:5a, b)[493]—for mankind will inevitably go to his *eternal home*,

---

[488] Most translations render *ḥēpheṣ* (12:1b) as "pleasure" or "delight" (cp. Ps 37:4). This nuance certainly fits the motif of enjoyment in 11:8-9 but it misses the broader sense of "purpose" that Qoheleth intends in the context of the reader's investment in the work of the Creator (cf. 11:5-6; 12:1-7): Given that mankind's intended *purpose* in life is to be found in the *purposes* of God (3:1, 17; 8:6a; n. 44), the earlier in life the reader *remembers* his *Creator*, the more time he has to invest his labor in order to realize those purposes (12:1).

[489] So NASB (NKJV misconstrues the intended sense of 12:2). If *light* and *see the sun* in 11:7a are figures for receiving the benefits of life (n. 470), then *darkening* of *light* from the *sun* and the lesser light sources (12:2a) signifies a **waning** of meaningful life. The metaphor continues in 12:2b, depicting the future prospect of a debilitated person who tries in vain to *see the sun*, since the *clouds* "keep returning" *after the rain* of adversity (cf. 8:6b). (Here, the *waw* consecutive pf. with *šûb* ["return"] is most likely a "habitual" imperfect, cf. Chisholm, *From Exegesis to Exposition*, 99).

[490] The phrase *in the day when* (12:3a) is followed by a sequence of *waw* consecutive pf. verbs that link the metaphors in 12:3-4 as simple future events (ibid., 100)—the impending debilitating consequences of aging. Thus, while the specific referents of these metaphors are controversial (Michael V. Fox, "Aging and Death in Qoheleth 12," reprinted in Zuck [ed.], *Reflecting with Solomon*, 381-99), they all portend the young man's (cf. 12:1) future "day" of incapacitation when all physiological functions inexorably wane.

[491] *The keepers of the house tremble* implies frail vulnerability, while *the strong men stoop* (NIV) denotes the loss of stature with age. The figures for chewing and sight signify the inexorable loss of physiological function.

[492] The four metaphors in 12:4 all relate to hearing; perhaps deafness incapacitates the elderly even more than blindness. The *doors on the street are shut* (NASB) should be read from the perspective of one who is inside and not outside; that is, normally audible *street* sounds, like *grinding*, can no longer be heard from behind the *shut doors*. Even a delicate sound like a *bird's* song will startle one as the hearing fails and all sounds (*the daughters of song*, NASB) *are brought low* (muted) and thus hard to distinguish.

[493] An opening emphatic *gam* ("indeed") governs a sequence of figures symbolizing total incapacitation; these figures are associated with *almond tree blossoms* (i.e., the *white hair* of old age, cf. n. 486) but their meaning is widely debated (cf. Fox, ibid.; Longman, *Ecclesiastes*, 265-66, 272). They all seem to portray some aspect of *paralysis:* The fear of heights and of the risks of traveling suggests paralysis of the *will;* the grasshopper dragging seems to portray *physical* paralysis; and if the caperberry is an aphrodisiac (cf. ibid., 272), then its loss of potency is a figure for *sexual* paralysis, perhaps the most appropriate figure of all to symbolize the final loss of one's capacity to act and enjoy life (cf. 1 Kgs 1:2-4; 2 Sam 16:21-23).

leaving those who remain behind to mourn (12:5c).[494] We should thus *remember* our *Creator before* we "break" as God's treasured instrument (12:6), our *dust returns to the earth*, and our *spirit returns to God*[495] *who gave it* (12:7).

The intent of this "collage" of metaphors is clarified by the two vantage points from which they are observed. The figures in 12:2-5 are visualized from the perspective of the young man seeking satisfaction in life,[496] while those in 12:6-7 reflect the view of his Creator, who has invested His stewards with great worth.[497] One can picture Qoheleth as Solomon in deep regret over the many wasted years when he failed to *remember* his *Creator*, now apprising his readers of how little time is truly left for them to enjoy life **and** exploit the opportunities that God presents in that life to fulfill His purposes.[498] By depicting how all future enjoyment and opportunity in life is so irrevocably foreclosed by debility and death, Qoheleth aims to crystallize our commitment to serve God's purposes as co-regents before we squander all our opportunity.[499]

---

[494] The *mourners* prefigure the steward's loss of earthly community at his death, while *his eternal home* is his intended destiny—to be in spiritual communion with his Creator (12:7; cf. n. 189).

[495] Reference to God as *Elohim* (cf. Gen 1) reflects mankind's nature and purpose as created in God's image.

[496] The figures in 12:2-5 are particularly persuasive from the perspective of the young man who stands to lose all further opportunity to fulfill his *purpose* in life (12:1b, n. 488); once this captures his attention, the figures in 12:6-7 shift the focus to the vantage point of *his Creator*.

[497] These metaphors reflect God's stake in what He created (cf. Job 10:3-13)— the first two signify mankind's **imputed** value to God (*silver* and *gold*), while the last two portray his **functional** utility in God's eyes. Such insight into God's vested interest should reaffirm the steward's hope of God's favor (9:4-10, cf. n. 400) and motivate him to realize his worth before he returns to God for his works to be judged (12:5b, 7b, cf. 11:9b; 12:14). Mankind's calling as a created "investment" is epitomized by Eph 2:10, "For we are His workmanship, created in Christ Jesus for good works, which God prepared beforehand that we should walk in them.

[498] Only an abiding awareness of the Creator's prerogatives (cf. nn. 483, 487) can ultimately sustain the incentive that one needs to "give a good account of his stewardship" (3:15, cf. n. 179; and below). M. Scott Peck's classic *The Road Less Traveled* (New York: Simon & Schuster, 1978) affords good insight into the connection between present enjoyment and provident awareness of the future in the prudent use of our resources. "To be organized and efficient, to live wisely, we must daily delay gratification and keep an eye on the future; yet to live joyously we must also possess the capacity...to live in the present and act spontaneously" (ibid., 64). Although not a Christian at the time, Peck remarkably acknowledged the critical constraint of "original sin" and our consequent need to recognize and respond to divine grace in order to make the most of these choices (ibid., 260-311).

499 This key strategic intent behind 11:9-12:7 is also the central feature of the parable of the unjust steward (Luke 16:1-13). The starting premise of the parable is that the steward is responsible to the master for administering his resources but has been squandering them (16:1). When the steward is judged unworthy and asked to account for his stewardship (Luke 16:2), he shrewdly takes stock of the resources available to him and the limited time he has to make the best of them before he is "decommissioned" by his master (16:3)—this is precisely what Qoheleth hopes his readers will do: The *young man* Qoheleth addresses may also have squandered a large portion of *his* resources (cf. Eccl 10:11-20) and consequently also need a "wake up call." It is this sense of impending termination of all opportunity to realize the master's purposes that especially resonates between the two passages—both emphasize the high stakes of failing to remain keenly aware of one's intended role as steward of the master's resources. When the shrewd steward "remembered" that his master's purpose was to reap dividends from invested resources, he immediately determined to settle accounts with a view to his future reward (Luke 16:4-7). In light of the coming *days of darkness* (11:8, cf. 12:2), Qoheleth's reader is likewise to *remember* his *Creator* and reckon early that his Master will judge his stewardship; he is to invest his God-given portion before he too has no further "purpose" as God's agent (Eccl 11:9-12:1, n. 488).

Epilogue

AUTHENTICATION

Words of Truth & Words of Purpose

Qoheleth's Authoritative Words of Wisdom (12:8-14)[500]

By describing how meticulously Qoheleth composed his work to convey God's truth for a specific purpose, **the frame narrator authenticates Qoheleth's instruction as accurate and reliable, because—like all true wisdom—it is inspired by God,** *so that students of wisdom might submit to Qoheleth's instruction to fear God and obey His commands and thereby inherit their intended legacy in the work of God.*

The epilogue can be distinguished from the body of the argument by the reemergence of the frame narrator at 12:8[501] after the conclusion of Qoheleth's observations and reflections (1:12-12:7). This reintroduction reminds the reader of the governing literary strategy, to cite Qoheleth's unprecedented wisdom and life experience as an *a fortiori* argument for the *futility* of all self-sufficient strategies to gain an advantage in life, the primary communicative intent of Eccl 1-6.[502] The text of the epilogue then consists of two pericopae, each initiated by the same opening marker[503] with a conspicuous shift to direct address ("my son") at 12:12.[504] The first pericope authenticates Qoheleth's textual arrangement of collected proverbs and reflections (12:9-11). This in turn warrants the concluding exhortation in the second pericope, which endorses Qoheleth's teaching as superior guidance for the student of wisdom (12:12-14).

Since Qoheleth's literary style and bold cynicism may have seemed out of place compared with other OT wisdom,[505] his readers

---

[500] This section draws significantly from the author's previous paper, "Words of Truth and Words of Purpose," delivered in Nov 2006 at the annual meeting of the Evangelical Theological Society (www.21stcenturypress.com/wisdom.htm).

[501] Some expositors assign 12:8 to the preceding text by *inclusio* with 1:2; however, the construction *vanity of vanities*, penned by the frame narrator, is best viewed as the opening marker for both the prologue and the epilogue—v. 12:8 initiates the **epilogue**, just as v. 1:2 initiates the **prologue** (not the main text, 1:12-12:7).

[502] *See* n. 124.

[503] The opening $w^e y \bar{o} th \bar{e} r$ in both 12:9 and 12:12 (n. 105) has a mildly adversative thrust ("but besides…").

[504] This view of the structure of the epilogue thus varies from that of those expositors who distinguish 12:13-14 as separate from 12:9-12 (cf. nn. 7, 11).

[505] *See* nn. 2, 4-7, 11 and related text in the Overview of Ecclesiastes.

would need some assurance that his teaching was inspired and his reflections worthy of their attention. The main thrust of the argument from Eccl 7 to 12 was to infer from Qoheleth's further reflections on *disillusionment in adversity* that life **does** have "purpose" after all, but only when lived in the *fear of God* ,as the frame narrator will confirm (12:13-14). Only the reader who along with Qoheleth had first faced his own disillusionment (12:8) and had honestly mourned the inadequacy of human self-sufficiency (Eccl 7:1-14) would then be receptive to Qoheleth's wisdom in Eccl 7:15-12:7, by which he *taught the people* (12:9) how to accept and enjoy their God-given portion and thus bring success in the inscrutable work of God (11:5-8, cf. 10:10b).

Thus, while this final section of the book may initially strike the reader as an awkward appendix to the argument it actually serves the crucial objective of validating the book's integrity and design.[506] That is, the frame narrator argues to convince the student of wisdom (*my son,* cf. 12:12) that Qoheleth's *words of the wise* were both *words of truth* and *words of purpose:* They were a *source of wisdom* so reliable (12:9-11) that the student of wisdom who aspires to a lasting legacy could confidently appropriate the *principal object lessons* of Qoheleth's "exercise in futility"[507]— object lessons developed in the enjoyment pericopae and now distilled by the frame narrator (12:12-14): *Fear God and keep His commandments.*

---

[506] *See* n. 13. Some expositors view the book as a "patchwork quilt" of miscellaneous proverbs and reflections (n. 5) to be used like a jar of assorted nuts and bolts to make impromptu repairs. If this were true it would contradict the frame narrator's attestation (12:9-14) to Qoheleth's unified and cohesive textual composition and even cast doubt on his **own** inspiration. Why then does the frame narrator defer such crucial authentication to the end of the book? If, as I have argued, Qoheleth's target audience is the inexperienced "student of wisdom" (n. 456), it makes sense for the frame narrator to wait until this potential steward has been fully persuaded to *fear God* and submit to His inscrutable purposes (cf. 11:9-12:1) before authenticating Qoheleth's words—only then would the student be concerned enough to verify their reliability and exploit their wisdom in order to maximize his own success in the work of God (cf. 11:1-8).

[507] Longman (*Ecclesiastes*, 38) insists that the frame narrator cited Qoheleth's teaching as *a foil* for "traditional" wisdom, which he then summarized in the final two verses (12:13-14) as a **correction** to Qoheleth's repeated inferences of futility. However, see nn. 7, 11 and the arguments below supporting the frame narrator's affirmations as an actual **validation** of Qoheleth's inferences of the futility of a self-determined search for meaning in one's labor.

A. Qoheleth's Reliability: *Inspired Words of the Wise* (12:8-11)

The frame narrator's "closing signature" at 12:8 clearly mirrors the "greeting" at 1:2 and reintroduces the opening theme of *futility* as the appropriate backdrop for the frame narrator's authentication of Qoheleth's[508] wisdom in 12:9-14: Not only did Qoheleth's proclamation of the futility of self-sufficiency epitomize his great wisdom (12:8), but he also used his wisdom to teach the people what he had learned in reflecting on life (12:9a);[509] He meticulously examined and set in order many proverbs (12:9b).[510] He looked for "words of purpose"[511] and to this end he wrote "words of truth" accurately (12:10);[512] his words were—like all "words of wise men"—designed to serve God's preordained purposes for the student of wisdom

---

[508] The use of the definite article with *Qoheleth* only in 12:8 seems designed to underscore his role for the reader (see n. 120).

[509] The sense is that Qoheleth's wisdom did not just benefit himself, thus giving the opening particle an adversative thrust (n. 502), "*But* besides being wise, Qoheleth also taught the people [his] knowledge...."

[510] The first of three Piel verbs here, *'āzān* is usually translated "hear, listen to" or "weigh, prove" (Longman, *Ecclesiastes*, 275 [fn. 62]; cp. the sense of the verbs *bārar*, n. 187; and *bûr*, n. 382). The context suggests the sense of an "audition": Qoheleth "listened to" (*'izzēn*) and *searched out* (*hiqqēr*) many proverbs and he *set in order* (*tiqqēn*) those that best suited his strategic intent in writing the book. If we read the first two verbs as a *hendiadys* (cf. NET fn. on 12:9), then Qoheleth "meticulously examined" his collected proverbs and "arranged" them in just the right way to yield "words of purpose" as he wrote "words of truth" (12:10).

[511] It is important to reiterate here that translations of Eccl often misconstrue the sense intended for *ḥēpheṣ* (n. 44), now seen here (12:10) in the genitive form ("of purpose"). The usual OT sense for *ḥēpheṣ* of "delight" (or "matter") does not fit the contexts of vv. 3:1, 17, or 8:6, which strongly imply that *ḥēpheṣ* refers to God's "purpose". Moreover, in the near context of the final pericope of Qoheleth's argument (11:9-12:7) the reader is urged to *remember your Creator*, for the time in life will come when he has no further *ḥēpheṣ* ("purpose," 12:1, n. 488), implying that there is *ḥēpheṣ* in life after all to replace the universal *hebel* ("vanity, futility") that Qoheleth had seen during his unparalleled empirical investigation (Eccl 1-6). Hence, the best sense in 12:10-11 is that the Qoheleth produced "words of purpose" (*dibrê ḥēpheṣ*) by accurately selecting "words of truth" (*dibrê 'ĕmeth*) from collections of the "words of wise men" (*dibrê ḥăkāmîm*).

[512] While Longman infers that "Qohelet sought [but failed] to write *words of truth*" (*Ecclesiastes*, 278, note 65, italics his), Bartholomew argues more plausibly for the reading "and he wrote" rather than "and he sought to write" (*Reading Ecclesiastes*, 161-2). The frame narrator is in fact **attesting** Qoheleth's meticulous selection and arrangement of proverbs (12:9b) as a reliable source of *truth* to achieve his intended *purpose* in the student of wisdom (12:10, n. 511).

(12:11a): Like *goads* these *words* provide direction and spur one to action;[513] their "great collections" make one sturdy and dependable, like *firmly embedded nails*.[514] Since the accuracy and reliability of Qoheleth's *words of truth* was guaranteed by the inspiration of *one Shepherd* (12:11b),[515] the frame narrator can now confidently recommend these words to his "son," so that they may become "words of purpose" in his own life as a student of wisdom (12:12-14).

B. Qoheleth's Refrain: *Fear God, Obey His Commands* (12:12-14)

With the repeated opening marker[516] the frame narrator now turns directly to the student of wisdom ("my son") and first warns him not to trust knowledge derived from sources other than the *words of the wise*—besides these,[517] there is no end to the many books that are written (12:12a), so incessantly scrutinizing such books for

---

[513] The imagery of *goads* portrays Qoheleth's readers as sheep lacking guidance and motivation—such was provided by his "pointed" imperatives (cf. esp. 9:7-10; 11:1-12:1).

[514] The imagery of nails denotes strength and stability and depicts the students of wisdom as buildings under construction, a fitting analogy for spiritual edification. The unique phrase "masters of collections" (cf. Murphy, *Ecclesiastes*, 124 [fn. 11.d]) may be idiomatic for "great collections." The chiastic parallel of this phrase with "words of the wise" in 12:11 (ibid.) suggests that the author was denoting "great collections" of "words of wise men." Thus, Qoheleth's meticulous arrangement of proverbs (12:9) had the same value as all "great collections" of wisdom literature—they are "like firmly embedded nails" (NIV).

[515] While the phrase "given by one Shepherd" has no specific antecedent (Longman, *Ecclesiastes*, 279), the parallelism of "words of purpose," "words of truth," "words of the wise", and their "great collections" in 12:10-11 (nn. 511, 514) suggests that all these "words" were "given by one Shepherd." This amounts to claiming that Qoheleth's wisdom was inspired by God (*contra* Longman, ibid., 279-281), which is comparable to other key Scriptural affirmations of divine inspiration (cf. Matt 5:18; 1 Cor 2:6-13; 2 Tim 3:16-17; 2 Pet 1:20-21).

[516] *See* n. 504.

[517] Lit. "But besides these, my son, beware..." (cf. NASB). The referent of "these" is the "great collections" of "words of the wise" in 12:11 (n. 514). The phrase implies a sharp dichotomy in accuracy and reliability between the "great collections" of "words given by one Shepherd" (like the words of Qoheleth, 12:9-10) and other books that were **not** thus inspired. The frame narrator's "son" is analogous to Qoheleth's "young man" (11:9) and represents all students of wisdom who need reliable truth to serve well as God's chosen agents.

life's answers will only "wear you out"[518] (12:12b). The author therefore concludes by recapping for his student "all he had heard" from Qoheleth (12:13a).[519] That is, since inspired words of the wise are the only reliable source of truth and guidance toward a meaningful life (12:9-11), the only sane approach to life is to heed Qoheleth's wisdom, all distilled into a single instruction: *Fear God and keep his commandments* (12:13b).

While the frame narrator's exhortation to *fear God* clearly denotes the same sense intended by Qoheleth,[520] some argue that the injunction *keep his commandments* is not consistent with Qoheleth's theology.[521] However, a review of Qoheleth's instruction on submission to authority suggests otherwise: While his readers were not literally enjoined to keep God's commandments they **were** to keep the king's commandment (8:5a; cf. 8:2a), which would exemplify their loyalty to God; i.e., to obey the king **was** to submit to God.[522] Furthermore, the incentive Qoheleth provides to obey the **king** (8:5b-6a) is the same incentive the frame narrator offers his "son" to submit to **God** (12:14): the awareness of impending judgment (cf. also 3:15b, 17; 11:9c).

---

[518] Lit. "and much study wearies the flesh." The opening particle w^{e-} is most likely inferential ("so"). The idea is that truth can never be "nailed down" (cf. 12:11) by non-inspired books, *so* the student who studies them will always have lingering doubt about their reliability and consequent need to keep studying in a futile attempt to derive the truth with certainty. This is the endless task of human philosophy and it reflects Qoheleth's own empirical but empty search—to "seek an explanation" (cf. 7:23-25)—of the meaning of life.

[519] The conclusion is introduced by the phrase (lit.) "The final word, all has been heard." The term *heard* most likely refers to the "son" who has "heard" all the truth that Qoheleth taught (12:12), even though it was the words Qoheleth *wrote* that the frame narrator had attested as true (12:10). In any case the text that follows (12:13b) is a **synopsis** of this truth, not a **correction** appended by the frame narrator (n. 507).

[520] The *fear of God* involves recognition of His sovereignty over all of creation, including all men's deeds and all the circumstances of life (3:11-15). It implies receptivity to God's word as a prerequisite for success in the *work of your hands* (5:6b-7). Only by *fearing God* can man overcome the consequences of sin to benefit from God's wisdom (7:16-20, 26) and "do well" before God (8:12b-13).

[521] Cf. Longman, *Ecclesiastes*, 282; Seow, *Ecclesiastes*, 394-5.

[522] Qoheleth had made it clear that obedience to the king was predicated on allegiance to God (8:2), so there is an implied parallel between God and the king (cf. nn. 44, 335, 337, 340): Since God, like the king, also "does whatever he pleases" (8:3), even more does it behoove the reader to also "watch *His* mouth" (cf. 8:2a, lit.) and "keep *His* commandments" (cf. 8:5a).

Therefore, the frame narrator's final injunction is best read as epitomizing Qoheleth's own teleology or "final" purpose: The awareness that mankind will one day have to reckon with God's judgment should compel us to *remember* our *Creator* (12:1); i.e., to *fear God* and *keep his commandments*. This is hardly the notion of blind obedience to fixed statutes or commandments but rather of fulfilling God's inscrutable purposes—whatever He pleases,[523] "for this is the whole of man" (12:13b):[524] We are commissioned as God's chosen agents to accomplish His inscrutable purposes. God will thus bring all our works to light, whether good or bad, to judge how well we—His agents—have fulfilled His purposes, in order to bestow His favor as a legacy for remaining obedient and account-able for our portion in these purposes (12:14).[525]

---

[523] It is tempting to infer from the phrase *keep his commandments* that the frame narrator is an ardent advocate of faithful obedience to the requisites of the Mosaic law (so Longman, *Ecclesiastes*, 282; Whybray, *Ecclesiastes*, 173). Yet the only other instance of the phrase *keep his commandment* in Eccl (8:5a) has nothing to do with Moses' law but is rather an object lesson regarding the king's unpredictable, unimpeachable whim (cf. 8:3b, n. 522). Qoheleth also emphasized near the end of his argument that we *do not know* what God is doing (cf. 11:1-6, esp. 11:5), so it is more plausible that the frame narrator used the term *miṣvâ* to refer to the unpredictable purposes of God, just as Qoheleth did in 8:5 with reference to the king (i.e., "your wish is my command"). Thus, God's "commands" like those of the king are unpredictable and newly received each day, and the mandate to *keep his commands* is invoked by mankind's ironic tendency to resist God's purposes, even though submission to authority is the wisest response in light of *judgment* (cf. 8:1-8; 10:4, 20 and related notes).

[524] The meaning of "this" (12:13b) is informed by Qoheleth's prior reflections on mankind's created image: Mankind is irrevocably named by God (cf. 6:10a) and valued (cf. 12:6-7) as His comissioned agent (cf. 1:13; 3:10-15). One's whole purpose as God's agent is therefore to accept his God-given portion—his intended work and legacy from God (5:18-20; cf. 9:1-10)—rather than contending for a different lot in life (cf. 6:10b).

[525] The sense is that God will judge all the works of man in accordance with His purposes (cf. 8:12b-13; 11:9c; nn. 345, 483). However, since God's agents cannot predict which of their works will meet with good outcomes (6:12; 11:2b, 6b) that serve God's purposes (3:1-13; 8:16-9:1; 11:5) they face the challenge of how to invest their God-given portion. Qoheleth had previously claimed that God already favors works that stem from one's God-given portion (9:7-10); it is now clear that the steward need not concern himself with the outcomes but with whether the works themselves are bad or good. It is the steward's works that determine judgment, with no punishment in view other than the absence of favor for "bad" works done in this life (cf. 1 Cor 3:12-14; Eph 2:10; 2 Cor 5:10).

POSTSCRIPT

The "Significance" of Ecclesiastes

Toward a Canonical Theology of "Human Agency"

A Personal Note

As I look back on life at the age of 58, it is now clearer to me how I have spent the vast majority of my life in the self-sufficient pursuit of a lasting legacy. Like Qoheleth, I shudder to think of all those whom I have "oppressed" in my striving for success and a "lasting reputation" or "remembrance." What is even more distressing to me, however, is that you would think that a man who began his in-depth study of the book of Ecclesiastes in seminary 27 years ago should have long since "gotten it right." Sadly, my choices in life continue to revert to the self-sufficient disposition so glorified by my culture[526] with its attendant "vexation," and I again find myself wondering how low I will go before I am so desperate for God that nothing else matters (cf. Psalm 42:1-2).

Qoheleth's answer to such a disposition is severe and decisive: The self-sufficient life is doomed to disillusionment and despair (Eccl 2-6). But God meets us at our point of need by permitting our own ambitious schemes to be frustrated as long and as frequently as it takes to instill within us the fear of God (3:14). If we react to disappointment by redoubling our efforts to achieve success we will only reap the oppression we sow (4:1-16). But if we are broken by disillusionment over the inevitable failure of ambitious schemes (4:1-6:12) we can wisely mourn the futility of our self-sufficiency (7:1-14), fear God (7:15-8:15), and enjoy the opportunities God gives us to invest our God-given resources in God's inscrutable work (9:4-10; 11:1-12:1).

These concepts are not difficult for me to grasp. But the notion of *fearing God*—deferring to His unpredictable will and depending on His inscrutable plans for fulfillment and satisfaction that only become clear in retrospect—too often seems like abandoning myself and my future to His whim. I have often asked, What can I show for all the time and energy I have expended since yesterday? (cf. Eccl 4:8b). This is hardly a man who does *not dwell unduly on the days of his life* (5:20). Consequently, even though I may "fear God" one day I may well revert the next day to the same self-sufficiency and

---

[526] A quintessential portrait of such glorified self-sufficiency can be found in the familiar poem *Invictus* by William Ernest Henley, appropriately quoted in Charles Swindoll's exposition of Ecclesiastes, *Living on the Ragged Edge: Coming to Terms with Reality* (New York: Bantam Books, 1985), 274.

then fall into the same predicaments. If I want to maintain the fear of God from one day to the next I find myself facing the same quandary that confronted the wandering Israelites: Do I accept my "portion" of just enough "manna" today to sustain me as I follow God's lead or do I yearn again in my own strength for something that seems at the time to promise more lasting fulfillment?[527]

It has not been unusual for me, especially recently, to be editing one portion or another of this commentary, deep in concentration, only to hear Qoheleth calling to me out of his own experience as a fellow self-reliant man striving to achieve success—"Hey, I'm talking to **you**." What is interesting about these "epiphanies" is that I never feel shamed by Qoheleth. Exposed as a "contender" with God (cf. Eccl 6:10)? Yes. But shamed? No. Then I ask myself what is "normal" for a man like me, and I realize that it is my lot to be reminded regularly by the very wise and self-aware "king" that I face the same personal challenges that he faced. It gives me another opportunity to mourn my self-sufficiency, submit myself under authority, and *remember* my Creator and that I am valued before it is too late (12:1ff). How many more opportunities will I have to serve Him?

These questions recur: **Who am I** today as I face the day's frustrations? …the self-sufficient creature who hopes today to perfect his own natural abilities, complete larger projects, and build a better kingdom than the day before? …or an agent who keeps his Creator's prerogatives in mind and embraces **His** opportunities? How long do I have before I am no longer privileged as His agent to avail myself of the resources he has provided for to me to do His work? When will I remember Him more consistently?

More important than the specific answers to these questions is the willingness and courage to keep asking them daily. They are the logical concerns of this reader who has reflected on Qoheleth's observations sufficiently enough for them to influence his life.

During my 20-year, on-and-off pilgrimage through the book of Ecclesiastes I have come to realize that I have not so much successfully interpreted Qoheleth, as the self-styled ancient "king" has successfully "interpreted" **me** and called me to the daily challenge

---

[527] A brilliant modern parable that illustrates this daily prerogative for the believer can be found in David M. Griebner, "The Carpenter and the Unbuilder," *Discipleship Journal* 44:8-9, 1988, reprinted from *Weavings: A Journal of the Christian Spiritual Life* 2 [No. 4] (Nashville, TN: The Upper Room, 1987).

of fearing God. As life unfolds each day to remind me of my own inadequacy, it takes courage to continue to allow myself to be exposed to such disappointment and let my disillusionment have its intended effect. This courage comes from the "living hope" that my Creator has something better in store for me (Eccl 9:4-10). While the prospect of completing this commentary has afforded me the profound personal satisfaction that comes from knowing more of the mind of the Author it has also served regularly to remind me of my own inherent fallibility and desperate need for Him.

One facet of my journey into mid-life depicts quite well how Qoheleth's reflections are finally beginning to leave their mark in my life. Ten years ago I took up distance cycling during a period of time when I felt somewhat bereft of lasting meaning in what I was "doing" for a living. On "good" days the weather and my cycling buddies afforded healthy and enjoyable times that would invigorate me for awhile. On "bad" days I would have to settle for spinning my wheels on a stationary bicycle to vent my pent up energy and at least feel that I wasn't losing too much ground; but I didn't feel like I was "getting anywhere." When I look back on that time I'm not sure I was "getting anywhere" even on "good" days. So, is there any more to my cycling than that? Is it lasting progress or just an enjoyable pastime to get from one day to the next? This question echoes Qoheleth's concern in the **first** half of Ecclesiastes.

As I reflected on the significance of cycling, a familiar image came to mind: *Mormon missionaries*. We all know the stereotype of two clean-cut young men with white shirt, tie, nametag, and black pants both riding bicycles as they slowly but deliberately go from one place to another to spread their message. Casting **their** bread on the waters. **Their** bicycles seem to be going somewhere. But **I** am intensely competitive and prefer racing bikes—can't stand to go slow. Yet to whom and for what would I bicycle? Can I enjoy going fast and still "go somewhere" as a successful Agent of my Creator? Would it result in "good" or turn out "bad" (Eccl 11:6)? While I don't have answers, the questions are a legitimate pretext for day-to-day decision making for the one who fears God—they speak from the **second** half of Ecclesiastes.

These reflections and frustrations have ultimately led me to consider the place of Ecclesiastes in the Bible and how it was meant by the Creator to be applied in the life of the contemporary reader. I will at least begin to address three related questions that influence how I should receive Qoheleth's message and respond.

First, considering the book's unique style and the vagueness of its historical setting, how does it "fit" into the Old Testament canon—what theological impact does it add to the Law, the Prophets, and the other books of Wisdom? Second, considering the virtual absence of any citations of Ecclesiastes in the New Testament, what role does the book serve, if any, as a backdrop to New Testament theology?

My third question derives from the first two and holds great promise for direct application in the life of the contemporary reader. Qoheleth's reflections seem designed especially to address the challenges that face man as a male created in God's image.[528] How does the approach taken in this exposition of Ecclesiastes relate to modern man? How likely is the average male to benefit directly from studying the book? Could it be that some men are called to emulate Qoheleth's mission to *teach the people knowledge* (Eccl 12:9) and communicate the important wisdom to their "sons" (Eccl 12:12)? As I reflect on my life, it strikes me as quite logical that the man who fears God is called, **first** to apply Qoheleth's reflections to his own life, and **then** to instruct his disciples or "sons" in the same wisdom. This commission will be explored in the final section of this *Postscript*.

The Place of Ecclesiastes in the Old Testament Canon

The temptation at this point is to build an extensive biblical theology of the book of Ecclesiastes upon the foundation laid in the initial *Overview*.[529] my purpose here, however, is to review the broader strokes of theological development that emerge from a cohesive view of Qoheleth's argument and show how they resonate with

---

[528] "The world that provides the illustrations for the message of the book is indeed predominantly the male world…, and it is a book that envisages men as its primary audience (e.g., 9:9; 12:12)" (Provan, *Ecclesiastes, Song of Songs*, 29). However, Qoheleth was not a misogynist (cf. 7:26-28, n. 326); he may very well illuminate the character of men on behalf of the woman most directly involved in a man's life, his wife, who is in the best position to edify him with *wise rebuke* (cf. Eccl 7:5, cf. 9:9). This is not the same as nagging (cf. Prov 19:13; 21:9; 27:15), but rather the kind of godly advice exemplified by Sarah, when Abraham—in a fit of self-sufficiency—insisted on establishing his legacy in Ishmael (Gen 21:8-14, cf. Gal 4:21-31). The wife who "knows" the self-sufficient male mentality is best equipped to provide such wisdom.

[529] *See* "Qoheleth's Use of Terms in the Argument." Cp. Roy B. Zuck, "A Biblical Theology of the Wisdom Books and the Song of Songs," in *A Biblical Theology of the Old Testament* (Chicago: Moody, 1991).

similar development in other books of the Old Testament. I have already pointed out some of these parallels in the footnotes to the exposition, wherever such correlation contributed to validating the interpretation. It is my conviction that this correlation is much more than coincidental—indeed, it reflects the canonical consistency and coherence of the Creator's inspiration of the entire literary corpus of the Old Testament (cf. Eccl 12:9-11).

Perhaps the most direct correlation can be recognized between Ecclesiastes and the early chapters of Genesis. Qoheleth's whole argument presupposes a foundational view of humanity as created by God to serve as His agents, to accomplish His sovereign plan (Gen 1-2). The counterfeit appeal of self-sufficient wisdom and achievement as an alternative strategy to faithful agency for God in our pursuit of lasting satisfaction (Eccl 1:12-6:12) is ultimately rooted in Satan's insinuation that God is unfair and in the intuitive logic of self-sufficient righteousness (Gen 3:5). Human suspicion that God unfairly withholds His goodness and the consequent ambition to forge one's own advantage—even at the expense of his fellow man (Eccl 4:1-5:10)—reflects the legacy of Cain: His ambitious pursuit of reputation and success with its attendant oppression of those he envied (Gen 4:3-24; cf. Eccl 4:1-4) was the conduit through which the natural appeal of selfish ambition spread from Adam to all humanity (Gen 5; cf. Eccl 7:29).

Given Qoheleth's apparent departure from "conventional" wisdom,[530] his blunt exposure of universal human depravity—the most daunting obstacle to our success (Eccl 7:15-29; 9:18-10:20)—identifies Ecclesiastes with other Old Testament wisdom more transparently than many expositors are willing to admit: Both the "intensive" and "extensive" aspects of human depravity are expounded throughout the Psalms (perhaps most familiarly in Pss 14; 32; 51), but this condition is presupposed in virtually all the other Psalms—indeed, throughout the Old Testament. Qoheleth is especially vindicated when such depravity is exemplified by the children Israel in their propensity to revert to self-sufficiency: It is seen in the pentateuch, the Judges, the Prophets, and—especially from Qoheleth's vantage point—the books of the Kings.[531]

Qoheleth's brilliant strategy of depicting the allure of self-sufficiency from the first-person perspective of the most gifted king of

---

[530] *See* n. 15.
[531] Cf. n. 208.

Israel is completely in accord with perhaps the most fundamental theological strain in Old Testament theology: *the rebellion of the kingdoms of man as Satan's surrogate strategy of choice in his attempt to usurp God's kingdom* (cf. Isa 14:3-21; Ezek 28:1-19). Such examples illustrate the *vain conceit* that attends the rebellion of ambitious nations against God's kingdom (Ps 2). By disclosing the futile outcome of such rebellion through the eyes of the most gifted king, Qoheleth makes the vanity of Satan-inspired competition with God's sovereign rule intensely personal: Such ambition yields only daily vexation and in the end an empty-handed return to dust (Gen 3:17-19; cf. Eccl 5:11-17).

The book of Job confronts the same concerns that afflicted Qoheleth,[532] especially the unjust oppression that attends human self-sufficiency. While Qoheleth epitomizes the self-sufficient man as eminently prone to **perpetrate** such oppression, Job depicts him as **victim** of oppression. Both books trace the problem of oppression to human contention with God for control over his own destiny,[533] so that our natural inclination to self-sufficiency is seen in both books to threaten our agency for God. The only solution to the agent's self-sufficient pursuit of lasting meaning in life is the *wisdom* that evolves out of the *fear of God;* thus, it is not surprising that Job and the other books of Wisdom so often proclaim *The fear of the Lord is the beginning of wisdom.* Indeed, throughout the Old Testament human self-sufficiency is viewed as antithetical to wisdom and to the fear of God, and as our title implies, *mourning* in adversity is the pathway God provides to forsake self-sufficiency and fear Him (Job 29-30; cf Eccl 7:1-4).[534]

As the influence of human depravity is overcome through the fear of God, wisdom's advantage then plays the key role in overcoming the uncertainty and mortality that still constrain the agent of God (Eccl 11:1-12:7). Although Qoheleth's concluding imperatives are primarily addressed to the "young man" (Eccl 11:9-12:7) they are particularly poignant from the perspective of the older man from whom youthful vigor has departed (11:10b) and whose time

---

[532] Note the plethora of cross-references in nn. 2, 28-29, 40-42, 142, 168, 230, 243, 250-251, 273-275, 286-287, 310, 325, 361, 367, 405, 497.

[533] See esp. Job:10:3-13; 13:13-19; 19:23-27; 23:10-12; Job 29-31; and Eccl 5:1-7; 6:10-11.

[534] See esp. Job 30:31; cf. nn. 39, 48-53, 74-76, 258-258, 265, 269, 285-286, 472.

has largely "run out." However, as long as we can exercise our God-given vital capacities we still have hope of benefiting from wisdom to make the best of our God-given portion (9:4-10). The Old Testament amply attests to the valued contribution of those men of God (including kings) who only late in life responded to His call as true agents.[535] The warning of Psalm 95, drawn from the example of the Israelites who were dying in the wilderness, should therefore appeal to one who only in mid-life or even later aspires to authentic agency for God.[536]

This all leads me to speculate—if I may be permitted to do so—on the likely place of Ecclesiastes in the Old Testament canon and propose a plausible candidate for the book's author. It is intriguing that the authors of the books of the Kings and Chronicles so often allude to "the rest of the acts" of the kings of Israel and Judah as recorded by other chroniclers and seers,[537] yet we have no extant copies of these other books. It is entirely plausible that one of these historians was sufficiently inspired by compiling his account of Solomon's life God to imagine then, using the corpus of wisdom available to him, how Solomon might have reflected after his death on the object lessons of his own life and the lives of the kings who succeeded him.

Whoever this "master of collections" (cf. Eccl 12:11, NASB) was, his mission was to exploit Solomon's unprecedented wisdom and draw inspired conclusions from the lives of Solomon and the other kings of Israel regarding mankind's self-sufficiency and his consequent need to fear God. It then stands to reason that this historian would have lived in roughly the same period as the authors of the last books of the Old Testament, the "Persian" period of the Chronicles, Ezra, Nehemiah, and Esther.[538] He may even have been

---

[535] This is arguably the main point of the accounts of the last phase of the lives of Samson (Judg 16); king Hezekiah (2 Kgs 20); and even the evil king Manasseh (2 Chr 33:1-20).

[536] At least two recent books addressed to the man in mid-life make specific mention of the central role of Ecclesiastes for such a man in adjusting his perspective and decision making to optimize his stewardship for whatever life remains. See Don Anderson, *Ecclesiastes—the Mid-Life Crisis* (Neptune, NJ: Loizeaux, 1987); and Bob Buford, *Game Plan: Winning Stategies for the Second Half of Your Life* (Grand Rapids, MI: Zondervan, 1997), 34. See also Paul Tournier, *Learn to Grow Old* (Louisville, KY: Westminster/John Knox, 1991) and the website www.finishers.org (with related links on-line).

[537] See 1 Kgs 11:41; 14:19, 29; 15:7, 23, 31; 16:5, 14, 20, 27; 22:39; and 2 Chr 9:29; 12:15; 13:22.

[538] See n. 6.

the prophet Iddo, was identified as the Chronicler who compiled the account of Solomon's life[539] and that would have enjoyed the advantage of retrospectively comparing Solomon with all the other kings of Israel and Judah (cf. 2 Chr 12:15; 13:22).[540]

Ecclesiastes as a Backdrop to New Testament Theology

Expositors often struggle with the apparent lack of harmony between Ecclesiastes and New Testament theology. They point out that Ecclesiastes is never formally cited in the New Testament and that the closest indirect allusion to the book is in Rom 8:20. In this passage *futility* serves as a backdrop to the redemptive hope of all Creation—a hope vested in the "sons of God" as His agents in a fallen world.[541] Thus, Paul mirrors Qoheleth's shift from deep pessimism[542] over the legacy of sinful man (Rom 1:18-3:20; 7:1-25; cf. Eccl 7:15-29; 9:2-3) to the hopeful promise that humanity can be transformed into successful agents of God's creative work and share in His promised inheritance (Rom 8:16-22; cf. Eccl 9:4-10; 12:1, 7).[543] It is the **nature** of this transformation (cf. Rom 12:1-2) that comprises the very fabric of New Testament theology.

Paul contrasts the futility of the foolish *wisdom of the world* (1 Cor 1:18-27, cf. Eccl chaps 1-6) with the self-effacing *wisdom from God* that only comes by faith (1 Cor 1:27-2:16; cf. Eccl chaps 7-12, esp. 9:11-18). For Qoheleth the prospective "agent" of God must become completely disillusioned with the failure of self-sufficient wisdom in order to gain wisdom's advantage for the work of God (Eccl 7:1-14). In the NT this process is depicted as admission of sin illuminated by God as light (1 Jn 1:5-10). Paul exemplified this in his own life (Acts 9:1-9) and reckoned his self-sufficient gain as

---

[539] If the author was Iddo the Seer (2 Chr 9:29; 12:15; 13:22) or a close descendant (Neh 12:4, 16; Zech 1:1, 7), it would place his writing at the end of the exile or within a few generations of the Israelites' return.

[540] This would explain Qoheleth's otherwise preposterous claim regarding "all [the kings] who were before me" (Eccl 1:16, 2:9; cf. n. 7).

[541] Paul and Qoheleth both saw their readers as valued agents of God's preordained purposes (Eph 2:10, cf. Eccl 3:10-15; 12:6-7; nn. 178, 179, 497).

[542] *See* n. 374 and related text (cf. also nn. 384, 388, 392, and 394).

[543] Qoheleth's notion of a "share" in life (n. 390) is the main focus of the book of Hebrews. Five of the six NT references to *metochoi* ("partakers" or "sharers") occur in Heb 1:9; 3:1, 14; 6:4; 12:8—it is the link between one's pre-ordained agency (Heb 2:5-8) and his hope of inheritance in God's kingdom (Heb 1:2, 4, 8, 9, 14; 2:3, 5-10; 3:1, 6, 14; 4:1-11; 6:7, 9, 12, 17; 9:15; 10:34-36; 11:8, 13, 39-40; 12:17, 28).

"loss" (Phil 3:4-8, cf. Eccl 5:10-17) in exchange for the righteousness of knowing God that comes through faith in Christ (Phil 3:7-10a).[544] The transformation mirrors Qoheleth's pivotal reflection that only by the *fear of God* can mankind escape the "dead end" of self-effort to prevail with true *righteousness* and *wisdom* (Eccl 7:16-18).[545]

This righteousness and wisdom characterizes the kingdom of God (Matt 5-7), and those who are blessed within it will *mourn* (Matt 5:4)[546] both the failure of self-sufficient strategies for success and the ambitious oppression of others to achieve that success (James 4:13-5:6). Like Qoheleth Paul urged his readers to learn from his precedent[547] and avoid *selfish ambition and vain conceit* (Phil 2:3 [NASB]; 2 Cor 12:20, cf. Eccl 4:1-6:12). The solution was to displace the vain conceit that fuels selfish ambition with single-minded dependency on the Father taught and modeled by Christ and the Apostles in the New Testament account that reflects the *fear of God* (cf. Eccl 5:7b).

Fearing God should neither destroy human ambition nor replace it with one that is completely foreign to our nature, for we are created in God's image with desires that are best fulfilled by accepting our unique calling and God-given heritage (Eph 1; 2:10, cf. Eccl 5:19; 6:10). The daily challenge for the steward who fears God is to remember our identity as agents of the Father (Phil 3:20-21, cf. Eccl 12:1) and submit to the instruction of His word (2 Tim 3:16-17; Col 3:16, cf. Eccl 12:13-14). In this way Paul exemplified how to fulfill one's calling by "forgetting what is behind" and persevering in the hope of God's favor as God's valued agent (Phil 3:11-14; cf. Eccl 9:1, 7; 11:9; 12:14).[548]

The ever-present danger of reverting to self-sufficiency is the subtext of the entire second half of Qoheleth's argument and clarifies why the frame narrator's concluding concern was that *the words of the wise* would find fertile ground in the future generations symbolized by his

---

[544] Peter Kreeft links Paul's testimony to Qoheleth's exposition of futility in self-effort, which had to come to nothing before Paul's life had meaning ("Ecclesiastes: Life as Vanity" [cited in n. 9], 27-29).

[545] *See* nn. 51, 76, 307, 310, 311, 366, 376, 383 and related text.

[546] Cf. Eccl 7:1-4 and n. 53.

[547] Cf. n. 124. Paul urged them to *imitate* him (1 Cor 4:17; 11:1; 2 Cor 1; Eph 5:1; Phil 3:17; 1 Thess 1:6; 2:14; cf. Heb 6:12; 3 Jn 11) not his prior example of selfish ambition (Acts 22:1-21; 26:1-29; Phil 3:4-17).

[548] Cf. n. 525. Cp. Phil 1:19-20; 1 Cor 9:24-27.

"son" (Eccl 12:12). Qoheleth understood that even after the reader was committed to serving God (7:1-14) one would need hope of God's favor to overcome the continued vulnerability of wisdom's advantage to his innate depravity, uncertainty, and mortality (7:15-9:10). Qoheleth hoped that with this confidence wisdom's advantage would prevail by overcoming these barriers (9:11-12:7) to bring success in the work of God.[549] This is the primary focus of John's repeated emphasis on "confidence"[550] and "overcoming"[551] in the believer's agency for God.

For Qoheleth, the wisest way to succeed in the work of God (cf. 9:10; 10:10b) is to *cast your bread upon the waters* and *sow your seed* at every opportunity (11:1-6), which somehow involves the need to *fear God and keep His commandments* (12:13). We are disturbingly intrigued as to what is meant by these concluding injunctions: First, to *keep His commandments* cannot reasonably be understood as referring to the "written code" of the Mosaic Law.[552] If we were to speculate on the ultimate goal of Qoheleth's exhortation to "keep His commandments," the most logical target in view of Qoheleth's quest would be to redeem mankind's legacy of unjust oppression and inhumanity to man (cf. Eccl 3:16-17; 4:1-3; 8:9-15).

---

[549] *See* nn. 408, 468 and related text.

[550] John repeatedly emphasizes God's favor in connection with bold confidence (Gk *parrēsia*) as His chosen agents of righteousness and love on earth (1 John 2:28-3:3; 3:21-22; 4:17; 5:14). Cf. n. 391.

[551] The NT concept of "overcoming" (Gk *nikaō*) is distinctively Johannine: Jesus inspired confidence among his fearful disciples by describing himself as having "overcome the world" (John 16:33). John reassured his "little children" that they also had overcome "the evil one" (1 John 2:13, 14), the "spirit of antichrist in the world" (1 John 4:4), and "the world" itself (1 John 5:4, 5). While John's allusions occur in the context of "external" opposition to God's chosen agents in the world (John 15:14-25; 17:14-19), it is equally clear that this opposition is exerted on the believer most powerfully through the world's "pull" on the "flesh" (1 John 2:15-17). *The world* in Qoheleth's terms is what is apparent *under the sun*, and it often appeals to the agent of God because of mankind's inherent proclivity for self-sufficient *folly* (i.e., depravity), his *uncertainty* over whether his labor will elicit God's favor, and his impending *mortality*. John makes it clear that this "leverage" on the agent of God is at Satan's disposal and is to be "overcome" by *faith* (1 John 5:4)—for Qoheleth, the *fear of God*. For John, faith is manifested by holding to *the word of God* and the *testimony of Jesus* (1 John 2:14; 5:5; Rev 12:11, 17). For Qoheleth, the fear of God is manifested by holding to the inspired *words of the wise* (Eccl 12:10-11) and the hope of God's favor (9:4, 7, cf. Rev 6:9f).

[552] *See* nn. 522, 523.

It thus stands to reason that the New Testament speaks so directly to such oppression with a view to reversing it with the love of God.

Again, of all the books in the New Testament First John may shed the most light on our understanding of what Qoheleth meant by *keep His commandments* in Eccl 12:13. Mankind's natural tendency is to hate (or "oppress") those whom he envies in the pursuit of his selfish aspirations; it is painfully evident that what is missing is *love* (1 Jn 2:3-11; 3:4-10). Since true righteousness and justice is presently unfulfilled (1 Jn 2:28-3:3, cf. Eccl 3:16-17), it comes as no surprise that John's own injunction *keep His commandments* is related to Christ's "new" commandment to "love one another" (1 Jn 2:7-8, John 13:34; 15:12). Consequently, John makes it clear that only those who "know God" can truly "keep His commandments" (1 Jn 2:3-4)—just as only those who *fear God* can *keep His commandments* (Eccl 12:13)—and avoid the oppression that so naturally attends ambitious self-sufficiency (Eccl 4:1-6).

This clarifies how Qoheleth's injunction to *cast your bread upon the waters* and *sow your seed* (Eccl 11:1, 6) is fleshed out by Christ's call to productive "investment" typified in Matt 6:19-34; 21:28-22:14; 24:45-25:30 and the parable of the shrewd administrator in Luke 16: Both Christ's call and Qoheleth's injunction attain their highest fulfillment when those agents who would succeed in the work of God respond in obedience to his charge and "invest" *sacrificial love* in the lives of others, having been warned to expect adversity by both Christ (John 15:18-25) and Qoheleth (Eccl 11:7-12:2; cf. 7:13).[553]

By the same token, both Qoheleth's injunction and Christ's challenge to sacrificial love and discipleship (Mark 10:32-45; Luke 9:57-62) can only be accepted because of the concomitant promise of joy (John 15:11; 1 Jn 1:4; Phil 4:1-7; cf. Eccl 11:7, 9) prefigured in Qoheleth's enjoyment passages.[554] When the challenge is met, God's agent prevails in wisdom and righteousness (Matt 10:16-26, cf. Eccl 7:18). The promise of joy paradoxically both **completes** and **begins** the steward's quest for a lasting inheritance in the work of God: It is completed in the sense that the steward can presently enjoy his God-given portion in the work of God (5:18-20; 9:7-10).[555] Yet it has only begun, in that we won't

---

[553] *See* n. 472.

[554] *See* n. 30.

[555] *See* Larry Crabb's *The Pressure's Off*, cited in n. 236.

see our full inheritance in God's work until God ultimately reveals the portion of our work that endures fire (1 Cor 3:10-15; 2 Cor 5:10, cf. Eccl 11:9; 12:14).[556]

The greatest risk of sacrificial love is that ambitious self-sufficiency appeals to humanity as a "safer," more life-giving option. This is precisely the concern that motivates John's first epistle—the tendency for young disciples to be seduced by the counterfeit appeal of the world's success (1 Jn 2:15-17). Vestiges of self-sufficiency gain their foothold in the steward whose ambition is rooted in presumption, as depicted in Eccl 5:1-9 and repeatedly exemplified in the example of Peter. John's mission can therefore be viewed as sustaining the knowledge of God among future generations of disciples (1 Jn 2:13-14), just as the frame narrator of Ecclesiastes intended for his "son" (Eccl 12:9-12). Christ modeled the same mission in John 17, to "sanctify" His disciples in the truth of the knowledge of God, that they may be unified in the Father's love.

Ecclesiastes relates more directly to New Testament theology than many are willing to accept. Given the contemporary culture of radical self-sufficiency and exposure of the contemporary church in America to multiplied counterfeit sources of knowledge (Eccl 12:12), Qoheleth's mission to "teach the people knowledge" (Eccl 12:9) is of profound relevance. In fact, the commission to "sanctify them by Your truth" (John 17:17) and to unify them in the "love of the Father" (John 17:22-23, cf. 1 Jn 2:15-17) may first require us to hear Qoheleth's message: Not until self-sufficient knowledge is exposed as utterly futile can the people of God perpetuate the *knowledge of God* (1 Jn 2:3-11); the task of discipleship is nothing less than equipping one's "sons" with this knowledge (Eccl 11:9-12:7, 11-12)[557] to live out New Testament truth.

The Indispensable Calling to "Teach the People Knowledge"

The epilogue to the book serves well as a template for the "fathers" among us to use Qoheleth's reflections to "teach the people knowledge" (12:9). If in fact Ecclesiastes was written primarily with man as male in mind[558] it would serve as an ideal mirror for the

---

[556] This explains the inherent uncertainty in Qoheleth's view of future reward (3:22; 6:12; 7:14; cf. n. 193).
[557] Cf. nn. 456, 517.
[558] Note 528.

"fathers" in the faith to teach "sons" (12:12), reflecting in their own lives the applicable life-changing object lessons illustrated by Qoheleth's unprecedented example. Each of these "fathers" would use Qoheleth's wisdom to redeem his "sons" from self-sufficient folly: This would expose their self-sufficient presumption and challenge them to mourn their inability and distorted relationships with God and others and to see themselves as stewards with a unique God-given "portion," deeply valued by the Creator.[559]

As the discipler exposes his disciples to this wisdom, leading by example through the book's challenges, distinctions of spiritual maturity would naturally become evident. A "reproductive cycle" of successive generations of "sons" would thus begin,[560] whereby one generation of spiritual directors trains others to lovingly invade the lives[561] of those mired in foolishness. Such training would become the platform for an ongoing spiritual journey rooted in the knowledge and confidence that one is an agent of the Creator on a lifelong quest to fulfill his portion or heritage in the work of God. On the journey the hope is that he would learn how to reproduce himself in the lives of others, challenging them to discover their respective "portions" as agents of God.

---

[559] Modern believers often seem unconvinced of their great value in the eyes of God (Eccl 12:6-7, n. 497) and the crucial role of their God-given portion (n. 29). John Eldredge creatively envisions how we can meet this daunting challenge in *Waking the Dead: The Glory of a Heart Fully Alive* (Nashville, TN: Thomas Nelson, 2003).

[560] This is entirely consistent with the frame narrator's objective to train his "son" in spiritual wisdom with the inspired words of "the wise" (Eccl 12:9-14), and Qoheleth himself addresses the "young man" in 11:9ff (cf. n. 456). It is my contention that the framework of First John is also designed to perpetuate this "reproductive cycle" of discipleship. John's stratification of all of his readers ("little children," Gk *teknia*, 1 John 2:12) into "fathers" (Gk *patera*) "young men" (Gk *neaniskoi*) and "children" (Gk *paidia*) (1 John 2:13-27) is conspicuously based on the level of their "knowledge" of God and their confidence in His Word as transmitted through the inspired authors of Scripture. These levels of "knowledge" in turn determine their spiritual capacity to resist embracing "the world," "the flesh" (self-sufficiency), and "the devil" (1 John 2:15-17) or being swayed by false teaching (1 John 2:18-27).

[561] Larry Crabb moves appropriately from the classical model of Christian counseling to a model based on existing relationships within the Body of Christ in *Connecting—Healing for Ourselves and Our Relationships* (Nashville, TN: Word Publishing, 1997); cf. also *The Safest Place on Earth: Where People Connect and Are Forever Changed* (Nashville, TN: Word Publishing, 1999); and *SoulTalk*, cited in n. 218.

To the self-sufficient reader this is one of the most potent challenges to transformation in all of Scripture but well worth facing: Qoheleth's message is based on an unchanging anthropology that accurately describes all men since the Fall and on a correct epistemology—the Truth given by "One Shepherd," and his message is meant to be viewed as a synthetic whole. Qoheleth's *a fortiori* strategy makes it difficult for the self-sufficient reader to "weasel out" of the convicting truths of the book; the testimony of one who has "been there, done that" mirrors the sinful underpinnings of the reader's choices and challenges one to admit his own failure.

Thus, the sequence of Qoheleth's reflections is cleverly designed to surface whatever stage of foolishness we may be suffering through in the "vanity" of our lives "under the sun." The reflections graphically portray the frustrated ambition and disillusionment that can break down the bastions of self-sufficiency and lead us to mourn our inability. We will be challenged to release self-sufficient strategies to gain a lasting legacy and replace them with the "fear of God" in our pursuit of meaning in life. In presenting these challenges the discipler will repeatedly be faced with the need to balance wise rebuke (Eccl 7:5-7) with encouragement and continued hope (9:4-10).

It is difficult to overestimate the importance of personal credibility to the effectiveness of such discipleship. Thus, the discipler who in his own life has faced life's adversity and disillusionment over the failure of self-sufficiency is best equipped as a "father" to "teach the people knowledge."[562] Disciples who are clinging to the illusory promise of self-sufficiency must gain the confidence that they will receive more life from God than from self-sufficient strategies before they release their grip. The credible foundation of the discipler's own experience enables him to move incisively into their lives[563] with both rebuke and encouragement and promote the

---

[562] This is the foundation of Paul's encouragement to the Corinthians after having gone through serious suffering and disillusionment of his own (2 Cor 1). Though it was necessary to sternly rebuke the suffering Corinthians (2 Cor 2:1-9; cf. Eccl 7:5), his own experience and example had made him trustworthy.

[563] Larry Crabb has illustrated what this entails, as his writing evolved over three decades from teaching *about* the need to forsake self-sufficiency to teaching *by example*. For example, cp. Crabb's *Effective Biblical Counseling* (Grand Rapids: Zondervan, 1977) with his landmark *Inside Out* and subsequent offerings that have quite effectively exploited the power of personal story, transparency, and brokenness. See the references cited in nn. 236, 258, and 561.

confidence to meet Qoheleth's challenge, thus redeeming their agency for God.

There is no guarantee that exposure to the message of Ecclesiastes will yield the intended transformation.[564] In fact, such biblical wisdom may have its greatest potential application in the lives of those already "flattened" by disappointment; such persons are more likely to be receptive to the unpleasant truth about their failure as created agents of God.[565] The books of Ecclesiastes and Job each afford templates for just such redemptive transformation of the oppressor and the oppressed, respectively, and several of the Psalms exemplify the biblical pattern for mourning. By so graphically illustrating the desired transformation as their primary literary strategy, these books are ideally suited for disciplers to walk their disciples through the same process.[566]

Sadly, the role of such "generational discipleship" in evoking personal growth and transformation is poorly appreciated in the western church, because the uncomfortable message of these books clashes with our rugged individualism and demand for comfort and convenience. Yet, we who aspire to lead and are "able to teach" (1 Tim 3:2) can ill afford not to "hold fast the faithful word as he has been taught, that he may be able... both to exhort and convict..." (Ti 1:9) and thereby promote authentic mourning over the failure of self-sufficiency. It falls on our shoulders to "teach the people knowledge" (Eccl 12:9)—but "not a new convert, lest he become conceited and fall into the condemnation incurred by the devil" (1 Tim 3:6, NASB).[567]

---

[564] This may be the main reason why the frame narrator waited until the end of the book to authenticate Qoheleth's wisdom as inspired by God (Eccl 12:9-14). If the reader was too blind to see the failure of self-sufficiency in his own life after being dragged through the disillusionment of the first 6 chapters, he would see no need to authenticate the challenges of the last 6 chapters. See n. 506.

[565] This may help explain why Christ's self-proclaimed mission (Luke 4:18) was "to preach the gospel to the poor...to heal the brokenhearted, to proclaim liberty to the captives and recovery of sight to the blind, to set at liberty those who are oppressed." It also explains why he was unsuccessful with other groups—they would not admit their true need before God, even when confronted by the Savior Himself. See Matt 11:4-6; 15:30-31; 21:28-32; Mark 6:2-6; Luke 10:8-16; 14:16-24; John 9.

[566] For example, Ruben Martinez has used Pss 32 and 51 to develop an appealing method to restore believers who have been paralyzed by serious sexual sin (unpublished D.Min. thesis, "Biblical Counseling and the Use of Community in Cases of Adultery," Westminster Theological Seminary, 2001).

Several years ago I had firsthand experience of the potential power of Ecclesiastes to be a catalyst for generational discipleship. As a military officer deployed to Southwest Asia in the aftermath of Operation Iraqi Freedom, I had a unique opportunity to teach the entire book of Ecclesiastes to a "captive audience" of primarily enlisted Air Force troops. These were ordinary American males from the ages of 20 to 40 who responded to the opportunity for a weekly small group Bible study (20 or 30 men per session) that lasted about 90 minutes each week. It would not be an understatement to conclude that a number of these men were riveted by this approach to the book, because the theological categories addressed them quite naturally as American males, and they were confined in close quarters with enough adversity to "get their attention."

By the end of the deployment, we had gone through the book in 14 weeks, and many of the men had embraced the message of the book as their own. I was particularly impressed by the testimony of the younger men in the study, how readily the message had opened their eyes to the crucial role of their agency for the Creator and the treacherous pitfalls of self-sufficiency. The *a fortiori* strategy of Qoheleth's approach to wisdom was intuitively obvious to these young men, and they soon came to see the inestimable value of the wisdom compiled in the book as a template for personal growth out of their common background of rugged western individualism. The study promised the answer to the disillusionment of modern life for them as Christians and opened up their hope to be full fledged Agents of the Creator.

So, exactly how would "fathers" or "elders" deploy Qoheleth's wisdom to teach their respective "sons" in this process of generational discipleship? This is the primary strategic advantage of recognizing the cohesive structure and logical progression in Qoheleth's *a fortiori* argument: Those men in the Body of Christ with the wisdom born of experience who aspire to become "fathers" or "elders" would do very well to study and absorb the message of Ecclesiastes. Assuming that these "fathers" have earned

---

[567] The great risk among contemporary church leaders of succumbing to the self-sufficient strategies indigenous to our culture raises the real question of how feasible it is to incorporate this priority into the "established" church at this late stage in the church age. "Elders" are all too often mainly interested in enjoying the "benefits" of retirement, a tendency that must be reversed. See Paul Tournier, *Learn to Grow Old*, and Bob Buford, *Half Time* (Grand Rapids: Zondervan, 1994). Thus, "He who has an ear, let him hear…" (Rev 2-3; n. 551).

their "sons'" trust, they could use Qoheleth's unprecedented experience as a "mirror" for the young man to recognize his own foolishness with a view to forsaking that foolishness in the fear of God to become wise and productive agents of their Creator.

Schooled in the message of Ecclesiastes, these "fathers" would direct their "sons" to those parts of the book that speak most directly to their individual life situations. If they respond to their fathers' "wise rebuke" (cf. 7:5) the sons will realize how they succumb to the appeal of seeking lasting satisfaction in pleasure, achievement, or material possessions (2:1-11), natural wisdom (2:12-17), workaholism (2:18-23), or prescribing good behavior to curry God's favor (3:1-22). Once the young man acknowledges how easy it is to presume on God and exploit others in his attempt to satisfy selfish ambition (4:1-6:12), the hope is that he will be disillusioned enough in adversity to mourn his inadequacy, forsake his vain presumption, and acknowledge God's inscrutable purposes (7:1-14). Yet disillusionment alone will not make us effective agents of God.

In order for wisdom's advantage (7:11-12) to be realized as success, the disciple must be so convinced that he cannot please God in his own righteousness or wisdom, that he can only *fear God* in his desperation (7:15-29). A wise "father" can teach his "son" that he will *do well* only by *fearing God* and realize wisdom's advantage only by remaining aware of the constraints of *time and judgment* in fulfilling God's purposes, even though he may not see these purposes fulfilled in this life (8:1-15). Thus, even when we can't predict what God is doing by what we see before us he will still receive God's favor by accepting the *portion* God has given us (8:16-9:10). This necessarily entails "rediscovering" that "portion" as we forsake self-sufficiency for the fear of God to joyfully walk in God's purposes.[568]

---

[568] When Qoheleth says *Whatever one is, he has been <u>named</u> already...and he cannot contend with Him who is mightier than he* (Eccl 6:10) he shows how our natural disposition of self-sufficiency leads to rejecting the "name" God has uniquely and individually given each of us as His agents. This text gives real life to the term *calling* (cf. n. 249) as a "birthright" of all who fear God and not only those we acknowledge as "leaders" of the people of God. One can hardly overestimate the critical importance of rediscovering this "name" in order to accurately discern what "portion" or "part" God originally intended for us to play as His agents in the fulfillment of His sovereign purposes. The power of this "rediscovery" is effectively captured by John Eldredge (*Waking the Dead* [cited in n. 559], 71-88), as he described how myth helped him to answer the key question "God, who am I? What do you think of me? What's my real name?" (ibid., 84). My own "rediscovery" began over 20 years ago when I began my in-depth study of

The long-term challenge is for the young man to remain aware that he is still God's chosen agent. Self-sufficient strategies for success will still appeal to the young man in adversity and threaten wisdom's advantage (9:11-18). "Fathers" recognize that reverting to self-sufficient folly will thoroughly subvert successful agency and they can remind their "sons" of this perspective to help keep them aware of their calling as agents of the Creator when tempted by folly's appeal (10:1-20). They remain aware of the inevitable constraints of *time and chance* (cf. 9:11c) on their opportunity to serve God's purposes: They *remember their Creator* and learn to invest their portion expediently as His highly valued and accountable agents, in light of life's unpredictable fortune and death's unavoidable finality (11:1-12:7).

Finally, as these "sons" assimilate this wisdom they too become wise and in turn teach their own sons and complete yet another cycle of generational discipleship (see above, cf. 12:8-14), so that the Creator may complete His sovereign work to the end of the age through the collective contributions of His chosen agents.[569]

Ecclesiastes and realized the profound irony in my own father's decision early in life to avoid being stigmatized by changing his middle name ("Solomon") to "Stuart." I was also given the name "Stuart," the consequence of my father's "contention" for a different name (cf. Eccl 6:10b). Ironically, in the process of capturing the mind of Qoheleth over all these years, I rediscovered the middle name I would have had if my father had kept his own, and God has used this to *keep* me *busy with the joy of* my *heart* (Eccl 5:20) as his chosen agent (cf. n. 237).

[569] It seems to me that this one profound implication of the epilogue to Ecclesiastes is the culmination of Qoheleth's repeated emphasis on accountability to the king (notes 522, 523) and that it goes a long way to inform New Testament theology of the Kingdom of God, especially the mysterious nature of its growth during the present age (cf. the parables of Matt 13). Perhaps the contribution of our respective portions to the Kingdom of God as "sons" (cf. Rom 8:18-21) will best be measured by how effectively we inculcate a passion for godly agency in our own "sons."

Selected Bibliography

Bartholomew, Craig. *Reading Ecclesiastes—Old Testament Exegesis and Hermeneutical Theory.* Analecta Biblica. Rome: Pontifico Istituto Biblico, 1998.

Buford, Bob. *Half Time: Changing Your Game Plan from Success to Significance.* Grand Rapids: Zondervan, 1994.

_____. *Game Plan: Winning Stategies for the Second Half of Your Life.* Grand Rapids, MI: Zondervan, 1997.

Crabb, Larry. *Inside Out.* Colorado Springs: Navpress, 1988.

_____. *Shattered Dreams—God's Unexpected Pathway to Joy.* Colorado Springs: WaterBrook, 2001.

_____. *The Pressure's Off.* Colorado Springs: Waterbrook, 2002.

Eaton, Michael A. *Ecclesiastes.* Tyndale Old Testament Commentary. Downers Grove, IL: InterVarsity, 1983.

Eldredge, John. *Waking the Dead: The Glory of a Heart Fully Alive.* Nashville, TN: Thomas Nelson, 2003.

Kreeft, Peter. "Ecclesiastes: Life as Vanity." In *Three Philosophies of Life.* San Francisco: Ignatius, 1989.

Longman, Tremper, III. *The Book of Ecclesiastes.* New International Commentary on the Old Testament. Grand Rapids, MI: Eerdmans, 1998.

Murphy, Roland. *Ecclesiastes*, Word Biblical Commentary. Dallas: Word, 1992.

Parsons, Greg W. "Guidelines for Understanding and Proclaiming the Book of Ecclesiastes. Part 1." *Bibliotheca Sacra* 160 (2003):159-72.

_____. "Guidelines for Understanding and Proclaiming the Book of Ecclesiastes. Part 2." *Bibliotheca Sacra* 160 (2003): 283-304.

Provan, Iain. *The NIV Application Commentary: Ecclesiastes, Song of Songs*. Grand Rapids: Zondervan, 2001.

Reitman, James S. "The Structure and Unity of Ecclesiastes." *Bibliotheca Sacra* 154 (1997): 297-319.

_____. "Words of Truth and Words of Purpose—Exegetical Insights into Authorial Intent from Ecclesiastes 12:9-14." Paper presented at the 58th Annual Meeting of the Evangelical Theological Society, November, 2006.
    Available at www. 21stcenturypress.com/wisdom.htm.

Seow, C-L. *Ecclesiastes*. Anchor Bible. New York: Doubleday, 1997.

Tournier, Paul. *Learn to Grow Old*. Louisville, KY: Westminster/John Knox, 1991.

Whybray, R. N. *Ecclesiastes*, New Century Bible Commentary. Grand Rapids: Eerdmans, 1989.

Yancey, Philip. "Ecclesiastes: The End of Wisdom." In *The Bible Jesus Read*. Grand Rapids: Zondervan, 1999.

Zuck, Roy B., ed. *Reflecting with Solomon: Selected Studies on the Book of Ecclesiastes*. Grand Rapids: Baker, 1994.

Scripture Index

Author Index

Foreign Term Index

(All foreign terms will be found only in the footnotes on the pages indicated.)

Subject Index

(Entries may be located in either the text or the footnotes on the pages indicated.)

368

frame narrator (see *literary genre*)
friend of God, 176
friends (Job's), 11-13, 26, 27, 39, 41, 42,
49, 51-58, 63, 65, 67-70, 73-75, 77-
87, 89-93, 95-103, 105, 109-111, 113,
116, 118, 123, 124, 126-128, 131,
133, 134, 136-140, 143, 144, 147,
161, 165, 166, 169-175, 264
futility, futile (see also *emptiness;
meaninglessness; vanity*), 6, 9, 12-
15, 22, 23, 25, 36, 43, 73, 75, 79, 83,
84, 88, 90, 103, 109, 111, 126, 140,
145, 158, 177, 182, 185, 187, 189,
193, 196, 198, 200-202, 207, 211,
212, 215-218, 221, 223-226, 237,
240, 242, 244, 246, 248-251, 253,
260, 261, 263, 264, 278, 287, 294,
314, 317, 318, 321, 327-329, 331,
335, 340, 342, 343, 346

good
    in God's eyes (sight), 194, 224-228,
        276, 280, 291
    what is good, 27, 133, 199, 250, 253,
        254, 259, 262, 268
goodness, 13, 64, 66, 68, 134, 136, 140,
    188, 190, 202, 221, 249, 251, 269,
    339
grammar (see *hermeneutics*)
grief (see also *vexation; mourning*),
    40, 66, 70, 75, 77-79, 81, 87, 94, 106,
    193, 196, 218, 222, 263

hand(s)
    grasping, 187, 193, 198, 216, 217, 225,
        239, 241, 243, 278
    imagery of, 135, 241, 244, 248
    nothing in his, 244
    of God, 85, 97, 109, 182, 195, 206,
        222, 223, 225, 273, 276, 290-293
    purity of, 57, 106
    work of one's, 90, 94, 147, 244, 248,
        298, 331
hate, hatred, 173, 292, 293, 295, 296, 345
heart (see also *wise of heart*), 10, 26,
    27, 55, 57, 79, 80, 87, 116, 118, 148,
    182, 183, 194, 196-198, 200-203,
    218, 220, 229, 245, 249, 251, 260-
    264, 266, 267, 274, 277-281, 283,
    285-287, 290, 293, 294, 296, 308,
    311, 316, 318-321, 347, 352, 353

heritage (see also *inheritance; legacy;
portion; reward*), 28, 65, 100, 110,
191, 196, 222, 234, 251, 253, 254,
267, 291, 295, 297, 343, 347
hermeneutic(s), hermeneutical (see also
interpretation; literary), 2, 3, 4, 25,
32, 34, 35, 4, 5, 9, 11, 14-20, 22-24,
35, 36, 188, 189, 197, 198, 270, 353
    application, 7, 9, 18, 21-25, 30, 32, 34,
        69, 264, 338, 349, 354
    as perlocution (see *hermeneutics,
        speech-act terminology*)
    as response (of reader, interpreter),
        21, 24
    contextualization, and, 24
    argument, the (author's)
        a fortiori (greater to lesser), 13,
            25, 28, 65, 96, 144, 160, 163,
            197, 204, 212, 217, 219-221,
            237, 242, 252, 286, 293, 327,
            348, 350
        logic (flow) of the, 22, 26, 28, 29,
            31, 33, 74, 89, 93, 103, 106, 107,
            111, 114, 127, 129, 130, 132,
            134-136, 138, 144, 145, 152,
            155, 156, 162, 175, 186-189,
            197, 199, 201, 205-207, 215,
            224, 226, 238, 242, 247, 251-
            254, 259, 261, 263, 273, 275,
            277, 284-286, 288-290, 292-294,
            296, 298, 301, 304, 308, 310,
            312-314, 316, 318-320
        of Ecclesiastes, 16, 177, 196, 199
        of Job, 15, 43, 44, 166, 169
        premise of, 107, 186, 201, 211, 222,
            224, 226, 275, 276, 287, 290,
            293, 324
    authentication, 6, 22, 26, 126, 127,
        325, 328, 329, 331, 349
    authorial intent, 4, 16, 17, 24, 25, 33,
        36, 188
    communicative intent, 17, 19, 24,
        29, 30, 34, 259, 290, 293, 327
    expressed in speech-act terminol-
        ogy, 24
    intended meaning, message
        (embedded in text), 9, 15-25,
        27, 29-31, 33, 34, 51, 82, 116,
        123, 169, 171, 190, 198, 233,
        262, 270, 284, 298, 306, 338,
        346, 348-351

occasion for the text, 19, 20, 67, 152,
228, 262, 287, 308, 315, 317
paragraphic units, 188, 199
premise(s), 18-22, 24, 186, 187
grammatical, 19-20
historical, 20
literal, 18, 19, 22
literary, 21
theological, 22
presuppositions, 16
purpose (see *hermeneutics, authorial intent*)
recognition of meaning, 17, 18, 20,
22, 29, 31, 34, 99, 196, 276, 331
semantic(s) (see also *hermeneutics, lexical*), 19, 20, 188, 189, 308
speech-act (see *hermeneutics, authorial intent*)
spiral, 3, 16, 17, 23, 24, 34, 35, 188,
197, 198
cycle(s) of, 3, 17, 22, 29, 31, 34, 73,
211, 212, 230, 347, 352
incremental understanding, and,
17, 31
iterative nature of, 22, 31, 34
mutually informing elements of,
18, 20
summary statement, 9, 25, 29-31, 33,
34
syntax, syntactical, 19, 28, 123, 169,
189, 231, 232, 248, 288, 310, 312
synthesis, synthetic, 4, 28, 29, 31, 33
teleology, 22, 332
textual
design (arrangement), 20, 21, 26-
30, 33, 34, 116, 146, 154, 187-
189, 192, 197-200, 211, 226,
239, 259, 276, 282, 301, 304,
306, 319, 327
evidence, 198
integrity, 16, 17, 33, 41
unity (see *hermeneutics, logical coherence*)
thematic emphasis, (pre)dominant
(key) theme(s), 143, 160, 187,
188, 199, 202, 203, 301
validation, criteria of, 9, 18, 23, 25,
29-32, 34, 277, 328
honor, 74, 81, 176, 183, 251, 252, 308-310
hope
false, 114, 215, 254

for an advantage, 238, 341
of God's favor, 6, 183, 232, 271, 283,
290, 323, 343, 344
of living (survival), 82, 93, 94, 100,
206, 240, 294-296
of resurrection (see *resurrection*)
of reward (legacy, inheritance), 99,
232, 273, 274, 291, 296, 342
of satisfaction, 192, 251, 273, 315
hopeless (see also *despair*), 82, 94, 98,
100, 192, 205, 240
hypocrisy, hypocrit(ical), 46, 84, 88, 90-
92, 102, 108, 117, 118, 161, 245, 246,
288

Iddo, 342
ignorance, 15, 47, 53, 76, 98, 134, 136,
140, 143, 147, 154, 155, 165, 172
image of God, man as, 115, 332, 338,
343
inadequacy, inability (mankind's), 41,
43, 76, 87, 108, 119, 130-132, 139,
147, 151, 157, 160, 183, 185, 194,
197, 199, 202, 204-206, 211, 260,
261, 273-276, 281, 301, 303, 328,
337, 347, 348, 351
indictment, indict, 55, 73, 85, 90, 107,
114, 118, 137, 140, 145, 154, 166
inheritance (see also *portion; reward;
wages; legacy; heritage*), 25, 27,
43, 47, 57, 58, 170, 174, 176, 177,
183, 191, 196, 265, 267, 268, 273-
276, 278, 295, 296, 342, 345, 346
iniquity (see *wickedness*)
inscrutable, inscrutability (see under
design; purpose; work of God)
instruction, teaching; instruct, teach
(see also *wisdom*), 12, 51, 56, 58,
83, 86, 92, 105, 109, 111, 112, 123,
124, 126, 127, 129, 131, 132, 136,
141-148, 152, 154, 156, 160, 165,
172, 174, 186, 198, 201, 208, 217,
262, 264, 296, 305, 314, 315, 316,
319, 327-329, 331, 338, 342, 346-352
intercession, intercessor (see also
mediation; mediator), 43, 53, 56,
57, 58, 98, 100, 106, 129, 143, 169-
174
interpretation (see also *hermeneutics*),
9, 14, 16-18, 20, 21, 23, 30, 32, 34,
35, 50, 188, 196, 284, 339

retribution (punishment) (see also *the-ology; vindictiveness*), 13, 55, 57, 59, 63, 64, 67, 68, 73-75, 81-89, 91-93, 95, 98-103, 105, 107-109, 117, 118, 126, 129, 134-136, 140, 147, 169, 171, 246, 284, 289, 332

reward (see also *inheritance; portion; wages*), 98, 115, 134, 169-171, 173, 174, 176, 177, 223, 226, 233, 275-277, 289, 291, 295-298, 321, 324, 346

  lasting, 223, 295, 297, 298

riches, 144, 203, 204, 244, 247, 249, 252, 253, 268, 304

rich man; the rich, 134, 145,, 249, 306, 307, 309, 314

righteous

  agency, co-regency (see *agency*)

  declared to be (forensically), 55, 89, 108, 130, 153, 162, 165

  morally, "moral man," moralist, 65, 83, 89, 108, 117, 225, 231-234, 289

  vindicated as (see *vindication*)

righteous, the, 64, 66, 92, 105, 106, 139, 142-144, 194, 195, 205, 206, 223, 231, 232, 273, 283, 289-294, 297

  works of (see *works*)

  the wise, and, 194, 195, 206, 223, 290-294, 297

righteousness, 15, 25, 43, 46, 56, 57, 59, 63, 65, 68, 82, 86, 98, 104, 108, 109, 117-119, 124, 129-132, 134, 138, 139, 142, 143, 147, 148, 153, 154, 160-162, 183, 195, 196, 273, 275-281, 287, 293, 339, 343-345, 351

  wisdom, and (see also under *fear of God*), 25, 196, 273, 275-278, 287, 343, 345

ruler, 134, 157, 192, 305-309, 314

sacrifice, 58, 130, 177, 246

  atonement, and (see *sin, atonement for*)

sarcasm (see *literary genre*)

Satan, 5, 15, 26, 27, 54-56, 58, 61, 63, 65-69, 73, 75, 78, 79, 83, 85, 87, 96, 102, 108, 110, 113-115, 124, 134, 137, 153, 160-164, 166, 167, 169-171, 173, 175, 177, 246, 339, 340, 344

  as Accuser, Adversary, 54, 55, 66, 96-98, 114

collusion (angelic) with, 161

complicity (human) with, 27, 54, 58, 153, 161, 166

deceptive strategy of, 26, 55, 58, 67, 68, 80, 114, 118, 124, 153, 166

defeat of (victory over), 5, 68, 75, 108, 124, 153, 163, 164, 167, 169, 171, 173, 175, 177

God's wager with, 15, 63, 65, 66, 78-80, 96, 108, 110, 114, 124, 151, 153, 161, 169, 175

subversive goals of, 54-56, 68, 80, 124, 153, 160, 161, 171

satisfaction, fulfillment; satisfy, fulfill, 9, 12, 13, 18, 20, 25, 27, 44, 54, 56, 57, 68, 69, 100, 106, 114, 131, 137, 161, 165, 170, 177, 185, 190-193, 195, 196, 198, 199, 202, 204, 206, 207, 209, 211, 212, 215-219, 221, 223, 224, 226, 227, 234, 237, 238, 241, 244, 245, 247-253, 255, 259, 267, 269, 273, 276, 291, 292, 295, 296, 312-315, 318, 319, 322-324, 332, 335-337, 339, 343, 345, 347, 351

  lack of (see also *restlessness*), 182, 191, 202-204, 212, 221, 242, 247, 250-254, 268, 292, 345

schemes (devices) of mankind (see *ambitious*)

search for meaning (see *meaning*)

self-deception, 216

self-destruction (see also *work of one's hands*), 56, 129, 131, 142, 143, 162, 172, 276

self-indulgence, 192, 218, 219, 242, 276, 278, 307, 308, 311, 313, 316

self-justification, 53, 86, 104, 108, 123, 124, 128, 149, 160, 161

self-righteousness (see also *presump-tion, self-righteous*), 5, 9, 26, 46, 47, 53, 56-59, 64, 68, 73, 75, 76, 82, 95, 104, 112, 113, 119, 124, 131, 133, 137, 138, 140, 145, 151, 152, 158-164, 166, 173, 273, 276, 278

self-sufficiency, self-sufficient (-reliant), 6, 13, 14, 23, 25-28, 32, 42-44, 49, 51, 56, 58, 83, 100, 114-116, 131, 140, 142-146, 148, 151, 152, 157, 164, 182, 183, 185, 192, 194-196, 200-202, 205, 207, 212, 215, 216, 218-222, 225, 227, 233, 234,